ACCELERATED
Learning for Break-through Results

ACCELERATED
Learning for Break-through Results

Whole brain, person and systems approach to accelerate learning, engagement, change and growth

By
Debbie Craig
and
Kerryn Kohl

KNO RES
PUBLISHING

2014

First published in 2014

ISBN: 978-1-86922-500-1
eISBN: 978-1-86922-501-8 PDF ebook

Published by Knowres Publishing (Pty) Ltd
P O Box 3954
Randburg
2125
Republic of South Africa

Tel: (011) 706-6009
Fax: (011) 706 1127
E-mail: orders@knowres.co.za
Website: www.kr.co.za

Printed and bound: MegaDigital, 5 Koets Street, Parrow Industria, Cape Town
Typesetting, layout and design: Cia Joubert, cia@knowres.co.za
Cover design: Cia Joubert, cia@knowres.co.za
Editing and proofreading: Adrienne Pretorius, Gemini Editing Services, pretorii@mweb.co.za
Project management: Cia Joubert, cia@knowres.co.za
Index created with: TExtract, www.Texyz.com

TABLE OF CONTENTS

Authors' Notes_____iv

Acknowledgements_____ v

Foreword _____ vii

About the Authors _____viii

About the Contributors _____ x

     Collaborators _____xi

Gamification On-boarding_____ xii

Icons used_____ xv

PART 1: Paradigm Shift for Accelerated Learning _____ 1

Chapter 1: The need for Accelerated Learning by *Debbie Craig*_____ 2

1.1 Introduction _____ 2

1.2 Global talent and change challenge _____ 5

1.3 South African talent and change challenge _____ 6

1.4 Making the shift_____ 8

1.5 Maintaining the foundations _____ 9

1.6 An Accelerated Learning framework_____ 10

1.7 Conclusion _____ 13

Chapter 2: The paradigm shift in learning by *Debbie Craig*_____ 15

2.1 Introduction _____ 15

2.2 Digital, mobile and social media trends _____ 16

2.3 Understanding today's learner _____ 18

2.4 Paradigm shift_____ 27

2.5 Conclusion _____ 40

Chapter 3: Insight into Accelerated Learning in South African organisations
     by *Debbie Craig*_____ 41

3.1 Introduction _____ 41

3.2 Challenges or opportunities _____ 42

3.3 Learning methodology trends _____ 46

3.4 Examples of Accelerated Learning programmes _____ 50

3.5 Leaders as learning champions _____ 53

3.6 Learning involvement in change _____ 53

3.7   Leadership skills needs_____54
3.8   Key messages_____55
3.9   Conclusion _____57

PART 2: Whole Brain, Whole Person Approach to Learning _____ **59**

Chapter 4: Unique learning profiles by *Debbie Craig*_____ **60**
4.1   Introduction _____60
4.2   Some basic principles_____61
4.3   Learning = Change _____62
4.4   Sub-conscious influences_____64
4.5   Learning influences_____66
4.6   Creating your own learning profile _____86
4.7   Conclusion _____87

Chapter 5: Neuroscience of learning by *Natalie Cunningham* and
        Debbie Craig _____89
5.1   Introduction _____89
5.2   What is neuroscience? _____90
5.3   Learning and neuroscience_____92
5.4   Workings of the brain _____94
5.5   The learning cycle_____98
5.6   Attention and memory_____102
5.7   The emotional and social brain_____107
5.8   Brain deception _____111
5.9   Environmental factors _____114
5.10 Conclusion _____116

PART 3: Creating a Learning Culture _____ **119**

Chapter 6: Creating a learning culture by *Debbie Craig* _____ 120
6.1   Introduction _____120
6.2   A tale of two companies _____121
6.3   A learning culture framework _____124
6.4   Embarking on a culture transformation journey _____139
6.5   Conclusion _____142

Chapter 7: Learning through coaching by *Natalie Cunningham* _____ 143
7.1   Introduction _____143
7.2   What is coaching?_____145

7.3 Why coaching? _____ 147
7.4 How do we go about coaching? _____ 149
7.5 Conclusion _____ 164

Chapter 8: Learning through authentic conversations by *John Gatherer* and
    Debbie Craig _____ 165
8.1 Introduction _____ 165
8.2 The context of the problem _____ 165
8.3 The imperative for holding authentic conversations _____ 166
8.4 Towards a culture of healthy conflict_____ 168
8.5 The learning imagery of holding authentic conversations _____ 170
8.6 The learning process of initiating and holding authentic
    conversations _____ 172
8.7 Conclusion _____ 175

PART 4: Designing Accelerated Learning Programmes_____ **177**

Chapter 9: Learning architecture by *Debbie Craig*_____ 178
9.1 Introduction _____ 178
9.2 The challenge _____ 179
9.3 A framework _____ 180
9.4 Understand – the strategic priorities and capabilities _____ 183
9.5 Design – the performance and competency standards _____ 188
9.6 Analyse – the proficiency levels and the needs _____ 198
9.7 Develop – organisational and individual plans _____ 206
9.8 Conclusion _____ 209

Chapter 10: Learning design by *Kerryn Kohl* _____ 211
10.1 Introduction _____ 211
10.2 Learning design for Accelerated Learning _____ 212
10.3 Design in practice _____ 217
10.4 Retention of learning_____ 225
10.5 Steps in the design process _____ 227
10.6 Methods and tools _____ 235
10.7 Conclusion _____ 242

Chapter 11: Gamification in learning by *Darryn van den Berg* _____ 243
11.1 What is gamification? _____ 243
11.2 Foundation principles driving the success of gamification _____ 244
11.3 Building a gamification strategy _____ 255

11.4 Gamification mechanics _____ 263
11.5 Examples of gamification _____ 266
11.6 Gamification lessons_____ 270
11.7 So what does all of this mean, and how can you apply it?_____ 271
11.8 Conclusion _____ 272

Chapter 12: Learning assessment by *Kerryn Kohl* _____ 275
12.1 Introduction _____ 275
12.2 Levels of assessment _____ 276
12.3 Strategic considerations in assessment decisions_____ 281
12.4 Designing assessment to be incorporated into Accelerated Learning
     programmes _____ 287
12.5 Assessment methods _____ 291
12.6 Assessment dilemmas _____ 294
12.7 Assessing the overall value of the ALP _____ 296
12.8 Conclusion _____ 301

PART 5: Making it Real – Case Studies of Accelerated Learning _____ 303

Chapter 13: How to guide – Learning to accelerate change
     by *Kerryn Kohl* _____ 304
13.1 Introduction _____ 304
13.2 A new perspective_____ 304
13.3 The learning landscape and audience _____ 306
13.4 The learning design _____ 308
13.5 Alignment with learning design principles_____ 312
13.6 Conclusion _____ 314

Chapter 14: Case Study: Breakthrough Learning for talent pools by
     Debbie Craig _____ 315
14.1 Introduction _____ 315
14.2 What is Breakthrough Learning? _____ 316
14.3 Why Breakthrough Learning?_____ 318
14.4 Setting up the programme _____ 320
14.5 High-level design _____ 321
14.6 Programme outline _____ 326
14.7 Selection of programme participants _____ 328
14.8 Assessments_____ 328
14.9 BL launch workshop _____ 329
14.10 BL learning modules _____ 330

14.11 BL project work _____ 331

14.12 Learning portal _____ 332

14.13 Final presentation and celebration dinner _____ 333

14.14 Final wrap-up: ensuring results and sustainability _____ 334

14.15 Conclusion _____ 334

Chapter 15: Case Study: Creating a culture of effective decision
   management by *John Gatherer* and *Debbie Craig* _____ 335

15.1 Introduction _____ 335

15.2 Context and rationale for effective decision management _____ 336

15.3 Background to the case study _____ 336

15.4 The company business case for decision management _____ 339

15.5 The learning themes and outcomes _____ 340

15.6 A robust process for WISE decisions _____ 342

15.7 Accelerated Learning principles _____ 344

15.8 Conclusion: _____ 346

Bibliography _____ 347

Index _____ 359

Endorsements from people who have read this book_____ 375

AUTHORS' NOTE

This book started as an idea, developed into a plan, expanded in content mind-maps, and then evolved into a collaborative project involving the creativity, energy and effort of many. We have constantly been amazed at the **power of collaboration** when one holds a vision in mind but **lets go** of one's own personal attachment as to how this vision can be achieved. This means staying open to ideas, exploring different approaches, following up on opportunities, learning from everyone, sharing widely, communicating often, accepting and responding to feedback, and allowing the process to **FLOW.**

The book and the wider learning community took on a life of their own and became a true example of Accelerated Learning in Action over about nine months. It appears before you in its current and evolving form. We hope that you join us on this Accelerated Learning-and-sharing journey and participate fully in the many suggested activities; rabbit-holes of additional learning nuggets; and shared resources to further your own understanding of learning how to learn for yourself and for others.

We hope that you share what you learn with your organisation, colleagues, family and community. We encourage you to share successes, case studies and lessons learnt with our online community through www.accelerated.co.za.

Debbie Craig and *Kerryn Kohl*

ACKNOWLEDGEMENTS

Heartfelt thanks and mountains of gratitude and appreciation go to the following people for their support and contribution to this book:

- *Kerryn* – for the original idea and for partnering me on the journey as co-author and committing to the end despite bringing a third child into the world in the same period.
- *Darryn* – for your amazing energy, creative ideas and courage to reinvent the boundaries of book writing and gamification.
- Natalie – for being a true collaborator and expert contributor and in working together so seamlessly despite some tough life challenges.
- *John* – for being such a committed and generous business partner, for your passion for learning, for your constant wisdom, and, of course, for your contribution to the book.
- *Andrew* – for your ever-present support in life and in business, particularly through the final weeks of long hours of writing and editing and listening equally to my joys and frustrations along the way. Thanks also for bringing your researcher strengths to bear and for the many hours and days of referencing, researching and editing.
- *Tuppy* – for being my other pair of hands and your selfless, reliable support in helping to co-ordinate so many aspects of my life, my business and this book. You are truly appreciated.
- *Knowledge Resources* – thanks to Wilhelm, Cia and team for being fantastic partners, collaborators and publishers, and for all your ideas and assistance in making this book a better end product.
- *Collaborators and Interviewees* – thanks for giving the readers an insight into Accelerated Learning in your organisations and to help make the book come to life.
- *Online collaborators* – thanks for your participation and for being early adopters and guinea pigs in testing our online strategy.
- *Catalyst clients* – thanks to all of our many clients, many of whom have become dear friends, who have opened their doors to us and partnered with us to build capacity and learning, and in so doing have helped us to grow and learn even more.

- *Friends and Family* – to all those very special family members and friends that support my dreams, generously share their time and wisdom with me and keep it real. I couldn't do any of this without you.
- *Debbie* – Thank you for your support and commitment to this book. You really are the glue that has held us all together. Thank you for your mentorship, and friendship.
- *Eaton*, *Ronan*, *Rhys*, and *Reilley* – thank you to my incredibly awesome family for your understanding and support of my goals and aspirations.

The Authors
October 2014

FOREWORD

Walt Disney was accredited with the inspirational, but profound quotation: "Think, Believe, Dream, and Dare!" If there was ever a quotation that symbolises the vision, imagination, creative development and tenacity associated with this new publication from Debbie Craig and Kerryn Kohl, Walt Disney aptly sums it up.

This work, entitled *Accelerated Learning for Breakthrough Results*, is an integrative and holistic chronicle on accelerated learning and contains a vast array of pragmatic learning applications, solutions, frameworks, tools, and case studies. I have had the pleasure of working with Debbie over the last fourteen years and with Kerryn over the last three years and I know that this project has been a special labour of love for both of them. From the early ideas and stirrings of commitment, to the forging of the concept design and content structure, to the insightful awareness of the dynamically changing business backdrop, Debbie and Kerryn have crafted a distinctive resource which will be invaluable to anyone who understands that learning and personal development are the biggest differentiators in achieving greatness.

This project has been a remarkable collaborative effort between the editors, the chapter contributors, and the heads of learning across business sectors – all of whom have provided seasoned experience, stimulating perspectives, novel learning techniques, and practical case studies within the publication. Having worked in the fields of Strategic Change, Talent Management and Management and Leadership Development for a number of decades, I believe that in today's fast-changing world, this is a definitive piece of work which positions and focuses learning and growth as a critical driver of excellence, which should appeal to leaders, managers, young talent, and technical and learning specialists alike.

Debbie and Kerryn bring with them a rich and refreshing blend of specialist expertise, knowledge and international business exposure and they are relentless in their insatiable appetite, drive and courage to "push the envelope" and make a difference within this important field of learning, growth and development.

It has been a privilege to be associated with this publication.

John Gatherer
Co- founder and Partner, Catalyst Consulting

October 2014

ABOUT THE AUTHORS

AUTHOR: DEBBIE CRAIG

Debbie has over 18 years' experience in the field of strategy, leadership development, change management, talent management, high-performance teams and organisational development. She has worked and consulted at leading local and global organisations in the private and public sector throughout Southern Africa and internationally in the UK, Australia, South East Asia, South America, Mexico, China, Canada, Europe and the USA. Debbie is a skilled strategist, design architect, and team builder, as well as a powerful facilitator, change agent and executive coach.

Debbie's passion is transformation and empowerment, which she facilitates through individual coaching and empowerment workshops, team-development workshops, corporate training and consulting assignments, and organisation-wide strategic change interventions. Debbie is the founder and Managing Director of Catalyst Consulting, which she has grown into a successful consulting company with her business partner, John Gatherer. She is also the founder of World Alive, a personal empowerment and transformation company. She is a registered Master HR Professional with the SA Board for People Practices (SABPP).

Debbie has published two books: *I am Talent* and *I am Alive*, written numerous articles, appeared on radio talk shows and presented at conferences. She also does public talks.

www.catalystconsulting.co.za | www.iamtalent.co.za | www.iamalive.co.za | twitter: @catalystsa

AUTHOR: KERRYN KOHL

Kerryn Kohl is the founder of The Coaching House ~ Talent Cultivation. Kerryn has a passion for learning, believing that it underlies any transformation or change that we wish to make. From this vantage point, learning is seen as not only the springboard to any culture transformation, but its foundational driving force.

Kerryn holds a Master's Degree in Adult and Community Education and an Honours degree in Psychology, all from the University of Johannesburg. She is a registered life and business coach with COMENSA (Coaches and Mentors of South Africa). Kerryn has consulted for a global management consulting firm and brings 14 years of valuable experience as a Talent and Organisation Performance professional to the table. Kerryn has experience across industries and her strengths lie in change management, workforce transformation, organisational learning, organisational design, performance management, and coaching. Kerryn is a strong leader and is skilful in motivating and encouraging others while taking the lead.

"My core value is integrity and I strive to maintain a highly Teachable Spirit." – www.thecoachinghouse.co.za

ABOUT THE CONTRIBUTORS

Natalie Cunningham is currently a Professional Associate of GIBS. She also runs her own consultancy – Origo – specialising in Leadership Development, Organisational Development and People Development. During 2013, she worked with Knowledge Resources to conduct a Leadership Development Survey of 150 companies/organisations in South Africa and their Leadership Development Practices.

Natalie was previously Director of the Leadership Development Centre at Wits Business School. She developed and designed the curriculum for a Masters in Management in Business and Executive Coaching. Furthermore, she set up a Coaching Supervision Certificate and Business Executive Coaching Certificate. Natalie also headed up all the coaching in support of the Leadership Development Programmes at Wits. She holds a BA (SW) Hons and an MBA from Wits. She is currently conducting her PhD research on "Developing theory on the coaching process based on the lived coaching experiences of executives".

John Gatherer has over 40 years' experience in the fields of HR, labour relations, training and development, leadership, and strategic change management. He holds a BA Hons from the University of Natal and a CPIR from WITS Business School. He is an affiliate member of IPM, a registered Practitioner with the SABPP, and a non-executive director of BIOSS SA.

John has held senior positions in Anglo American plc and the De Beers Groups, working as Training Consultant to the Anglo plc Group and serving on the Executive Committee of De Beers as Group Manager – Human Resources between 1999 and 2005. He also headed up a Global Centre of Expertise in leadership development and talent management for De Beers.

John joined Debbie Craig at Catalyst Consulting as Chief Operations Manager, and together they have forged a consulting business, specialising in strategic change, leadership development and talent management, working locally and internationally with a variety of clients from a range of business sectors. John brings a deep specialist knowledge and expertise to his roles as facilitator, consultant and executive coach as well his ability to think strategically and design innovative solutions.

He has also co-written a book, *I am Talent*, on optimising potential and career aspirations, has written numerous articles, and has presented at conferences. John's other passions include photography and travelling and he has published a number of photographic books.

Darryn van den Berg is the visionary founder and MD of the group P4D (Passion4Development). He has been involved in pioneering new, alternative and effective learning and development solutions for over 13 years. He applies best practice and new, cutting edge initiatives that guarantee increase in productivity of the workplace, and is proud of the fact that training in these initiatives is seldom required. P4D is a constantly growing, dynamic organisation where new, exciting ground is broken frequently and where Darryn and his staff live by their values. Passion is his brand and persona, and he thrives on living on the edge, innovating, and causing change in business and life!

COLLABORATORS

Angela Donnelly, Head of Learning and Development, Rand Merchant Bank (RMB)

Ilka Dunne, Senior Learning Architect and head of young talent development, Rand Merchant Bank (RMB)

Boni Gantile, Executive Human Resources: Functional Competency Management, Telkom

Candida di Giandomenico, Head of Learning and Development, AVI Limited

Gawie Herholdt, Group Effectiveness Manager: Talent Performance and OE, Harmony Gold Mining

Nicolene Hogg, Head: Develop Dimension Data

Hester Jardine, Talent Manager, Harmony Gold Mining

Andrew Johnson (Dr), General Manager: Eskom Leadership Institute, Eskom

Marc Kahn, Head of Human Resources and Organisation Development, Investec

Taryn Marcus, Head of Talent Management and People Development, Liberty Group

Brent Nestler, Learning and Development Manager Ricoh South Africa

Dean Retief, HR Executive: People Development, Nedbank

Shaun Rozyn, Executive Director: Executive Education, Gordon Institute of Business Science (GIBS)

GAMIFICATION ON-BOARDING

"Gamification uses the stuff that makes play fun and irresistible and applies these into non-game contexts. Engaging 'players' through Feedback, FUN and Friends" – Darryn van den Berg

We are offering something to **YOU**, the reader, that is completely NEW and **DIFFERENT**. Come and join us on this exciting journey to **ACCELERATE YOUR LEARNING** and **HAVE FUN**, while exploring the topic of Accelerated Learning – not only in this book, but through a **RABBIT HOLE** of awesome resources.

Your Quest … should you choose to accept it …

Engage (with the AL community), learn (in an accelerated way which is fun), share (your experiences and insights), and earn (rewards).

This is how it works.

ENGAGE	1	LEARN	2	SHARE	3	EARN	4
Sign-up to connect, learn and share		Gain access to a rabbit hole of resources		Comment on Facebook or Twitter		Each step earns you more points, status, and entry into reward draws	
Track your progress		Specially selected by our contributors		Visit www.accelerated.co.za		Engage – points for opting in and tracking progress	
Earn status and great prizes		Fast-track your learning by completing activities		Share experiences and insights		Learn – points for activities	
Join the AL community						Share – points for sharing	

What's in it for you?

Not only does this gamification opportunity increase your level of engagement in the topic and accelerate your learning; it also opens up the opportunity to build new relationships, practise virtual collaboration, and join a community of practice. In addition, you stand the chance of winning numerous rewards such as books, coaching, one-on-ones, workshops, resources, and various learning options. To find out what rewards you can win, visit www.accelerated.co.za. There are automatic rewards, prize draws and surprise rewards for exceptional contributions and for finding hidden messages (Easter Eggs). We dare you to find them…if you can!

It is easy to become eligible for status and rewards; just follow the four steps above. Sign up, tell us how you are doing on your journey, engage with the authors, complete different FUN Brain Breaks, and share your progress and your insights.

Tracking your progress

We have provided two different ways to track your progress, using a low-tech (manual) or a high tech (online) Leader Board.

1. *Low-tech progress*: You can track your own progress on our AL Excel progress chart (see example below). This can be downloaded from www.accelerated.co.za. Find the quest for each part and chapter and then update your progress on the Excel document as you achieve. When ANY of the tasks is completed, you can email the updated Excel doc to progress@accelerated.co.za.
2. *High-tech progress*: You can track your own progress on our AL online progress tracking tool. Find the quest for each part and chapter and then update your progress online.

We will consolidate all submissions and uploads on a monthly basis to our online leader-board, available *www.accelerated.co.za*. Keep an eye out on the AL Facebook page for notices and updates.

Look for these signs on the Leader Boards to guide you to achieving your REWARDS!!

Set your goal: This is where you write out your goal for reading the chapter. Make it REAL!

Activities to complete: Throughout the chapters, there are different **optional** activities to complete. If you want the reward, you need to complete at least ONE activity for EACH chapter.

Rate yourself: This is a self-rating on how you completed the activity/activities. Track how well you are doing by circling the star that demonstrates your achievement of that activity topic (1 star being Novice, up to five stars being Guru).

Brain Breaks: As part of the fun of Accelerated Learning (and Gamification), these are fun, random activities for you to break your reading. These are dopamine rewards, and you will know what they are (and IF you have won them) only after you have completed them and told us on our AL Facebook page.

Hidden messages: These are hidden within every chapter and make up a phrase for every PART. You will win when you find the phrase for the PART and send it to us.

xiv

ICONS USED

Look for these **ICONS** in the book to guide you.

	Reflection questions
	More information
	Gamification
	Activities
	Video resources
	Tips
	Reading resources
	Examples or case studies

PART 1

PARADIGM SHIFT FOR ACCELERATED LEARNING

Chapter 1: The need for Accelerated Learning by *Debbie Craig*

1.1   Introduction
1.2   Global talent and change challenge
1.3   South African talent and change challenge
1.4   Making the shift
1.5   Maintaining the foundations
1.6   An Accelerated Learning framework
1.7   Conclusion

Chapter 2: The paradigm shifts in learning by *Debbie Craig*

2.1   Introduction
2.2   Digital, mobile and social media trends
2.3   Understanding today's learner
2.4   Paradigm shift
2.5   Conclusion

Chapter 3: Insight into Accelerated Learning in South African organisations by *Debbie Craig*

3.1   Introduction
3.2   Challenges or opportunities
3.3   Learning methodology trends
3.4   Examples of Accelerated Learning programmes
3.5   Leaders as learning champions
3.6   Learning involvement in change
3.7   Leadership skills needs
3.8   Key messages
3.9   Conclusion

CHAPTER 1

THE NEED FOR ACCELERATED LEARNING

By Debbie Craig

"The ability to learn faster than your competitors may be the only sustainable competitive advantage." – Arie De Geus

1.1 INTRODUCTION

We are born to learn. From the moment we come into this world, we are learning how to survive, who to love, what to eat, what to avoid and how to get around. As we grow we learn new things every day. We learn about choice, boundaries, consequences and power. We learn about competition, co-operation, independence and group dynamics. We learn how to set goals, and experience how it feels to fail. We have an innate capacity to observe, absorb, interpret, integrate, test and learn from feedback. We are living, breathing, learning machines. We develop new thought patterns, emotional responses, beliefs and mind-sets which form our fundamental programmes of how to manage our lives.

So why is it that organisations struggle so much with getting people to learn and change and make better decisions? What happened? What changed? What are we missing?

We are faced with a global talent crisis of massive proportion. There is just not enough depth of "ready now" candidates to fill the critical leadership and technical positions in the future. It is without fail in the top three risk categories in organisations worldwide, and one of the top three strategic challenges which organisations are investing resources to address.

If we know what talent we need and know who we have got, why can't we match learning pathways to strategic challenges and ensure that we engage, nurture, develop and retain the talent we need?

Research from *Thinking Fast and Slow* (Kahneman, 2011) and *Decisive* (Heath & Heath, 2013) highlights the following frightening statistics:

- 1 in 5 doctors are misdiagnosing ailments.
- 44% of lawyers advise against a career in law.
- 40% of senior managers are pushed out, fail or quit within 18 months.
- 83% of mergers and acquisitions fail to create value for shareholders.
- We don't save sufficient funds for retirement.
- We get into relationships that are bad for us.
- We reverse tattoos – 61 500 tattoos were reversed in 2009 in the US.
- We still don't seem to be able to get work–life balance correct.

We still seem to be unable to harness the value of large-scale change interventions, with only a 25 per cent success rate. Although change, uncertainty and complexity are a consistent part of our business world, we still find that change results in resistance, derailment, demotivation, disengagement, lower productivity, and losing good people.

If we know what needs to change and who needs to join us on the change journey, why can't we utilise people's natural learning ability to move nimbly, responsively and creatively through the change process?

We consistently make bad decisions, despite being able to learn, adapt and correct.

This is because we are irrational beings, our brains are flawed instruments, and our gut instincts are full of questionable advice. The Heath Brothers in the book *Decisive* (2013) describe the four villains of decision making as:

- **Narrow framing** – unduly limiting the options we consider
- **The confirmation bias** – seeking for information that bolsters our beliefs
- **Short-term emotion** – being swayed by emotions that will fade
- **Over-confidence** – having too much faith in our predictions.

If we know what leads to poor decision making, which impacts on all areas of our lives daily, why can't we learn to address these flaws and automatic programmes and make better decisions?

Recent research from the Corporate Executive Board (2013) highlights the three key trends in the new work environment: **frequent organisational change, more independent work** and **more knowledge work**. They say that in order to cope with change, the three key capabilities for the new high performer are the ability to **adapt to change, to work collaboratively** and to **apply good judgement in decision making**.

Three key capabilities for the new high performer

Adapt to change: High performers use their knowledge of the organisation and their role to adjust quickly to work environment changes. Adaptive employees are also proactive; they are not paralysed by change, and they are willing to take action and move projects and priorities forward.

Work collaboratively: High performers are good collaborators, working well with and through others. They have the teamwork skills necessary to work with a wide range of people across the organisation. They use their technical expertise to influence stakeholders and contribute to collaborative projects.

Apply judgement: High performers use strong analytical skills to prioritise their work, assess problems, and make decisions. They rely on their expertise, experience and knowledge of the organisation to apply judgement to their problems, decisions and their work.

The 10 competencies for the new high performer: The competencies that make up these capabilities are prioritisation, teamwork, organisational awareness, problem solving, self-awareness, proactivity, influence, decision making, learning agility, and technical expertise.

Our challenge as learning professionals and leaders is to ensure that these competencies are learnt and applied, as quickly as possible.

Retention of learning

In this age of being over-whelmed and overloaded, it is becoming more and more difficult to retain information and learning. *How many telephone numbers can you remember now compared to 10 years ago?*

Studies have shown that two days after a training session we remember only about 20% of what we have learnt, and it decreases after that. We need to find creative ways to build in repetition, recall, review and reinforcement to optimise the retention of learning over the short and long term. See more on this in Chapter 10.

This book is about exploring answers to these questions, and examining leading practices and case studies for possible approaches and techniques that we can craft together into creative solutions in the future.

1.2 GLOBAL TALENT AND CHANGE CHALLENGE

Globally, the war for talent, or, as we call it, "the Perfect Talent Storm", continues to rage. Leadership failures and the inability to respond to a changing world continue to appear long after the lessons of Enron, WorldCom, the space shuttle disaster and the dot.com era have been learnt. The BP oil spill in 2010 was a very public example of poor judgement and lack of empathy and responsiveness. Long-term industrial giants, such as General Motors, can also fail if leadership is not in touch with change on the ground.

The financial sector has not fared much better in the last few years, with the Eurozone crisis and the bankruptcy of the Lehman Brothers in the US impacting on both local and international financial stability. Too often, high-level business and political leadership is fraught with ego, power and greed, and endures only in the short term.

In the 2014 *Global Human Capital Trends Report* by Deloitte Consulting, a number of key talent and leadership challenges emerge:

* Companies face an **urgent need to develop leaders at all levels** – from bringing younger leaders online faster, to developing leaders globally, to keeping senior leaders relevant and engaged longer.
* **Leadership remains the number 1 talent issue** facing organisations around the world, with 86 per cent of respondents rating it as "urgent" or "important". Only 13 per cent of respondents say they do an excellent job developing leaders at all levels – an exceptionally large "readiness gap".
* 21st-century leadership is different. Companies face new leadership challenges, including **developing Millennials** and **multiple generations of leaders**, meeting the demand for leaders with global fluency and flexibility, building the ability to innovate and inspire others to perform, and acquiring new levels of understanding of rapidly changing technologies and new disciplines and fields.

When asked how they are doing in managing this leadership and talent readiness gap, only 13 per cent of companies rate themselves "excellent" in providing leadership programmes at all levels. 66 per cent believe they are "weak" in their ability to develop Millennial leaders, and over half (51 per cent) have little confidence in their ability to maintain clear, consistent succession programmes. Only 8 per cent believe they have "excellent" programmes to build global skills and experiences.

The survey further emphasises that **building the leadership pipeline** takes financial investment, time, and expertise, and that there are **no shortcuts to building a leadership team** that is broad and deep. A new leader typically needs

18 months before feeling fully comfortable in a new role, while for a mid-level leader, the time period stretches from 24 to 36 months. High-impact companies in the United States spend more than $3 500 per person each year to develop mid-level leaders and over $10 000 to develop senior leaders.

Corporations now **compete globally** for increasingly scarce technical and professional skills. Organisations need to create a global skills supply chain in the quest for workforce capability. While 75 per cent of survey respondents rate workforce capability as an "urgent" or "important" challenge, only 15 per cent believe they are ready to address it. Companies that succeed in building a global "supply chain" for skills will be positioned for success in innovation and performance.

1.3 SOUTH AFRICAN TALENT AND CHANGE CHALLENGE

The dynamics of leadership and talent shortages in **South Africa** are compounded by a legacy of poor education, poverty, and economic disempowerment in certain population groups.

Unemployment rates are some of the highest in the world, with up to 50 per cent of our youth (18–25) unable to find employment and only about 30 per cent of women succeeding in doing so. Poor quality and infrastructure in **education** lead to a low attendance and high drop-out rate, and a skills mismatch between what business needs and what the education system is producing.

How do we accelerate the quality and relevance of education in South Africa in order to optimise skills the economy needs while creating employment and income through an entrepreneurial mind-set?

Employment equity legislation, while well-intended, has led to unintended consequences of what we call a "revolving door" effect, with new hires moving on to the next company approximately every 1.5–2 years, without building the requisite depth of skill by seeing strategies and projects through to implementation and sustainability.

How do we accelerate the learning path of employment equity employees, and still build the requisite experience curve into the mix?

The other challenge is that many industries in South Africa have an **ageing workforce**, with the average age of engineers, artisans and employees in the mining, manufacturing and heavy industry sectors being between 50 and 55 years old. Specialist skills and institutional knowledge are not being passed on fast enough to prevent a significant loss of technical and company-specific expertise over time. Even where skills are being transferred, we often lose these scarce skills to local and global competition for them.

How do we accelerate the transfer of skills and knowledge to the younger generations fast enough to replace those retiring soon, with dignity and recognition for all involved, and in so doing retain these skills in our businesses and the economy?

Another factor impacting on the availability and quality of our leadership and specialist talent is the **credibility and competence of the learning or training function** in South Africa. Industry standards have until recently not been well defined, managed or regulated, and the training or learning function is taking a long time to move from its traditional administrative, curriculum-based role to that of a strategic value-adding partner. The *2013 Leadership Development Survey* by Stout-Rostron, Cunningham and Crous (2013) reports that the largest obstacles to leadership development are inadequate internal resources to deliver leadership programmes, and programmes not being aligned to the vision and strategy of the organisation. Another is the lack of ability to evaluate development against "hard" criteria such as ROI or organisational goals. This factor constrains investment in the right technology, talent and resources. Most private companies rate their programmes as either not effective (2) or just effective (3) on a 5-point scale. Only a very small minority (less than 5 per cent) of respondents rated their current programmes as totally effective (5/5). The major problem seemed to be the difficulty in applying new knowledge and skills owing to lack of opportunity to transfer the knowledge, a lack of follow through, not making time to implement what has been learnt, and lack of top leadership support.

How do we accelerate the credibility and competence of the learning function in order to create value-adding business partners and ensure that learning is transferred and applied for performance?

Lastly, in the South African context, the **National Qualifications Framework (NQF)**, the **Sector Education and Training Authority (SETA) system**, and the **Broad-Based Black Economic Empowerment (BEE) Codes of Good Practice** have an impact on how training and development investment decisions are made. As with most legislation, the intention, which is to improve the standard of education and skills in the country and to give recognition to those who have the skills but may not have a qualification, is laudable. Unfortunately, in practice, learning decisions can become limited to a narrow SETA context, focusing on how to maximise levies or points. Planning of learning activities ends up being channelled into the annual Workplace Skills Plan process, which doesn't cater for learning activities that are strategic, customised, not linked directly to unit standards, and happen outside the skills cycle. The process of working through sometimes tedious outcomes-based programmes, collating a portfolio of evidence and being assessed and audited is time consuming and resource intensive for both the learner and the organisation, thereby slowing down the whole learning process and reducing access to the learning process.

Activity 1

What are the three (3) biggest challenges that could benefit from Accelerated Learning in your organisation, project or community?

1

2

3

Submit your answers for points. See On-Boarding Info at the beginning of the book or go to www.accelerated.co.za

---

1.4 MAKING THE SHIFT

It is time to change the tide, to embark on a fresh approach, to identify and remove the barriers to the natural inherited learning process, and to embrace what unleashes true talent, latent potential, natural curiosity, and the motivation to learn and change.

> *"Problems that are created by our current level of thinking can't be solved by that same level of thinking." – Einstein*

Much of what we learn in structured or formal training sessions is outdated within a few years. "We need to **revolutionise the learning environment** to be more strategic, co-ordinated, learner centric, and using more on-line and mobile platforms," reads the *Global Human Capital Trends Report* (Deloitte Consulting, 2014). More than 66 per cent of companies in this survey see this trend as "urgent" or "important", yet only 6 per cent believe that they have mastered the content and technology capabilities needed to make online learning an accessible tool and a compelling experience for their employees. "We need to empower employees to become equal partners in the learning process, and foster a culture of learning and growth – driving performance, engagement, and career development." (Deloitte Consulting, 2014.)

Gone are the days where learning can be limited to a planned event that is scheduled for some time in the future. Single-session classroom-based learning sessions with tedious PowerPoint® presentations and thick manuals are outdated and ineffective. Learning needs to be immediate, interactive, continuous and accessible 24/7. We must think creatively and weave the learning process back into how we live and work as human beings. Let's remind learners of the ease and joy of learning and the thrill of mastering a new skill. It can be really empowering to embrace the humility of not knowing it all, trying, risking, failing. and building the resilience to get up and try again until we get it right.

High-performance organisations must develop leaders to become masters of talent, competence and change and build learning pathways towards a strategically planned future. Understanding how individuals, groups and communities learn and change will become a core competence. In order to engage staff, it will be necessary to create an environment that stimulates interest and passion for learning and growing – as whole people with a balanced life. Learning interactions in the future will be designed to optimise whole brain, whole person learning, utilising the latest research in Neuroscience and positive psychology – including understanding people's natural strengths, the power of collaboration and team coaching, and reshaping the stories we tell.

We need to integrate learning into work, and teach every manager to be a coach and every person to be a learning "buddy". Let's allow the younger generation to teach us how to interact simultaneously, on multiple platforms, with information and relationships all over the world. Let's appreciate the assistance of the older generation in keeping us focused, respectful, reliable, and able to deliver quality products on time. Let's make learning colourful, fun and flexible, and customise learning for individuals – making it available wherever you are, for people on the move, and creating multiple opportunities for practice and repetition in a "safe" space.

Brain Break: Close your eyes, take a deep breath, and reflect on what you can contribute to making the shift.

1.5 MAINTAINING THE FOUNDATIONS

While we need to evolve, adapt and make the shift to online, mobile, interactive relating, sharing and learning, we still need to continue to develop the skills of dialogue, conversation, rapport, empathy, emotional intelligence, relationship building, giving and receiving feedback, and conflict management – still the foundation for personal and work success. We need to hone our ability to focus in a world of ever-increasing information overload and distraction. And we need to build and enhance our skills, emotional maturity and "grit" continuously in order to flow with the change that bombards us every single day.

It is very important to keep on dreaming of a better world, working in a better company, being a better person and living a better life, in order to keep us motivated into continuously improving our thinking, our skills, and our ability to learn. Purpose and passion are key ingredients for generating energy, for pursuing creative options, for trying again when we fail, and for staying the course until we get results.

We hope that this book will refresh some old perspectives, break some outdated paradigms, reinforce the beliefs that empower you, and inspire you to reinvent your own learning journey, and those learning journeys that you have an impact on in some way.

1.6 AN ACCELERATED LEARNING FRAMEWORK

We have developed a visual framework containing the elements to consider when planning for and designing Accelerated Learning programmes. See figure 1.1.

Individual, team and organisation

We need to consider the individual (with unique learning needs and learning profile), the group or team (with group learning needs such as team effectiveness and collaboration) and the organisation or community (with strategic learning priorities and a learning culture).

Competencies and proficiency levels

We need to determine the competencies required for learning (knowledge, skills, behaviour, and mind-set) and the proficiency levels required (novice, competent, experienced, expert).

A short summary of the elements of the AL framework as shown in Figure 1.1 follows:

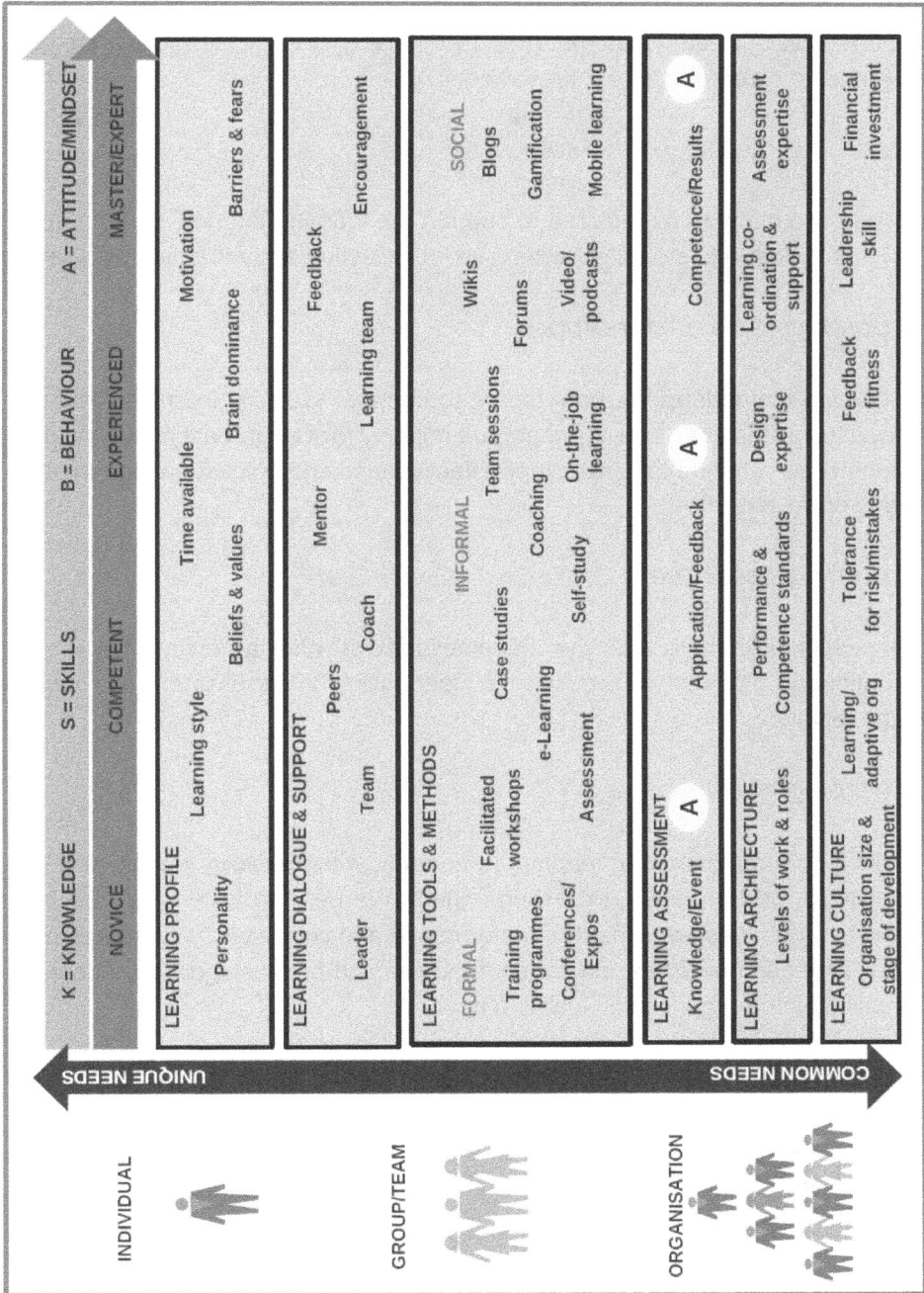

Figure 1.1: Accelerated Learning framework

Learning profile

Every individual learns differently and we must customise learning where possible or at least cater for different preferences.

Learning dialogue and support

There are many roles required to support the learning journey, and the important skill of dialogue to create opportunities for reflecting and reframing perspectives.

Learning tools and method

Learning methods range from formal to informal to social learning. Methods are evolving all the time, and it is important not only to stay abreast of new techniques, but also to continue to assess their effectiveness and not just get caught up in the fads of the day.

Learning assessment

Assessment is more than the "happiness factor" after an event. It is a planned, continuous process with application, feedback and assessment of competence and results.

Learning architecture

This is the foundation for learning to happen, without which the learning may be pointless, ad hoc, and lack lasting impact. We need to know what the strategic learning priorities are, what the performance and competency standards per level look like, and how to assess for competence and proficiency in order to establish individual and organisation learning needs.

Learning culture

Lastly, learning cannot happen in a vacuum. The culture and leadership style, the investment in learning, and the tolerance for risk or mistakes all play a role in the effectiveness and impact of learning.

Activity 2

Look through the Learning Framework and identify 3 areas that could do with some more investigation and focus in your organisation, project or community.

1

2

3

Submit these answers for points. See On-Boarding Info at the beginning of the book or go to www.accelerated.co.za

1.7 CONCLUSION

This book is designed to cover each of these aspects through the following parts and chapters, ending in some case studies that will show how all of it can be pulled together to create real, high-impact learning for breakthrough results. You can read the book from cover to cover or dip into the book in areas that catch your interest.

Don't forget to opt in to join our on-line community. See On-Boarding Info at the beginning of the book or go to www.accelerated.co.za for tons of additional resources, links, tools and templates ... AND gain access to great learning rewards.

PART 1: Paradigm shift for Accelerated Learning

1. The need for accelerated learning – what is the critical need, and what holds us back from sustainable learning and results?
2. Paradigm shifts in learning – understanding the evolving world of learning, with current and future trends
3. Insight into Accelerated Learning in South African organisations – a summary of challenges, trends and Accelerated Learning programme examples from interviews with Head of Learning and Development

PART 2: Whole brain, whole person approach to learning

4. Unique learning profile – understanding how people learn and change, and how to customise learning to individuals and create the right environment for accelerated learning
5. Neuroscience of Learning – understanding latest research on cognitive, emotional and social brain responses to different stimuli and situations

PART 3: Creating a Learning Culture

6. Creating a learning culture – what are the ingredients of a learning culture that continually adapts, learns and grows?
7. Learning through coaching – how everyone can be a coach by building key skills and tools
8. Learning through authentic conversations – how leaders can build critical skills required to accelerate learning in themselves and others

PART 4: Designing Accelerated Learning programmes

9. Learning architecture – understanding the performance and competency standards, proficiency levels and needs to inform your learning solution
10. Learning design – exploring foundational and new learning design principles and methodologies in order to enhance and accelerate the learning process
11. Gamification in learning – how to capture the interest and attention of learners throughout the learning journey by using gaming mechanics
12. Learning assessment – how to ensure learning translates into measurable business and behavioural results

PART 5: Making it real – case studies of accelerated learning

13. Case Study: Breakthrough Learning for talent pools – a case study on the design and implementation of an Accelerated Learning programme for key talent (potential successors)
14. Case Study: How to guide – learning to accelerate – a case study on how integrated learning can accelerate the change process in a large scale change intervention
15. Case Study: Creating a culture of effective decision management – a case study of collaborative design and implementation of an Accelerated Decision Management Programme

CHAPTER 2

THE PARADIGM SHIFT IN LEARNING

By Debbie Craig

2.1 INTRODUCTION

"Learning and innovation go hand in hand. The arrogance of success is to think that what you did yesterday will be sufficient for tomorrow." – William Pollard

A typical day

Here is an example of a typical Monday morning as I was writing this book. The day started with checking my smartphone from my bed for new messages, tweets and mails, and looking through my diary for the day. I caught up with my 22-year-old stepson Jason's weekend activities through Facebook and made a mental note to ask him about the Joburg social event where his Gen Y group of friends get paid for partying, taking photos and videos, and spreading the word through social media.

Later at my desk, I checked in, connected and updated Linked-in with a post on thoughts from my weekend research on the importance of focus in our distracted lives. I responded to urgent mails and checked an online weather site for weather in India for my trip there in three days' time. I searched Google maps on my smartphone on the way to my client, listened to the news on the radio, and had a conversation with a friend while negotiating traffic. During the day, in between meetings and documents, I ordered a baby gift online and found a restaurant for an anniversary celebration that night. I also used my network to get some best practice articles on performance management and passed these on to clients struggling with this issue. I did some more online research for this book and was amazed at the quantity of information available.

At about 11am, back at my home office, Sarah, my 20-year-old stepdaughter, surfaced, and we discussed her day of job-hunting, which included Internet searches on various career and corporate sites. She had had a late night because she had been chatting on Skype to her friend studying medicine in China. She had also received a few late-night texts from friends, which she always answers regardless of the time of day or night. When asked how long she would last without her phone without an anxiety attack, she laughed and made a guess of about two days.

That evening, I received a call from my 70-year-old mother, commenting on my recent activities she had seen on Facebook and updating me on her Skype chat with my brother in the UK, the new book she is reading on her Gobi reader, and the volumes of emails she had to process after her trip to the bush. Her husband (85+) shouted hello from the background, currently looking at the share market on his iPad. He would later play Sudoku on his electronic handheld device. Just two weeks earlier I had witnessed him using the Roberts Bird app on his iPad on a birding outing, showing us how to compare three similar but different birds and their calls. As the evening came to an end, Andrew was skimming through the news on FlipBoard and MyBroadband, and I was watching a series that Jason had downloaded from Netflix. I closed down my day with a quick squiz at my Facebook updates and reading on my Kindle, while Andrew finished up a level on his computer game.

What did I learn?

I learnt about what my family and friends were up to. I learnt about key news headlines. I learnt how to get to where I was going, which new restaurants were open and popular, and about the weather in Mumbai, India for the next week. I learnt more about performance management, mobile usage rates, shifts in learning, millennial learning style, and how the brain retains learning. This was all just-in-time learning.

"Our phones and other mobile devices have become part of our DNA. Think about it for a minute. We never leave home without them. They are always on. We check them an average of 34 times per day; panic if we lose them; and a large percentage of us sleep with them within arm's reach. They have become part of who we are and how we interact with the world around us." (Enders, 2013)

This is the world we live in now. Three generations in my own family were all actively searching, receiving, uploading, downloading, interpreting, summarising, playing and interacting online, on-the-go, each with their preferred devices, apps, programmes or search engines.

2.2 DIGITAL, MOBILE AND SOCIAL MEDIA TRENDS

Reports from many research houses and leading digital providers show an ever-increasing demand for mobile devices and a massive explosion of connections, data services and social media usage. Mobile access to information at our finger-tips will both lead and stimulate the transition to both online and mobile learning with consistently increasing adoption rates of online and mobile learning platforms (Cipolla, 2013).

Mobile devices (notebook PCs, tablet PCs, smart phones and phones) – global sales are growing at an incredible rate with tablet PCs and smart phones having the highest annual growth rate of 35 per cent and 18 per cent respectively (Canalys, 2013).

Social media – monthly global mobile users of the most popular sites in 2013 were found to be: Facebook at 680 million, Twitter at 120 million, Foursquare at 30 million, and LinkedIn at 46 million (Kearney, 2013:9).

Mobile data – volumes are also increasing exponentially with a 66 per cent growth over the last five years (Kearney, 2013:9).

Emerging markets (including South Africa) remain more active on social networks compared with developed countries.

The worldwide market for **mobile learning products and services** is also growing significantly with an annual growth rate of 18.2 per cent over the last 5 years. Developing countries (including South Africa) will have the highest forecast growth rates (up to 30 per cent), making mobile learning an essential strategy to improve education in these dynamic economies (Ambient Insight, 2013). There is also an explosion in **mobile learning value-added services (VAS)** products which deliver learning content over mobile networks.

Participation in **computer games and online gaming** continues to expand leading to more interest in bringing all the positive, learning and engagement aspects of gaming into the marketing and learning environments. The overall market for **gamification** is predicted to grow to $1.6 billion, up from $100 million in 2011. Within the next 5 years, a gamified service for consumer goods marketing and customer retention will become as important as Facebook, Twitter or Amazon. Already a number of organisations are using gamification to train workers, educate students, solve problems and generate new ideas and concepts (Kapp, 2013). See more on gamification in Chapter 11.

The most popular **devices used for learning** today, and which will evolve, integrate and grow, are smartphones, tablets, e-readers, handheld gaming systems, and portable media players. Each of these has the ability to deliver learning content either via text, podcasts, videos or interactive games or apps that facilitate learning. Size of screen and keyboard are no longer considered barriers to usage. SMS or text messaging can be used to reach even learners who have only a standard feature phone. Learning has become a extension of our everyday lives.

The biggest challenge for learning and change specialists in the corporate world is to channel attention and focus on specific content or behaviours that need to change or be learnt. Structured and outcomes-focused learning is competing with billions of other snippets of information that stream into our awareness every second. How do we both harness the accessibility of learning content in an engaging, fun and interesting way while maintaining attention through the learning process, in order to ensure that real skills are retained, embedded and applied back into work contexts?

> Watch this video on YouTube: **10 Hot Consumer Mobile Trends 2014**
> http://www.youtube.com/watch?v=n4xW8BNTpag
> (© Inbj | Dreamstime.com - You Tube Logo And IPhone Photo)

2.3 UNDERSTANDING TODAY'S LEARNER

So what do we need to know today to assist us with designing accelerated learning solutions both now and in the future?

Three key differentiators that can be used to understand today's learner are:

- Their generation
- Their technology user type
- Their motivation to learn.

2.3.1 The generation gap

Generation Theory has been around for a number of years and helps us to understand that people who have lived through different eras, defining events and ways of life develop different value systems which then influence the way they act and interact. While there will always be exceptions to the rule, and everyone is unique, it is quite useful for determining strategies for targeted segments as a whole, and then to adapt from there.

The generations commonly accepted are the Veterans (or traditionalists), the Baby Boomers, the Generation Xers, the Generation Ys (or Millennials), and the youngest generation, the Generation Zs. Four of these six categories are active in the workforce today. Generalising broadly, each of these generations has a particular learning history and style which will potentially have an impact on the way they learn today. As learning professionals and leaders, we need to understand where people are coming from, in order to help accelerate their learning process in a positive and encouraging way.

Table 2.1: Generation Theory: Description of the generations (adapted from Hart, 2008)

Generations	Description
Veterans or traditionalists (born 1925–1945)	Grew up in times of economic hardship, which led them to become disciplined and self-sacrificing. They place duty before pleasure, believe patience is its own reward, see work as an obligation, and as workers, are loyal, hard-working, and dedicated. They respect authority and work within the system. Some of the youngest of this generation are still in the workforce. *We learnt through experience and the life of hard knocks. Being at school meant sitting on hard benches listening to stern-faced teachers following a set syllabus with little room for creativity or interaction. The privileged few went on to a higher education, which was very expensive, while the rest of us learnt a trade through apprenticeship or started working from the bottom.*
Baby Boomers (born 1946–1964)	These are members of a large generation which grew up in economic prosperity after World War II in strong, nuclear families with stay-at-home mums. They are competitive, optimistic, and focus on personal accomplishments. They are workaholics, who "live to work", and often take work home. Their job or profession defines them, and they like to feel valued and needed. They have no work–life balance; many have sacrificed a home life for a career, and for those who have tried both, it has been a juggling act. This generation has dominated the workforce for many years, and now its members hold significant positions within it. *We learnt primarily in formal institutions such as school classrooms, colleges and universities. We learnt from teachers and experts in their field, using textbooks, library books and encyclopaedias. Once we had an education, we applied our skills and learnt further on the job. Careers had to be chosen while very young, and stuck to for life, with little room for change, which would have meant starting again.*

Generations	Description
Generation X (born 1965–1979)	Grew up in very different circumstances. For many, having divorced parents and mothers at work was the norm. This led to their characteristic resilience, independence, and adaptability. At work, they take employment seriously and have a pragmatic approach to getting things done. They "work to live, not live to work", and move in and out of the workforce to accommodate their family and children.
	We were encouraged by our parents to get an education and build a career. We joined industrial bodies, networked, and attended further education and conferences to expand our learning over the years. Corporates invested a lot of money in our development. Computers started to become an extension of our work tools and we had to learn a whole new world of technology later on in life. In addition, we started learning about the world and other cultures through black and white TV, which later progressed to colour.
	These are the children of Baby Boomers, who indulged them and gave them lots of attention. They now display a high level of self-confidence. This generation grew up in good times, and spent more time in full-time education than any previous generation. Because they have known only economic prosperity, they do not fear unemployment. They are self-reliant and very social. Friends are very important to them, and they have a large network. They like to multi-task, and are always moving on to the next thing. They question everything, hence their alias: "Generation Why?" In the workplace they are not afraid of challenging managers (Baby Boomers). Work for them is a means to an end; it is a place, not their identity. They want flexible working hours, to be able to work from home, and to have time off for travel. Gen Y-ers are quite happy to leave a job if it doesn't come up to expectations. They think they can have it all and are not embarrassed to ask for it. They are happy to job hop until they find what they want.
	Gen Y's spend more time online(for leisure or work) than watching TV, mostly downloading music, video and movies before they hit the stores. They are the highest users of mobile social networks such as Web 2.0 i.e. blogging, file sharing, location-based socialisation services, chat, and so on.

Generations	Description
Generation Y or Millennials (born 1980–1995)	*We learn as we go and when we need to, using technology and contacts. We know that information is a click away, so there is no point in learning stuff now for which we can't see a use. Some of us have learnt through home schooling and at private colleges; the rest of us have dragged ourselves through school not understanding the point of it all, and actually learning about life and the world through TV and the Internet. Some of us have followed our parents' wishes by going to university, but many of us have preferred the experiential route of testing a lot of things to see what fits in between gap years, gaming and chill sessions. Learning is not limited to an age or an event, but is a continuous process of discovery.*
Generation Z (born 1996 onwards)	These members will start appearing in the workforce in five or so years. They are digital natives who grew up with the technology. They are "native speakers" of the digital language of computers, video games, and the Internet. Because of this, they "think and process information fundamentally differently from their predecessors". Digital natives share a common global culture that is not defined strictly by age, but by certain attributes and experiences related to how they interact with information technology, information itself, one another, and other people and institutions.
	We learn almost everything through technology. The world-wide web is part of our identity and expression and as natural to explore and use and our fingers. Our phones and tablets are an extension of our limbs and go with us everywhere, with uncapped data and continuous Wi-Fi being the norm. Education will most likely be through online multi-media interactive courses enhanced with gamification techniques to keep us stimulated and interested.

Worth reading: There is a very good overview of the different generations' values, learning motivation, delivery methods and feedback preferences in Learning Style, Defence Centres of Excellence (Defence Centres of Excellence, nd). *Visit www.accelerated.co.za for more information.*

Table 2.2: Generational Learning Style: (adapted form Defence Centres of Excellence, nd)

	Traditionalists	Baby boomers	Generation X	Millennials
Ages	Ages 66+ Born prior to 1946	Ages 47–65 Born 1946–1964	Ages 29–46 Born 1965–1982	Ages 18–28 Born 1983–1993 (Roughly 26% of the population)
Values	• Respect authority • Conservative values • Conformity • Discipline	• Optimism • Involvement • Hard work	• Scepticism • Fun • Informality • Self-reliance	• Realism • Confidence • Extreme fun • Social and networking
Values (continued)	• Formality • Structured environment with clear expectations			• Structured environment with clear expectations
Learning motivation	• Knowledge of history and context • Public recognition • Training relevant to organisational goals • Leadership opportunities	• Public and peer recognition • Training relevant to career goals • Training by invitation as a perk	• Training relevant to personal goals • Recognition from instructor • Mentoring opportunities	• Training as fast track to success • Structured assignments with tight deadlines • Networking opportunities
Delivery methods	• Accustomed to classroom-based lectures • Dislike role plays and learning games; they fear feeling foolish	• Accustomed to lecture and/ or workshops • Small group exercises • Discussion may elicit "safe" rather than honest answers	• Accustomed to eLearning • Experiential learning, such as role play activities • On-the-job training and self-study, allowing them to multi-task	• Accustomed to eLearning leveraging wikis, blogs, podcasts, mobile applications • Hands-on learning and collaboration leveraging technology
Feedback	• Assume they are meeting objectives unless they receive contrary feedback	• Prefer well-documented feedback all at once	• Prefer regular feedback	• Prefer frequent, on-demand feedback

The impact of Millennials

Jane Hart in *Understanding Today's Learner* (2008) eloquently describes Millennials as follows:

"Millennials comprise approximately 25 per cent of today's workforce with the percentage growing each year. This is a substantial group of people who have grown up in a world very different from the other generations, whose lives are saturated in technology, who are wired differently and have startling attitudinal differences and preferences. New research is showing that their brains are evolving due to the constant influences of technologies. This is the generation that does not write; they keyboard. They are in constant multi-tasking mode, and whose friends are no longer limited by the proximity of their neighbourhoods, schools or even cities. Their social networks are their lifelines and they don't hesitate to reach out and ask their network how to find a job, solve a problem or access resources. This is the generation that expects their work environment to be at least as tech savvy as they are. It is no longer possible to think workers have the same approach to life, work, or learning as their bosses. In fact, Time *magazine reported that Generation Y is forcing a cultural shift on companies and managers. As such they are becoming change agents, forcing organisations to rethink and improve their methods of recruiting, training, and management. If we don't create an environment that embraces and provides tools to support this generation's professional growth, they will move to another organisation that does. Not only do you need to consider the Millennials when designing learning solutions but include them in the solutions' design and development process."*

> Watch this video on YouTube: **Leading Millennials: How to Motivate and Engage the Future Workforce:**
> http://www.youtube.com/watch?v=HgD1P33o4xU
> (© Inbj | Dreamstime.com - You Tube Logo And IPhone Photo)

2.3.2 Technology user types

Technology users can typically fall into 2 categories with some obvious exceptions (like my 80+ stepfather): digital natives and digital immigrants. The students of today are digital natives; they are all "native speakers" of the digital language of computers, video games and the Internet.

So what does that make the rest of us? Those of us who were not born into the digital world but have at some later point in our lives become fascinated by and adopted many or most aspects of the new technology are, and always will be when compared to them, digital immigrants (Prensky) 2001.

Table 2.3: Technology user types

Digital immigrants	Digital natives
• Members of the older generations • Learnt to use the technology to adapt to their environment • Always retain, to some degree, their 'accent', i.e.their foot in the past • May embrace computers, Internet, mobile devices, and so on, but use the technology very differently from the younger generations • Can be just as connected, if not more so, than their younger counterparts through goal-directed effort and amount of time invested (experimentation and practice)	• Grew up with the technology • Technology is a natural extension of their environment • Native speakers of the digital language of computers, video games, and the Internet • Inseparable from their mobile devices. Think and process information fundamentally differently from their predecessors • Share a common global culture that is defined not by age, but by how they interact with information technology, one another, and institutions

Whether someone is a digital immigrant or a digital native, they **may** have very different patterns of engagement with technology and social media, depending on:

- Level of engagement – how they interact with the tools,
- Frequency of engagement – how regularly they use it
- Scale of engagement – range of tools they use.

Three types of engagement are outlined in Table 2.4 below.

Table 2.4: Engagement types (adapted from Hart, 2008)

Engagement Types	
Readers (passive consumers)	Users who simply browse websites, blogs, and wikis, watch videos, listen to podcasts, and so on
Participants (active contributors)	Users who contribute to content in blogs, wikis and other websites, share links using online bookmarking services or from their RSS readers; or otherwise connect with others using instant messaging, SMSs, micro-blogging, and social networking services

Engagement Types	
Creators (pro-active producers)	Users who create and share their own content such as photos, videos, and other files and documents, as well as build their own blogs, wikis, social networks, and so on, in order to encourage connections and discussion with others

Learning design must cater for both digital immigrants and natives, as well as for the different engagement preferences.

2.3.3 Motivation to learn

To accelerate and design learning experiences effectively, we also need to know that learning (which takes effort) will generally be individually motivated only in a moment of need. Seven of the main moments of need are explained below. They should be identified and the approach adjusted for each specific need.

Table 2.5: Moments of need (adapted from Enders, 2013)

Aspect	Description
New	Learn how to do something for the first time
More	Expand the breadth and depth of what has been learnt
Apply	Act upon what has been learnt, including planning, remembering or adapting learning to a unique situation
Solve	Solve problems: When things break, or don't work the way they were intended to, or when confronted with unexpected challenges
Change	Learn a new way of doing something, requiring a change in mind-set or skills that are deeply ingrained in performance practices/behaviour
Who	Learn who to connect with, consult with or gain decisions from in an organisation, client and community network. Usually required with a new hire, transition, restructuring or M&A (mergers and acquisitions)
How	Learn how things are done within the culture of the organisation. Usually required with a new hire, transition, restructuring or M&A

2.3.4 A profile of today's new breed of learner

Aggregating all the characteristics identified so far, we can build a profile of the new learner of today as someone who is:

• Most likely to be under 30 (and a member of Generation Y or Z) but may also be older than 30 (and a member of Gen X, Baby Boomer, Veterans)
• A digital native (or a very tech-savvy digital immigrant)
• Connected 24/7 via a PC and/or mobile device, and
• A highly engaged user of a broad range of social media tools on a frequent (daily) basis.

Some features of the new breed of learner

• They prefer hyperlinked information coming from many sources.
• They are skilled multi-taskers, and they parallel process. They are used to working with different content and interacting with others simultaneously.
• They are highly visual learners, preferring to process pictures, sounds, and video rather than text.
• They are experiential learners who learn by discovery rather than being "told". They like to interact with content in order to explore and draw their own conclusions. Simulations, games, and role-playing allow them to learn by "being there", and also to enjoy themselves and have fun.
• They have short attention spans, so prefer bite-sized chunks of content (on either a PC or an iPod).
• They are very social, and love to share with others. They enjoy working in teams. Interaction with others is key to their learning, and they want to be part of a community, collaborating, sharing, and exchanging ideas.
• They are happy to take on different roles in their learning, as a student, or even as an instructor or facilitator or supporter of others, and switch between the roles.
• They prefer to learn "just in time", that is, have access to relevant information they can apply immediately.
• They need immediate feedback, responsiveness, and ideas from others, as they are used to instant gratification.
• They are very independent learners, and are able to teach themselves with guidance; they don't need sets of instructions like their predecessors – they found out how to use their iPods or Google in just the same way.
• They prefer to construct their own learning, assembling information and tools from different sources. (Hart, 2008)

Activity 1

Describe your technology engagement type:

- Generation: veteran, baby boomer, Gen X, Gen Y, Gen Z
- User type: digital immigrant or native
- Engagement type: reader, participant, creator
- Favourite platforms and apps for learning and engaging

Share via e.mail or Facebook to level up. See OnBoarding for more info on how to do this.

2.4 PARADIGM SHIFT

The first paradigm shift in learning occurred over 500 years ago and involved the move from oral language to written text. The current paradigm shift is just as significant, moving from text-based learning to Internet-based multi-media, social learning and collaborative tools. This shift has already and will continue to change fundamentally the way in which knowledge and skills are acquired and how learners interact with content, teachers, "experts" and co-learners. This new paradigm opens up tremendous opportunities for both efficiency and effectiveness of the learning process, and accessibility to the masses; hence the potential to accelerate learning worldwide. However, it also presents a considerable challenge in transforming mind-sets and habits that are hard-wired into our preferences and behaviour if we are to make the transition quickly and successfully (Treadwell, 2013).

There are many aspects to this paradigm shift. I have chosen eight of these to highlight their impact on our ability to accelerate the learning process. They are shown in Figure 2.1 below.

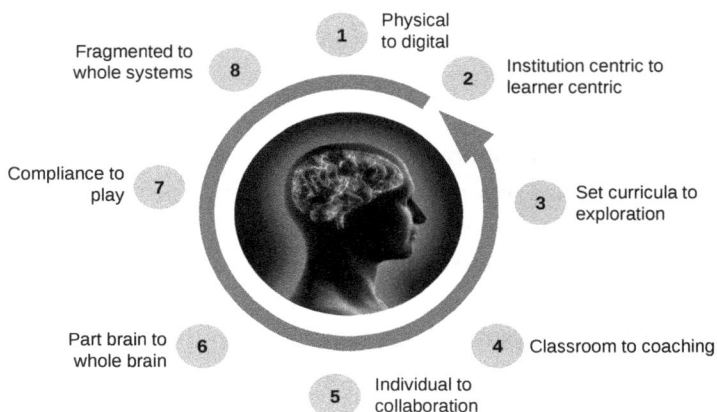

Figure 2.1: Paradigm shifts in learning

2.4.1 Physical to digital

Physical (paper-based) books, text-books, learner guides and hand-written exams are gradually becoming a thing of the past. Most of our future learning experience will happen on a digital platform, using multiple sources of online material, research assignments, typed up "portfolios of evidence" and virtual assessments. This requires digital literacy to be able to navigate the masses of data available, to distinguish fact from fiction, to differentiate solid research from public perception, and to analyse, interpret and integrate findings into useful insights and recommendations. It is also no longer necessary to be at a physical location for learning to take place.

Lectures and seminars are now occurring through webinars, virtual classrooms, video-conferencing, pod-casts, YouTube videos, downloadable items or posted DVD sets. When everyone is connected digitally with cameras and sound, learners can interact, ask questions, get answers, comment, blog, vote, rate, and correspond directly with the educator. Informal learning can also now occur among communities of interested parties, without "educators", as we now have access to "experts" who wish to share and interact with communities, such as: social media gurus, software developers, executive coaches, neuroscience professors, survivors of incurable disease, innovators, and even doctors and lawyers. People spend many hours of their discretionary time (often without pay) creating content, solving problems, responding to queries, and connecting on community forums.

The physical age of the university or business school campus experience is also changing rapidly. Already many Massive Open Online Courses (MOOCs) are being offered.

> *Worth reading: Shift Learning – The History (and Future) of MOOCs* (Imber, 2014). *Visit www.accelerated.co.za for more information.*

While digital learning ticks the boxes of efficiency and effectiveness, accessibility, cost, just-in-time, volumes, learner driven, and so on, it also has its challenges in building and sustaining real emotional connection and motivation with the learning (an important component of whole brain learning). Physical learning institutions will always have their place in fostering intellectual stimulation and debate, group collaboration, and social learning. The way in which they construct the learning experience will, however, change dramatically.

Don't wait for a magic bullet in choosing your digital platforms. Investigate different digital platforms and devices. Challenge your policies with regard to personal applications and mobile integration. Assess your own comfort with learning in the digital age and expand your boundaries into interacting and creating your own content. Learn from the pioneers who have gone before you in order to avoid making early adopter mistakes. It will most probably be a steep learning curve, which you can't miss out on if you want to be a learning organisation one day.

Massive Open Online Courses (MOOCs)

"A MOOC is an online course aimed at unlimited participation and open access via the web. In addition to traditional course materials such as videos, readings, and problem sets, MOOCs provide interactive user forums that help build a community for students, professors, and teaching assistants" (*Wikipedia*, 2014).

MOOCs first came into being in 2008 as pioneers in distance-learning technology. There was an unprecedented growth rate explosion in 2012 with as many as five million students undertaking a MOOC in 2012 across three leading providers alone. There are for profit and not-for-profit MOOCs, many offering the learning modules for free, although assessment and certification come at a cost. Some predict that online courses spell the demise of universities, while others say they could be key to maintaining a competitive edge, although at a huge cost. Harvard and MIT invested $30 million each into edX programmes. With their high development cost, for MOOCs to be successful in the future, they need to generate some form of revenue, authenticate and certify students as appropriate, and offer an enjoyable experience.

2.4.2 Institution centric to learner centric

The focus of learning solutions development used to be institution driven. Schools, colleges, universities, organisations, private learning providers and professional industry bodies were the ones who were setting the standards, prioritising content, establishing criteria for access or success, and investing their resources accordingly. Once a learner had chosen their preferred supplier of learning, they were pretty much stuck in the system and had to follow the process to get a recognised result or certificate.

While traditional learning is still offered and invested in, the focus is shifting to customised learner-centric solutions. Learning providers are now offering multiple options within their learning framework, allowing individuals to choose how and when they learn, what content they wish to focus on, which format will they be assessed on, and encouraging unconstrained research on their chosen topic (without being limited to an "acceptable" list of sources). As long as the learner can produce the evidence of knowledge, skills or behaviour acquired and applied, the learner can achieve success by optimising his/her own learning style and life-style.

Even classroom-based learning caters for the individual by allowing more choice. Learners can choose facilitators, topics, application projects, groups to work with, which pre-work to focus on, which sources of information they will access, and how to build their portfolios of evidence.

This approach certainly does challenge the traditional institutional way of thinking and requires additional investment in learning platforms, options, and up-to-date content. It is frightening to think that learners can sit in a class and google multiple other research studies and theories from around the world, and challenge their lecturer in the moment. Educators and learning designers need to build new competencies to stay up to date with these new trends and remain current and relevant.

2.4.3 Set curricula to exploration towards outcomes

Learning will no longer be limited to set curricula. I remember being posted my thick, heavy MBA manuals from an international business school and being able to write my exams by just reading, summarising and remembering what was in these books. Learning material that is developed today can be outdated within months or a few years depending on the industry. Learners will be encouraged to explore, research, experiment and experience the full gamut of a topic, so that learning becomes embedded and integrated in the brain as opposed to being placed in short-term recall memory that fades over time.

In organisations, learning will be both a targeted and a continuous process. For specific short-term skills acquisition (for potential successors, scarce skills or large-scale change), there will be many planned events and experiences over a period of time, sometimes called a learning chain, spaced learning or interval learning.

Modern learning theory and new insights from neuroscience show that the format of single-event presentation of materials is not very effective for long-term memory formation. More effective is seeing the new materials over time, in bite-sized chunks, in different formats, and then seeing them again at a later time, particularly as a review or test. This leads to greater retention and ability to apply the new knowledge or skill.

A great example of the application of this thinking is the redesign of the online fellowship, the Master Psychopharmacology Program at the University of California.

Worth reading: Play it Again: The Master Psychopharmacology Program (Stahl et al, 2010).

> **The Master Psychopharmacology Program (MPP) (University of California)**
>
> This is an online learning programme in the field of psychopharmacology designed to enhance retention of new information and to facilitate its transfer into clinical practice. It has been programmed to do this by applying the principles of adult learning such as maximising encoding of new information at the time of original presentation of new materials, followed by adapting interval learning techniques to repeat new information in various formats, including tests, and over various time intervals. Specifically, original presentations of content are designed to be delivered in multiple novel online formats; to be bite sized; to take only minutes to complete rather than an hour; and also to require interactivity constantly. Also, online testing is extensively integrated into the MPP, both as an assessment tool and as a learning tool during iterations of the original content. Finally, numerous additional activities are made available for self-directed learning so that participants can choose additional sources of information either to help them to encode difficult-to-learn materials or to provide them with additional mechanisms to repeat and thereby to consolidate easier-to-learn materials in another format and upon demand.

Continuous learning will also be encouraged and recognised to ensure skills remain relevant, sharp and continuously improve performance and prepare for the next level of work. Organisations will be providing social and mobile learning opportunities and applications to access information, networks, experts, coaches, forums, lessons learnt, etc. in industry and organisation specific products, services and processes. Personal development plans will be less rigid or course/event based, and more learner driven and outcomes focused, with the end result being able to demonstrate competence. Learning specialists will need to enhance the ability in leaders to guide or facilitate this exploration and to assess outcomes and competence, without relying solely on the external certification process of the past.

Learners will have access to multiple sources (instead of a few recommended sources), many experts (instead of one teacher/lecturer) and will not only absorb content, but may actually generate and share content that will assist other learners. The competitive advantage of organisations will no longer be in protected Intellectual Property but in the skills of employees to absorb, interrogate, innovate, integrate and apply knowledge to create newer, better and faster offerings and solutions as compared to their competitors.

2.4.4 Classroom to coaching

Globalisation, competition, access to information, speed, complexity, and change all result in overwhelming demands on our time. There seems to be less and less time available to be out of the office, off-site or offline for more than a few hours at a time. Gone are the days of luxurious week-long learning programmes or three-day strategy sessions. Knowledge is acquired mostly online, skills are learnt are applied on-the-job with often immediate feedback, and behaviour is practised wherever possible with the support and feedback of a coach to keep us honest with ourselves.

Ten years ago, it was a challenge to get leaders to admit that they needed the assistance of a coach, never mind suggesting that they could be a coach or mentor to others. Now there is hardly an executive or senior manager who is not in or has not been in some sort of coaching relationship. The benefits have been demonstrated over and over again, with the primary benefits being that coaching is time efficient and individually focused. It also encourages reflexive learning and builds the skills to think about our thinking, which leads to mindfulness, emotional intelligence, awareness of choices and impact, and therefore enhanced decision making. The coaching process often includes gaining feedback from peers or managers, which opens up the Johari Window of self-discovery, and aligns self-perceptions with the views of others allowing greater insight and therefore impact.

Most online learning experiences and organisational accelerated learning programmes are supported by some form of coaching: lecturers, teaching assistants, co-ordinators, mentors or coaches. If learning specialists and leaders are not open to and actively embracing coaching (for themselves and others) as a means to accelerate the learning process, they will find themselves way behind the curve.

> The coaching industry has mushroomed and grown in leaps and bounds over the last 10 years, as indicated in a 2012 report by the International Coach Federation. In the *2013 Leadership Development Survey* by Stout-Rostron et al (2013), mentoring (67 per cent) was seen as the tool most valuable to develop decision-making skills and problem-solving skills in leaders. This was supported by action learning and coaching by external coaches (57 per cent).

2.4.5 Individual to collaborative learning

"Social learning is a natural continual process of learning with others and from others. It is nothing new. But with the help of modern social technologies, it is now possible to enable and support it in powerful new ways." – Jane Hart (2011)

Our previous heritage of learning occurred primarily as individuals facilitated through a trainer in a classroom. This progressed to e-learning facilitated through online content rich courses and a learning management system (LMS). Next came blended learning, whereby classroom training and e-learning were combined to optimise time out of the office. While group work has always been part of the classroom experience, the learning was still largely individual in focus. In the last decade, a more social and interactive form of learning has emerged to keep up with the progressively digital nature of learning. Social learning became the trend, using social media applications in both training and e-learning to enhance the social element of learning, and to encourage learners to interact with each other, despite not being in physical proximity to each other. This was especially popular within distance-learning institutions as a support mechanism among learners in different regions. It also gained ground in large multi-national organisations where networking, building relationships and sharing information while learning virtually was important.

The current paradigm has been coined "collaborative learning" (CL).

Collaborative learning (CL)

"CL is an umbrella term for a variety of educational approaches involving the joint intellectual effort from small group projects to the more specific form of group work known as cooperative learning. CL suggests a way of dealing with people which respects and highlights individual group members' abilities and contributions. There is a sharing of authority and acceptance of responsibility among group members for the groups' actions. The underlying premise of CL is based upon consensus building through co-operation by group members, in contrast to competition, in which individuals best other group members" (Laal, 2011).

This approach departs radically from the traditional learner–teacher relationship, treating learners and teachers as adults (equals), each with his/her own unique experience and ideas to contribute. Collaboration can occur either in the classroom (face to face) or virtually through online discussion via forums, chat rooms, Skype, and so on. Learners collaborate with each other to research, write papers, complete group projects, solve joint problems, design innovations, challenge and expand critical thinking, and manage project stakeholders, among others.

The trend towards collaborative learning is premised on the Smart Worker. Jane Hart (2011) says that the Smart Worker:

- Recognises that she learns continuously as she does her job.
- Wants immediate access to solutions to her performance problems.
- Is happy to share what she knows.
- Relies on a trusted network on friends and colleagues.
- Learns best with and from others.

- Keeps up to date with her industry and profession.
- Constantly strive to improve her productivity.
- Thrives on autonomy.

Teachers or facilitators therefore become less of experts or transmitters of knowledge and more of expert designers of learning experiences for learners – acting more as coaches or midwives of a more emergent learning process.

> *"Through social media, mobile learning, blended learning, eLearning, and other inherently connected learning experiences, it is possible to leverage the potential of inter-dependence and crowds. This occurs simply through crowd-sourced knowledge (e.g., Quora, Wikipedia, learnist), visually through curation (e.g., scoopit, Pinterest, MentorMob), and long term through digital communities (e.g., Twitter, Google+, Facebook)"* (Heick, 2013).

> *"Social media can help to support and enhance learning, but the presence of social media doesn't necessarily mean social learning will take place." – Hart (2008)*

Collaborative learning sounds interesting, interactive and fun. However, it takes a significant mind-set change, especially for the older generations. While it may be interactive, it still takes time and effort, not always leading to direct rewards. Contributions may end up being unequal; people may not deliver their pieces on time; or they may leave the learning space halfway through a programme as a result of resignation, promotion, transfer, life crisis, and so on.

Building and maintaining an interactive, creative, user-friendly virtual workspace is also very costly and requires on-going maintenance, upgrades and updates. In addition, adoption rates for social learning platforms are slow. Offering a new corporate platform is only a piece of a very large puzzle. People are used their own platforms, applications and mobile devices and use them in a certain way (for example, Facebook, Twitter, WhatsApp, Pinterest). Changing this behaviour requires well-thought-through change management strategies and a long-term outlook. Dean Retief, the CLO of Nedbank South Africa, says that adoption rates for their social platforms is one of their big challenges.

Watch this video on YouTube: **Learning Collaboration**
http://www.youtube.com/watch?v=9IpouFsyGMw
(© Inbj | Dreamstime.com - You Tube Logo And IPhone Photo)

2.4.6 Part brain to whole brain (neuroscience of learning)

Learning is a continuous, lifelong process and is happening consciously and unconsciously all of the time. New neural pathways are being formed and old, outdated programmes deleted or adjusted. A whole brain approach to learning is not new per se. There are many models that encourage us to use whole brain techniques including Dr Ned Herman's *Whole Brain Thinking*, Kolb, Honey & Mumford's *Learning Styles*, and the Neurolinguistic Programming (NLP) representation systems (see more on this in Chapter 4).

Recent developments in our understanding of the brain have led to major shifts in understanding how people learn and how to optimise this. Learning theory is no longer based just on theories or models but also on validated scientific evidence achieved through new advances in brain-mapping technologies.

> *"Up until the 1980s, scientists thought the structure of the brain developed during childhood and that once developed, there was very little room for change. Scientists now know that the brain possesses enormous capacity to change. People's ability to process widely varied information and complex new experiences with relative ease can often be surprising. The brain's ability to act and react in ever-changing ways is known as neuroplasticity"* (Maritz Institute, 2010).

The latest research into Neuroscience helps us to identify specific brain functioning and processes for learning. If learning experiences are designed with the whole brain in mind, they can be accelerated, be more efficient, and be much more fun. Instead of spending most of our time focused on delivering content, we could be focusing on optimising the learning process. This will result in greater engagement and motivation, better retention and memory recall of knowledge, positive emotional association with the learning, and the confidence to apply the new thinking or behaviours. See Chapter 5 for further interesting applications of Neuroscience to learning.

You can start immediately by reviewing the learning design of current learning interventions and providers. Assess them against the principles of whole brain learning. Search for opportunities to bring more playfulness into training situations. Experiment with simple gamification to engage learners more. Brush up on your own understanding of neuroscience and how people learn and change. Teach your leaders how to optimise the environment for learning and avoid the emotionally charged traps that put learners into the limbic response pattern of flight, fight or freeze.

Brain Break: Turn your book upside down and read like this for 5 minutes (this helps shift your brain patterns).

2.4.7 Fragmented to whole systems learning

While the concept of systems thinking and the learning organisation has been around for many years, the majority of organisations still admit to not learning fast enough, not being sufficiently strategic in learning framework design, not being able to inculcate a culture of learning, not successfully equipping leaders with a learning organisation mind-set, not responding fast enough to industry and global changes, and still being way behind the curve on skills, talent and change readiness.

What Is systems thinking?

"Whenever I'm trying to help people understand what this word 'system' means, I usually start by asking: 'Are you a part of a family?' Everybody is a part of a family. 'Have you ever seen in a family people producing consequences in the family, how people act, how people feel, that aren't what anybody intends?' Yes. 'How does that happen?' Well ... then people tell their stories and think about it. But that then grounds people in not the jargon of 'system' or 'systems thinking' but the reality – that we live in webs of interdependence" (Senge, 2012).

There have been many attempts at addressing and implementing a systems approach to learning. Some organisations seem to be getting it right: Disney, Zappos and Apple. Many are still stuck in the past with event-based learning, ad-hoc planning, outdated didactic "training" courses, and personal development plans that read like a wish list of courses to attend without direct impact on the job. A few brave souls have stepped out and experimented with building learning organisations, but are still struggling with the complexity and relentless energy and effort required for sustainable leadership and culture transformation.

An organisation's ability to adapt and respond to its environment (system), is a product of its ability to think (as individuals and collectively), to be skilled at creating, acquiring and transferring knowledge; and at modifying its behaviour to reflect new knowledge and insights. Learning is the foundation to improve products, processes or services continuously and is the critical link between strategic intent and results, between thinking about doing something and getting it done.

Peter Senge, who popularised the concept of the learning organisation in his book *The Fifth Discipline: The Art and Practice of the Learning Organization*

(1990), suggests five learning disciplines that provide vital dimensions in building organisations that can truly learn. These are: personal mastery, mental models, shared vision, team learning and systems thinking. These dimensions develop separately, although each dimension is critical for the others' success. These five disciplines represent approaches for developing three core learning capabilities: fostering aspiration, developing reflective conversation, and understanding complexity.

Five disciplines of a systemic learning organisation

Personal mastery – a discipline of continually clarifying and deepening our personal vision, of focusing our energies, of developing patience, and of seeing reality objectively.

Mental models – deeply ingrained assumptions, generalisations, or even pictures of images that influence how we understand the world and how we take action. This includes the openness needed to unearth shortcomings in perceptions

Building shared vision – a practice of unearthing shared pictures of the future that foster genuine commitment and enrolment rather than compliance.

Team learning – starts with dialogue, the capacity of members of a team to suspend assumptions and enter into genuine thinking together. This includes the skills of groups of people to look for the larger picture beyond individual perspectives.

Systems thinking – the Fifth Discipline that integrates the other four.

Learning organisations are rare because these five disciplines are difficult to implement. Overwhelming change, time constraints, short-termism, egos, politics, power and competition still plague the domain of organised business. If building a learning organisation using the whole systems approach is taken seriously, **senior executives** need to be fully committed to these five behaviours. This would entail first of all working on their own personal mastery (and blind spots) and challenging their own mental models and assumptions. It would mean shaping a shared vision and values of continuous learning throughout the entire organisation. Priority would need to be given to building an effective, aligned, high-performance executive team that is able to have regular and robust individual and team crucial conversations. And finally, it would require the investment of time and resources to think systemically and strategically in their approach to learning frameworks, architecture, culture, leadership, processes and people. This would require the willingness to enter into not just change, but personal and organisational *transformation*.

This is not a quick fix, but a long-term investment in learning how to learn, building mindfulness and reflexive thinking muscle, and being willing to take risks, open up to feedback, learn from mistakes, and grow through the process. Individual learning leads to team learning which leads to organisational learning in an ongoing systemic cycle.

"The concept of intelligence we need will never be achieved by a handful of smart individuals. It's not about 'the smartest guys in the room'. It's about what we can do collectively. So the intelligence that matters is collective intelligence". – Peter Senge (2012)

2.4.8 Compliance to play (gamification of learning)

Play and playfulness

Traditionally, learning has been a serious business. We used to choose a career, identify the qualifications required, understand the outcomes to be learnt, and focus years of our lives in the pursuit of an education. Then we joined the corporate world, and continued the very serious business of learning about and complying with leadership or technical competencies. Classroom learning required sitting still, listening and discipline. Only the talented few who stand out from the crowd are eligible for additional learning and promotion opportunities.

Compare this to how we learn as children., Play forms an integral part of the early development of children; they play to explore, to learn new things or to practice a skill. They also play to build relationships or just to have fun. They use their imagination, their creativity and their experiences. They also use heroes, props, space and expression. Research findings show that play in children increases problem solving ability, creative capacity, emotional expressiveness, reading and storytelling competency, literacy, language skills, writing ability, cooperation with other children, and produces better behaved children.

However, as the child matures into an adult, play and playfulness are given less attention in the teaching and learning process and we allow less and less fun, spontaneity, connecting, silliness, goofiness, creativity and imagination. Studies show that encouraging play in the learning environment has multiple benefits and stimulates the parts of the brain that enhance creativity, connection, memory, positive emotion and appropriate risk taking. While participants say that playfulness leads to fun, enjoyment, and laughter, it also leads to cognitive gains in terms of engagement, retention, and understanding (Tanis, 2012). In this evolving digital world, the more we can encourage self-directed learning and allow learners to "play" with information, platforms, and ideas, the more benefits are possible. This requires user-friendly, playful, colourful interfaces with many options and choices for unique individuals to learn through the process of exploring, finding, experimenting, interpreting, proposing, and so on. We can also do more to bring play into classroom learning, through fun activities, creative role plays, competitive or collaborative games, art, music, colour and movement.

Gamification

The phenomenal popularity of computer games worldwide has stimulated learning designers to apply some of the techniques that engage and absorb gamers into learning experiences though play. Some of these techniques include a narrative (story), player control, immediate feedback, opportunities for collaborative problem solving, scaffolded learning with increasing challenges, opportunities for mastery, and levelling up and social connection. With so many issues demanding our attention on a daily basis, and being in contact 24/7 on our mobile devices, we struggle to really engage or focus on any one thing, to do it properly. A key feature in learning design in the future will be capturing the interest of learners and inspiring them to continue learning.

Gamification techniques have been used in simple ways to increase completion of pre-work, workshop attendance and participation and post-workshop action learning assignments. Gamification strategies can be used in classroom learning through the use of leader boards, prizes, puzzles, games, voting, online chat forums, levelling up, and additional rewards for finding new ways of applying the learning. Incorporating elements from games into classroom scenarios is a way to provide students with opportunities to act autonomously, to display competence, and to learn in relationship to others.

You will even notice how a few simple gamification techniques have been woven into this book!

More sophisticated gamification has been used to teach armed forces to prepare for or adapt to different scenarios; to teach medical staff how to diagnose and treat different diseases; to train security officers to act safely in the workplace; to teach vehicle technicians how to fix or maintain different makes of cars; to train counsellors how to counsel effectively with empathy, assess cognitive potential, and allow leaders to experiment with business scenarios, and so on. See more on gamification in Chapter 11.

Within the **South African context**, it could be argued that learning is becoming limited to a narrow Seta context. Companies and organisations are implementing learning and development activities based on the advice of BEE consultants as to how to gain maximum advantage from learning activities, without giving learning a context. Many organisations believe that they are learning organisations because they are complying with requirements. The context of a learning organisation is much wider than isolated learning "events" (Fourie, 2012).

2.5 CONCLUSION

"It's challenging enough to manage a traditional learning environment where the curriculum is handed to you, and meetings are set, and you're simply there to manage; adding more ingredients to the mix seems like asking for trouble. But the truth is, it's becoming increasingly difficult to educate people in the face of such radical technological and pedagogical progression. The good news is, many of the elements of a progressive learning environment – e.g. digital literacy, connectivism, and play – conveniently, and not coincidentally, work together. And better yet, collectively they can reduce the burden on those managing the learning because they place the learner at the centre.

While it's possible to try out these ideas on a traditional classroom, and then sit back and wait for the clouds to part and the sun to shine brilliantly, you'll likely be waiting a while. These aren't single tools to "try", but new ways to think about how learners access media, how educators define success, and what the roles of immense digital communities should be in popularising new learning models.

"None of it is really complicated – it just requires new thinking"
– Heick (2013).

Activity 2

Which 2 paradigms does your organisation need to shift in order to accelerate learning?

1
2

Which 2 paradigms do you need to shift in order to be able to learn faster?

1
2

Share via e.mail or Facebook to level up. See OnBoarding for more info on how to do this.

INSIGHT INTO ACCELERATED LEARNING IN SOUTH AFRICAN ORGANISATIONS

By Debbie Craig

3.1 INTRODUCTION

"What counts in life is not the mere fact that we have lived. It is what difference we have made to the lives of others that will determine the significance of the life we lead." – Nelson Mandela

In preparation for writing this book, we wanted to get an insight into what SA organisations were up to in the Accelerated Learning space. We aimed for a cross-section of industries and to talk to people who were active contributors in the industry. We asked them about their Accelerated Learning challenges, what new learning methodologies and tools they were experimenting with, what current Accelerated Learning programmes they were running, and how ready they felt their leaders were to be learning and change champions. The intention is to offer you, our reader, a snapshot in this space of insight into what South African organisations are up to, and perhaps how your organisation compares. It will also give you a sense of some real examples of Accelerated Learning programmes and methods. Thanks to all the contributors for sharing and being part of the collaboration to make this book real and relevant.

The insights are from the following organisations: Nedbank, RMB and Investec (banking); Dimension Data (Information Technology/ITC); Eskom (Infrastructure/ Electricity); AVI (Manufacturing/FMCG); Harmony Gold (Mining); Ricoh (document management/services); Telkom (Telecommunications); Liberty Group (financial services); and GIBS (Business Education).

> If you would like to share and build on this body of knowledge, please opt in on www.accelerated.co.za, and join the other collaborators in Accelerated Learning.

3.2 CHALLENGES OR OPPORTUNITIES

The biggest challenges that the learning function is facing with regard to accelerating learning in the next three years are numerous. We have categorised these into the top seven most common challenges, together with a few additional but less common challenges, mentioned below.

3.2.1 Challenge #1: Building a learning and leadership culture

This was the most common and prioritised challenge from every organisation. Nicolene Hogg from Didata emphasised that "culture is a strategic business enabler and must be owned by business and supported by learning. L&D cannot do it alone". Most of the interviewees felt that leaders need to build the capacity to become talent and learning champions, realise the value of learning, be great coaches, and create learning environments where people aren't afraid to make mistakes or receive feedback. Nicolene continued by saying: "Organisations and leaders need to embed lifelong, continuous learning beliefs and practices into the business (for example, the 70/20/10 approach and After-Action Reviews – AARs)."

It is a challenge to find the balance between organisation-led learning and learner-led learning, which requires a certain maturity of both learners and leaders. Gawie Heroldt from Harmony says: "We need to shift the leaders' mind-sets of: 'Not invented here – my business unit is different'; 'This is how it's done here; forget what you have learnt'; and people not being released from jobs due to pressure to perform and focus on targets only." Shaun Rozyn from GIBS says: "There needs to be a deep expectation and commitment to extract the benefit from learning from the sponsors of the initiative and the line managers." Mark Kahn from Investec says that they are aiming to create an environment which is not manageable i.e. one that is "Out of the Ordinary", innovative and entrepreneurial. This means that they need to create a context for learning, not out of the workplace, but in the workplace. The challenge is to create a learning journey that is continuous, live and for all people, all of the time. He says: "Talent that can be managed is not really talent."

3.2.2 Challenge #2: Moving learning from the classroom to the job and performance

The bandwidth of executives and managers continues to decrease, as organisations face information overload, fast pace of change, multiple distractions, lean structures and greater global complexity. Angela Donnelly from RMB says:

"There is less and less appetite for taking time off for learning away from the job and a greater necessity for on-the-go, just-in-time, relevant, accessible learning options." Candida from AVI commented: "We find out learners are tired of traditional learning approaches. Boredom thresholds are much higher than ever before and time out of office is a tough ask particularly when people will report only retaining around 10–15% of what was covered anyway." Getting people into the classroom is getting harder and harder. Business is saturated with many programmes and continuous change and new challenges. As Dean Retief from Nedbank says: "We need to get learning out of the classroom and into the boardroom."

3.2.3 Challenge #3: Fast-tracking specific experience and skills

With the business world, technology, and products changing so rapidly, the predominant question at the top of our minds is: How do we fast-track specific skills and experience within a global context? A key question raised was: How do we fast-track experience? In other words, how do we build judgement, decision making and wisdom so that learning can be applied in multiple unique situations and contexts? Another question was: How do we develop systems thinking, complexity management, and leading in chaos? Context becomes more important than content at senior levels. Another challenge is up-skilling to keep up with changing business models which require new skill-sets such as a move from hardware to software, IT, and consulting skills. Brent Nestler from Ricoh says: "We need to keep up with project management, change management and service management to create a uniform experience with global clients. We also need to keep up with global roll-outs of new products, services, pricing models or clients and get these knowledge and skills to the front-line sales and support staff as quickly as possible."

In addition to the above, we need to get everyone up to speed in their current roles which are evolving all the time, for example, new systems training. With existing leaders, how do we continue to build technical depth while also developing leadership capability? As Dr Andrew Johnson from Eskom says: "Technical problems can be easily solved until people are involved." He adds: "We need to look to the future and plan to fill the leadership and technical pipeline in a changing world. We need to accelerate the development of leaders of the future (such as engineers, power-station managers, business unit managers). How do we prepare young graduates today to become the leaders and change agents for the future and become capacity builders themselves?"

3.2.4 Challenge #4: Learning to shift paradigms and mind-sets

Most of the interviewees mentioned the importance and challenge of designing learning experiences to shift paradigms and mind-sets. Ilka Dunne from RMB says: "We need triggers and hooks to engage people and motivate them to learn." Many spoke of the leaders needing to believe in the importance of self-leadership as the foundation for all learning and helping people to build self-awareness, find purpose and meaning, understand their impact, and create a legacy. People are blind to their faults and require learning experiences to help them grow.

3.2.5 Challenge #5: Making learning relevant and valuable

Individualising learning is a big challenge to most organisations. The question is how to position the value of learning for each individual so that they understand the "what's in it for me?" (WIIFM). How do we match and target learning opportunities to people and their roles, and not adopt a whitewash approach? We need to make learning relevant and time efficient. A big challenge is to assess the critical gaps of an individual on their talent development path, and make sure there is a healthy base from which to grow – both functional and leadership skills. Also, how do we communicate with everyone and inform them what is available in a self-driven learning environment, when people don't read much? Shaun Rozyn from GIBS says: "It is important to position a learning intervention within the ecosystem of an organisation. Does it fit best as a talent initiative, an OD intervention or an enabler to a strategic thrust. Any accelerated learning program must encompass what is needed to deliver real results, It must also balance individual and business needs and ensure that learners are integrated back into the workplace successfully."

3.2.6 Challenge #6: Alignment of individual values and expectations with the culture

Another complex challenge is how to ensure that the learning process assists integration and alignment of individual values and expectations with the organisational culture. This is particularly relevant to the induction of employment equity (EE) candidates so that they stay. How do we build resilience and coping skills with new entrants and talent champion skills with their leaders? This also applies to MBA students, who have a reputation for leaving within 18 months of completing their studies. How do we ensure transfer of knowledge from old to new generations through mentoring and avoiding the mind-set of "We got here the hard way, so we don't want to make it easy for the youngsters." How can we build a "leaving a legacy" mind-set? The challenge works both ways, as organisations are faced with a sense of entitlement and arrogance from some of the younger generations, which doesn't make it easy for the people transferring the knowledge.

3.2.7 Challenge #7: Increasing adoption rates on technology platforms

At least five of the organisations interviewed have started their virtual and social learning platforms. Their challenge was to get adoption rates up and get people actually to use the platforms, create content, share knowledge, and interact. A culture shift is needed to migrate the organisation strategically to a new way of learning and behaving.

3.2.8 Challenge #8: Strategic re-alignment of learning to support a changing strategy

Organisations that have significantly changed to their strategy, such as moving from a consolidation to a growth strategy, or shifting the focus of their offerings, require a different skills set, both now and in the future. These organisations need to articulate the skills and talent they need far into the future, in order to set up the developmental processes to grow, nurture and retain them. Taryn Markus from Liberty says: "In many cases technical experts are required to become leaders who lead growth and change. Leaders often struggle to articulate what skills they will need in the future (not just now) and face a dilemma in identifying who can make the shift."

3.2.9. Other challenges

Other challenges included how to leverage knowledge across functions and levels and how to ensure deeper alignment across senior managers in order to ensure understanding of decisions and avoid topics which are better left undiscussed. Some companies were struggling with balancing company versus country requirements. For example, people need certification or qualifications on SAQA, but the unit standards are not always relevant or current. Companies in shrinking industries such as mining were facing development opportunity challenges with limited scope for growth and limited resources. Another company is struggling with the Transformation agenda, and accelerating the development of women and Previously Disadvantaged Individuals (PDIs). A company with many programmes was thinking through the best way to select individuals for accelerated learning programmes: Do we ask managers to select (candidates may perceive that they have been selected because "I am lacking")? Or do we ask individuals to self-select (volunteer)? (But think about the ones who need it but don't put themselves forward.) We need to ensure fairness and honesty in feedback and a clear rationale for learning. Lastly, a company ahead of the curve is asking how they can integrate talent, transformation and learning in reporting to show return on investment (ROI).

3.3 LEARNING METHODOLOGY TRENDS

The interviewees were asked to comment on **trends in learning methodologies** that are having an impact on the way in which they plan, design and implement learning. We also asked for specific feedback on some of the global trends below.

*   **e-Learning:** All the companies we interviewed had been using e-learning for a while, but to different degrees. Some have comprehensive content modules for their business, while others have focused on induction and safety modules. Investec uses e-learning mainly for technical and compliance learning, but not for relational issues. Liberty has a well-established e-learning platform in their sales environments. Some use business school platforms and modules, but struggle with adoption rates and usage. Only 10 per cent of Telkom's learning is delivered through an e-learning platform; 90 per cent of their learning is still delivered through instructor-led training methods. GIBS have their own content portal but have shifted their focus more to technology enabled learning (rather than pure content) to ensure the dynamics of dialogue and team learning is not lost. Some such as RMB are re-establishing their e-learning platforms to integrate them with social learning and more video-based options. Didata for example, has been using a lot of virtual and online learning and is now planning to bring in more video-based learning and gamification. Nicolene says: "A key need is to up-skill learning designers and facilitators to operate in an online environment." Ricoh says that globally they are moving toward breaking longer modules into JIT ("just-in-time") short-burst modules of a few hours, or possibly a video. Overall, there is a shift towards more visual, video, interaction and mobility in e-learning.

3.3.1 Social learning and collaboration platforms

Less than half of the companies interviewed have implemented social learning platforms, many of which are only in roll-out phase. Didata uses "Saba People Cloud" and Ricoh uses "iEngage", a collaboration portal and platform built on Jive technology, both of which are driven through a global implementation. Nedbank has a platform and a five-year strategy to migrate the organisation to online and collaborative learning, but is still struggling with adoption rates. For example, all

SAP training is now linked to virtual learning. RMB has various platforms including SharePoint portals, encourages the use of Twitter to connect experts with learners, and is now looking into Panopto as a video-focused platform. Liberty has been using Yammer for a few years with a gradual increase in use, primarily in the projects environment to share ideas, information and gather data through surveys. GIBS uses tools such as Google Hangout, LinkedIn, Yammer and Webex. Investec spent years developing a comprehensive internal Facebook and LMS called iExpress and are still struggling to get adoption rates above 5%. Overall, this is still a very new trend in learning and requires a significant change in mind-sets and behaviour with the current generation to use company-based platforms for learning. Generation Y and future generations will probably naturally gravitate to these platforms for learning in the future, once user-interface issues have been ironed out. Change management is a critical component for success of these platforms.

- **Mobile learning** – Very little is happening with mobile learning tools in the companies we chatted to. Globally, Ricoh is using smartphones (tablets in future) for people in the field to encourage more collaboration and dialogue and therefore learning. Field marketing (AVI) has built a virtual store and an online programme on a tablet to help train their store staff.

- **Gamification of learning** – There was much mixed feedback on gamification. Everyone had heard of it, but most did not yet have a strategy or project to explore seriously and some were waiting to see if it is just a fad or a real value-add. RMB had taken gamification the furthest by building gamification mechanics into many of their learning programmes, conferences and staff engagements. For example, they have an evening quiz show to build technical skills. Some use it selectively, for example, in induction programmes or where it is fit for purpose and proves its value over time. Nedbank has elements of gamification in some of the e-learning modules.

  Spitz (AVI) Customer Service for Retail Program used a Doodles video case study and board game with characters, team names, moola which can be earner during the running of the 4 day course and then traded ins at a Spaza shop, dice and a variety of questions on the business and learning taken from the programme to accelerate their customer service training. Liberty has introduced gamification into their sales e-learning programs. Investec has used gamification in their various Leadership Development Programs and are investigating building a comprehensive "game" to run the country to build understanding of systems thinking, consequences, economics and financial management.

- **Positive psychology tools such as Affirmative Inquiry, Strengths Finder, world cafés:** Positive psychology is still a very new trend, with a few companies having experimented with it in pockets of the business where the leadership appetite has allowed. There seems to more of a focus on self-leadership and helping people to discover purpose, meaning, strengths, beliefs, blind-spots and impact before embarking on large-scale positive psychology interventions. Nedbank uses Gallup Strengths Finder with new entrants; Harmony uses Affirmative Inquiry questioning in its culture transformation initiative; and a variety of the businesses within AVI have used world cafés and held Affirmative Inquiry workshops which have included many positive psychology approaches. Investec has embraced positive psychology and has been using techniques such as deep democracy, process-based facilitation and open spaces for many years. GIBS uses Socratic learning, questioning and facilitation across the board.

- **Neuroscience ,of leadership:** This is also a very new field and we didn't find many examples of where the latest Neuroscience thinking had been incorporated into leadership programmes. Some had a small module in stress management programmes; one company had a module in a leadership programme; and another company had run an ad-hoc session with their leaders. It was interesting to hear that Eskom had taken their top 100 leaders through a programme on Mindful Leadership which included reflective practice, journalling, meditation and Qigong. GIBS uses Neuroscience principles and behavioural economics in the design of its programs, such as action learning, personal projects, PDPs and Happiness at Work aspects. GIBS has also built an iLab, which is a creative space, to accommodate whole brain and Neuroscience principles.

- **Coaching skills for line managers:** Coaching has become main stream, with all organisations offering executive coaching to their senior leaders. Many have progressed to training line managers to lead with a coaching style of leadership and some, such as RMB and Nedbank, have invested a lot of time and effort in training their line managers as coaches, including offering comprehensive training and qualifications and using their internal coaches on many of their internal leadership programmes. Coaching roles are formalised in some organisations but not in others. Ricoh uses a lot of peer-to-peer coaching. Didata is now moving coaching training down to their first-line leaders. GIBS uses Business Impact Coaching, whereby coaches assist learners to develop their personal business case for coaching – taking PDPs to a whole new level. Learners are expected to report back to the organisation on the impact of the coaching program. Investec has embraced coaching as a philosophy and encourages everyone at all levels to dialogue, inquire and learn continuously. They run internal coaching training programs and use external coaches. All OD practitioners are expected to be qualified and experienced coaches.

- **Accelerated learning programmes for key talent pools:** Most of the organisations have talent management and succession planning in place, although in a few it is very new and still being piloted and tested. About 50 per cent of the companies have comprehensive Accelerated Learning programmes in place which have run for a year or more and include the elements of Accelerated Learning such as action learning projects, coaching, outside-in thinking, and modules to develop leadership or technical skills (see the examples below). These organisations typically have AL programmes at each tier of leadership or for particular mission-critical talent segments.

  Another 30 per cent have small scale AL programmes such as fast-track induction, sales, and young talent or global leadership programmes. These are all shorter in nature, for example, two weeks and include a blended learning approach and practical application. The other 20 per cent are still working on talent strategies and gaining leadership commitment to investing time and money in comprehensive accelerated development programmes.

  One of the companies has just cancelled two of its AL programmes because of resistance from the business (such as complaining of relevance, time off work, people leaving after the programme or not completing assignments); leaders not supporting time or integration of learning; and the learners not wanting to give up evenings and weekends to learn.

- **Cross-functional collaboration:** This is not so common. The only organisation that gave specific examples was RMB, which has two initiatives that cater for cross-functional learning. They use the IDEO method, which uses cross-functional teams to solve real business problems through a learning approach (challenge, observations, insights, experiments, and product). The Accelerated Learning XL programme encourages cross-functional teams to work together on their strategic projects and share team learning across the whole group (you can read more about this in the case study in Chapter 14).

Other interesting trends mentioned were the following:

- **Nedbank** have gone back to basics to create an enabling environment in order to increase current performance and prepare for future performance. They are focusing on clear job expectations, learning plans, feedback, and ensuring that various functions within HR are aligned and working together to solve business challenges, and not working in isolation. They are also focused on providing real world just-in-time learning that can be applied immediately, for example, simulations, action learning, and tools to apply immediately. This implies a move away from content learning (which can be done online with technology platforms) and a greater focus on attitude and culture.

- **Eskom** have been spending some time exploring cognitive psychology, and Chris Argyris work on discussables and undiscussables.

- **Harmony** are busy revamping their performance management process which they believe will lead to more focus on learning. They have also started including KPIs for learning in certain functions where leaders are passionate.

- **Spitz (AVI)** have a creative "adopt a store" programme where head office managers and staff each adopt a store over the busy holiday festive season and mentor, motivate and or help out store staff where they can, specifically to enable them to reach targets and stay focused at peak. In FMCG, AVI's learnerships are moving towards a more customised and tailored approach in which delivery is not only provider led. Internal experts and customised content allow them to meet SETA and organisational requirements in a very collaborative way. **Investec** has brought learning into live Deal Forums, using a fishbowl approach. Identified learners are invited to observe critical meetings, and the Chair is trained to pause occasionally and to facilitate a learning moment. Interest in the process and accelerated learning results so far have been exceptionally positive. They call this a "LearnScape" and are looking into application into other areas such as the Call Centre environment.

- **Investec** also spends a lot of time facilitating alignment of people and teams across geographic, divisional or functional boundaries, trying to get the "Glocal" balance right.

Brain Break: Go outside or find a window and look into the distance for 5 minutes before reading again. Feel the difference when you begin again.

3.4 EXAMPLES OF ACCELERATED LEARNING PROGRAMMES

We have summarised a few key features of some of the Accelerated Learning programmes we have come across.

Table 3.1: Features of Accelerated Learning programmes

Examples	Brief description of the programme
RMB: TEAM – The Evolving Art of Management (managers of others); 1 year, part-time	Aligned to the business cycle e.g. modules prepare for strategy, innovation, diversity, budgeting, people and performance etc. Action-learning projects are real-life business requirements. Includes thought leadership and coaching. On-line portal for virtual interaction and collaboration. In second year
RMB: XL – Accelerated Learning for Operations & Technology potential successors (managers and technical specialists, cross-functional): 9 months, part-time	Competency-driven to develop exposure and competence at the next level of work. Includes leadership and technical competencies and exposure. Team-based strategic action learning projects with regular executive exposure. Number of contact modules over the year interspersed with coaching and project work. 360° feedback. Online portal for virtual interaction and collaboration. In second year
RMB YSA – (Leaders of self): 1 year, part-time	Number of contact modules over the year interspersed with coaching and project work
RMB LEAD RMB – (Senior Leaders): 8 months, part-time	Coaching focused (internal coaches) to grow introspection and self-awareness. Intent is to build the RMB leadership brand and a cohesive leadership cadre at senior levels. Incudes building personal purpose, fingerprint, worldview and leadership capability. 360° feedback.
Eskom – Top Engineers programme (graduate engineers with 1 year's tenure): 18 months, full-time	Cream of engineering graduates, selecting only 18 out of 300 applications. Released full-time onto programme. 1–2 week contact modules spread over 8 months with practical application. 60/40 split between deep engineering consulting skills and leadership skills. In second year
Eskom – Top Generation Managers programme (future senior leaders in generation): 1–3 months, full-time	Released full-time onto programme. 60/40 split between deep technical expertise and leadership skills. Lots of deep reflection into self and others. Inter-woven every day e.g. what are the blockages to learning. In second year
Eskom – BDAL for future leaders (high potentials): 1–3 months, full-time	Contact sessions and action-learning projects provided by senior managers (short-term critical problem – divisional or cross-functional). Full exposure to business leaders. Intra and inter-personal focus. Use outside in thinking. 3 x 3 days' contact sessions at business school. Action-learning coach (external). Take projects up to proposal stage and tie the sponsors (middle and senior managers) in to accept the proposal

Examples	Brief description of the programme
Harmony – Junior Engineers programme (new entrants): 2 years full-time plus 1.5 years to certify.	Practical on-the-job-training for 2 years
Harmony – HR development programme (new entrants with 1 year tenure), 2 years, full-time	Practical on-the-job training for 2 years
Didata – Global leadership programme (future senior leaders): 2 weeks full-time	GIBS, IE business school, consultants
Didata – Emerging Talent Pool (high-potential future leaders, Gen Y): 2 years	Exposure to business value chain, contact sessions in blocks with virtual classrooms and online learning in third year
Ricoh – Sales Fast Track programme (new entrants): 2 weeks	Multi-layered sales programme to fast track new entrants e.g. induction, product knowledge, systems knowledge, company knowledge, peer-to-peer mentoring, individually customised. External providers for sales skills. Learners assessed by managers' discussing KPIs
Telkom	ALPs targeting African females and different grade levels Programmes for the supervisor and manager level that target increasing their technical skills and commercialisation skills. These programmes aim to bridge the gap between technical staff and business Young women – Internet protocol skills delivered through Cisco Whole workforce is currently transforming from fixed line to converged infrastructure – driven project by project to transform general knowledge of converged infrastructure

Examples	Brief description of the programme
GIBS – Accelerated Leadership Program 4-6 months part-time. Facilitates programs for corporates eg. Anglo American, SAB	3 phases: Initiation – personal assessment of leadership and learning styles and identification of action learning projects Active learning – 3 blocks of 5 days every 4-6 weeks. Content tailored to projects. Second block designed by the learners. Coaching – per team, must have process expertise, be an industry specialist and have functional experience. Continue post program for transition back into work. ROI – some companies do a full post-program evaluation including competency shifts, individual impact and business improvement impact.

3.5 LEADERS AS LEARNING CHAMPIONS

The interviewees were asked to what extent **leaders** are **equipped** with knowledge, skills, behaviours and mind-sets to be **learning champions.** We described a learning champion as someone who could create a learning environment, do personal profiling, assess learning needs, plan learning opportunities, be a great coach, give constructive and regular feedback, hold crucial conversations, empower others, and believes in the importance of learning for growth and performance.

Overall, most organisations felt that only about 20-30% per cent of their leaders were ready to be learning champions Many mentioned that there were pockets of passion and natural coaching styles of leadership, but still many old-style, autocratic or arrogant leaders who believed in recruiting for performance and not developing for performance. In general, senior leadership was considered more ready, with access to more exposure and development than lower down. Senior leaders were often willing to share experiences at leadership programmes. Some of the companies have done a lot of culture work and understanding the impact of leaders on others with feedback through 360° feedback and engagement surveys. Others are still catching up. A particular problem area was middle managers, whose attitude varies with experience and whether they have a technical or managerial preference. Robust conversations are still seen as an enormous challenge in all companies. Most companies said they are have not yet mastered the skill of developing leaders. Career ownership is also a new trend, training staff to empower themselves and manage their own careers and build skills such as self-leadership, awareness of strengths and derailers, emotional intelligence, assertiveness, influence, and personal branding, and navigating career choices and transitions effectively. Making learning an option for self-driven learning through career portals is also starting to appear.

3.6 LEARNING INVOLVEMENT IN CHANGE

We were keen to establish how traditional boundaries of OD/change management versus learning/development were changing. Interviewees were asked to what extent the **learning function** is involved in accelerating learning in large-scale **change processes**. Responses were widely varied. Some organisations still have very clear boundaries between OD/change and learning, with OD or a change office handling the planning. Learning is there only to implement specific training modules. Other organisations have started to consult proactively with learning in the planning stage of large-scale change interventions, although this happens more as a result of relationships than a standardised approach. The learning function was a key part of the RMB Corporate Banking culture transformation project team In order to ensure that learning is built into all streams and activitiesLearning was involved at Spitz (AVI) in creating a customer-centric organisation and was able to integrate the use of early morning sessions, SMS campaigns, climate surveys and café conversations to create the shift in thinking and behaviours. There is a realisation that learning functions still need to communicate more to the business about what they offer, how they can assist, and what capacity they have. Some companies were exploring how these two functions could be combined in future. Investec has merged OD and learning to facilitate learning within the business context. Liberty is looking at building OD capacity in all HR practitioners. A minority of the organisations still say that it is a big challenge to get business to buy into proactive change management and involvement of learning. It needs to be driven from the top and be part of how we do business. Didata recognises that they need a standardised project and change approach to help global clients have a consistent experience.

3.7 LEADERSHIP SKILL NEEDS

Our last question was: What are the three most important **leadership skills** that need development in the near future? There was a lot of commonality here, with the skills listed in order of frequency:

- Self-leadership – deep intra-personal insight and Emotional Intelligence
- Relationship building with others – trust, honesty, caring for others
- Inspirational Leadership – the ability to inspire and influence communities (project teams, teams) and deliver results
- Crucial conversations – hard feedback
- Strategic and proactive thinking – to operate at the right level of work and ability to cope with the complexity of operating at GM or C-suite level.

- Critical thinking and decision making – wisdom, judgement and application across multiple contexts, understanding unintended consequences
- Coaching and mentoring – to accelerate emerging talent, for performance and for engagement
- Building partnerships – for long-term win–win business relationships
- Global leadership – how to lead and manage in a phase of growth in a global world and global strategy, managing virtual workplaces, balancing geographic differences, etc
- Innovation and entrepreneurial thinking – less risk averse
- Accountability – holding self and others accountable, role clarity, managing expectations and giving clear feedback
- Collaboration – learning how to share, communicate, involve, co-create and still deliver on time
- Cultural sensitivity – both in the local context and cross cultural across global organisations
- Curiosity – being interested in life and the world beyond the work you do
- Strategic alignment – cross-functional and global
- Creating a sustainable future – mind-set, attitude, beliefs
- First-line leadership
- Change management – adapting, responding and accelerating change

Worth reading: Chief Learning Officer: Three Trends Shaping Learning {Plater, 2014)

3.8 KEY MESSAGES

We asked each interviewee if they had a key message for business and the learning industry. Here are their comments, listed in order of the interviews.

- **Dean Retief (Nedbank):** At an organisational level we need to ask if we are being true to our profession as learning professionals. Do we truly appreciate what the purpose of learning is? Do we enable learning and performance? Do we help to address strategic learning challenges? Do we understand the complexity of strategic objectives of the business and deliver real value to the business through earning interventions? The role of the learning function is to enable leaders to take ownership of creating a learning environment for their staff. The Chief Learning Officer needs to spend more time at executive and board level to ensure that learning plays a strategic value-adding role.

Learning needs to become a shared environment between the learning function and line through collaboration, innovation and more ownership and control by line.

- **Nicolene Hogg (Didata):** Our key role as learning specialists is to create a learning organisation. L&D needs to change the way it operates from being the expert or go-to person and become an enabler and create tools and platforms for self-driven learning. We need to develop leaders and the organisation to become self-sufficient. L&D are not the owners of learning. Learning is the role of every manager in the company and needs to be built into practices and real people development skills.

- **Angela Donnelly (RMB):** We need to be more aware of and concerned with culture. We don't tap into the value of culture enough to move organisations forward by creating purpose, meaning, happiness at work, and engagement. It needs to come from leaders and be driven by leaders. We need to realise the role and value of Human Resources in business results and spend a sufficient amount of time on people issues.

- **Ilka Dunne (RMB):** Business is about people. The only way to have a real impact on people is to help them grow – to become better than yesterday. Our natural instinct is to want to grow. We need to give our people opportunities to discover their potential. The national impact would be huge. Large-scale opportunities are good, but we mustn't lose sight of individual influence and impact. We need basic technical and functional skills BUT we need to "touch" people to really unleash a learning mind-set.

- **Gawie Herholdt** (Harmony Gold): SA needs education as a means to create a future. We have a poor record of integrating education into results. It is a lever to create a sustainable SA – the need to have learning as part of our DNA. We are not doing anyone a favour by developing them. It is our job and our responsibility and our duty to leave a legacy.

- **Hester Jardine (Harmony Gold):** If you want to change your circumstances and improve your opportunities in life, you need to embrace lifelong learning.

- **Candida di Giandomenico (AVI):** There is no appetite for fluffy stuff and large scale, costly training rollouts. We have to have our fingers on the pulse of the business and understand deeply what is needed to deliver a result and ensure the benefits of the intervention. This requires us to customise for their context because today one size doesn't fit all. You need to reinvent yourself as an L&D specialist – be a chameleon or even an alchemist – what may have worked 10 to 15 years back is not going to cut it today. The learners have changed, as have the times, technological advancements, available resources (or the lack thereof) all paly a roll and the business world is continually changing at an exponential rate. We need to be flexible, creative and sharp and find ways to make learning meaningful and relevant to all the stakeholders. Keep interventions simple and useful, provide line with the skills and competence to engage around on the job and informal learning to really enable and empower staff. Trade off lecturing, unnecessary detail and complexity with user-friendliness and simplicity.

• **Brent Nestler (Ricoh):** We need a deep understanding of learning principles and how important these are to the culture and leadership of the organisation. Learning interventions need to be collaboratively supported by leaders and embedded in the organisation. We need executive sponsorship for real involvement (not disengagement), collaborative developmental space for people to learn and coaching for support and feedback. We need to be dynamic, open, and flexible, to embrace technology, to move away from spending days in the classroom, and to be fully interactive in the way we do things.

• **Taryn Markus (Liberty):** You've got to know your business, the strategy and what it is trying to achieve. It is not about your own technical expertise, principles or models. It is about using business language and strategic priorities as the foundation for conversations and then weave in the people agenda to show a strategic solution.

• **Shaun Rozyn (GIBS):** Business that are most successful are able to think strategically, deliver and execute relentlessly and truly inspire their constituents. Learning practitioners need to be comfortable sitting at the Boardroom table, engaging with thought leaders and academics to get scientific updates and interacting with all levels of learners. We will earn respect when we can do this and craft customised solutions and empower them to deliver business results.

3.9 CONCLUSION

Activity 1

How does your organisation compare with the ones featured above?

Bonus rewards – remember to share your case studies or examples with us (see Chapter 17).

PART 2

WHOLE BRAIN, WHOLE PERSON APPROACH TO LEARNING

Chapter 4: Unique learning profiles by *Debbie Craig*

4.1   Introduction

4.2   Some basic principles

4.3   Learning = Change

4.4   Sub-conscious influences

4.5   Learning influences

4.6   Creating your own learning profile

4.7   Conclusion

Chapter 5: Neuroscience of learning by *Natalie Cunningham* and *Debbie Craig*

5.1   Introduction

5.2   What is neuroscience?

5.3   Learning and neuroscience

5.4   Workings of the brain

5.5   The learning cycle

5.6   Attention and memory

5.7   The emotional and social brain

5.8   Brain deception

5.9   Environmental factors

5.10   Conclusion

CHAPTER 4

UNIQUE LEARNING PROFILES

By Debbie Craig

4.1 INTRODUCTION

> *"Learning is one of the defining aspects of being human. Truly profound learning experiences change who we are – we change through learning. All learning involves thinking and doing, action and reflection. Learning changes what we can do – it is always active – you haven't learned to walk until you walk." – Peter Senge*

Everyone is unique. If we could design a world in which everyone's needs, preferences, personalities, motivations, goals, expectations and aspirations could be catered for, it might look quite spectacular. In *Trends Reshaping the Future of HR* (2013), Cantrell and Smith wrote about t how to customise and design a talent strategy to suit each individual. "Organizations of all types have long excelled by treating customers as 'markets of one' – offering them personalized buying experiences." Why not with people?

Cantrell and Smith (2013) say: *"When it comes to managing talent, one size no longer fits all. Customization has transformed everything from marketing to medicine, and is poised to revolutionize the way organizations manage their people. With customization, organizations will no longer treat their workforce as a single, monolithic entity. Instead, they will treat each employee as a 'workforce of one'."*

This is particularly relevant to the field of learning. If I am an extrovert, visual, pragmatic (hands-on), optimistic learner who thrives on attention, competition and recognition, surely I would learn fastest and most enjoyably in a group learning setting, where there are a lot of visual, colourful stimuli. I could have fun solving real-life problems or case studies, and rise to the challenge of doing it better and faster than the competing groups, in order to win some kind of incentive.

This scenario would, however, make my husband cringe. He is an introvert, an intellectual (he loves to understand the theory behind things) and an idealist (he imagines how things could be – not how they actually are). He is also fiercely independent and prefers having time to think, research and reflect, and learn at his own pace. He hates any form of exam (he believes they are demeaning) and just wants to learn what he needs to get on with his work.

How then, would you structure a learning experience for the two examples above, with limited time and resources (a reality in the world of work)? In the past, you might decide to throw all team members in a classroom with a trainer or facilitator and expect them to be happy to have the privilege and opportunity. In today's world there are more options, higher expectations for individuality, and we are more informed about how people learn and change through some great research and many years of experience. This chapter explores the balance of understanding and catering for individual preferences AND creating unique group-based, blended method, accelerated learning experiences to optimise economies of scale and the important interactive nature of group learning.

4.2 SOME BASIC PRINCIPLES

Understanding the dynamics of how and why we think, feel and act the way we do is a discipline all on its own. A few fundamental principles that I have found useful in the context of learning are the following:

- We are born with inherent genetic programmes, cognitive potential, personality-based preferences, brain-based dominance, and learning styles.
- We absorb and integrate programmes of thinking, feeling and doing (assumed to help us survive) which become automatic and subconscious – including values, beliefs, habits, motivations, mind-sets, and world-views.
- Our subconscious programming, of which we are unaware most of the time, drives much of our responses and behaviour.
- We learn and develop throughout our lives, building capabilities to enhance our natural born talents, strengths and tendencies – including emotional intelligence, resilience, leadership, and so on.
- Learning is about creating meaning from what we experience.
- Learning is a lifelong natural process. We learn, grow and change continuously as we move through life. Our natural tendency is to gravitate towards comfort and the known. Learning brings the unknown and the discomfort of trying new things and potentially failing or looking incompetent (especially if externally imposed). We need to build our level of awareness, insight, willingness and action to make a significant change and to overcome fear and resistance to the change.
- The more we practise and repeat thought patterns and behaviours, the more the learning pathways are embedded in our memory, the better we get at them, and the more automatic (instinctive) they become. These apply to both "good" and "bad" habits or behaviours.

- We have an optimal state called "flow" in which we are fully immersed in what we are doing and feel absorbed, engaged, fulfilled, competent and motivated. This is also called "the zone" or being in "the groove" as explained by Csíkszentmihályi in his book *Flow: The Psychology of Optimal Experience* (2008).

Learning requires that we change the way we think, what we think about, the depth or breadth of thinking, and the timeframe of our thinking and learning in order to understand the systemic interconnectedness of things. Learning requires us to change the way we feel and what we believe, especially when our paradigms, assumptions and stereotypes are challenged. Learning requires us to become more aware of our choices, our behaviour, the consequences of our actions, and our impact on others. Learning requires us to leave the safe haven of the known, and embark on an uncomfortable but exciting journey of trying new things, feeling foolish, incompetent and humble. Learning requires letting go of the old disempowering beliefs, assumptions and ways of working and embracing the new, more empowering approaches to living life and achieving success in a balanced, sustainable way.

4.3 LEARNING = CHANGE

"The real voyage of discovery lies not in seeing new landscapes, but in having new eyes." – Marcel Proust

Change (and therefore learning) requires awareness, insight, willingness and action. Change cannot happen without **awareness** (it's not working, so something needs to change), without insight (something I am thinking/feeling/doing needs to change), without **willingness** (I am willing to make the effort and be uncomfortable in order to change), and, of course, change cannot happen without repetitive **action** and practice (I am doing what I need to every day, to make the change part of my life). See Figure 4.1 below, which illustrates the cyclical nature of learning and change.

Activity 1

Choose a specific behaviour or habit that you would like to learn to do differently for better results. Some leadership examples can include: listening more (interrupting less); more emotional control (less temper or being reactive); being more assertive (learning to say no); feeling greater empathy and compassion; being more strategic in thinking; being more consultative (less independent) when working in teams, and so on. You could also choose a personal habit or lifestyle that you would like to change, such as changing your eating, exercising or stress management habits.

Share via e.mail or Facebook to level up. See OnBoarding for more info on how to do this.

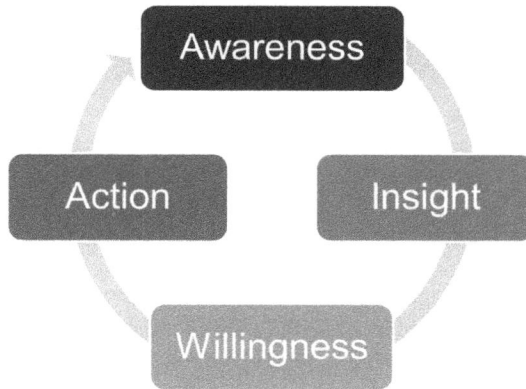

Figure 4.1: Cycle of learning and change

Table 4.1: Behaviour aspects

Change aspects	Rating 1–100%	Actions to increase rating
What is your current level of **awareness**?		
What is your current level of insight?		
What is your current level of willingness?		
What is your current level of action?		

HOT TIP Here are some pointers so that you can consider and rate each area fully.

Awareness

- Are you clear about what is expected in your role – or do you have a role model?
- Have you asked for feedback from multiple people (including your family) in order to understand your strengths and gaps?
- Have you stood in front of the mirror and looked yourself in the eye and asked: "Am I truly happy with my behaviour and with my life?"

HOT TIP

Here are some pointers so that you can consider and rate each area fully. (Continued)

Insight

- Have you fully acknowledged that you and only you can change your behaviour?
- Do you still blame others for lack of opportunity, training or coaching or the right environment to start building a new skill or behaviour?
- Have you looked deep within yourself to understand how your own habits, beliefs, assumptions, behaviours, blind-spots and perceived pay-offs influence your current behaviour?

Willingness

- How willing are you to move out of your comfort zone and enter into the zone of uncertainty and potential risk and ridicule?
- Have you identified which fears (for example, fear of failure) may cause resistance and an approach to building courage and overcoming these fears?
- Are you willing to forgo the pay-offs of the old behaviour (for example, previous confidence and success, delicious fattening food, sleeping in)?
- Are you willing to make the practice of the new behaviour a priority in your life and spend time every day thinking about it, doing something about it, and telling others about it?

- Are you taking daily action to learn or practise new skills or habits?
- Do you have a learning partner to hold you accountable, such as a coach, a friend, or a family member?
- Are you sticking to your calendar appointments with yourself or your learning partner?

4.4 SUB-CONSCIOUS INFLUENCES

Nerve cells (dendrons) that fire together, wire together!

If you keep repeating certain habits, such as avoiding conflict or getting upset when you receive criticism, these become automatic habits. The more we repeat good or bad habits, the stronger and more automatic the responses become, especially when we are tired or stressed. Breaking these habits and adopting a different response to the same stimuli requires daily repetition and practice to carve out a new neural pathway which will strengthen with use.

Daniel Kahneman, a psychologist and Nobel Prize Winner in economics, says in *Thinking, Fast and Slow* (2013). "We are blind to our own blindness." In other words, we have a self-confirming bias and believe what we want to believe, ignoring sometimes obvious facts or feedback. We draw conclusions with amazing ease, without the requisite analysis and facts. We don't even realise the many intuitive feelings and opinions we have about almost everything that comes our way. We are on automatic pilot.

Kahneman (2013) summarises the impact of our subconscious programmes and the conscious aspect of our minds as System 1 and System 2, as follows:

 **SYSTEM 1: The Subconscious**	 **SYSTEM 2: The Conscious**
• Inituitive (fast)	• Effortful (slow)
• Little of no effort	• Attention and concentration
• Automatic	• Self control
• Recognition	• Focus and attention
• Orientation	• Searching
• Fight or flight	• Recall

Figure 4.2: Systems 1 and 2 (© Klektadarya | Dreamstime.com – People Working In Call Center Photo)

System 1 (sub-conscious, automatic) works at an irrational, intuitive level with rapid thought processors (directed by the amygdala or primordial brain). We automatically respond to a loud sound or show a disgusted face when we are shown a disturbing picture. This part of the mind runs 24/7, never gets tired, and is instinctive (in other words, the response is automatic, and there is no choice available).

System 2 (conscious, attentive) works at a rational level with slower, calculating thought-processing capability (directed by the pre-frontal lobes or executive brain). We consciously allocate attention, assess two choices and make decisions. This part of the mind allows us to fill out tax forms, do comparison shopping or monitor our behaviour in a social setting. When we are relaxed and focused, we have a choice as to where to direct our attention and how to allocate our rational thinking capacities. However, the conscious mind has a limited capacity for attention and for handling issues.

Unfortunately, much of our lives is not in flow or relaxed or focused. We tend be stressed, overwhelmed, overloaded and distracted by the many conflicting demands we face daily. This level of stress reduces the resources available to deal with problems rationally (at a chemical level) and we then default to system 2 and follow the Law of Least Effort – we use our intuition rather than analysis. For example, we act on subconscious preferences or programmes to decide if we like a particular item (for example, a car, a motorcycle, a man or a woman) rather than analysing the safety record, resale value or financial stability of the choice. Have you ever noticed how talking stops when driving with someone in wet, misty or challenging conditions? Our mind automatically allocates the limited resources to the activity that will ensure the self-preservation of the person. As you become more skilled at a task such as driving, its demand for energy diminishes. Another way of seeing this is: as talent goes up, effort comes down.

> *"We do not think as long as things run along smoothly for us. It is only when the routine is disrupted by the intrusion of a difficulty, obstacle or challenge that we are forced to stop drifting and to think what we are going to do." – John Dewey*

To make these changes, it helps to understand the foundations of neuroscience and how the brain works with learning, memory, recall, integration and application. See Chapter 5 for more on this.

The rest of this chapter will outline the various learning influences and give you an opportunity to understand your own learning profile or work with someone else to establish theirs.

4.5 LEARNING INFLUENCES

> *"To learn is not the special province of a single specialized realm of human functioning such as cognition or perception. It involves the integrated functioning of the total organism – thinking, feeling, perceiving, and behaving." – David Kolb*

We may be wired by personality (cautious versus bold), social conditioning (competition versus collaboration), leadership role models (autocratic versus engaging), personal values (loyalty versus self-interest), thinking styles (big picture versus detail), information processing (visual versus auditory), our generation (what information we seek or trust), motivations (status versus achievement), fears (financial versus credibility), and many other factors such as worldview, job type, location, social status, and so on. See Figure 4.3 below, which summarises the key factors affecting the way we learn.

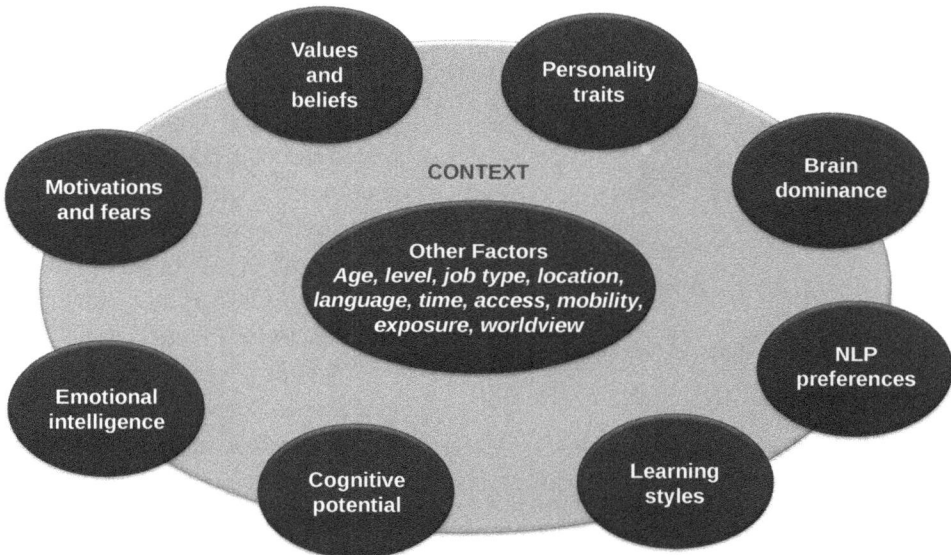

Figure 4.3: Learning influences

Unique learning profile

This section offers you the option of completing your own unique learning profile or the profile of someone whom you are supporting on a learning journey. Each aspect will give you some insight into preferences and activities to enhance learning for an individual or for a team of people with different styles. There may be some overlaps as you work through these different influences. However, each aspect is unique and underpinned by research and practice. For a template to complete the full profile. you can find a downloadable template on *www.accelerated.co.za*. Remember to opt in, on-board and join the journey for many additional resources, links and downloads.

Share via e.mail or Facebook to level up. See OnBoarding for more info on how to do this.

4.5.1 Values and beliefs

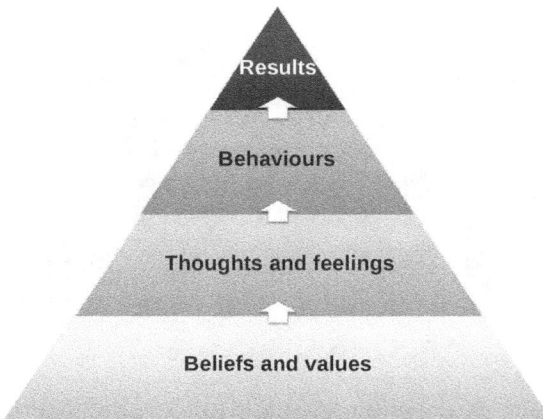

Figure 4.4: Factors governing our capacity to learn

Fundamental to your capacity to learn are your underlying beliefs about learning and your personal values which guide your decisions. Your behaviour and results are a sum total of all beliefs, values, thoughts, feelings and attitudes, as depicted in Figure 4.4.

Values also guide our behaviour and choices by providing direction and a point of reference along our journey to a purposeful life. If we were sailing across the ocean with no sign of land, then our values would be our compass and our destination would be our purpose. Values that encourage learning are: continuous improvement, personal growth, adventure, challenge, creativity, excellence, expertise, knowledge, curiosity, wisdom, and courage, among others. These values will help you to seek out situations and opportunities for learning and experimenting.

Values that encourage you to help others to learn and grow are: sharing, collaborating, teamwork, contribution, making a difference, leaving a legacy, helping others grow, and so on.

If, however, your value system centres on money, achievement, power, competition, risk mitigation, status, independence, pleasure, reputation, and so on, it may be harder for you to make the time and effort to create a learning space for others.

Table 4.2: Values

Support learning			Discourage learning		
Continuous improvement		Excellence		Money		Status	
Personal growth		Expertise		Achievement		Independence	
Adventure		Curiosity		Power		Pleasure	
Challenge		Wisdom		Competition		Reputation	
Creativity		Courage		Risk mitigation		Taking it easy	
Other:		Other:		Other:		Other:	

If you believe that learning is a quintessential aspect of everyday life and you believe that it is acceptable to try and fail and try again, then you will behave in this way. Similarly, if you believe that life will teach you what you need to know, when you need to know it, you may not prioritise learning activities which can significantly accelerate your knowledge, skill and effectiveness. You also do not want to look silly or incompetent in front of your colleagues, so avoid learning situations where you need to practise new skills in a group context. Beliefs also relate to our own sense of what we can and can't do. As Henry Ford said: "Whether *you think you can*, or *you think you can't – you're right*." You will have beliefs around the organisation's roles in your learning, in the ability of a particular facilitator or coach, and even in how much time should be spent on learning activities as opposed to doing your job.

Activity 2

Draw a table similar to the one in Table 4.3. Write down some values and beliefs that support or discourage your own learning.

Table 4.3: Beliefs

Support learning	Discourage learning

Recent brain research confirms that we can learn and change, even at a fundamental value or belief level, as long as we are willing to challenge our existing paradigms and embark on a learning journey of repetition, recall, review and reinforcement to embed new neural pathways that support our survival and purpose.

4.5.2 Personality preferences

Our inherent personality preferences certainly influence how we like to learn. One of the most widely used personality assessments is the MBTI (Myers Briggs Type Indicator), which is based on over 50 years of research, with more than two million people taking the test every year. The MBTI is based on four continuums, where you have a natural preference for a clear, moderate or slight preference for one side or the other of the continuum. Take a look at the continuum and the descriptions below, and decide for yourself where your preferences lie. You can test your personal view by comparing it to that of people who know you well.

Table 4.4: MBTI continuum

Strong	Medium	Slight	Slight	Medium	Strong
The way you get energised					
Extrovert if you are sociable, outgoing, expressive, like people interaction, think out loud			**Introvert** if you are quiet, prefer talking one on one, enjoy being alone, keep thoughts private		
What you pay attention to					
Sensing if you are factual, realistic, practical, in the "here and now" and operate from experience			**Intuitive** if you are conceptual, imaginative, future orientated, enjoy new ideas and consider possibilities		
How you make decisions					
Thinking if you are logical, curious, analytical, questioning, prefer objective and rational approach and seek knowledge			**Feeling** if you are genuine, compassionate, base decisions on personal values, relationship centred and harmonious		
The lifestyles you adopt					
Judging if you are decisive, organised, plan ahead, set goals and meet deadlines, prefer order and routine			**Perceiving** if you are flexible, adaptable, enjoy change, spontaneous, like to keep options open		

Learning Preferences

Have a look at the table below and identify your own learning preferences. List your preferences below:

Table 4.5: Learning preferences

Typical learning preferences	
Extrovert Wants to talk through their ideas in order to clarify them Likes action and being kept busy Prefers active learning and group projects Learns by teaching others	**Introvert** Gathers information from numerous sources Likes to reflect and clarify before speaking Prefers to have others do the talking Prefers lectures and structured tasks Likes to understand
Sensing Focus on facts, details and the known Likes structured sessions, guidelines and objectives Likes learning to be practical and relevant Likes real life examples and are drawn to realistic and practical applications Prefers memorisable facts, and concrete questions	**Intuitive** Interested in the patterns and relationships between the facts Likes to learn by discovery and then develop new original solutions Like simulations or experiments Prefer concepts and theories which can give greater play to imagination and inspiration Prefer interpretation and imagination
Thinking Likes to understand the theory behind concepts Likes to solve problems and analyse case studies Likes tests to measure progress Likes to take an objective approach and emphasise logic and analysis in their decisions Prefers objective feedback, and thrive when there is pressure to succeed	**Feeling** Like small group exercises where they can connect with others Like activities that stimulate positive emotions Give greater weight to relationships in their learning process and decisions Prefer positive feedback and individual recognition
Judging Prefer orderliness, structure and organisation Appreciate any resources that can help them to plan their work Prefer clearly defined strategies to achieve goals Like closure and a feeling of completing tasks in time Work well within clear and reasonable deadlines	**Perceiving** Prefer flexibility, adaptability and freedom to choose Often postpone doing work until the very last minute Seek information until the deadline (and often beyond) Like to consider all sides to a problem Love opportunities to be spontaneous

For more information on each of the types or to do a free assessment (based on Jungian types) visit http://www.humanmetrics.com/cgi-win/jtypes2.asp.

Other popular personality profiling tools include: 16PF, Insights, Social styles, Enneagram, Kiersy Bates, The Wave and OPQ. Visit this site for a brief overview of the many instruments available: http://www.ashridge.com/Website/Content.nsf/wELNPSY/Psychometric+Instruments+available?opendocument.

4.5.3 Brain dominance

Our brain dominance impacts on the way in which we pay attention to stimuli; take in information; process information; access memory; integrate different sources of information; utilise our imagination;, and, finally, interact with others about the information. In his brain dominance model, Dr Ned Herrmann identifies four different modes of thinking, aligned with the right and left hemispheres of the brain, which impact on learning and change, as described below.

Activity 3

Take a look at the four thinking style quadrants and descriptions below, and identify where you have a low, medium or strong preference. Most of us will have at least one or two dominant (strong) natural preferences, with the others being by default less strong. You can test your personal view by comparing it to that of people who know you well.

Table 4.6: Thinking styles

LEFT BRAIN	RIGHT BRAIN
A. Analytical thinking (Analyser)	**D. Imaginative thinking (Conceptualiser)**
Key words: Auditory, logical, factual, critical, technical and quantitative	*Key words:* Visual, holistic, intuitive, innovative, and conceptual
Preferred activities: Collecting data, analysis, understanding how things work, judging ideas based on facts, criteria and logical reasoning	*Preferred activities:* Looking at the big picture, taking initiative, challenging assumptions, visuals, metaphoric thinking, creative problem solving, long-term thinking
Learning style: Research, accurate facts and details, material presented in a neat and professional way, time to think and reflect on all possibilities, work independently	*Learning style:* Big picture, long term, variety, change, experiment and try new approaches, not too concerned about the practical details, visuals, colours and games, spontaneity, fun and humour
B. Sequential thinking (Organiser)	**C. Interpersonal thinking (Personaliser)**
Key words: Safe-keeping, structured, organised, complexity or detailed, planned	*Key words:* Kinaesthetic, emotional, spiritual, sensory, feeling
Preferred activities: Following directions, detail orientated work, step-by-step problem solving, organisation and implementation	*Preferred activities:* Listening to and expressing ideas, looking for personal meaning, sensory input, and group interaction
Learning style: Organised approach, clear objectives and deadlines, clear process to be followed, detailed summaries, practical applications and case studies can get stuck in the detail or implementation issues	*Learning style:* Talk about the topic, connect with and discuss with others, link learning to personal and emotional experiences, group-work, movement, music, role plays

Learning preferences

Have a look at the learning preferences in your dominant thinking quadrants. List your preferences below:

Ultimately, Dr Herrmann encourages us to practice *Whole Brain Thinking* and cultivate flexibility in our thinking styles, so that we can use all four styles of thinking depending on what the situation calls for. For more info, see www. herrmannsolutions.com

Another useful resource to understand the 4 quadrants and 8 dimensions of thinking is the Neethling Brain Instrument (NBI) developed by Kobus Neethling. See www.nbiprofile.com

You can also understand the 4 thinking mode preferences and 20 item profile through Mindex developed by Dr Karl Albrecht. See www.KarlAlbrecht.com/mindex/gallerypage-mindex.php

4.5.4 Neuro-Linguistic Programming (NLP) preferences

Neuro-Linguistic Programming (NLP) is a technique that explores the relationships between how we think (neuro), how we communicate (linguistic) and our patterns of behaviour and emotion (programmes). Through the study of excellence, we can model new and more effective patterns of thinking, communicating and behaving. These new, preferred patterns can be programmed into our subconscious and with practice and repetition can become our default responses for greater success. NLP is used in business, psychology, coaching, sports, police forces and personal development.

From a Neuro-Linguisitic Programming perspective, there are four main ways of taking in and processing information. The learning methods best suited to each of these different types are shown below in Table 4.7.

Activity 4

Look at the four different NLP types and think about which are your primary and secondary preferences.

Table 4.7: NLP types

Visual	Auditory	Kinaesthetic	Auditory–digital
Likes to see things visually and in pictures	Likes to hear things or see the words	Likes to experience things through the five senses	Likes to analyse, process, use logic and understand
Learns through pictures, diagrams, colours, drawings, DVDs	Learns through reading, workbooks, audio tapes, music, being spoken to or discussion	Learns through practical application, touching and feeling, practice and feedback	Learns through information gathering, thinking, analysing, theorising and testing logic

Learning preferences

Have a look at the learning preferences in your dominant NLP types. List your preferences below:

When designing a learning experience, it is suggested that you aim to cater for all of these styles by providing colourful visuals for the Visual types (PowerPoint slides, posters, using colourful wall-chart activities); discussion activities and additional resources for reading and listening to for the auditory types (pre-reading, workbooks, music, podcasts, discussions); experiential activities, sharing and feedback activities for the kinaesthetic types; and analytical research and problem-solving activities for the auditory–digital types. Providing all these activities will allow each type to find their groove, and also stimulate different parts of the brain to build greater flexibility in learning style in the future.

4.5.5 Learning styles

Learning styles based on the work of Kolb were developed by Peter Honey and Alan Mumford (2000), who identified four distinct learning styles or preferences: Activist, Theorist; Pragmatist and Reflector. These are the learning approaches that individuals naturally prefer and they recommend that in order to maximise one's own personal learning each learner ought to understand their learning style and seek out opportunities to learn using that style. There is a learning styles questionnaire; however, you can also do a quick self-assessment using the table below.

Activity 5

Look at the four styles summarised in Table 4.8 and identify your primary and secondary styles.

Table 4.8: Learning styles (adapted from Honey & Mumford, 2000)

Reflector	Theorist	Pragmatist	Activist
Learns by observing and thinking about what happened	Likes to know the theories and principles behind the learning	Likes to learn only what is immediately relevant to their life	Learns best by doing
Likes to reflect and think deeply before responding with questions	Likes models, concepts and facts in order to engage in the learning process.	Likes to find practical application to any new knowledge	Likes to test knowledge through direct experience and action, and get immediate feedback
Prefers to stand back and view experiences from a number of different perspectives, collecting data, and taking the time to work towards an appropriate conclusion.	Prefers to analyse and synthesise, drawing new information into a systematic and logical "theory".	Abstract concepts and games are of limited use unless practical	Likes to get his/her hands dirty, to dive in with both feet first.
		Likes to experiment, trying out new ideas and techniques to see if they work.	Has an open-minded approach to learning, involving him-/herself fully and without bias in new experiences.
• Paired discussions • Self-analysis or personality questionnaires • Observing activities • Feedback from others • Coaching • Interviews	• Models • Statistics • Stories • Quotes • Background information • Applying theories	• Time to think about how to apply learning • Case studies • Problem solving • Discussion	• Brainstorming • Problem solving • Group discussion • Puzzles • Competitions • Role-play

Learning preferences

Have a look at the learning preferences in your dominant learning style. List your preferences below.

4.5.6 Cognitive potential

When assessing people for development, a career path or job fit, identifying the way in which they think and learn is very important. Cognitive potential is an indicator of both the level of complexity that an individual has the potential to master both now and in the future, and how a person approaches learning about new and different environments and tasks. Ultimately, if a person's cognitive preferences can be matched to both work role and developmental activities, there is a greater chance of achieving the identified potential and of job satisfy action, self-actualisation and work performance.

Cognitive Process Profile (CPP)

A very valuable instrument to measure cognitive preferences and potential is the CPP or Cognitive Process Profile, which was developed by Dr M Prinsloo from Cognadev Ltd (http://www.cognadev.com). It is used widely both locally and internationally and is aligned with the Stratified Systems Theory, based on the work of Elliott Jaques (http://www.requisite.org/). Among other constructs, the CPP results predict, in a valid and reliable manner, intellectual functioning related to:

- Specialist versus generalist applications
- Visionary and strategic capabilities
- Integrative, big picture views and the tendency to contextualise issues
- Judgement capability and executive decision making capacity
- Managerial structuring and monitoring tendencies and skills
- Knowledge reliance, acquisition and access, and
- Learning orientation, curiosity and flexibility.

The CPP will indicate to you the strengths and development areas of thinking and learning across the fourteen dimensions.

Activity 6

Have a look through the following fourteen dimensions and get a sense of your strengths and development areas. A full assessment and debriefing with a specialist is highly recommended in order for you to understand more about the cognitive impact of your learning style and how to optimise your potential.

Table 4.9: Cognitive Process Profile (adapted from Prinsloo, 2010)

Category	Dimension	Strength	Develop
Exploration	Exploration – The investigation of a problem to identify important information.		
Analysis	Analytical approach – A disciplined, detailed, and rule-based approach.		
	Checking – Repeatedly revisiting detailed issues – often to "make sure".		
	Clarification – Interpreting, judging, weighting and prioritising unclear information.		'
	Precise and systematic approach – Work with accuracy, applying a detailed and precise approach.		
Structure	Abstract conceptualisation – Expressing conceptual thinking by using creative, abstract language.		
	Big picture view – Conceptualising and understanding a situation in terms of the wider and long term context. Here clarification and judgement is regarded as a prerequisite.		'
	Extracting core elements – Identifying and pinpointing key issues.		
Transformation	Logical verification – The tendency to search for logical proof.		
Memory	Memory strategies – Use of techniques and aids to assist memory functioning.		
Metacognition	Intuition – Basing judgement and insight on complex internalised information structures.		
	Learning – Improving one's understanding by adjusting, expanding and integrating information structures in a self-aware manner.		

Category	Dimension	Strength	Develop
Metacognition (continued)	Self-monitoring – Comparing own performance to appropriate criteria and rules in a self-aware manner.		
	Strategising – Careful planning on how to approach a problem.		
Implications for learning Jot down the possible implications for learning and how you can optimise strengths and manage or develop developmental areas:			

4.5.7 Emotional Intelligence

Another very significant influence on our ability to learn effectively is our emotional intelligence. Research findings using the EQ-i™ indicate that the most powerful EI contributors to work performance are:

- The ability to be aware of and accept oneself.
- The ability to be aware of others' feelings, concerns and needs.
- The ability to manage emotions.
- The ability to be realistic and put things in correct perspective.
- The ability to have a positive disposition and outlook on life.

EQi

The EQi is a highly regarded EQ self-assessment that compares your Emotional Intelligence to norm groups. For more information visit: http://ei.mhs.com/InternationalDistributorsInfo.aspx

Activity 7

Have a look through the following thirteen dimensions and get a sense of your strengths and development areas.

Table 4.10: EQi dimensions (adapted from BarOn, 2007, 2011)

Dimension	Description – when feeling confident and competent	Under pressure or stress …	Strength	Develop
Intra-personal				
Emotional self-awareness	Aware of one's feelings and emotions	Egocentric Self-absorbed		
Assertiveness	Expresses feelings, beliefs, and thoughts in a constructive way	Submissive Withdrawn		
Self-regard	Accepts one's perceived positive and negative aspects and possesses inner strength and self-confidence.	Self-conscious Foolish Clumsy		
Self-actualisation	Realises one's potential capacities. Involved in pursuits that lead to a meaningful, rich, and full life.	Sense of failure		
Independence	Functions autonomously versus needing protection and support.	Dependence		
Inter-personal				
Empathy	Aware of, understands and appreciates the feelings of others and displays empathy	Insensitive Aloof		
Interpersonal relationship	Establishes and maintains mutually satisfying relationships characterised by intimacy and by giving and receiving affection.	Conflictual or withdrawal		
Social responsibility	Shows up as a co-operative, contributing, and constructive member of one's social group and takes on community-orientated responsibilities.	Selfish Couldn't care		
Adaptability				
Problem-solving	Identifies and defines problems, generates ideas and implements effective solutions. Balances need for info versus risk taking. Confronts problems.	Disorganised Confused Stuck		

Dimension	Description – when feeling confident and competent	Under pressure or stress …	Strength	Develop
Reality testing	Continuously tests own experience (thoughts, feelings, perceptions) against what objectively exists. Accurately "sizes up" situations.	Out of line with others perceptions		
Flexibility	Adapts to unfamiliar, unpredictable, and dynamic circumstances and agile, synergistic, and capable of reacting to change without rigidity.	Rigid		
Stress management				
Stress tolerance	Withstands adverse events and stressful situations without "falling apart" by actively and positively coping with stress.	Stressed Highly strung		
Impulse control	Has self-control and emotional control and is able to resist or delay an impulse, drive, or temptation to act. Also called self-regulation or delaying gratification.	Reactive Explosive		
Implications for Learning				
Jot down the possible implications for learning and how you can optimise strengths and manage or develop developmental areas:				

4.5.8 Motivators and fears (SCARF)

Our approach to learning and the speed at which we learn is highly influenced by our motivators and fears. While various motivation theories abound, I have found the **SCARF** model developed by David Rock, founder of The NeuroLeadership Institute, to be highly useful in understanding deep influences from neuroscience relating to the way in which people interact and respond in social environments such as learning. The SCARF model is premised on two themes:

- Motivation driving social behaviour is governed by an overarching principle of minimising threat and maximising reward

- Five domains of social experience draw on the same brain networks to maximise reward and minimise threat as the brain networks used for primary survival needs (that is, our need for **s**tatus, **c**ertainty, **a**utonomy, **r**elatedness and **f**airness = S-C-A-R-F).

The five domains have been shown in many studies to activate the same reward circuitry that physical rewards activate, such as money, and the same threat circuitry that physical threats, such as pain, activate (Rock, 2008). If you are a leader, coach, learning specialist or learner, understanding the impact you and others have on these motivators or fears can assist you in creating the most enabling environment for learning. When we are motivated and feel safe and secure, we engage more with the learning process, are more creative, take risks, experiment, and are open to listening and feedback. However, when we are feeling threatened or fearful, we withdraw and narrow our thinking and exposure, our working memory is reduced, we are less intuitive and insightful and less compassionate, and we become more pessimistic and risk averse. This has implications for the way in which leaders make decisions and solve problems; stay cool under pressure; collaborate with others; and facilitate change.

Activity 8

Look at the descriptions below and identify which of the 5 SCARF factors motivate or threaten you the most. Usually we can identify 2–3 primary motivators/fears even though we still experience some of the others some of the time. Notice how you can adapt or influence your learning environment by using the tips provided and ensure that the learning process maximises the feeling reward and motivation and minimises possible threats and fears.

Table 4.11: SCARF factors (adapted from Rock, 2008)

	Motivators	Fears	Tips for learning
Status	Relative importance to others	Fear of criticism, exposure, failure, loss of power/status	Safeguard others' status by what you say and do, maintain dignity and self-esteem, give recognition for incremental growth, balanced constructive feedback, offer rewards for reaching certain milestones Avoid comparison with others, encourage beating personal bests rather than competing against each other, avoid public criticism, or situations that may cause rejection, avoid destructive or one-sided feedback
Certainty	Being able to predict the future	Fear of uncertainty, chaos, not knowing, loss	Be as clear and as consistent as you can be, give clear objectives and process, communicate often, assist immediately to remove barriers to learning or unnecessary frustration, offer alternative resources and support, create a safe place to practice new skills
Autonomy	Sense of control over events	Fear of authority, loss of control, loss of freedom	Provide choices, give parameters and allow individuality and space to experiment. Allow mistakes within reason. Avoid micromanagement, especially while learning new skills or behaviours. Set clear boundaries and standards.
Relatedness	Sense of safety with others, of friend rather than foe	Fear of rejection, disappointment, betrayal, not being accepted	Strive for inclusion and connectedness. Connect people together and build a sense of belonging to a group through team-identity exercises and encouraging communication between sessions. Start with ice-breakers and getting to know you exercises (in buddies or small groups) to reduce the "stranger" response. Avoid situations where people may feel ostracised or side-lined. Use group activities to increase collaboration and info sharing

	Motivators	Fears	Tips for learning
Fairness	Fair exchanges between people	Fear of unfair treatment, inequity, not being recognised	Be transparent in decisions affecting learners. Give clear explanations of changes and reward/certification criteria. Set clear expectations, allow groups to set own rules. Treat people equally. Use objective criteria to assess competence or performance.

Implications for Learning

Jot down the possible implications for learning and how you can optimise the motivators and manage or the fears

4.5.9 Other factors

Apart from the various learning influences mentioned above, a number of personal and environmental factors also affect our interest in and ability to learn. Some of these are outlined below, together with some things to consider.

Table 4.12: Other factors influencing learner profiles

Factor	Consideration
Age	Our brains change as we age. The good news is that latest research shows that we can continue to learn and create new neural pathways with the right attitude, process and environment. Our age may relate to our generation and have an impact on how we view learning as well as how we learn. See Chapter 2 on generational preferences in learning.
Job type and level	Some roles are highly hands-on, allowing little time off the job for learning. Learning needs to be structured in such a way that job performance is not impacted. As leaders rise up the corporate ladder, many assume that they have what they need, without acknowledging the significant change in thinking and relationships required at different levels with higher levels of proficiency.
Location	If you are far away from the corporate office or where training events are taking place, you may miss out on some of the regular events, group discussions or spontaneous learning activities that happen when people are in close proximity. Learning may need to be more self-driven and virtual. You may also need to set up regular communication and feedback sessions to stay in the loop and add your ideas.

Factor	Consideration
Language	Global companies continuously face the language challenge. People learn more easily in their mother tongue, but often training programmes are offered in the business language, which may be a second or third language to learners. Where possible, have materials translated into a language of choice and offer translation services if the group is highly diverse.
Time	Time constraints are one of the biggest barriers to learning in this day and age. People are finding less and less time to read, study, and attend learning programmes. Work demands are overwhelming and roles in an uncertain economy are stretched to breaking point to contain costs. Work–life balance doesn't exist. Unless learning is a value and positive beliefs about learning are encouraged with evidence on performance and satisfaction improvement, we will struggle to entice people into learning sessions and activities
Access to tools	The new paradigm of learning encourages individualised learning, using digital content on mobile devices and using apps which are great fun. This assumes that learners have access to these tools. Many developing countries are still way below the curve, with poor infrastructure, limited bandwidth, and a lack of resources for learning. This is a critical consideration when designing learning interventions for all types of people.
Mobility	Often learning entails travel to a different destination, local or international. Mobility constraints need to be considered, including people with small children or who are care-givers, people with disabilities, access to transport, and travel funds.
Exposure	Exposure to previous learning must be understood when designing a learning programme to ensure that there is no unnecessary repetition of content or process.

Implications for Learning

Jot down any factors above that may impact your ability to learn or access to learning and how you can manage these:

Brain Break: Draw a picture to reflect what you have learnt in this chapter so far.

4.6 CREATING YOUR OWN LEARNING PROFILE

Activity 9

Now that you have insight into all the different influences on learning, you can create your own learning profile or work with someone to create theirs. You can find a downloadable template on *www.accelerated.co.za*. Remember to opt in, on-board and join the journey for many additional resources, links and downloads.

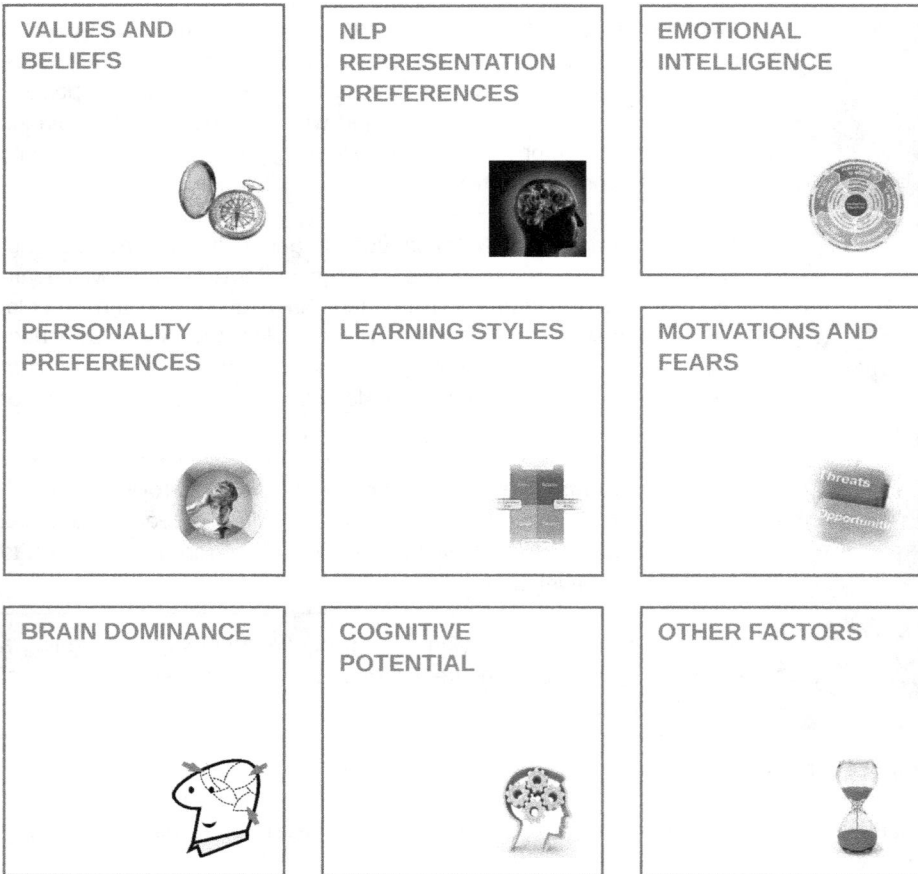

VALUES AND BELIEFS	**NLP REPRESENTATION PREFERENCES**	**EMOTIONAL INTELLIGENCE**
PERSONALITY PREFERENCES	**LEARNING STYLES**	**MOTIVATIONS AND FEARS**
BRAIN DOMINANCE	**COGNITIVE POTENTIAL**	**OTHER FACTORS**

Figure 4.5: Learning profile

4.7 CONCLUSION

Ultimately, if we really want to accelerate the learning process and cater for individual needs, we need to get into a state of FLOW. Csíkszentmihályi (2008) describes flow *as* an optimal state of intrinsic motivation where the person is fully immersed in what he or she is doing, characterised by a feeling of great absorption, engagement, fulfilment, and skill – and during which temporal concerns (time, food, ego-self, and so on) are typically ignored. You could also refer to it as being in "the zone" or in "the groove".

In order to achieve a flow state in learning, a balance must be struck between the challenge of the learning task and the skill of the learner. If the task is too easy or too difficult, flow cannot occur. Both skill level and challenge level must be matched and high; if skill and challenge are low and matched, then apathy, boredom or worry results. The more we can assess and understand each person's own unique styles and learning preferences, the more we can customise learning, cater for dynamic team differences, and optimise the flow experience. See more on flow in Chapter 11, which deals with Gamification.

CHAPTER 5

NEUROSCIENCE OF LEARNING

By Natalie Cunningham and Debbie Craig

"The human brain is the most complex living structure in the known universe. It has a capacity to store more information than a supercomputer and to create a network of connections that far surpasses any social network. The brain has enabled humans to achieve breath-taking milestones – walking on the moon, mapping the human genome, and composing masterpieces of art, literature, and music." – Brainfacts.org

5.1 INTRODUCTION

The United Nations called the 1990s "the decade of the brain" because of the amount of brain research that was being done. Since 2004, the explosion has been even more phenomenal, with over 1 000 papers in the field of Neuroscience being published monthly in various scientific and accredited journals.

However, scientists have barely scratched at the surface of what the brain is capable of. It is the most remarkable body organ apart from the heart. It controls every physical, physiological and psychological function of the body, ranging from heart rate and appetite to emotion, learning, and memory. It also controls the immune system's response to disease, and determines how our body systems will respond to medical treatment (Brainfacts.org, 2014). Apart from these physical functions, the brain "shapes our thoughts, hopes, dreams, and imaginations, and … is [w]hat makes us human" (Brainfacts.org, 2014).

This chapter will explore the relationship between Neuroscience and learning and how the brain responds to internal and external stimuli, what it pays attention to, and how it integrates and stores information and memories. We will also aim to understand how emotions sway our thinking, how the brain can deceive us, and how we can design learning to optimise our natural thinking and processing capacities.

> *Brain Break: Put on some soothing music (for example, Baroque) while you read.*

5.2 WHAT IS NEUROSCIENCE?

Neuroscience is the *scientific study* of the function of the brain and *the nervous system*.

Neuroscience is a diverse field using brain research to explore anything from schizophrenia, depression, autism, dyslexia, attention deficit disorder, and a host of other human neurological, psychiatric, and developmental disorders. It is also used in an attempt to understand individual behaviour, motivation, creativity, learning, and social interaction. The emphasis of Neuroscience is on the "How?" Neuroscience explores questions such as:

- How do cell circuits enable us to read and speak?
- How and why do we form relationships?
- How do we think, remember, despair, or motivate?

The aspect of Neuroscience that has an impact on the world of work and learning is Social Cognitive Neuroscience.

- The **social level** is concerned with social, motivational and interpersonal factors that have an impact on behaviour and learning, such as the impact of group pressure on learning. For example, if learning is seen to be an aspirational aspect of a group, the willingness and motivation to be part of a training programme would be higher.
- The **cognitive level** is concerned with the information-processing mechanisms that give rise to social level phenomena. For example, what happens if you receive an assignment and you have an "F" for "fail" written on the front page? The information processing could transition through a number of interpretations, as indicated in the diagram below. The cognitive process makes the transition from a purely cognitive thought: *"I have an F"* to a social aspect: *"Everyone else did badly too."*

- The **neural level** is concerned with the brain mechanisms that drive cognitive level processes and what is happening to the neurons and the connectivity. The goal is to understand the links between social, cognitive and neural levels and how this relates to learning.

Initially the brain was assumed to be an information processor that performed work without context. Early brain research was about mapping the patterns of the senses: sight, hearing, and taste; and what happened in the brain from an information-processing perspective. Subsequently, with technological advances and interdisciplinary discoveries, a more systemic paradigm of Neuroscience emerged. One of the most significant developments was a machine called the functional Magnetic Resonance Imaging machine or fMRI machine. The American Psychological Association states: "While a conventional MRI results in snapshots of what's inside the body, the fMRI produces movies starring the brain." The MRI looks at the structure of the brain, while the fMRI looks at what lights up in the brain as people perform different mental tasks. This technology is enabling the answers to questions such as:

- How do people make decisions?
- What's the best way to motivate people?
- Why is it so hard to lose weight?

The images below show the difference between the fMRI results of a person looking at a picture of a face (animate, personal) versus a house (inanimate, impersonal) and which parts of the brain light up as they observe the inanimate objects as opposed to animate objects.

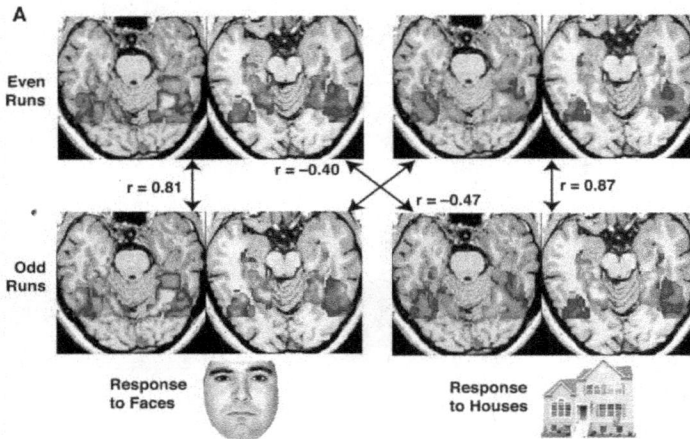

Figure 5.1: fMRI images

Some interesting facts have been discovered through the use of fMRI machines. Remember to opt in, on-board and join the journey for many additional resources, links and downloads. See the On-boarding section or www.accelerated.co.za.

The power of what we can learn from the fMRI is vast and this is why the field of Neuroscience has seen such growth.

5.3 LEARNING AND NEUROSCIENCE

As we emphasised in Chapter 4, **learning = change**. We are continuously learning, both consciously and unconsciously. We often do not even realise how our brains are being altered by what we observe, how we interact with the world and our role models and influencers. Learning changes the physical structure of the brain and results in its organisation and reorganisation. The past 15 years of research in neuroscience have produced some profound insights into the ways that learning occurs.

For many years, the focus of learning interventions has been on the **content** (in other words, what learners need to learn) and how we can effectively transfer the learning content to the learner in the shortest amount of time at the lowest cost. Not much attention has been given to the **context** (that is, how they will learn). This has resulted in dismal learning retention and application and continues to exacerbate the global and local leadership and skills crisis. Content-focused learning fails to engage learners in a way that stimulates the development of new neural pathways, the integration of learning into long-term memory, and the ability to apply learning to multiple situations and contexts.

The **paradigms of learning** within the world of work are also changing rapidly, as outlined in Chapter 2. Information overload, 24/7 connectivity, divided attention and rapidly evolving technologies all increase the barriers to effective learning. As a result, the learning styles of the **Millennials** are shifting too, and they require a much more active and interactive approach to learning, rather than being passive absorbers of material and theories presented to them. Not only do they want to interact, but they want to be involved and to contribute in a meaningful way to the learning process. They want to co-create their ideas of the future.

Powerful new insights into the workings of the brain can help us **create learning experiences** that are both more effective and more efficient. Neuroscience offers a new way to think about the design of learning activities and programmes and how to tap into the way in which the brain naturally learns, and avoid its shutting down. It offers us a way of understanding how to gain and guide attention, how to utilise and regulate emotion, how to stimulate and embed memories, how to use visual cues and symbols for greater absorption of ideas, how to give space and time for reflection and integration, how to build mindfulness practice to help focus the mind, and how to make better learning choices.

The six key aspects having an impact on learning from a Neuroscience perspective are outlined in the diagram below and will be described in the rest of the chapter. Although each aspect will be addressed individually, in reality they are all interrelated.

Watch this video on YouTube: **Neuroscience and Learning**
http://www.youtube.com/watch?v=oO3T6Ep5I0g

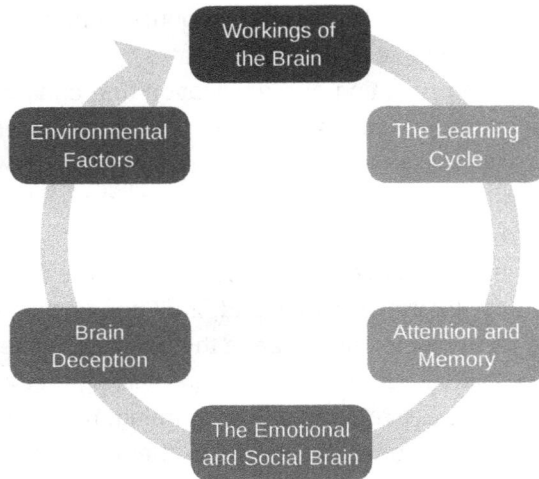

Figure 5.2: Aspects of Neuroscience which have an impact on learning

5.4 WORKINGS OF THE BRAIN

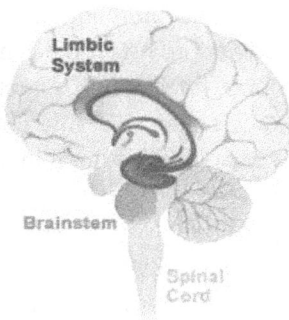

Figure 5.3: The brain,
showing the limbic system

The brain has several components but for the purpose of this section we will focus primarily on two parts of the brain, the limbic system and the pre-frontal cortex.

The first part is the **limbic system**, or the reptilian brain, located in the centre of the brain. It is the most primal part of the brain and is concerned with survival and managing fear or threats. It is also called the "emotional brain". It reacts first to stimuli. It never matures and its primary purpose is to scan all information and determine the level of safety or risk. If all is "safe", then the brain remains calm. If, however, a threat is detected (whether rational or irrational), it moves into flight, fight or freeze mode, anxiety rises, and the brain immediately focuses all its attention on the threatening situation and diverts resources accordingly (see Figure 5.3).

The second part is the **prefrontal cortex** or the executive decision function, located in the right front hemisphere of the cerebral cortex.

This is also called the "thinking brain", which is slower to respond as it first filters and processes information – it assesses, evaluates and chooses a more mature response. The pre-frontal cortex is the seat of concentration, motivation and working memory. It is where inputs from all cortical areas are projected onto and integrated or connected. It is the driver of conscious action. This is the part of the brain that learns, integrates, assesses options, prioritises and makes choices (see Figure 5.4).

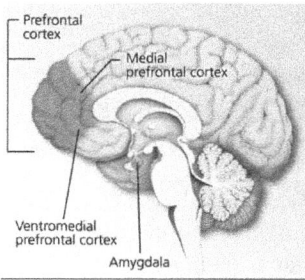

Figure 5.4: The brain, showing the pre-frontal cortex

When a person experiences a significant amount of stress or intense fear, social judgment and cognitive performance are negatively impacted. Some stress is necessary to meet challenges and does potentially lead to better thinking and learning, but beyond a certain level it has the opposite effect. Boyatzis (2013) speaks about the **sacrifice cycle** which occurs when we experience too much stress. A stress overload triggers the arousal of the sympathetic nervous system (SNS), leading to a brain shut-down of non-essential neural paths. It leads to people being less open, less flexible and less creative. People with an aroused SNS feel anxious, irritable, and frustrated, and often out of control. Physically older neurons get stimulated and shrinking of neurons occurs. It has been found that perceptions become distorted and it feels as though the world is conspiring against you when you are in this state. Things people say or do are seen as threatening, judgemental and negative (Cunningham, 2014).

Fundamentally, the brain loses the capability to learn. Learning designers, specialists, educators and leaders must make it their business to avoid this debilitating state when planning or implementing learning experiences.

Some of the science

The Central Nervous System (CNS) consists of the Somatic Nervous System and the Autonomic Nervous System. The somatic nervous system is concerned with purely physiological or bodily functions. The autonomic nervous system consists of the **Parasympathetic Nervous System (PNS)** and the **Sympathetic Nervous System (SNS)**. It is these two systems that are relevant to our understanding of the brain in interaction with the environment.

Remember to opt in, on-board and join the journey for many additional resources, links and downloads. See the On-boarding section or *www.accelerated.co.za*

Here is a useful summary of these two important components and their impact on thinking, learning and long-term health.

Table 5.1: Comparison of SNS and PNS

Flight – Fight – Freeze mode (reflexive)	Executive Decision mode (reflective)
Limbic system (emotional brain) – Reacts within 1/5 of a second	Pre-frontal cortex (thinking brain) – slower to respond
Manage fears or threats (stress) for safety and survival	Seat of concentration, motivation, working memory – evaluates, integrates, chooses
Sympathetic nervous system (SNS) – amygdala, brain shut-down of non-essential neural paths, releases hormones (cortisol, noradrenalin)	Parasympathetic nervous system (PNS) – vagus nerve, slows heart rate, releases hormones (oxytocin, vasopressin, dopamine)
Feel anxious, fearful, irritable, frustrated, out of control, distorted perceptions (threatened), judgemental, negative,	Feel positive emotions, optimism, well-being, compassion, energised, greater intuition, heightened learning state, social judgement, in flow
Rapid heart rate, increased blood pressure, sweating and an increased respiratory rate	Reduced heart rate, calm, deeper breathing, relaxed
Less open, flexible, creative, learning, memory, risk tolerance	Less anxiety, fear, stress
Reduced immune function and general metabolism	Greater long-term health

"Courage is about learning how to function despite the fear, to put aside your instincts to run or give in completely to the anger born from fear. Courage is about using your brain and your heart when every cell of your body is screaming at you to fight or flee – and then following through on what you believe is the right thing to do." – Jim Butcher, Ghost Story

5.4.1 SNS Triggers to avoid – SCARF

David Rock's SCARF model described in Chapter 4 is a useful approach to help us understand the particular triggers of the SNS. As a reminder, SCARF is an acronym derived from the initial letters of Status, Autonomy, Certainty, Relatedness, and Fairness. It is derived from studies showing that much of our motivation driving social behaviour is governed by an overarching organising principle of minimising threat and maximising reward. You will remember, as you read in Chapter 4, that the brain cannot separate social threats and physical threats – it reacts in exactly the same way, regardless of whether the trigger is physical or social. See examples of rewards and threats and their impact in Table 5.2 below.

Table 5.2: SCARF rewards and threats

Response	Traditional primary factors activate the response	Social factors activate the response	Results in
Approach (Reward)	Rewards in form of money, food, water, sex, shelter, physical assets for survival.	Happy, attractive faces. Rewards in the form of increasing status, certainty, autonomy, relatedness, fairness.	More cognitive resources More insight More ideas for action Fewer perceptual errors A wider field of view
Avoid (Threat)	Punishment in the form of removal of money or other resources or threats such as a large hungry predator or a gun.	Fearful, unattractive, unfamiliar faces. Threats in the form of decreasing status, certainty, autonomy, relatedness, fairness.	Increased motor functions Reduced working memory Reduced field of view Generalising of threats Erring on the side of pessimism

When we are feeling **rewarded**, we are more open, creative and insightful and have more cognitive resources available for good decisions. When we are feeling **threatened**, however, we cannot solve problems effectively or make good decisions (or sometimes even any decisions). We also struggle to be empathetic and have healthy relationships with others. For example, someone feeling threatened by a boss who is undermining his/her credibility is less likely to be able to solve complex problems and more likely to make mistakes.

In other words, the SNS is triggered when people are feeling that their **status** or position of power is under threat, when they are **uncertain** or confused about the future, when they sense a **loss of control** or autonomy over their lives, when they experience **isolation** or **rejection**, or when they perceive **unfair** treatment. These five domains are activated in social or work situations. You can use the table in Chapter 4 to understand how these five domains motivate us and make us fearful, and how to manage these for an optimal learning environment.

Some more science – Good and Bad tags

When a person encounters a stimulus his/her brain will either tag the stimulus as "good" (engage or approach), or "bad" (disengage or avoid). If a stimulus is associated with positive emotions or rewards, it will likely lead to an approach response, and vice versa. For example, the brain encodes one type of memory for food that has tasted disgusting in the past, and a different type of memory for food that has been good to eat. It uses similar circuitry for interacting with the social world (Rock, 2009).

Remember to opt in, on-board and join the journey for many additional resources, links and downloads. See the On-boarding section or *www.accelerated.co.za*.

Learning principles

- Design programmes and interactions with people to maximise rewards and minimise threats.
- Help learners, leaders and facilitators to understand their threat and reward triggers and how to be sensitive to others' triggers
- Monitor body language and behaviour of learners for possible disengagement arising from SCARF factors.
- Be continuously aware of how others may be evaluating what you say and do in relation to reward or threat. This is not a conscious process, but it happens at a very basic instinctive level.

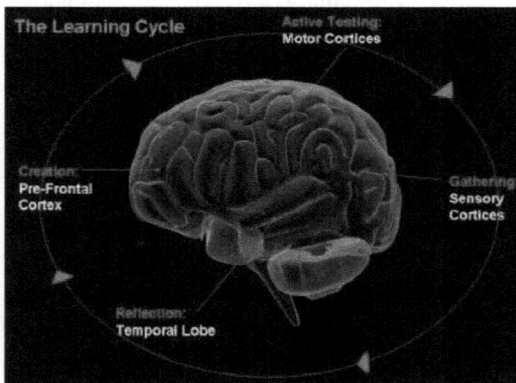

Figure 5.5: The learning cycle

5.5 THE LEARNING CYCLE

Neuroscience has also taken the understanding of the learning cycle to a new level. Further development on the experiential learning cycle of Kolb (1984) and Honey and Mumford (2000) by educator and biologist Zull (2002) has linked the steps in the learning cycle with different regions of the brain, these being the sensory cortices, the temporal lobe, the pre-frontal cortex, and the motor cortices.

The brain processes learning through four regions or stages of gathering, reflection, creation and active testing. This involves gathering sensory experiences through the sensory cortices; engaging in reflective observation; drawing on the temporal lobe; creating new concepts in the pre-frontal cortex; and actively testing through our motor cortices. (This is obviously an over-simplification of a much more complex and interrelated process.)

The complete cycle of learning arises from the very structure of the brain and results in new and lasting physical connections. Zull suggests that the power and duration of learning is proportionate to how many regions of the brain are engaged. The completion of the entire cycle is required for true change in behaviour and performance.

It is important to remember learning begins with connecting with what we already know – our **prior knowledge.** Every fact, idea, belief, worldview, habit or action is part of a network of neurons in our brain. We must therefore assess and enable access to prior knowledge even before we embark upon the learning cycle. Each person's network is unique and requires an individualised approach to access this prior knowledge in order to empower the learner and to avoid disengagement through boredom or insult.

The four stages of learning according to Zull, are summarised and described in Table 5.3 (adapted from Hendel-Giller in collaboration with Hollenbach, Marshall, Oughton, Pickthorn, Schilling & Versiglia, 2010).

Table 5.3: Four stages of learning

Step 1: Gathering	Step 2: Reflection	Step 3: Creation	Step 4: Active testing
• Gather sensory experiences (information) through the sensory cortices • Inputs are received through sight, hearing, touch, position, smell and taste	• Reflective observation by engaging the temporal lobe • Integrates the sensory information received during the gathering stage • Searches for connections	• Creates new concepts by engaging the prefrontal cortex • Creates knowledge in the form of abstractions such as ideas, plans, concepts and symbolic representations	• Actively tests through engaging the motor cortices • Allows the brain to make the abstract concrete by converting mental ideas into physical events – into action

Step 1: Gathering	Step 2: Reflection	Step 3: Creation	Step 4: Active testing
• Concrete experience is first recorded in the brain and gathered for further stages	• Internal, private and requires time and space for learners to pause and digest • Works better when sensory inputs are shut out and brain can focus attention on integrating information • Reflection is necessary for insight formulation, creativity and innovation • Reflection can happen both within and between learning activities	• Manipulates and organises information in working memory to create new relationships and new meaning and link back to prior knowledge. • Creation is unique to each individual – must be allowed to create their own understandings and make meaning in their own ways • Gives space and choice and "trusts the brain to think"	• Any action inspired by ideas qualifies as active testing
Examples: Reading, explanations, presentations, course content, experiences	*Examples: Reflection questions, integrative assignments, time out between learning events for relaxing, disconnecting and sleeping*	*Examples: Creation often involves language, so really important for a learner to explain something "in your own words" e.g. "tell me your plan for action", draw your own framework or picture, describe the usefulness of this in your workplace*	*Examples: Reading another book on the topic; talking to someone about the book; explaining and talking about what was learnt; hearing what someone else thinks; searching the topic on the web; seeking out people who live the topic and talking to them; setting up experiments to test.*

Without **reflection**, learning will be disconnected and shallow. Research clearly demonstrates the benefits of **spacing** versus massing practice and training (Zull, 2002). Until learners actively **create** their own ideas, and create or assign personal meaning, learning has little chance of enduring. Multiple studies have found that promoting creation of knowledge rather than passive studying of content result in longer lasting learning (Richland, Bjork, Finley & Linn, 2005). The very act of **recalling** information reinforces and embeds learning. Activities that ask learners to retrieve learning within the learning process can be very powerful (Bjork & Linn, 2006).

5.5.1 Progressing from novice to expert

When designing a learning experience we must remember that novices and experts learn differently. Experts who are normally experienced in the content have many neural connections and the interconnections are stronger and much better organised. It is thus easier for experts to access, retrieve and integrate knowledge. Often training is designed in the same way regardless of whether the learners are experts or novices. We need to respect the existing knowledge and neural pathways of experts and build this into our training design. Experts are thus able to move more easily from working memory (which is limited in capacity) to long-term memory.

Novices, however, have far fewer prior neural connections and pathways and struggle to contain new knowledge. Both the novice and expert will breakdown their information into smaller chunks, with one significant difference: novices cannot identify which are important; whereas experts are able to spot quickly which are important. It is therefore critical to help novices to develop a way of sifting through the details and to aid them in choosing what is important. When designing learning events for novices, it is important to look at the world through their eyes. This is often difficult, as the learning designer is normally an expert and assumes that the learner will look at things through the same set of eyes or world-view. We need to remember, however, that every person is a novice in some areas and an expert in others.

Learning principles

- Design learning processes with space and **time for gathering, reflection, creation and retrieval** to match the way the brain learns.
- Actively help learners to make meaningful connections and tap into **prior knowledge and experience** e.g. through use of metaphors, analogies and stories.
- Customise training to **match the level of expertise** of the audience.
- Help people to **create connections** between new information and what they already know, and between the big picture and the details.
- The **traditional barriers between formal and informal learning must be less rigid**, with reinforcement being embedded into on-the-job, informal learning.
- Learners must **make meaning of their own learning.** They need maximum control of their learning experience in order for deep learning to occur.

5.6 ATTENTION AND MEMORY

"We live in an age of information overload, where attention has become the most valuable business currency." – Thomas Davenport and John C Beck, The Attention Economy

5.6.1 Continuous partial attention

In today's world we are living in a space where we have **"continuous partial attention"**, a term coined by Linda Stone, former Microsoft vice president. We are looking at Facebook, having lunch, answering an email, and engaging in a face-to-face conversation. No one activity has our full attention. "We pay continuous partial attention in an effort not to miss anything. It is an always-on, anywhere, anytime, anyplace behaviour that involves an artificial sense of constant crisis" (Stone, 2008).

In a 24/7, always-on world, continuous partial attention used as our dominant attention mode contributes to a feeling of being overwhelmed, to over-stimulation, and to a sense of being unfulfilled. We're so accessible that we're inaccessible. The latest, greatest powerful technologies have contributed to our feeling increasingly powerless … We have focused on managing our time. We need to focus rather on how to manage our attention (Stone, 2008).

5.6.2 Neurons that fire together wire together

The way the brain engages and manages attention is the way in which it filters information. Your brain becomes what you focus on or, as stated in the well-known phrase, *"neurons that fire together wire together"*.

Learning affects the brain in two different ways – either by altering existing connections or by creating new connections. Every memory, thought and idea is made up of a set of connections between neurons, and these connections create a **map of connecting highways** in our brain. The maps are constantly competing for resources as there is not enough energy for all the neurons to connect with each other at every moment. The brain is therefore continuously "pruning" neurons. We can therefore not remember the exact quantities of the ingredients to bake a chocolate cake, if we bake only once a year. But if we bake regularly, we will remember the quantity of each ingredient, but may possibly not remember the title of a book that we read a year ago. If however, we are a publisher or editor, we would be more inclined to remember book titles because of our interest in books. In fact, in the age of Google and smart phones, our brains have become "lazy" as we no longer feel the need to remember information, just how to search for it.

Over time, the **connections** we make based on what we are **paying attention to become hard wired** and form the basis for how we behave. Conscious decisions have an impact on our attention and awareness and in turn trigger different neural connections. Schwartz and Begley (2002) call this process "self-directed neuroplasticity". Self-directed implies a choice, and neuroplasticity implies that the brain is able to change.

Neuroplasticity

"Up until the 1980s, scientists thought the structure of the brain developed during childhood and that once developed, there was very little room for change. Scientists now know that the brain possesses enormous capacity to change: People's ability to process widely varied information and complex new experiences with relative ease can often be surprising. The brain's ability to act and react in ever-changing ways is known as neuroplasticity.

"Neuroplasticity is perhaps the single most important concept in terms of learning and the brain.

"The knowledge that our brain is constantly changing and growing – that cortical plasticity extends throughout the human lifespan – shifts our understanding of what is possible for adult learners. Learning is not just changing external behaviour, but changing the very wiring of the brain as it relates to those behaviours. Deep, lasting change is possible at all ages."

(Hendel-Giller in collaboration with Hollenbach *et al*, 2010)

5.6.3 Harnessing attention

In order to engage learners in the learning cycle, we need to **harness the energy of the learners**. The word "harness" is deliberately used, as learners will be all be paying attention to something (friends, Facebook, food) all the time. The brain is designed to **filter all incoming sensory stimuli** immediately and select only those that are relevant at that moment so as to encode them. It will discard or ignore information that doesn't fit these criteria. David Rock (2009) calls it the spotlight effect. For example, if we focus on the faults of an individual, we will be hard wired to see the faults constantly, as is often the case in failed relationships. Similarly, if we focus on positive characteristics and gratitude, we are more likely to notice these. We therefore need to design learning experiences that quickly, effectively and powerfully grab the learner's attention and then maintain that attention throughout the learning process.

5.6.4 Attention density

The **quantity and quality of attention** determines the strength of connections in our brain. This is also called **attention density**. We get more of what we pay attention to. The **quantity of attention** refers simply to the number of times focus is directed to the desired circuit.

The quality of attention is affected by the intensity of **emotional reaction** as well as reflective **questions**. By asking people to engage with a question, we get them to recall what they know, which can trigger auditory and visual memory circuits, thus improving the quality of recall. See Chapter 7 for some good tips on questions.

5.6.5 Energy, chunking and multi-tasking

Some uses of the brain also **use more energy** than others such as conscious prioritising, which uses considerable energy. This suggests that we should spend time prioritising when we have energy, not at the end of a day or strategy session when your brain is tired. It has also been proved that the brain can't attend to two or more attention-rich stimuli simultaneously – simply put, **multitasking** doesn't work, so make focused time for important tasks.

Recent research indicates that working memory has a capacity of about **four "chunks" of information** in young adults (and fewer in children and older adults). This is fewer than the original seven. We must therefore build "chunks" of content into the learning design or we may get cognitive overload. It is interesting to note that the brain has an extraordinary capacity to remember **images**. People can recall seeing hundreds, even thousands, of pictures (Standing, Conezio & Haber, 1970). **Pictures** seem to operate as "chunks", and while the brain can hold only a few chunks in working memory at a time, visual images allow the brain to hold and enlarge the scope of those chunks.

5.6.6 Novelty, shifting attention and engaging the senses

Novelty is a powerful strategy for harnessing attention. People show increased production of dopamine, a neurotransmitter linked to pleasure and reward, when shown something new (new could indicate a possible reward). They also recall information more easily when new information is combined with familiar information.

While we generally think that focus is good, it can exhaust certain neurons. Scanning can be useful as well as **shifting attention** through looking at things from many different angles, or even moving around the room. We can also shift attention by changing from one topic to another or exposure to a different facilitator. Just remember that shifting attention requires three discrete brain processes: disengaging, moving and re-engaging, which take time and energy; and we must therefore allow learners sufficient time to make these shifts (Wright & Ward, 2008).

Engaging the senses through multimodal learning does make a difference in learning. Presenting material in two media – pictorial and verbal – is generally superior to presenting material in only a single medium. Science shows that **visualisation** of an action or an activity engages the same parts of the brain that actually doing that activity activates in the brain. This is why athletes often engage in mental practices – because they have physical benefit.

5.6.7 Mindfulness

We tend to live not in the present moment, focusing on the sensory experiences, but rather in our heads. Siegel (2007) has found that by being mindfully aware, attending to the richness of our experiences, it creates a change in the brain physiology and improves our sense of well-being. Siegel believes that while mindfulness is a form of attentional skills processing that focuses our minds on the present, ultimately it is a form of a healthy relationship with ourselves. Practising mindfulness means focusing our attention on a particular thing or thought in a very conscious way. It means that we are immersing ourselves in the very moment, "waking up from life on automatic".

The benefits of mindfulness have been shown to be an improved capacity to regulate emotions, improvement in the quality of thinking and subsequent decision making, and reducing negative mindsets. Empathy, intuition, morality and self-insight have together all been found to be enhanced by mindfulness.

"The practice of mindful leadership gives you tools to measure and manage your life as you're living it. It teaches you to pay attention to the present moment, recognizing your feelings and emotions and keeping them under control, especially when faced with highly stressful situations. When you are mindful, you're aware of your presence and the ways you impact other people. You're able to both observe and participate in each moment, while recognizing the implications of your actions for the longer term. And that prevents you from slipping into a life that pulls you away from your values." –
Bill George

Watch this video on YouTube: **The Neuroscience of Memory – Eleanor Maguire**
http://www.youtube.com/watch?v=gdzmNwTLakg

Activity 1

Imagine that you are designing a learning programme which is classroom based. Choose a topic with which you are familiar and address each of the attention elements in the design process. Use the template below. Try it on your own at first, to support true learning principles, and use examples to stimulate your thinking if you find yourself stuck. Refer to the notes above to remind you of the principles in each area.

Share via e.mail or Facebook to level up. See OnBoarding for more info on how to do this.

Attention techniques	Proposed activity/ Guide
Chunking – 4 elements	
Sensory stimulation	
Novelty	

Attention techniques	Proposed activity/ Guide
Shift attention	
Images	
Mindfulness	

Learning principles

- Actively incorporate attention management strategies during learning design.
- Provide learners with awareness and skills training in attention management.
- Eliminate multitasking in order to facilitate more efficient and effective encoding of knowledge.
- Minimise the load placed on working memory by limiting distractions and avoiding asking learners to process vast amounts of information at one time.
- Manage attention shifts, allowing learners sufficient time and space to disengage and re-engage.
- Utilise novelty and surprise while allowing learners to make connections with existing knowledge.
- Remember to access all senses in the learning experience.
- Using visual images and asking learners to visualise will increase learning retention.
- Teach learners how to be more mindful in everyday life.
- Help learners apply attention management strategies back on the job. These strategies include changing expectations that inadvertently encourage the productivity-sapping practices of multitasking and continuous partial attention. For example, organisations may need to allow employees time for focusing on tasks without interruption, or give them permission to respond to email or voicemail in a manner that suits them.

5.7 THE EMOTIONAL AND SOCIAL BRAIN

"There can be no knowledge without emotion. To the cognition of the brain must be added the experience of the soul." – Arnold Bennett

Over two thousand years ago Plato declared that *"all learning has an emotional base"*. Evidence now proves that emotions are powerful and inevitable parts of life and learning. Neuroscientific research has revealed that emotion and cognition are not neatly divided in the brain. Virtually all mental activities involve both emotion and cognition (LeDoux, 2000). There are positive and negative aspects to emotions and the link to learning.

5.7.1 The "Aha!" moment

One of most powerful triggers that motivates people to learn is a positive emotion or an illumination – **the "aha!" moment** – the moment of insight that comes with the understanding of a new idea. The brain loves this learning experience. The energy rush we feel is a new set of connections happening in the brain supported by neurotransmitters such as dopamine, adrenalin and serotonin. At the moment of insight, strong gamma bandwaves are transmitted as the brain simultaneously processes information across different regions. A new map is being created across the brain, linking many parts of the brain. This energises the individual.

5.7.2 Not too hot, not too cold

Just the **right amount of emotion** is needed for learning – not too much, and not too little, or as Goldilocks liked her porridge – not too hot, and not too cold. Learning is maximised in a moderate state of arousal, often referred to as "relaxed alertness" and related to the alpha brainwave state. If learners are not aroused at all, they will not engage. However, if they are too aroused (or anxious), they will be unable to stay focused. A moderate level of arousal triggers neural plasticity by increasing production of neurotransmitters and neural growth hormones, enhancing neural connections and cortical reorganisation (Cozolino, 2006).

5.7.3 Self-regulation

Managing one's emotions is one of the key skills of being an effective learner. **Self-regulation** is one of the most important behavioural skills needed. Emotions direct (or disrupt) psychological processes, such as the ability to focus attention, solve problems, and support relationships. Emotional states induced by fear or stress directly affect learning and memory. Brain studies have illuminated how **negative emotions block learning** and have identified the amygdala, the hippocampus and stress hormones (glucocorticoids, epinephrine and norepinephrine), as playing a crucial role in mediating the effects of negative emotions such as fear and stress on learning and memory. Simultaneous bodily events such as an increased heart rate, perspiration, and elevated adrenaline levels also occur (Damasio, 2000; LeDoux, 2000), and in turn influence cortical activity.

But other less extreme **sources of stress** can have a parallel impact, such as aggressive teachers, bullying students, or incomprehensible learning materials. If students are faced with situations that trigger fear or stress, their cognitive functions are affected. These stressors can operate at a conscious or sub-conscious level. Openness to learn is greatly diminished when there is a perception of threat or when learners sense a potential for loss of control as described in the SCARF section above.

"When it comes to shaping our decisions and our actions, feeling counts every bit as much as – and often more than – thought."
– Goleman

5.7.4 Memory blocks

Emotion also affects our memory. We remember emotionally charged events better than neutral events (Bechara, Tranel, Damasio, H, Adolphs, Rockland & Damasio, AR, 1996). However, strong emotion can also impair memory, and prevents us from remembering clearly something that happens after an emotional event. We need to be sensitive to the emotional climates that we create during learning experiences and tune in to the emotional states of learners.

5.7.5 Positive Emotional Attractors (PEAs) and Negative Emotional Attractors (NEAs)

When designing the learning experience and engaging with learners, we need to be cognisant of the Positive Emotional Attractors (PEAs) and Negative Emotional Attractors (NEAs) stimulated by our human need to survive (primary driver) and thrive. The survival need activates the SNS and is triggered in response to perceived stress or even potential stress, for example, thinking of a potentially difficult conversation one has to have with a manager or an employee. The conversation may go well and be much better than anticipated, but the anxiety about the possibility of what could go wrong would result in the SNS kicking into action prior to the conversation. The person would enter the meeting in an aroused SNS state, with all the associated dysfunctionality.

Table 5.4 below provides a few examples of PEAs and NEAs and demonstrates the predisposition to focusing on positive scenarios (possibilities) as opposed to more limiting or negative scenarios (criticisms, gaps).

Table 5.4: Emotional attractors

Positive emotional attractors	Negative emotional attractors
Ideal self	Real self/Social self
Strengths	Gaps and weaknesses
Focus on the future	Focus on the past
Hope	Fear
Possibilities	Problems
Optimism	Pessimism
Learning agenda and goals	Performance Improvement Plan

5.7.6 Social brain

In addition to the brain being emotional, it is also social. It requires and thrives on interactions with other brains. In fact, the brain develops in concert with other brains – and requires those other brains to develop.

> *"Like every living system, from single neurons to complex ecosystems, the brain depends on interactions with others for its survival. Each brain is dependent on the scaffolding of caretakers and loved ones for its survival, growth and well-being ... The brain is an organ of adaptation that builds its structure through interactions with others." – Cozolino (2006:15)*

5.7.7 Mirror neurons

During neuroscientific research with monkeys Italy in the 1980s, the researchers, led by Giacoma Rizzolatti, accidentally discovered that some of the neurons they recorded would respond when the monkey saw a researcher pick up a piece of food as well as when the monkey picked up the food. This later became known as the mirror neuron system and through fMRI studies a similar mirror neuron system was detected in humans. Research shows that newborns as young as 42 minutes old match gestures shown to them. Before infants can see their own faces, or see a reflection in the mirror, they are already mirroring the behaviour of other humans (Meltzoff & Prinz, 2002). Learning from others happens more directly, more automatically and more powerfully than was ever imagined.

Some scientists speculate that a mirror system in people forms the basis for social behaviour, for our ability to imitate, acquire language, and show empathy and understanding. It also may have played a role in the evolution of speech (Society for Neuroscience, 2007).

HOT TIP **Learning principles**

- Design learning so as to create a strong **emotional pull** for learner engagement.
- **Avoid** creating an overly charged emotional environment that will have a negative impact on the learner.
- **Anticipate learners' potential emotional triggers** (for example, prior negative experiences with formal training) that might have an impact on their ability to learn and use insights from SCARF to manage these triggers.
- Recognise the influence of the facilitator's and fellow learners' mood (**mirror neurons**) and use the notion of mirror neurons positively and proactively. Enthusiasm can be contagious.
- Consider the **organisational environment** and its potential for enhancing or impeding learning.
- Careful consideration must be given to how we build **human interaction** into learning solutions in the digital age, for example, by using blended solutions and **leveraging connections between learners**.

5.8 BRAIN DECEPTION

Schwartz, a leading neuroscientist and psychiatrist, says that one of the greatest things having an impact on our changing and growing is our own thought patterns (Schwartz & Gladding, 2011). We can have positive programmes or disruptive programmes. He calls the negative or inhibiting programmes or ways of thinking, **"deceptive brain messages"** which as "false or inaccurate thought or any unhelpful distracting impulse or urge that take you away from your true goals and intentions in life."

A deceptive brain message leads to you feeling a sense of discomfort. You try to reduce the discomfort habitually. It is not even necessarily a conscious process and can include dysfunctional responses such as addiction, avoidance, getting into an argument, shutting out the world and whatever behaviours you may have tended to do in the past. On a deep, subconscious level there is almost the hope and thought that if you practise this behaviour, the feeling will go away. What you are dealing with is an **emotional sensation** which is different from an emotion. **An emotion** is a true and appropriate feeling. In other words, if someone you love dies and you feel sad, that would be appropriate. These feelings must not be supressed. An emotional sensation is an emotion that does not have its foundation in truth. An example may be that if you felt you were unlovable, despite evidence to the contrary, and that led to your feeling sad, the sadness would be based on a deceptive brain message – not recognising that your friends and family care for you. This leads to dysfunctional, unhealthy behaviour. True feelings need to be honoured and felt, but emotional sensations rooted in false beliefs need action. Some examples of these deceptive brain messages are listed below in Table 5.5.

Table 5.5: Distortion impacts

Cognitive distortions	Impact
All-or-nothing thinking	I set high standards for myself/I am never satisfied
Catastrophising (big catastrophic event in your mind)	I worry and am always exhausted
Discounting the positive	Depression – feeling I am not good enough
Emotional reasoning	Hopelessness – will I ever feel better?
Mind reading	I will do whatever I can to control things
"Should" statements	I disappoint myself
False expectations	I feel inadequate
Faulty comparisons	I feel shame

The "brain" learns that when you feel or experience that painful sensation, for example, "nobody loves me" (even if deceptive and false) and you perform a persistent action in order to avert or distract yourself from that sensation (such as isolating yourself), the brain will keep performing those persistent actions and repeating the behaviour. It will not stop to discern whether this is good or bad for you, unless you consciously make your brain do so.

Schwartz and Gladding (2011) suggests a four-step strategy to counteract the deceptive brain messages. These four steps are summarised in Table 5.6 below.

Table 5.6: Counteracting deceptive brain messages

Relabel	Identify the intrusive thought and urges as uncomfortable and call them what they are
Reframe	Label the deceptive brain message as a deceptive brain message saying something along the lines of: "This is not me. It is just a deceptive brain message"
Refocus	Direct your attention to something else and do another ore constructive behaviour.
Revalue	Do not take these thoughts at face value. Recognise that they were simply sensations caused by deceptive brain messages.

CASE STUDY

Let us illustrate with an example:

You find yourself thinking: *"If my boss valued me, he would have invited me to play golf with him this weekend. He invited Gary, my colleague. He must value Gary more than me."*

Table 5.7: Example of how to counteract deceptive brain messages

Relabel	I do not know if this is fact. This is just a perception. I am feeling uncertain so I am labelling it as my boss does not value me but I do not know that for certain.
Reframe	Maybe my boss values me, maybe my boss likes playing golf with different people at different times. There are a number of explanations. My brain has decided there is only one. I reject that brain. There may be other reasons
Refocus	Let me work on this proposal I was busy with instead of fretting about golf
Revalue	I need to chat my boss and check out what he enjoys and values about my work and what he does not. I need some facts.

Activity 2

Pick one of the deceptive brain messages that you can relate to and work through the 4 Rs:

Relabel:
Reframe:
Refocus:
Revalue:
Share via e.mail or Facebook to level up.

Learning principles

- Trainers, managers and coaches must **challenge assumptions** that learners bring into the learning process and check the truth and **appropriateness of emotions**.
- Emotions such as inadequacy, shame and guilt will impede learning and these emotions must be counteracted by focus on emotions of **possibility, hope and potential**.

5.9   ENVIRONMENTAL FACTORS

Environmental and physical factors such as sufficient nutrition, exercise, natural light, oxygen and sleep can also play a significant role in the quality of brain functioning. These seem obvious and so are often overlooked when designing learning programmes.

5.9.1 Sleep

Historically, some companies and business schools designed intensive learning programmes where participants were pushed with ridiculous group activity deadlines into the night, only to present the next morning with little or no sleep. These team challenges were designed to test their ability to cope with stress and reveal their derailing behaviours in stress situations. Neuroscience research shows that the brain cannot function at maximum capacity when tired, so if learning is the aim, boot-camp type training programmes will not lead to sustained learning. If, however, the aim is to assess and identify behaviours, this kind of experience can still be useful.

The power of sleep

- Ariana Huffington, in her latest book, *Thrive* (2014), talks about the power of sleep and its impact on our lives. "Creativity, ingenuity, confidence, leadership, decision-making; all of these can be enhanced simply by sleeping more".
- "Sleep deprivation negatively impacts our mood, our ability to focus, and our ability to access higher-level cognitive functions,, the combination of these factors is what we generally refer to as mental performance." (Division of Sleep Medicine, 2007)
- They also point out that lack of sleep was a "significant factor" in the Exxon Valdez wreck, the explosion of the Challenger space shuttle, and the nuclear accidents at Chernobyl and Three Mile Island.

5.9.2 Natural light and air

Many conference and training rooms (especially in hotels) are designed to have no distractions. They are either situated deeply within a building or have closed windows, heavy curtains and air conditioning. This means that no natural light or air reaches the learners. Research is now showing that space to view natural light and breathe fresh air is conducive to a better quality of thinking.

5.9.3 Nutrition and exercise

What we eat can energise or de-energise us. Many learning session breaks are filled with sugar-laden delicacies, much to the delight of the delegates (muffins, sandwiches, biscuits, croissants, fried nibbles, and cakes). Research suggests that excessive glucose in the form of refined sugar can be very detrimental to your brain, ultimately affecting your attention span, your short-term memory, and your mood stability. So perhaps we should be more mindful of the types of snacks and treats provided during learning sessions.

Movement and exercise also increases the quality of thinking by improving blood flow to specific areas of the brain. Recent research indicates that regular exercise can improve brain function in ageing adults (Chapman et al, 2013). Build some movement time into learning interventions. These can be as simple as a few stretches, dancing or games to get the body moving. Even better, take the group for a walk or activity outside, where they can benefit from both fresh air and movement.

Overall, it is good to be clear on the learning objectives of all interventions and sessions. A whole brain, whole person, integrated design for learning programmes that recognise the close interdependence of physical and intellectual well-being will go a long way toward both accelerating the learning process and making it more fun.

 **Learning principles**

- Influence the context and physical environment as much as possible in the design and choice of venue and learning activities to ensure maximum light, air, and nutritious food
- Build movement and mindfulness activities into the programme
- Alert learners to environmental factors that are within their control e.g. sleep, exercise, nutrition, breaks

5.10 CONCLUSION

Neuroscience gives us new ways to think about learning and is a very exciting field that is discovering new insights each month. However, we need to move ahead with some caution. As Hendel-Giller in collaboration with Hollenbach *et al* (2010) says: *"… At the same time as we are excited and see great potential, we need to remain very aware of the nature of the field that we are exploring. While neuroscience research has produced more knowledge about the brain in the last decade than in all history prior, this is still a very new field. Consider that over 90 per cent of neuroscientists who have ever lived are still alive and practicing today!"*

The brain is fashionable and the prefix "Neuro-" appears in front of many disciplines. Popular appeal, however, can lead to potential pitfalls, with the general mass of popular literature being less discerning than true scientific research. This has given rise to the concept of "neuromyths", which are often based on some element of sound science, but drive an agenda where there is vested interest in perpetuating the myth. Two common examples of neuromyths are:

- "We use only 10 per cent of our brain".
- "I am a left-brained person and she is a right-brained person".

Neuroscience research now shows that the brain is 100 per cent active, and no area of the brain is inactive, even during sleep. In terms of the right/left hemisphere debate, no scientific evidence indicates a correlation between the degree of creativity and the activity of the right hemisphere. Scientists think, based on the latest research, that the hemispheres of the brain do not work separately but work together for all cognitive tasks, even if there are functional asymmetries. The brain appears to be highly integrative.

In summary, Neuroscience research is happening at a phenomenal rate and we need to ensure that we base our leadership programmes, culture change programmes, and our human capital strategies on science that is valid and true. If we do this, we can make a meaningful impact on sustainable growth in people and in our organisations.

PART 3

CREATING A LEARNING CULTURE

Chapter 6: Creating a learning culture by *Debbie Craig*

6.1   Introduction

6.2   A tale of two companies

6.3   A learning culture framework

6.4   Embarking on a culture transformation journey

6.5   Conclusion

Chapter 7: Learning through coaching by *Natalie Cunningham*

7.1   Introduction

7.2   What is coaching?

7.3   Why coaching?

7.4   How do we go about coaching?

7.5   Conclusion

Chapter 8: Learning through authentic conversations by *John Gatherer* and *Debbie Craig*

8.1   Introduction

8.2   The context of the problem

8.3   The imperative for holding authentic conversations

8.4   Towards a culture of healthy conflict

8.5   The learning imagery of holding authentic conversations

8.6   The learning process of initiating and holding authentic conversations

8.7   Conclusion

CHAPTER 6

CREATING A LEARNING CULTURE

By Debbie Craig

6.1 INTRODUCTION

"Learning organisations are organisations where people continually expand their capacity to create the results they truly desire, where new and expansive patterns of thinking are nurtured, where collective aspiration is set free and where people are continually learning how to learn together." – Peter Senge (2006)

The learning organisation, the adaptive organisation, the resilient organisation, the high-performance organisation, the flourishing organisation. There have been many attempts over the years to label and explain an organisation that grows, adapts, learns and thrives, continuing both to produce extraordinary results AND build a great place to work. Examples abound, with organisations such as Google, Apple, Disney, Amazon, Zappos Shoes, WL Gore, Southwest Airlines, Semco, Dell, Toyota, Whole Foods, IKEA, ANZ bank, and many more. In South Africa we have companies such as Old Mutual, Flight Centre, Virgin Active and Microsoft SA which are recognised as Best Companies To Work For. There are just as many organisations that fail to adapt and learn, including GM, Sony, AOL, Yahoo, Sears and Starbucks.

As organisational development consultants, we partner with many companies on a journey of transformation toward high performance and high engagement, often over a number of years. We have experienced the exceptional, the good, the bad and the ugly, each with its own unique characteristics, capacity and willingness to change. Most often we get called in to help change the "culture". We are told: "We need a more innovative culture, or a high-performance culture, or a culture where people challenge boundaries"; or: "We need a culture where people take accountability or a culture where leaders are really committed to growing and retaining talent". Executives are flummoxed, after many mediocre or failed initiatives, as to why they haven't quite made the impact expected. They wonder why things haven't changed, why people still resist the change, why strategic projects don't have the required traction, or why the engagement survey results haven't improved. Here are two real-life examples of two very different organisations with which we have worked.

Watch this video on YouTube: **Martin Carver: Creating a Learning Culture**
http://www.youtube.com/watch?v=oSFf_Gf2eeY

6.2 A TALE OF TWO COMPANIES

6.2.1 Company A

CASE STUDY

When we started discussions with Company A, the CEO really listened, and questioned and debated the issues with us. He was not shy to share both the successes and challenges in the company without being defensive. He was quick to involve his executive team in the possibilities of change. There was no hesitation to invest the necessary time and money in an important leadership alignment session in order to identify, as a team, the real strategic challenges and opportunities and to start the process of building capacity in the top team. He invited the next level of leaders to participate in the session to ensure that there was clear buy-in and commitment to the change process across all key functions.

The outcomes and decisions from the initial workshop were communicated and put into action. Strategic project teams were set up to investigate and propose changes to the culture, talent management, processes, efficiencies, innovation, and business expansion aspects of the business. Quarterly reviews were scheduled; capacity building sessions were initiated (innovation, talent management, leadership, strategic project management); and communication mechanisms were set up to ensure that information was available and shared at the right levels at the right time.

The CEO started every session with a passionate emphasis on and story around the vision and the values of the company and how the culture was being developed by every single word, facet of behaviour or action that each person displayed. He also shared business results, linking the results to organisational drivers and behaviours. The leaders embraced creative and alternative methods of sharing and learning together such as strategy expos, café conversations, movie and popcorn nights, "6 hats" thinking sessions, innovation games, collaboration stations, and so on. Visual reminders of the vision, values and strategic projects were placed throughout the company, and reinforced through newsletters, the intranet, at company meetings and at year-end functions. All leaders participated in a series of leadership development workshops, assessments, coaching, and action learning projects. All staff participated in self-leadership workshops and those with high-potential talent were identified and included in strategic project teams.

The CEO was not afraid to confront key leaders if their behaviour was not in line with the core values, and encouraged his team to do the same. He also asked his team regularly for feedback on his own derailing behaviours. He started a culture of reading and sharing books and articles on high-performance culture and leadership, expecting his team to read and share insights into their teams.

A new position was created to co-ordinate and track all strategic projects and all strategic talent forum actions. The person holding down this role was also responsible for ensuring that key events forming part of the transformation journey were scheduled, logistics arranged, communication sent out, and outcomes published internally. Project tracking and information sharing systems were implemented.

The Innovation team, after arranging an international Innovation Champions training session, decided to take innovation to their key customers and arranged joint Innovation Workshops, resulting in a number of new business opportunities for the customers and the company.

The culture team embarked on bringing in some of the international best practices from the global company, such as trained facilitators to run team alignment sessions, project start-up sessions, problem-solving sessions and talent forums. Leaders underwent 360° feedback on their leadership competence and behaviour.

The success of the process was self-evident, as the results continued to show. Sales increased and profitability improved significantly. Talent mobility increased dramatically in the first two years as an outcome of talent forum decisions, including international exposure in global workgroups, secondments and transfers. Engagement survey scores increased. Innovation projects were implemented with excellent ROI. New market initiatives were initiated in Africa, and unique sales and distribution methods were devised. Products were streamlined, production efficiencies improved, and the Green Environment project resulted in huge savings in water and waste management and CO_2 emissions.

With the success of the South African division over the two years, the CEO decided to accelerate the journey across the South East Asia and China divisions, with even more spectacular results. The company was able to adapt quickly to the economic crisis in 2008, replacing some of the strategic projects with cash and cost management projects. As soon as was prudent, the longer term, higher investment strategic projects were back on track. Over a three-year period, two of the three divisions on the transformation journey achieved their Big Hairy Audacious Goals (BHAGs), which were 15 to 20 per cent higher than their normal targets would have been. The third division achieved their BHAGs only a few months after the deadline, mostly due to huge industry upheaval of their key customer base. The international executives were so impressed by what they saw in the Global Roadshow that they embarked on a worldwide roll-out across nine regions of key components of the journey, in particular the leadership and talent management aspects.

Despite the uncertain economy and many senior leadership changes, the organisation continues to survive, adapt, learn and thrive. In recent years, they have undergone value stream analysis, restructuring, streamlining, global SAP implementation, global ADKAR, training and many other challenging processes. They still, however, continue to invest in their people with strategy, leadership and staff refresher programmes such as strategic review sessions, strategic thinking, coaching for managers, 3Es of leadership (engage, enable, empower), Wise Decision Making, 5S principles for workplace efficiency (sort, set in order, shine [clean thoroughly], standardise, sustain) and I am Talent for career and self-empowerment. As one CEO replaces another, the new leader takes up the mantle and continues the learning journey.

6.2.2 Company B

We arrived on a consulting assignment at Company B after six months of protracted discussions, presentations, competitive bids and about five different proposals, as the executive team were trying to gain clarity on what they actually wanted. The new CEO was keen to make a difference and fix some of the problems that he had experienced in working his way up the organisation to the key leadership position. The executive team was small and seemed keen to embark on this journey of transformation. As we started to engage with some of the other leaders during our diagnostic phase, we were told repeatedly that this would be just another initiative and they joked that we wouldn't last long as they were so stuck in the old traditional ways of doing things and highly resistant to change.

Initially things looked really encouraging. Commitments were made to have a strategic alignment session with their top 30 leaders. It was a positive session, with much learning and excitement about the possibility of making the changes agreed to. Strategic projects were initiated (Talent and Competency Management, Operational Excellence and Market Growth). Capacity building sessions were arranged to empower the chosen teams. Communication structures were set up to ensure that the strategic plans and projects were reviewed and meetings were held at the right levels with the right people. Functional scorecards were drafted, work-shopped, finalised and cascaded down through the organisation into team and individual scorecards. Roadshows were held across each of the operating areas, with the CEO introducing the vision, the strategic intent, the desired culture, and the strategic projects supported by the various executives. Stakeholders at the Group head office were informed and involved with much interest in using the company as a pilot.

The Talent and Competency project team got off to a good start with regular meetings well attended, strategies, processes and toolkits drafted, training held, and implementation plans developed, all in consultation with line managers. The Operational Excellence team held a strategy session, developed a framework and sub-projects. The first Steering Committee (Steercom) meeting was held to review progress. The first strategic review and leadership development session was held, but crucial conversations started to occur and be noticed.

And then, as we handed over the reins to the executive and project teams, the momentum slowed. Steercom meetings were postponed and not rescheduled, despite repeated reminders. No time could be found for strategic review sessions. Implementation of talent and competency management (role profile sign off, career discussions, talent forums, leadership competency assessments, and development) ground to a halt. The Operational Excellence project limped along, with some sub-projects getting some air-time, but no co-ordinated decisions could be made across all operations. The Market Growth project came up with a plan, starting with a restructuring, which took years to get off the ground. The executive team, although encouraged, reminded and even pushed, did not take up the executive coaching and team alignment sessions suggested, and the team retreated into its silos, and the "polite" conversations resumed.

HR embarked on a strategic re-alignment process as a result of a credibility crisis raised during the talent project sessions and the diagnostics. Although it was initiated with best intentions and buy-in from the Exco, final important investment decisions (key roles required, competency assessment and development, and technology support) were rejected, resulting in a new, leaner structure but without the competence level and administrative and technology support to service the business effectively.

When we managed to get time for review meetings, the various executives blamed each other or Head Office for lack of budget, or the economy, or their key client that was taking all their attention. In the occasional workshop that did get off the ground, for example, HR strategy, the talent management refresher training, and so on, staff complained about the leadership, about lack of decision making, about micro-management, and about things not changing. Despite our best efforts, and the good intentions of many good people, this organisation just couldn't make the shift to a high-performance, adaptive, learning organisation.

What went wrong? Was it…

- … the economy?
- … the impact of a key client threatening to cancel contracts?
- … the head office influence?
- … the leadership style of the new leader?
- … the lack of alignment and true commitment of the executive team?
- … the lack of follow-up and accountability?
- … the complacency culture of the company, without much local competition?
- … the lack of experience and competence of certain key leaders?

Let's explore some of the ingredients of building an organisation culture that encourages and recognises the importance of learning for individuals, in teams, across teams, as an organisation, and with the external community for growth and success for all.

6.3 A LEARNING CULTURE FRAMEWORK

I have been an avid reader, explorer and experimenter with learning, leadership, culture and change over the years. Although many frameworks exist, my own experience has led me to focus on the following seven aspects when assessing, customising and building the foundation for a high performance, high engagement culture that that has learning at its core. See Figure 6.1 below.

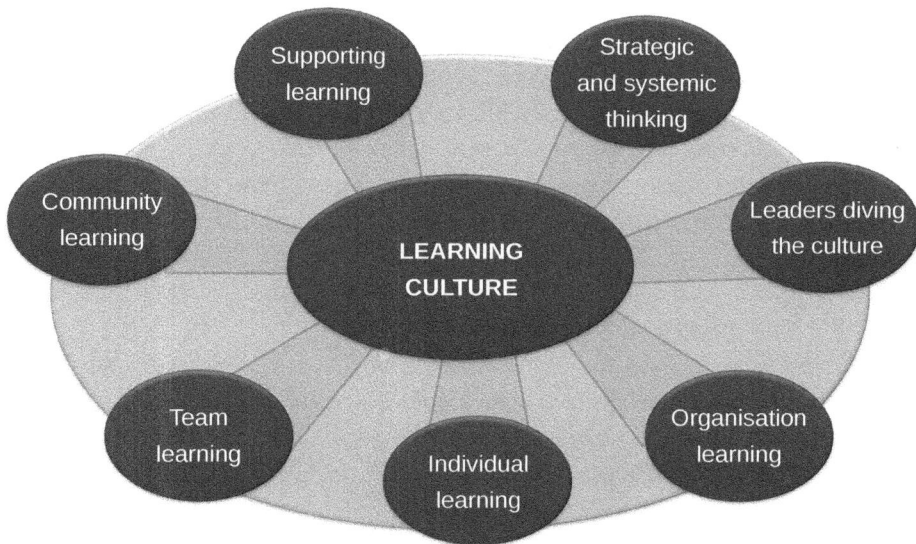

Figure 6.1: Seven aspects of a learning culture

6.3.1 Strategic and systemic thinking about learning

Learning design needs a strategic and whole systems approach to ensure a holistic, integrated learning strategy and architecture. Learning activities and opportunities touch every part of the business and all aspects of people's lives. These touch points can be identified and optimised through systemic thinking and building the systems and tools to support learning at all levels. Learning can be woven into all strategies, systems, processes and policies and made visible and accessible through effective communication and engagement mechanisms. Lastly, learning requires a long-term view when making budget decisions, and it is wise to avoid short-termism when costs need to be managed. Have a look at the suggestions below for opportunities in your own organisation.

- There is a clear **strategy** for learning (and creating a learning culture) which has a scorecard with goals, measures, targets and timelines and is aligned with the organisation and HR strategy.
- Learning strategies and approaches are **continually reviewed**, aligned to best practice, possibilities explored, and key lessons from the past shared and integrated into future plans.
- **Systemic and strategic thinking** are core competencies of senior leaders who understand the various factors having an impact on an organisation's ability to adapt and change.

- There is a **Chief Learning Officer**/Head of Learning who reports directly to the CEO and sits on the executive committee.
- There is buy-in and commitment to the learning strategy and the **executive support** it requires by all senior leaders in the organisation.
- There is a **learning structure** that supports the strategy with sufficient specialist resources that are competent to deliver on the strategic goals.
- There are appropriate **infrastructure, systems and tools** to drive learning, such as a Learning Management System (LMS), mobile and social learning platforms and applications, physical facilities, virtual learning facilities, and a variety of learning content and tools.
- Learning is seen as a **long-term investment** and there is sufficient budget allocated to both strategic and operational learning activities required to create a learning culture and deliver the strategic goals.
- **Learning policies** support the strategy and are clearly communicated to all staff, for example, further education policy, time off work for learning, provision of technology, and so on.
- **HR strategies and policies** support the creation of a learning culture.
- Learning is **built into every system**, process, technology, function and daily activities.
- Learning is made **visible, accessible and encouraged** through visual symbols, communication, events, recognition, stories, invitations, newsletters, and so on.

New roles in learning

Chief Learning Officer (CLO)

Companies that are serious about building a learning culture are employing or promoting a key strategic role reporting directly to the CEO and a Chief Learning Officer (CLO). Learning is too important and too specialised to fall into the general HR arena and be represented through the HR Executive. The responsibility of the CLO is to drive the corporate strategy and align the development of people with the business goals of the organisation. Skills need to include business analytics, technology, learning theory, performance consulting, and scientific inquiry. CLOs need to understand and sometimes manage other critical aspects of modern business such as talent management and change management, and play a critical role in leadership development.

In the 1990s, Jack Welch, then CEO of GE, made Steve Kerr his CLO, making GE the first company to have such an officer (http://en.wikipedia.org/wiki/Chief_learning_officer). The University of Pennsylvania has its own Doctoral Program under their Graduate School of Education, called the Penn CLO Executive Doctoral Program. It specially prepares Chief Learning Officers and other senior-level human capital executives for success in their roles as learning and talent development leaders,

Learning and performance specialists (L&P specialists)

A new role is appearing in many progressive organisations. Learning and performance specialists are a new breed of learning specialists who understand how people learn, what it takes to be competent, and the link between learning and on-the-job performance (both now and in the future). L&P specialists are excellent at diagnostics and designing learning interventions. They also ensure there are clear learning outcomes, application opportunities and assessment methods built into both learning and performance reviews. They are also great advisers and business partners to line managers, ensuring that learning and performance are integrated and make business sense. Some of the role players may develop through the HR function, but many more of them come from line roles.

Are your Learning and Development specialists transitioning and transforming to design and lead accelerated learning programmes and culture in your organisation for real measurable performance and business results?

Activity 1

What can you do to start this journey of development?

6.3.2 Leaders are capable of and committed to driving a culture of learning

Research has shown that leaders impact culture by up to 70 per cent. They are therefore critical elements in the culture journey that can either make it or break it. Every leader joins an organisation with his/her unique values, vision for the future, personality, skills, behaviours and blind spots. If we let each leader do his/her own thing, it is unlikely that we will create a unified culture that encourages lifelong learning, mistakes, honesty, and openness to feedback and learning. It is important that the learning organisation and the leadership values and behaviours supporting it are defined, developed and monitored, with ongoing feedback and learning loops built into the system.

Read through the suggestions below to identifyr opportunities in your own organisation or for you as a leader.

- The organisation's **purpose** is meaningful, inspirational and people centric, and is linked to learning at all levels.
- Organisational **values and behaviours** are clearly defined and drive a learning culture.
- The **leadership brand** of the organisation is clearly defined and includes leadership behaviours required to drive a culture of learning.
- Leadership sessions are held to explore and challenge **beliefs, paradigms and mental models** around learning. New beliefs are reinforced at meetings, at events, and through communication channels.
- All leaders participate in a constructive multi-rater **feedback process** to assess perceptions of how they live the leadership brand and organisational values.
- Leaders create an environment in which people are **allowed to fail** and learn from their mistakes.
- Leaders at all levels participate in **leadership development and coaching programmes** designed to accelerate learning and to build capacity in creating a learning culture: the 3 Es of leadership (engage, enable, empower), coaching, and crucial conversations.
- Leaders are encouraged and enabled to adopt a **coaching style** of leadership.
- Leaders are **confronted** when their behaviour is out of line with the leadership brand or values.
- Leaders have measures on their **scorecard for learning** and are held accountable for specific results.
- **Culture champions** are identified and developed to ensure that a culture of learning is embedded.
- **Culture surveys** are completed annually, with results pertaining to specific areas given to leaders, and action plans developed in consultation with senior leaders.

Building a culture of feed-forward

One of the most powerful learning methodologies is receiving input and observation on your behaviour and impact. Although usually labelled "feedback", a different spin on things is to call it "feed-forward", that is, information that helps you grow and *move forward* toward your goals. There are many ways of creating opportunities for feed-forward. These include: performance reviews; psychometric assessments; assessment and development centres; postbox feedback in a leadership development context; 360° leadership behaviour surveys; start–stop–continue behaviours in a team; peer review of strengths and development areas; honest conversations; and one-on-one discussions. The most important ingredient for feed-forward is the attitude of the giver and receiver. If feed-forward is given with the spirit of growth and caring in a coaching style, then it can never be wrong.

What are you doing in your organisation to encourage a culture of feed-forward?

Activity 2

Name two people whom you will be asking to give you some feed-forward input.

6.3.3 Organisational learning

For a whole organisation to be learning, adapting, responding and growing, structures and processes need to be set up to guide and support these behaviours. Aspects such as learning design, change management, decision making and communication strategies need to incorporate accelerated learning principles. Communities of Practice require leadership and co-ordination and knowledge management must be supported by platforms and behaviour change to make it work. Collaboration and social learning are new approaches to the business world and new competencies and habits can be encouraged and rewarded. A different level of dialogue is required when assessing readiness for talent and succession and how to go about accelerated development. How do you turn every employee into an Insight worker that contributes real insight toward important business decisions?

Have a look at the suggestions below for opportunities in your own organisation.

- **Accelerated Learning** is built into the fabric of learning programme design.
- **Change management** is a core competence of leaders, HR and learning specialists and built into all change projects.
- **Change resilience** and responsiveness is a core competence of all staff who are exposed to training in personal effectiveness, change resilience and stress management.
- Communication strategies and mechanisms are well-developed and effective.
- Leaders are clear on levels of authority, decision-making parameters and trained in effective, collaborative decision making skills to avoid the traps of decision making **(see Chapter 15)**.
- Leaders understand the power of **collaboration**, are trained in the key skills of collaboration and have the tools to enable collaboration (such as SharePoint, SAP Jam, Cyn.in, Socialspring).
- **Communities of practice** are encouraged and recognised to capture, build and share specialist knowledge throughout the company.
- There is a **knowledge management** system that is actively used and encouraged to ensure learnings are captured from projects and accessible to new people and teams.
- There is a culture of **innovation** supported by Innovation strategies, process, tools and skills to ensure ideas are captured, filtered, assessed and feedback, resources and budgets allocated accordingly.
- **Social learning** is enabled through internal and Internet-based platforms and applications such as yammer, TidWit, Curatr, and so on.
- **Talent forums** are considered an important strategic event in which leaders learn about the talent in the company. Robust talent discussions are held about how to accelerate learning and readiness for future positions and address performance, learning or behaviour challenges. Talent forum actions are tracked and reviewed on a quarterly basis and form part of leaders' scorecards.
- Employees are empowered to be **insight workers** and convert data to information, to knowledge, and eventually to insight that is useful and relevant to organisational decisions. This includes boundary workers who engage with the external world, industry, customers, suppliers, government, the community, and so on on a regular basis.

Are knowledge workers being replaced by "insight workers"? (Lesser, 2001)

Peter Drucker coined the phrase "knowledge workers" in 1959 to describe the shift in workforce trends and the increasing value of those who accumulate expertise within a given domain. The term has served us well for half a century, but it will become increasingly obsolete in the years ahead. We are in the early stages of the decline of knowledge workers, because knowledge is becoming increasingly ubiquitous. We see this in our personal lives already: "Are you smarter than a 5th grader?" used to be a slam dunk for most educated adults. Give a sharp 5th grader an iPhone or an Android device, and that same adult now has no chance.

Expertise was, and in many places still is, highly valued. Drafting a legal brief, closing the financial books, or writing a market research report are all important tasks that provide thousands or even millions of well-paying jobs. Yet within each of these professions and many others, there are really two different sets of activities. The first is the ability to gather and synthesise knowledge into coherent and useful observations. The second is translating those observations into insights that can deliver impact – win a trial, improve the economics of a business, take market share from competitors.

While the aspirations of most professions are concentrated on driving outcomes, much of the actual work, particularly by entry- and mid-level workers, concentrates on creating and synthesising knowledge. And here is where the challenge will be greatest. Knowledge workers are coming under siege, and this trend will accelerate as computers enhance their abilities to analyse vast amounts of data, process language, make real-time judgements, and integrate different data sources. It will not happen overnight and it will move at different paces in different areas, but we are at the beginning of a trend that will accelerate in the years to come.

This change will have a profound impact on many professions and in turn will place new challenges on educators and employers. If what we need are insight workers more than knowledge workers, then we need to develop talent of all ages differently -- with more emphasis on problem-solving, more emphasis on collaboration, more skills in translating information and ideas into impact. Many educators and employers are already identifying these needs, but most are probably not recognising how fast these new requirements will be upon us.

Last month, an IBM computer beat the two top Jeopardy champions of all time in a practice match. As this technology expands and approaches ubiquity, how will the average knowledge worker compete?

6.3.4 Individual learning

Individual learning can be optimised by providing the information for employees to assess and develop their own performance, competence and potential. Effective on-boarding, role profiling, performance feedback and career development are critical foundations to anyone's learning journey. Combine a good system with the right behaviours and you have a winning recipe. Give employees ample opportunities to build their personal mastery capabilities and tap into what really motivates them. Support learning outside of work as an effective retention strategy and individualise learning wherever possible. Offer support in the form of coaching and on-the-job application options. Have a look at the suggestions below for opportunities in your own organisation or for yourself.

- Individuals all participate in **on-boarding** activities that ensures they understand the culture of learning.
- Individuals all have user-friendly, updated **role profiles** with performance standards and competencies against which they can assess their current performance and competence.
- Individuals have access to **career development information** including the requirements for roles at different levels and functions in the organisation.
- Individuals are encouraged and enabled to take initiative and **drive their own career** and role development.
- **Personal mastery** is a core competence of all staff who are encouraged to grow and develop skills such as self-awareness, emotional intelligence, assertiveness, influence, accountability, and so on.
- Individuals have an opportunity for regular **performance and behavioural feedback** from their managers at least four times per annum.
- Leaders understand the **three key motivators** – autonomy, mastery and purpose – and aim to provide as much of these as possible.
- Leaders understand the **whole brain, whole person, whole systems** approach to learning and are able to plan learning with their staff for accelerated results – repeat, revise, recall, reinforce.
- Leaders support individuals with **integrating learning** from learning activities back into their work lives.
- Learning is used as a **retention strategy**. Organisations are willing to pay for learning even if learning is not linked to the current or future potential role, for example, guitar lessons, Spanish lessons, and so on. Research supports this approach, showing that senior leaders are more likely to stay with an organisation that provides unbounded learning opportunities.

Research: On learning and retention

In an Accenture research report (2008), the survey results show that investment in employee's skills and competencies that make them more marketable actually make them stay. This may sound counter-intuitive. Logic would argue that building employability would increase the risk of leaving, but this is not so. A global study of managers and executives, found that organisations can strengthen their executives' intentions to stay by equipping them to leave. This is particularly relevant in today's uncertain economic environment. Rather than guaranteeing employment security, businesses can provide opportunities for employees to accumulate skills and experiences that both improve company performance and enhance employees' employability in the labour market. This "employability approach" encourages and often expects individuals to take greater personal responsibility for their careers.

CASE STUDY

Semco

Ricardo Semler (2004) has been breaking traditional business rules as the CEO of Brazil-based Semco for 25 years and achieving success with it. Semco, which has over 3 000 staff members, grew from $35 million in revenue to $212 million in just six years. Along the way, Semler asked himself: "If the work week is going to slop over into the weekend ... why can't the weekend, with its precious restorative moments of playtime, my time, and our time, spill over into the work week?" He says businesses are set up to fail once they have "burned out their employees and burned through ever more manipulative and oppressive strategies".

Semler believes that a company that puts employee freedom and happiness ahead of corporate goals can still achieve profit, sustainability and growth that surpass the competitions. He has implemented an idea at Semco that allows each individual to take half a day a week as personal time, while exchanging it for half a day post-retirement. This allows people to explore their passions, interests and special family moments at the prime of their lives AND sets them up with a purpose and the ability to contribute later on in life. It is a true win–win.

6.3.5 Team learning

Learning within and across teams is often underestimated as a means for shifting awareness and insight. High performance teams continually assess their effectiveness and give each other feedback and hold each accountable. There are many mechanisms and tools to support team learning including team review and alignment, team sharing, team feedback, team skills and team tools. Cross-functional team sessions are also useful for unleashing value to the internal or external customer and learning new ways of doing things for greater impact. Have a look at the suggestions below for opportunities in your own team or organisation.

- **Team alignment** or team-building sessions are built into the annual calendar of every team.
- Teams have the opportunity to **get to know each other** and understand their team member's personalities, strengths, weaknesses, expectations, preferences, pet hates and aspirations.
- Leaders are trained in **team facilitation techniques**.
- There are **trained facilitators** available to design and facilitate or co-facilitate team sessions.
- Team members give each other **feedback and suggestions** to improve individual and team performance and behaviour.
- Teams have sessions to raise and address **crucial team conversations** that may be standing in the way of high performance and learning.
- Teams have regular **team-sharing sessions** to share projects, new approaches, information gathered and lessons learnt.
- **Cross-functional team sessions** are encouraged to share issues and learnings across boundaries.
- Teams continually ask who else they could **consult with or collaborate with** for superior results.
- **Cross-functional learning projects** are a regular feature of accelerated learning programmes.

Buckman Global: Team facilitators and team tools

CASE STUDY

Buckman, a US-owned global family business for over 65 years, has long been recognised as a learning organisation and is still in the top 50 of US learning practices. One of their non-negotiables is to run a team alignment session every time a new leader joins a team or the team is restructured, or there is a significant change in the team. This applies to both functional and project teams. Buckman invests significant time and money into training team facilitators who undergo extensive training, practice and co-facilitation to master the art of true facilitation. While some of these trained facilitators are from HR, the majority hold senior line management positions in the business.

The facilitators are also trained on Buckman-specific team tools which are a standard at all team meetings and workshops. These include tools such as team meeting agendas and outcomes, team charters, team one-page progress updates, team energisers, after-action reviews, and team behaviours. Throughout Buckman, their values and behaviours are guided by what they call the seven principles of teamwork. These are 100% Responsibility, Trust, Clear communication, Healthy conflict, Commitment, Accountability, and Focus on results. They are refreshed at every major induction, training session or workshop or as required in performance and career discussions.

Buckman takes teaming very seriously and sees it as the lifeblood of their organisation which operates with global workgroups, cross-functional teams, strategic project teams, global customer account teams, and many other teams.

6.3.6 Community learning

Sometimes we forget how much additional knowledge, experience and ideas exist in the spaces around our organisation. We can learn from other organisations (competitors and non-competitors) about their products, processes and services. We can build relationships and learn from the local communities how to be ethical and sustainable into the future. We can offer learning experiences to leaders and staff through CSI programmes and community leadership interactions. We can involve highly experienced retirees in building knowledge and capacity in others for a win–win solution to scarce skills. Have a look at the suggestions below for opportunities in your own organisation and community.

- Senior leaders all have a clear idea of the **various communities** which have an impact on and on which the organisation has an impact. These includelocal government, local villages or towns, community upliftment projects, board members, shareholders, unions, suppliers, customers, industry players, and so on.
- There is a detailed **stakeholder management plan** with activities and owners who implement and report back on the plan.
- There is **regular dialogue** with important communities in order to learn and share together.
- Create time for learning sessions with **Board members and shareholders**. Many of them come with years of experience and ideas. Instead of seeing them only as authority figures to appease, and board sessions being tense affairs, create a learning environment for two-way sharing and learning.
- Opportunitiesfor**sharingandlearning**fromnon-competing organisations are identified and developed; fpr example, Buckman facilitates innovation sessions with key customers in order to explore further use of products and services.
- Companies can also **learn from competitors** by observing how they do things or by using their products, such as Sam Walton from Wallmart (Heath & Heath, 2013).
- Staff have the opportunity to participate in **Corporate Social Investment (CSI) projects** in the community and to learn through their interactions and build meaning in their lives.
- Semi-retired or **retired employees** have the opportunity of adding value back to the organisation, for example, by providing mentoring roles, project advisory roles, training roles.
- **Families of employees** are invited to participate in certain learning experiences where it makes sense, for example, retirement counselling, self-development or emotional intelligence programmes, and entrepreneur programmes

- There are programmes to identify **high-potential learners** from the local schools, colleges and universities and offer them bursaries, internships or work experience.
- There are **leadership programmes** that involve interacting with local community leaders for a mutual learning experience, such as Partners for possibilities (see www.pfp4sa.org), RMB entrepreneurs programme.
- There are **employment programmes** for low-skilled contract workers in the local community.
- **Company facilities** can also be used for community projects during non-work hours.

CASE STUDY

Buckman SA: Innovation with Key Customers

A great example of an organisation taking learning and application to the next level is the Buckman SA Innovation team. A strategic review session a number of years ago launched the need for greater innovative thinking and processes in the company. A strategic project was set up which developed an Innovation strategy in consultation with the senior leadership team. Innovation Champions were identified in each division and trained on how to facilitate various innovation sessions (idea generation, idea funnelling to different levels, idea prioritisation, and communication with the Innovation Forum.) Through this training the idea was explored about how to collaborate with key customers and suppliers for greater innovative ideas and business possibilities.

Buckman approached two of their largest customers to help facilitate customer-focused innovation sessions with what they had learnt. Both customers welcomed the idea and invited many key players to participate. The sessions were co-facilitated by the Buckman Innovation Champions and supported by us. The sessions were a resounding success, with many ideas leading to win–win business opportunities for the customers and Buckman. Buckman also enhanced their reputation as not only high-quality, reliable suppliers, but also innovative thought leaders in their field.

Many customers and suppliers over the years have requested visits to Buckman, not just to see their products or facilities but to find out how they manage to engage their staff and build a culture that is always learning and stretching the boundaries of possibility.

6.3.7 Supporting learning

There are various roles which can support the learning process by providing support, feedback and encouragement along the learning journey. We can learn from managers, mentors, coaches, consultants and colleagues. We can also learn with our friends and families. We can utilise technology to support and remind us and help track our learning. Have a look at the suggestions below for opportunities in your own organisation or life.

- **Personal Board of Directors** – this is an imaginary group of five to seven people who, if you could invite them into your board room or living room, would give you the best possible advice for your own greatest success and highest potential. Some people choose famous icons such as presidents and CEOs; some choose people they deeply respect and admire, such as grandparents and people they have actually met before. These are people who embody the core values and standards you aspire to live up to. You can turn to these "elders" for guidance at times of ethical dilemma, life transitions, and when difficult choices have to be made. You can ask questions, pose dilemmas, and then imagine and reflect on the advice these people might give. Remember that the imagination is an exceptionally powerful mechanism for learning and creativity (Collins, 1996 – see www.jimcollins.com/article_topics/articles/looking-out.html).

- **Manager** – your manager is the person often closest to observing how you perform and behave. Your manager has most probably been in your role before and so understands what is required. Managers are in the ideal position to give you honest feedback on what they observe and suggestions for improvement. While some managers may feel threatened by you or not have a learning approach, most managers are dedicated to continuous improvement of the position and the people with whom they work. So give it a try and ask for feedback and assistance with activities that will enhance your skills.

- **Coach or mentor** – as you will see in Chapter 7, which deals with coaching, having a coach and being a coach are fundamental components of accelerated learning. A coach helps you set learning goals; helps you talk through what you are learning; provides additional perspectives; facilitates feedback; and holds you accountable for the learning journey. While a professional executive coach will add significant value, don't be surprised at how much value a colleague (younger or older than you) can add if you having coaching conversations with each other.

- **Learning department** – the learning department or HR business partner that looks after learning in your area is also a good source of support. They have specialist knowledge in understanding competence and behaviours and will have access to a wide array of learning ideas, tools and resources. They can also assist you with finding a coach or learning partner.

- **Learning partner** – just like our manager, our colleagues and friends are the ones who see us in action on a daily basis (even more so than a busy manager). If you have a good relationship with a colleague or friend who has a particular skill that you admire, or has a certain ability to be insightful and wise, don't be shy to ask them to be a learning buddy. Set up a specific session where they will be your learning buddy and ask some questions, give your feedback, and hold you accountable for certain behaviour. Give them permission to come to you after a presentation or meeting to share what they observed so that they can give you more insight into your own body language, attitudes, behaviours, and the impact you have on others.

- **Family members** – our close family members know us the best out of everyone. They see us at our best and at our worst. They experience our impact when we are fulfilled and loving. They also know our de-railers and blind spots intimately. Who better to get some feedback from regarding a leadership or learning programme than our own families? Not only will it help you increase your Johari window of self-knowledge; it will also demonstrate a humility and willingness to be vulnerable and open to difficult conversations – and hence deepen these very important relationships. (See www.mindtools. com/CommSkll/JohariWindow.htm.)

- **Suppliers and consultants** – most organisations work regularly with suppliers and consultants in the project, change and learning space. Many of these consultants have made it their business to specialise in their field and will have useful models, summaries, tools, articles and tips to help you accelerate your learning. Optimise your time with them in team meetings or set up individual sessions to ask questions, discuss ideas, request additional reading, and even ask for advice, feedback or coaching.

- **Technology support** – we use technology all the time for scheduling wok and personal activities and reminders. How about using technology to enhance our learning by scheduling activities and reminders that will encourage learning? These could be actual events such as workshops or coaching sessions, but also time set aside for reading, reflection, summarising, testing, action learning projects, cross-functional visits, etc. As we discovered in the Neuroscience chapter, reflection and integration activities are just as important as reading about or listening to new content in order to embed the learning into memory and be able to recall it and apply it in a variety of different environments.

- **Tracking and measuring** – it is important to know how you are doing when building competence to improve performance and results. Feedback and assessment at certain stages of the learning process helps us keep track, do a reality check, feel encouraged and motivated when there is progress and up our game when we realise that we haven't quite mastered the topic yet. Assessments can be in the form of feedback form others or through assessment activities which test knowledge, skills or behaviours such as questionnaires, tests and demonstrations. If you are completing a formal training programme or course, assessment is usually structured into the process. However, if you are adopting a self-driven learning journey, then you will need to build in the tracking and measuring yourself.

Learning partner – with friends and colleagues

Have you ever asked a good friend or colleague to have a coaching session? A while ago, as I was exploring more about coaching and the multitude of opportunities that exist to learn from others, I approached a friend and asked if we could have coffee and a coaching session. This shifted the paradigm from just a mutual catch up to my friend being able to ask some really insightful questions and share observations that made me sit up and take notice. It helped me realise some of my blind spots and it gave me some ideas on how to start making changes. The success of this one session led to both of us giving each other permission to go into coaching mode when it was deemed necessary. Instead of always being in coaching mode (and not relaxing and just being ourselves), we came up with a phrase: "May I ask you a coaching question?" Most of the time, we agree; but sometimes, it is not the right time or mood, and we just laugh, and say: "Maybe another time."

This friendly arrangement can be mutually beneficial in any relationship, as long as the permissions have been discussed in advance. In our business we often have a coaching debrief after a client meeting or workshop to tell each other what went well, and what we could have worked on for greater impact in the future. This is done with a real intention of helping the person to develop awareness and grow. It is very helpful for continuous learning as we are never too old or too experienced or successful to learn from others.

Activity 3

Draw a mind-map of the learning culture in your organisation or your current social network.

Share via email or Facebook to level up.

6.4 EMBARKING ON A CULTURE TRANSFORMATION JOURNEY

Changing organisational culture takes time. It requires an inspiring vision, commitment from senior leaders, investment in the financial and people resources to make it a reality and the drive and resilience to stay the course.

If we use the Prosci framework of ADKAR in order for cultural transformation to occur, it requires the following at all levels:

- **A**wareness of the need to change – everyone at every level needs to understand the vision and burning platform for the shift in culture.
- **D**esire to participate and support the change – there must be visible leadership commitment to the change and clear benefits for the change for all employee groups to stimulate a desire for the change
- **K**nowledge of how to change (and what the change looks like) – a clear description of the journey must be communicated to all levels, with specific customised versions of what the change means for me and for my team.
- **A**bility to implement the change on a day-to-day basis – Employees must understand and be competent to implement the change. This includes having the knowledge, skills, behaviours, and mind-sets necessary for the change. It also means that work processes need to be aligned to the new process, including new policies, processes and procedures.
- **R**einforcement to keep the change in place – new processes and behaviours need to be monitored and measured to ensure the change takes place. Positive progress can be recognised and problem areas can be addressed.

Building a learning culture requires a cross-functional strategic project team to drive activities toward the clearly defined outcomes. Simply giving your head of HR or Learning the KPI to deliver this is not sufficient. This requires a cross-functional, multi-level effort to shift mind-sets, processes and behaviours toward a new reality. It requires confrontation, overcoming of resistance, and getting people out of their physical and mental comfort zones and paradigms. It requires leaders at all levels to role model the learning culture and culture champions in order to stimulate dialogue about it throughout the organisation. Ivory towers, old boys' networks, cliques, egos and political agendas need to be dismantled and a new order of meritocracy, humility, open feedback and honest conversations must prevail. A professional project management approach and governance is necessary to ensure success, including organisational prioritisation, budgeting, steering committees, project streams, project communication, and team reviews. Multiple project streams will be required such as strategic alignment, leadership development, employee engagement, learning architecture, communication, and change management.

Here is an example from a company embarking on a culture transformation journey.

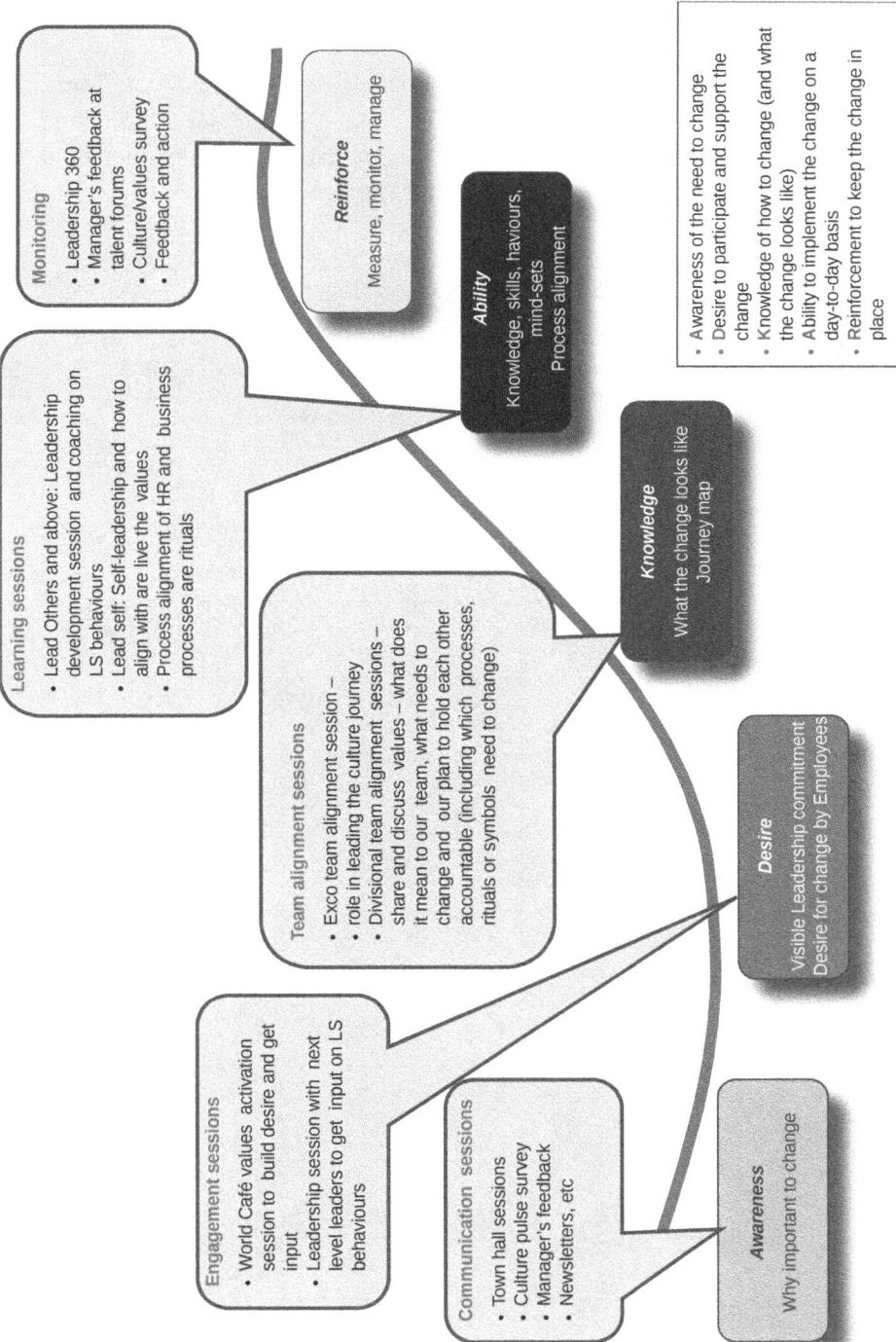

Figure 6.1: Culture transformation journey

Monitoring
- Leadership 360
- Manager's feedback at talent forums
- Culture/values survey
- Feedback and action

Reinforce
Measure, monitor, manage

Ability
Knowledge, skills, haviours, mind-sets
Process alignment

Learning sessions
- Lead Others and above: Leadership development session and coaching on LS behaviours
- Lead self: Self-leadership and how to align with are live the values
- Process alignment of HR and business processes are rituals

Knowledge
What the change looks like
Journey map

Team alignment sessions
- Exco team alignment session – role in leading the culture journey
- Divisional team alignment sessions – share and discuss values – what does it mean to our team, what needs to change and our plan to hold each other accountable (including which processes, rituals or symbols need to change)

Desire
Visible Leadership commitment
Desire for change by Employees

Engagement sessions
- World Café values activation session to build desire and get input
- Leadership session with next level leaders to get input on LS behaviours

Communication sessions
- Town hall sessions
- Culture pulse survey
- Manager's feedback
- Newsletters, etc

Awareness
Why important to change

- Awareness of the need to change
- Desire to participate and support the change
- Knowledge of how to change (and what the change looks like)
- Ability to implement the change on a day-to-day basis
- Reinforcement to keep the change in place

6.5 CONCLUSION

The transformation toward a learning organisation must survive CEO and staff changes, economic uncertainties and crises. A learning culture is the foundation on which the future adaptability, innovation and success is built and it should be a high priority, non-negotiable item on the strategic agenda.

Brain Break: Think about how you can influence the learning culture in your organisation.

CHAPTER 7

LEARNING THROUGH COACHING

By Natalie Cunningham

7.1 INTRODUCTION

"The Conductor doesn't make a sound. He depends on others to play their instruments for his power. And his power is great, but he cannot play the instruments for them." – Ben Zander, Conductor, Boston Philharmonic Orchestra

Coaching has experienced a phenomenal growth rate as an accelerated learning and development tool. In a recent survey conducted in South Africa by Knowledge Resources on leadership development practices (2013), coaching was the second most used modality for leadership development. Formal classroom training came in at 89 per cent, followed by coaching at 60 per cent and assessments at 54 per cent. Having a coaching style of leadership and being an effective coach appears in the leadership brand or top 10 leadership competencies of many leading organisations in South Africa and globally. The number of accredited coaches is increasing exponentially on an annual basis, leading to estimated annual revenue of roughly $2 billion globally, as recorded by the International Coach Federation (ICF) in 2012. In addition to accredited coaches, many organisations are training internal managers to improve their coaching skills and identifying certain leaders to undergo extensive coaching training to become accredited internal coaches.

The value of coaching

The International Coach Federation (ICF), which has over 1 2000 credentialled coaches, states: *"Coaching deepens learning. Coaches help clients reach goals through a discovery process to deepen learning. Coaches skilfully draw out a client's wisdom, help them recognise it, and yield forward momentum via accountability."*

There are many opportunities for coaching in the workplace. In the learning context, coaching is specifically useful as a leadership tool to accelerate the learning process before, during or after a learning intervention. Prior to an intervention, a leader can assist an employee in moving through the change cycle of awareness, insight, willingness, leading to the action of participating fully in the learning process. During a learning session a facilitator can assist learners to manipulate the brain's natural learning cycle of gathering, reflecting, creating and active testing. Back in the workplace, active testing can be further encouraged by a leader or coach in order to increase retention of learning and plan activities for repetition, recall, review and reinforcement. Coaching is also used in support of online learning.

Coaching is repetitive and reflective – both key components of learning. It is also time efficient, occurring in short bites of time once or twice, reducing the need to take large blocks of time out of work for learning.

The person receiving the coaching can be called a coachee, coaching client, learner, or learning partner. These terms will be used interchangeably. This chapter will explore coaching and its associated benefits with regard to accelerating learning, and will answer three questions:

- What is coaching?
- Why is it useful for learning?
- How can it accelerate learning?

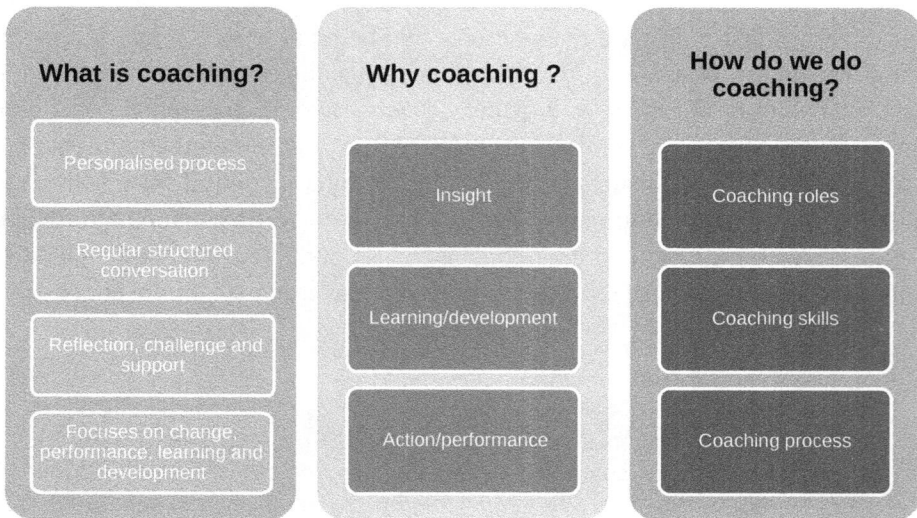

Figure 7.1: Key aspects of coaching

7.2 WHAT IS COACHING?

The two primary types of coaching are business coaching and life coaching. Life coaching is focused on building awareness and skills to live a more fulfilled and successful or purposeful life. Business coaching is focused on attaining required behaviours and results in the business world, but with a strong emphasis on aligning personal and business goals and values. We will be exploring business coaching in this book.

Business coaching is a **personalised process** facilitating performance improvement. While much of training is generalised for the majority, coaching is unique and specific to each individual. For example, assertiveness training would teach everyone the same content such as what assertiveness is; passive versus aggressive behaviour; the impact of self-esteem; and techniques to be less aggressive or more challenging. Coaching, on the other hand, personalises assertiveness for the individual. Kathy, for example, may struggle with assertiveness because of her great need for recognition and approval; whereas Susan, who tends to be aggressive, could realise through coaching that her aggressiveness is a defensive mechanism that allows her to feel in control. Both Kathy and Susan would use some of the techniques from the classroom training, but the coaching process would allow for reflection on and personalisation of the learning.

> *"Business coaching is the process of engaging in regular, structured conversation with a client: an individual who is the recipient of business coaching. The goal is to enhance the client's awareness and behaviour so as to achieve business objectives for both the client and their organisation." – WABC (2008)*

An important aspect of the above definition is that coaching conversations must result in **enhanced self-awareness and insight**. This is achieved through questioning and exploring as opposed to telling and explaining, which do not lead to enhanced self-awareness. Coaching is behaviourally driven and must lead to change in actions and behaviours and, of course, achieve business **objectives**. Business coaching is also a great way to bring individuals into **alignment** with their own goals and aspirations AND link them to the needs, goals and aspirations of the organisation.

Key assumptions that underpin business coaching are the following:

- Coaching is a **systemic process** and takes places within a context. It is driven by an organisational purpose and strategy and is often in support of leadership development and talent management initiatives, as well as assisting people through transitions such as business promotions.

- Coaching is a **collaborative process**. Research has shown that it is very important that the coachee wants to receive the coaching and does not see it as punishment or remedial. If coaching is seen as something that happens to poor performers, it could result in resistance to the coaching process. Coaching needs to be positioned as a collaborative developmental process and it is important to take the time to position and frame coaching prior to the start of the coaching relationship. While the motivation of external professional coaches won't often be questioned, the willingness of internal managers to be in a different type of relationship – a more equal, collaborative relationship – must be made clear and is a key success factor. The word **collaborative** comes from a combination of two words – "co", which means "together or with", and "labor–laboris", which has its origins in the word "labouring", which means working So ultimately coaching is "working together". The ethos of coaching is that of a partnership.
- Coaching is about helping individuals **understand their own thinking and emotions**, and how their worldview, mind-sets, perspectives and behaviour have an **impact** on the working environment, relationships and ultimately, performance. **Enhanced performance** is sustainable only if the underlying drivers of performance are addressed at more than a superficial level.
- Coaching also needs to take place **over a period of time** in order to cement the learning (Stout-Rostron, 2009:14).
- Business coaching enables coachees to **understand their role** in achieving business success, and to enhance that role in ways that are measurable and sustainable. The **dual focus** of business objectives of both the coachee and the organisation is what distinguishes business coaching from other types of coaching. The business coach helps the coachee to discover how changing or accommodating personal characteristics and perspectives can affect both personal and business processes.

Table 7.1: Characteristics of the coaching relationship

Key characteristics of the coaching relationship
• Trust
• Safety
• Challenge
• Support
• Accountability
• Willingness
• Space to reflect
• Action orientated
• Egalitarian relationship

"Coaching is an on-going relationship which focuses on clients taking action toward the realization of their visions, goals and desires. Coaching uses a process of inquiry and personal discovery to build the client's level of awareness and responsibility and provides the client with structure, support and feedback. The coaching process helps clients both define and achieve professional and personal goals faster and with more ease than would be possible otherwise." – International Coach Federation

7.3 WHY COACHING?

All learning involves thinking and change. As Peter Senge says:

"Learning changes what we do – it is always active – you haven't learnt to walk until you walk." – Peter Senge

Learning involves thinking, doing and reflection. Coaching supports learning in each of the elements as outlined in more detail below.

Thinking – coaching creates the space where you can stop and think about what you are doing, how you are behaving and why you are making the choices you are making. It is a space that moves away from a pure operational focus to the focus of understanding why we do what we do – thinking about our thinking.

Doing – it is recommended that coaching be spaced over several weeks, which allows the coachee to experiment, try the new behaviour in action, and then reflect on what has worked or not worked. The spacing of sessions encourages the doing and the action.

Reflection – it is only through reflection that insight can occur. The quieter space of coaching and the nature of reflective questions allow someone to move to insights and deeper understanding, which are a critical component of learning.

Insights are a specific type of thought. Kiefer and Constable (2013) in their book *The Art of Insight – How to Have More Aha! Moments* define insights as fresh thoughts that deepen understanding. Insights are not just intellectual understanding. They include intellectual understanding, but go further. A new cognitive structure is formed that is greater than the sum of its parts, and it usually calls for a different action. So a person may have been considering going down path A, but after an insight, he/she may realise path B is a better choice, and understands why.

Insights result in changed perceptions. Michael Cavanagh, a lead coaching researcher in Australia, developed a model on coaching (2013) and coined the phrase Perspective Taking Capacity (PTC). He defines PTC as the capacity to understand, critically consider and integrate multiple competing thoughts into a bigger perspective that enables more effective action. A more complex perspective enables us to:

- See more of the system and how it is connected.
- See the challenges differently.
- See more options for change.

Reflection and sharing reflections in a coaching conversation appears to enhance this perspective-taking ability. The spaced practice of coaching also allows time for in-between reflection which can occur while exercising, sleeping, walking and relaxing. Often providing a coaching question to consider between sessions or even an assignment can broaden the learning experience.

> **CASE STUDY**
>
> One coach gives his coachees a disposable camera and asks them to take photos of things beautiful and true between sessions. One client reminisced, saying: "I took photos of my children, the garden and books because I love knowledge. And then I took photos of food and friends. And then I was stuck. I thought: is that it? Family, friends, learning and nature … did anything else matter?"
>
> This indicates both reflection and insight and will be different for different people.

From a neuroscience perspective, brain studies have shown that when we are reflecting we are not thinking logically or analysing data, but rather using a part of our brain which makes links across the whole brain. We are thinking in an unusual way, allowing our unconscious brain to work, and not just relying on our working memory.

Much of this process is facilitated through the coach asking questions and giving observations and feedback. A coach may observe as follows: *"I have noticed that you keep saying I should have .., I ought to have … it was my fault … (and so on). It seems to me as if you shoulder a lot of responsibility with the use of your words such as I should, I ought to, and so on. Would you say you take on a great deal of responsibility?"*

This may be followed up with: *"Do others give you this responsibility, or do you jump in and take it on willingly?"*

Feedback is a mechanism for an individual to see his/her blind-spots by holding up a reflective mirror. Many coachees say that their coach helped them to look at the world through different eyes or see things through a different lens, or challenged their assumptions.

Brain Break: Take off your shoes and walk on the grass/ground/ barefoot to stimulate the nerve endings in your feet.

7.4 HOW DO WE GO ABOUT COACHING?

"Coaching is face-to face leadership that pulls people with diverse backgrounds, talents, experiences and interests; encourages them to step up to responsibility and continued achievement; and treats them as full-scale partners and contributors." – Nancy Austin and Tom Peters, A Passion for Excellence – the Leadership Difference (1985)

7.4.1 Coaching roles

Coaching can occur in an **informal** way as part of a coaching style of leadership or be **formalised** into a coaching relationship with specific goals, sessions and timelines. Informally, a leader may use questions to encourage critical thinking, reflection, awareness and insight when working with an employee or team. With good coaching skills, a leader can naturally and effortlessly enhance the learning process in any interaction where there are challenges or opportunities for improvement or out-of-the-box thinking. Coaching can happen "in the moment" with a quick few questions or observations, or it can happen in a scheduled one-on-one discussion to review performance or development needs.

Coaching can also be formalised to the point where a coach and coachee are matched, a contracting session occurs to assess the needs and agree the process and the goals, and then a number of sessions are scheduled to work through the various coaching goals. There will most likely be some sort of progress reporting and feedback, especially if a large amount of money is being invested in external coaches or in the training of internal coaches.

Coaching can be done by **internal** coaches who have been trained or **external** coaches who are contracted to the company and provide the service. Line managers can also play an informal coaching role as described above. There are upsides and downsides to each of these approaches, which are most often combined and used for different target groups.

Table 7.2: Types of coaches

External coaching	Internal coaching (full or part-time)	Line managers as coaches
Upside: Specialised skills, experience and accreditation Objective view and not affected by politics Confidentiality allowing open sharing of issues	Upside: Understand the context and ethos of the company Cost effective because once trained, can be used for many years Builds relationships outside the direct reporting lines Can help identify issues in the company–manager–employee relationship and enhance problem solving, engagement and retention	Upside: Understand the context and ethos of the company Most managers have a desire for their staff to learn and grow Direct access to observable behaviours and performance One-on-one conversations for performance and development are part of their role anyway
Downside: Expensive as a result of expertise and demand Less flexible in scheduling (cancellation fees) Limited resource for specific high-value talent	Downside: Allocation and matching of coaches is a challenge, as is balancing demand and supply Part-time coaches may not have the time to dedicate to coaching	Downside: May not have the right mind-set toward coaching Require more skill development, which can cost time and money Line relationship may have an impact on the honesty of the coaching conversation (fear of judgement) Managers often feel pressurised to achieve targets rather than invest time in coaching

Overall, coaching is a cost-effective, continuous learning process. HR and learning and development specialists also encounter many situations where coaching conversations occur spontaneously. Coaching skills are very useful in spontaneous situations as well in the classroom. Aside from the possible coaching roles mentioned above, there are many other opportunities to accelerate your learning by listening, sharing, questioning, and reflecting with your colleagues, your family members, a mentor, or anyone else in your network. Don't be shy to suggest a coaching or mentoring relationship and indicate your willingness to learn from them or mutually. Some different coaching relationships are depicted visually below.

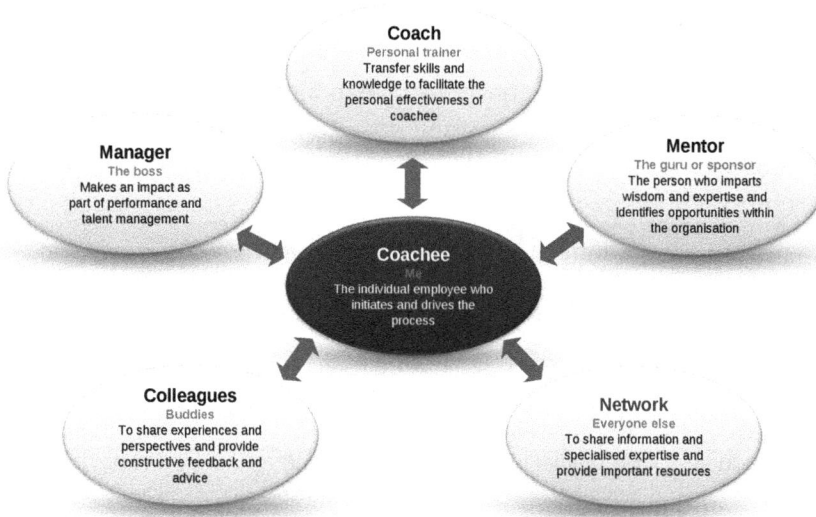

Figure 7.2: Coaching roles

The foundation for both formal and informal coaching is a set of skills that with practice can become part of the repertoire of relating to others and helping them to grow. The ultimate aim is to move the relationship to a self-directed one to ensure the highest level of ownership of the learning and therefore performance.

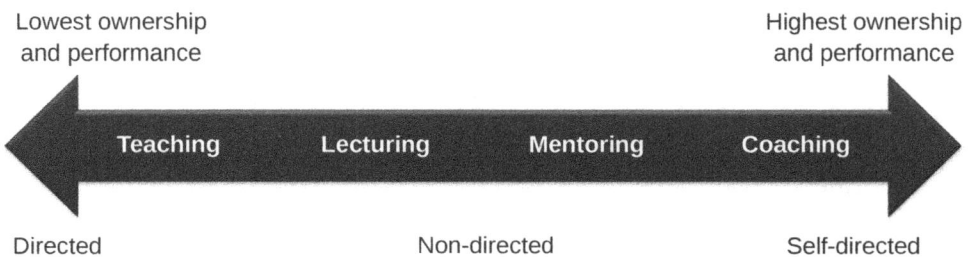

Figure 7.3: A coaching continuum

This section will describe some of these key skills that any leader, coach or facilitator can use, and then describe the nature of more formal coaching relationships that require a process of initiating, contracting, managing and eventually dissolving.

7.4.2 Coaching skills

Some of the key skills that any coach needs can be summarised as follows:

Table 7.3: Coaching skills

Brain and behaviour change skills	Emotional intelligence	Conversation skills	Business results orientation
Personal profiling – personality, learning styles, motivation, and so on Situational diagnostics Understanding the change cycle and personal transformation Neuroscience of coaching	Self-awareness Self-management Self-motivation Empathy Social skills Optimism	Building rapport Listening Reflecting Interpreting Summarising Questioning Giving feedback Story-telling	Goal setting, planning and prioritising Problem solving Decision making Conflict management Crucial conversations Impact and influence Drive, energy, passion

Building a safe, confidential and trusting relationship

These skills will help the coach to create a safe, confidential, and trusting relationship. In the section on Neuroscience we learnt about the impact anxiety has on learning, reducing our ability to think creatively or laterally. Coaching should be a space where a person feels safe to experiment, ask foolish questions, and think outside the box, and where the parasympathetic nervous system is activated. This involves creating a focus on hope, possibilities, dreams, purpose and goals, rather than limitations and constraints. If a coach does need to challenge or confront derailing behaviours, this must be done in a compassionate and non-judgemental way. An appreciative inquiry approach can be used to ask a challenging question such as: *"If there were no inner voice saying no, what would be possible?"*

Building rapport, empathy and support are key aspects of creating this trusting learning space, as well as the ability to engage in active dialogue using conversation skills such as deep listening, questioning, reflecting, interpreting (reframing) or summarising. Not everyone can be a coach. If people have exceptionally judgemental control agendas, they cannot coach effectively.

Rapport	The degree of sameness, I feel at a subconscious level- body language, dress, voice, beliefs, values, interests. hobbies. Amount of warmth, comfort, related, connected, relaxed.
Body language	Body language (55%), voice/tone (38%), words (7%) Awareness, eye contact, affirmation (nodding), open, relaxed. Mirror, match, lead.
Listening	Cosmetic, conversations, active, deep listening- listen with all senses to the whole person (step into their world).
Reflecting	Reflecting is one way of expressing to the person that we are in his internal frame of reference and that we recognize his deep concerns. Reflect feelings, experience, content. E.g. "It sounds like you are really worried/frustrated/ anxious/angry about....
Summarising and interpreting	Tying together several ideas and feelings at the end of a discussion/session to summarise discussion and move on Helping the person see their problems in new ways or from a different perspective.
Questioning	Open Q's: what, how, when, where (avoid why?). Closed Q's: to move ahead, gain confirmation, decisions or ending sessions.
Giving feedback	Creating awareness of performance or behavioural impact through questioning, sharing perceptions and giving specific feedback from others. Assertive. Empathetic. Sandwich technique. Encouraging.

Figure 7.4: Conversation skills summary

Out of all of these, questioning is the most difficult and most important to master and is the key component for moving away from giving advice or telling. Expand your questioning approach with some additional approaches, tips and traps of questioning below.

Activity 1

Look through the list of skills above. Do a self-assessment and identify three skills that you are really good at and three that require additional focus and learning.

Good at:

Can work on:

Figure 7.4 contains a brief summary of the fundamental conversation skills for creating a conducive coaching space.

Remember to opt in, on-board and join the journey for many additional resources, links and downloads. See *www.accelerated.co.za* or OnBoarding for more info on how to do this.

When thinking of questions to use in the coaching context, it is better to use more open questions, such as What, Why, Where, Who, When, Which, (How), rather than closed questions, in order to encourage sharing more personal feelings and thoughts. "What" is probably the most powerful question, since it is the most open of all and leads to the greatest disclosure of new information by the other person? For example:

- "What is it about…?"
- "What is your reason for…?"
- "What makes you think…?"

When you wish to deepen a relationship it is recommended that "Why" questions are avoided as they imply criticism and threats. Closed questions are useful for confirming information such as: "Have I got that right?"; moving the conversation along: "Can we continue?"; or closing a conversation down: "Have we finished?"

Activity 2

Suppose that John says he is very stressed at work and would like to be less stressed. He comes to you for coaching. Write down the coaching-type questions you might ask him.

Share via e-mail or Facebook to level up. See OnBoarding for more info on how to do this.

David Rock discusses in his book *Quiet Leadership* (2006), the type of questions that we ideally need to ask and the traps we fall into often when trying to ask good questions.

Questioning traps

Giving advice but phrased as a suggestion – In the example above, you may ask: *"Have you thought of taking up yoga or doing exercise to help you?"*

When you give advice, even if in the form of a question, you are drawing very much from your own life experience and what has or has not worked for you. You are assuming that the person has similar needs or preferences to you, which is often not the case. In the event that the suggestion is helpful, you are still doing the thinking for the person and taking responsibility for their choices. This can result in lack of accountability and blame down the road if it doesn't work out, and it creates a sense of dependency.

Asking questions about the problem or the detail about the problem – in the above example, you may ask: *"Tell me more about what causes you to be so stressed?"*; or *"Does this happen every day?"*

When you focus on the problem, you are activating the sympathetic nervous system, which heightens anxiety. You are giving attention to the factors that could inhibit an insight or focus on a solution.

Using questions to rush to solutions – in the above example, you could ask: *"What are you going to do about this situation of being so stressed?"*

Rushing into action does not allow thinking, the acknowledgement of feeling, or learning to take place.

Asking broad questions – a question such as: *"What are some of the big problems?"* may lead to interesting dialogue and possibly a good venting session, but will not be exceptionally useful to enhance thinking and learning.

Questioning tips

We really want coachees to recognise the quality of their thinking and to identify patterns that occur in their thinking. This increases self-awareness and helps people to learn. They can then manage future dilemmas in a similar way.

None of the following questions focuses on detail or problems; nor do they tell people what to think, but rather encourage a deeper thinking (Rock, 2006).

Table 7.4: Thinking questions

Examples of thinking questions	
• How long have you been thinking about this? • How often do you think about this? • How important is this issue to you on a scale of 1 to 10? • How clear are you about this issue? • What priority is this issue in your work or life right now? Top 5, top 3 or top 1? • What priority do you think it should be? • How committed are you to resolving this? • How motivated are you to resolve this? • Can you see any gaps in your thinking? • What impact is thinking about this issue having on you? • How do you react when you think that thought?	• How do you feel about the resources you have put into this so far? • Do you have a plan for shifting this issue? • How clear is your thinking about this plan? • What are you noticing about your thinking? • What insights are you having? • How could you deepen these insights? • Would it be worth turning these insights into a habit? • Do you know what to do to turn insights into a habit? • Are you clear about what to do next? • How can I best help you further?

7.4.3 Coaching process

In more formalised coaching relationships, coaching moves through a number of phases, each of which is an important step. These steps are visually depicted and described in Figure 7.5.

Initiating

If your company assists you with initiating a coaching relationship, then initiating is not a big challenge. Here it will be important to ensure that the person selected as a coach is respected by you and perceived as having real value to add. Initiating often includes a matching session, where you may have more than one coach to choose from. Where coaching is more informal, it may take courage and initiative to ask someone you admire to be your coach. You may fear rejection or being perceived as impertinent. In most cases, good leaders will handle these requests with grace and either accept your request or give good reasons why not. For example, they may already be coaching six others, and may suggest an alternative.

You can also offer yourself as a coach to a young talented person to whom you relate well, or to a colleague who is struggling with a particular skill that you have mastered, such as managing upwards, or even using Excel. This also takes courage, and you may fear being seen as arrogant or presumptuous. These fears are mostly unfounded, unless the person you approach has very low EQ and openness to learning.

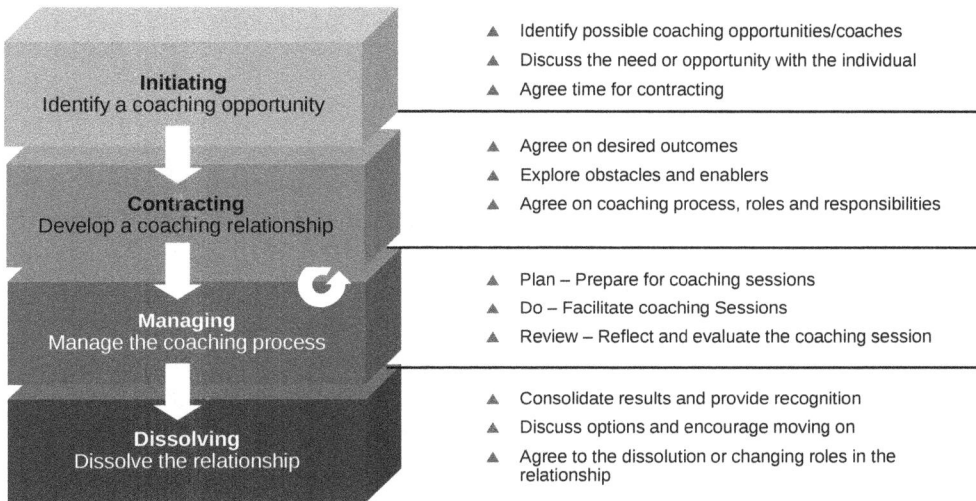

Initiating
Identify a coaching opportunity

- ▲ Identify possible coaching opportunities/coaches
- ▲ Discuss the need or opportunity with the individual
- ▲ Agree time for contracting

Contracting
Develop a coaching relationship

- ▲ Agree on desired outcomes
- ▲ Explore obstacles and enablers
- ▲ Agree on coaching process, roles and responsibilities

Managing
Manage the coaching process

- ▲ Plan – Prepare for coaching sessions
- ▲ Do – Facilitate coaching Sessions
- ▲ Review – Reflect and evaluate the coaching session

Dissolving
Dissolve the relationship

- ▲ Consolidate results and provide recognition
- ▲ Discuss options and encourage moving on
- ▲ Agree to the dissolution or changing roles in the relationship

Figure 7.5: The coaching process

Contracting

Business coaching is not just a conversation between friends and has a specific purpose and objective leading to behavioural and performance improvement. To avoid misunderstandings or unmet expectations, it is important to contract the nature of the coaching relationship upfront. Each relationship is unique. This contract may be written or not but it needs to be clear to both the coach and the person being coached. The contract would address the practical applications, which are the following:

- **Frequency and duration of coaching sessions** – one hour, once a month
- **Length of engagement of coaching** – number of sessions or months
- **Dissolving process** – how to end it
- **Modality** – face to face, phone or Skype
- **Location**– ensuring privacy and lack of interruptions.

Equally important is to contract on the psychological expectation of the process. This includes having the discussion of what coaching is and what it is not, and expectations of the coaching relationship, such as: *"I as coach will not be taking responsibility for solving your challenges. We will be equal thinking partners. It is similar to being a mid-wife. I will be there to help birth the baby, but it's your baby."*

Lastly, it is important to contract with regard to measures of success and outcomes, and to agree to this up front before you begin coaching. A useful question to ask is: *"How will we know that the coaching has been successful, and what in your behaviour, relationships or thinking will be different?"*

Managing the coaching process

The coaching requires a certain amount of managing and nurturing. It also requires preparation. It is best if you can spend some quiet time prior to the session releasing any of your own personal challenges and stresses and becoming present, so that you are in the right mind-space for the coaching session. This is not always possible with spontaneous coaching moments, but can be achieved with scheduled sessions. Preparation also requires you to refer to your coaching notes and contract, especially if there has been some time between sessions. You also need to refresh your memory on the specifics of the coachee's context, current issues and coaching goals. When preparing for and facilitating a coaching conversation, it is quite useful to keep some basic principles in mind and follow a rational process that will help you reach clear outcomes.

You can choose from a number of different coaching processes for different types of coaching. There are frameworks for "in-the-moment" coaching, regular coaching and transformational life coaching.

An example of a one-page A3 contracting template is shown in Figure 7.6:

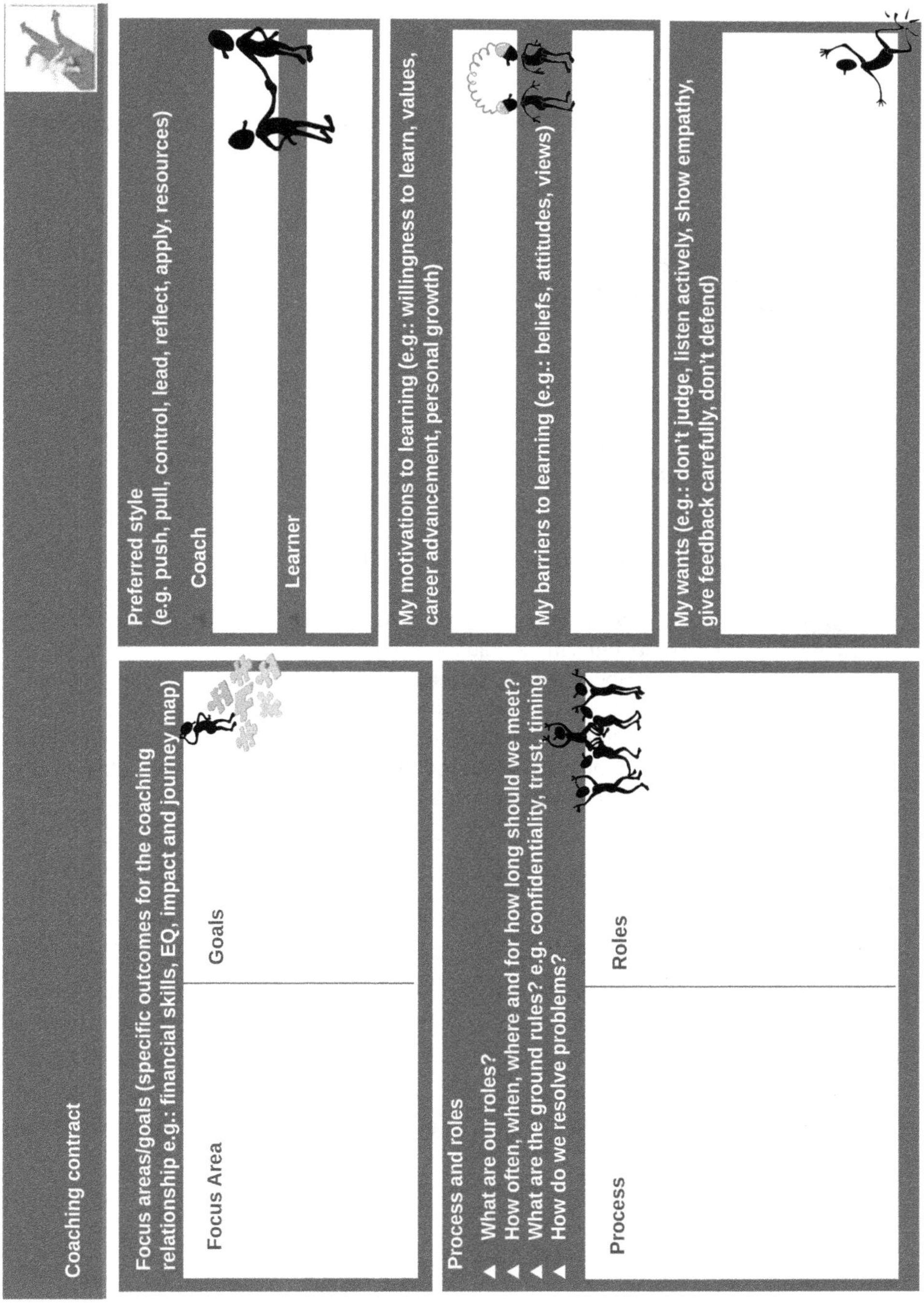

Coaching contract

Preferred style
(e.g. push, pull, control, lead, reflect, apply, resources)

Coach

Learner

My motivations to learning (e.g.: willingness to learn, values, career advancement, personal growth)

My barriers to learning (e.g.: beliefs, attitudes, views)

My wants (e.g.: don't judge, listen actively, show empathy, give feedback carefully, don't defend)

Focus areas/goals (specific outcomes for the coaching relationship e.g.: financial skills, EQ, impact and journey map)

Focus Area	Goals

Process and roles

◄ What are our roles?
◄ How often, when, where and for how long should we meet?
◄ What are the ground rules? e.g. confidentiality, trust, timing
◄ How do we resolve problems?

Process	Roles

Figure 7.6: A sample contracting template

In the moment coaching

A simple framework adapted from *Tao of Coaching* by Landsberg (2003) for in-the-moment coaching is to reflect on the following three aspects of a problem:

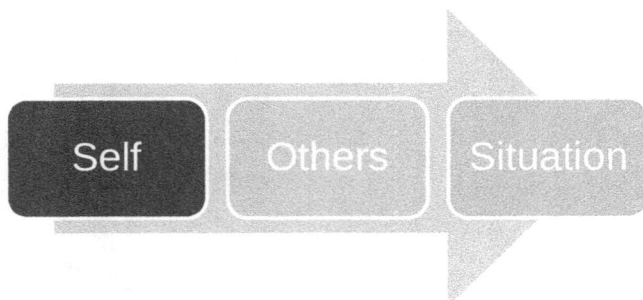

Figure 7.7: Aspects (adapted from Landsberg, 2003)

Questions for a coach to ask can include:

- **Self:** How are you contributing to the problem? What barriers in you could be inhibiting a solution? What can you change?
- **Others:** How are others contributing to the problem? Who could help with perspective toward a solution? How can you involve them?
- **Situation:** What are the other systemic factors in the situation that are contributing to the problem? What have you not considered that may help in finding a solution? How can you view this from a fresh perspective?

Scheduled coaching

There are many different models and approaches to coaching. Most of them have acronyms such as GROW – **G**oal, **R**eality, **O**ptions, and **W**rap up. We have chosen in this chapter to focus on a framework using the COACH pneumonic, adapted from Julie Starr's *Coaching Manual* (2003) and developed further by Catalyst Consulting (www.catalystconsulting.co.za). This framework is shown below and contains process suggestions as well as specific statements and questions to help you along.

Climate and context	Outcome	Actual situation	Consider options	Hand-over
• Greet the coachee warmly • Establish rapport with topics of interest – observe, match and mirror • Deal with logistics e.g. timing, refreshments, potential interruptions, etc. • Acknowledge and appreciate	• Clarify what the coachee wishes to achieve • Explore and clarify SMART goals – short and longer term where necessary • Encourage coachee to 'own' the direction and content of the conversation through questions • Build a positive expectation of success	• Explore the current reality i.e.. Issues impacting coachee • Ask questions to clarify • Invite self reflection to develop insight into the coachee's own role and impact • Add possible perspectives • Provide feedback where you have sufficient information to help coachee face reality	• Cover wide range of options – keep digging • Acknowledge coachees own insights or options • Encourage out the box thinking • Guide them towards empathy – other person's shoes • Offer suggestions carefully • Explore consequences • Reflect, summaries and interpret if required • Ensure choices are made and agree specific actions	• Summarise session discussion, progress and outcomes • Ask coachee what the next steps are • Clarify SMART goals • Identify possible barriers • Identify support required • Build confidence and encourage possibility thinking
Useful phrases: • Thanks for making the time • I am looking forward to hearing how it has been going	**Useful phrases:** • What would you like to achieve/discuss? • How will this help you? • It will great when you are doing this naturally	**Useful phrases:** • Tell me more about. • What is your take on the situation? • What is happening at the moment? • What effect does this have? • How might … see the situation?	**Useful questions:** • What could you do to change the situation? • What alternatives are there? • What are the benefits/risks of this option? • What ideas have you tried in the past? • How might people respond if you chose this? • Would you like me to make a suggestion?	**Useful questions:** • What are your next steps? • What resources and support do you need? Who do you need to enroll? • By when do you want to achieve this?

Figure 7.8: Catalyst Consulting Coaching framework (adapted from Starr, 2003)

The process is not static; nor is it necessarily sequential. The coach will often need to backtrack to explore situations in more detail or consider additional options before ensuring that the coachee takes full responsibility for the actions agreed.

Activity 3

Use this coaching template to prepare for and have a coaching conversation with an existing coachee or someone whom you approach to agree to be your coachee for this practice session.

You can find a downloadable template on *www.accelerated.co.za*. Remember to opt in, on-board and join the journey for many additional resources, links and downloads.

Share via e.mail or Facebook to level up. See OnBoarding for more info on how to do this.

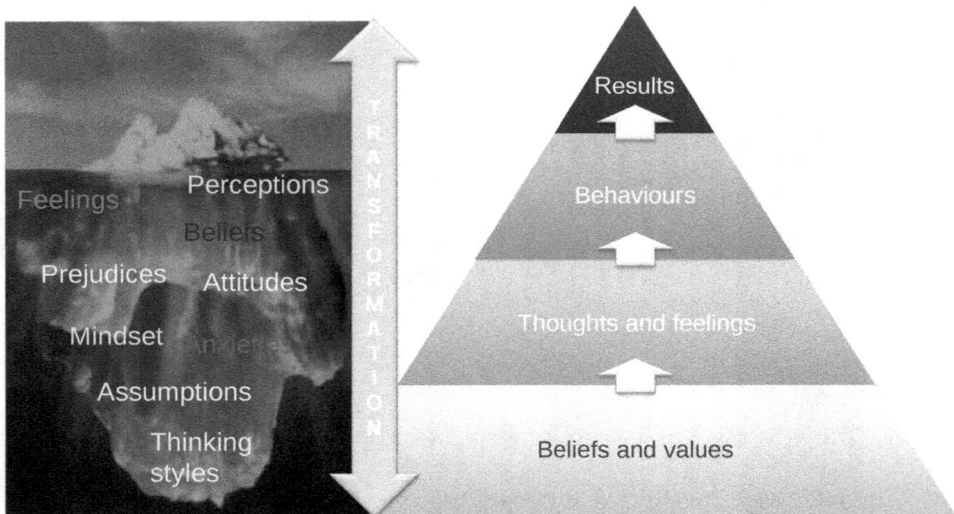

Figure 7.9: Iceberg of factors having an impact on behaviour

Transformational coaching

Coaching is a learning space that provides an opportunity to reflect and gain insights which lead to changing behaviour, growth and performance. We need to recognise that if we are focusing only on visible behaviour, we are in reality dealing with the tip of the iceberg and not addressing the real underlying issues. The diagram below shows how we as coaches need to draw on the beliefs, assumptions, paradigms, prejudices, feelings, thoughts, behaviours and experiences of people in order to lead to personal transformation and sustainable learning.

> **HOT TIP** **Questions for a coach to ask that help to unpack the issues below the water level can include:**
>
> - What result would you like to change?
> - What is the specific behaviour that is leading to those results?
> - What feelings may be leading to those behaviours?
> - What thoughts may be leading to those feelings?
> - What beliefs or assumptions may be leading to those thoughts and feelings?
>
> **Once underlying beliefs or factors are identified, questions can include:**
>
> - What beliefs or assumptions could be more useful to achieve the results you want?
> - What thoughts, feelings and behaviours would this result in?
> - How would this impact on your results in future?

This transformational approach can be very powerful in helping people to see how their own inner sub-conscious programmes have an impact on their own thinking, behaviours and results.

> *"People's behaviour and results are a sum total of all – beliefs, assumptions, values, thoughts, feelings and attitudes."*

Throughout the coaching relationship, keep these coaching principles in mind.

Coaching principles

- Don't position yourself as an expert.
- Allow the person to take full ownership.
- Be still; allow things to happen.
- Recognise the individual's ability to learn.
- Provide the space for practice and risk taking.
- Allow ambiguity to provoke thinking, questioning, and self-discovery.
- At critical moments, provide a strong intervention which enables self-insight.
- Share experiences in order to create "shared experience".
- You can't coach if you don't have the other person's interests at heart.
- Maintain your commitment to supporting the individual.
- Coaching relationships are built upon truth, openness and trust.
- Coachees are responsible for the results they are creating.
- Coachees are capable of much better results than they are currently generating.

- Maintain focus on what the coachee thinks and experiences.
- Accept that coachees can generate perfect solutions.
- Coaching conversations are based on equality.
- Always remove your own ego and agenda

At the end of each coaching moment or session, it is good practice to review the effectiveness of the session, think through the conversation at a different level of awareness, and notice what has been said (or not said): body language signals, how effective and balanced your questioning or suggesting was; and the need to have an attitude of continuous improvement.

> Watch this video on YouTube: **How Coaching Works**
> http://www.youtube.com/watch?v=FXj4wSsRUgo

Dissolving coaching relationships

Coaching relationships can be dissolved for two reasons. The first is that the agreed number of sessions has come to an end. It is important in this case to review the goals and outcomes of the coaching and for both the coach and the coachee to feel good about the results and about moving on. The second reason for dissolving the relationship is when it is not working out because of time constraints; a change in circumstances; or when there is a mismatch of expectations. This is more difficult to address. It is best to have this conversation face to face or telephonically if face to face is not practical. As a last resort it can be done through a carefully worded e-mail that maintains the dignity of all parties. Avoid leaving relationships hanging in no-man's land, as this leaves a very uncomfortable space to negotiate at a later stage.

7.5 CONCLUSION

In conclusion, we would like to encourage you to look at the powerful impact of coaching conversations on enhancement and acceleration of learning.

> Watch this video on YouTube: **Building Coaching Cultures in Organisations**
> http://www.youtube.com/watch?v=ybxh1X-LiOU

CHAPTER 8

LEARNING THROUGH AUTHENTIC CONVERSATIONS

By John Gatherer and Debbie Craig

"Authenticity is a collection of choices that we have to make every day. It's about the choice to show up and be real. The choice to be honest. The choice to let our true selves be seen." – Brené Brown,
The Gifts of Imperfection

8.1 INTRODUCTION

Why is it that we struggle to speak our minds and challenge other people on issues that we feel strongly about? Why is it that we avoid expressing a viewpoint that we sense will trigger an argument or emotional reaction – even though we know that we are in the right? If and when we do end up in a verbal slanging match, why do the heated exchanges typically drain our energy and rarely result in resolving the issue of dispute? These situations all relate to the practice popularly known as holding difficult or crucial conversations – but what we prefer to call authentic conversations. This chapter outlines an approach to help individuals confront their difficult relationship realities and fast track their skills, expertise and confidence in holding successful authentic conversations.

8.2 THE CONTEXT OF THE PROBLEM

In our work with Leadership Development and Talent Management, spanning different countries and business sectors across the world, it is not surprising that one of the most common, universal needs expressed to us is how to hold difficult or authentic conversations! We can all relate to the subject. You know that you need to talk to someone about an important issue, but you keep delaying it and even sugar-coating it! Often you resort to your best brand of humour, cynical gibes or caustic sarcasm, but the person seems to have an inability of getting the message, especially as a result of your veiled feedback and walking on eggs! On a few occasions when you were pushed to the limits of exasperation you tackled the offender – resulting in defensive behaviour, highly charged outbursts and an aftermath of a "no-speak" atmosphere!

What makes our discomfort and inadequacy worse about not expressing our honest feelings, speaking up and confronting reality is the intense feelings of guilt that it creates. How often have we replayed incidents and exchanges in our mind, sometimes in the middle of the night, and considered the consequences and alternatives of standing our ground, presenting our view and having the courage of our convictions – in the moment of truth!

People do not like any situation that heightens interpersonal sensitivities and leads to disagreement and conflict. Yet every organisation is characterised by a pressurised, changing work environment, in which bottom-line results are a function of the company's goals and targets, customer needs, supplier deadlines, performance standards, people diversity and relationships. That's quite a crucible of highly charged factors already and that is before you add the other ingredients of personality type, thinking style, cultural differences, generation gaps, power and politics!

When things don't go as well as expected, how do we, as leaders and team members, address these important issues and use them as a learning experience? Authentic conversations need to occur when the stakes are high and strong emotions are involved – a time when values, views or expectations are sure to differ. People's natural reaction to many of these unresolved issues is to ignore them, avoid them or handle the conflicting viewpoint during a flashpoint of emotion. In today's world of high-performance organisations, it is imperative to confront the "other party" in the relationship by addressing and working through those difficult issues.

8.3 THE IMPERATIVE FOR HOLDING AUTHENTIC CONVERSATIONS

Many times we are faced with difficult situations and dilemmas that are not clear cut, do not have an obvious solution, and are surrounded by a plethora of complexity, perceptions and potentially diverse world views.

All four situations are screaming at you for attention – silence and avoidance is certainly not the option! You need to hold an authentic conversation, confront the reality and get involved. The response required is engagement – face-to-face, eyeball to eyeball dialogue and there is no escaping it. In recent times, leadership engagement has been referred to as one of the most essential practices of **the authentic leader** – holding continuous discussions and reciprocal exchanges with direct reports, colleagues, customers and suppliers. It is essential that the leader not only masters the skill and process of addressing conflict and difference, but creates a culture where all team members feel safe and comfortable in speaking out or challenging points of view. This is a critical skill and practice in creating a learning culture.

Activity 1

Review the following situations. Write down how would you handle these scenarios?

A senior manager has been sliding backwards in his performance, never quite enough to be serious, but personal effort and attitude are inappropriate and his half-hearted work is not going unnoticed. You know he has a "short fuse" but needs some direct, candid feedback regarding his contributions. You also know that the conversation will be potentially explosive.

Your action plan:

A colleague of yours who you've invited to your project team because of his special expertise is a "serial late-comer". On most occasions that you hold project review meetings, he dashes in late, with a smile and an inane apology, and does not seem aware of his disruptive behaviour, let alone the loss of respect from the junior members of the team. You've approached him once before about the need for punctuality but he dismissed it out of hand, citing his" pressurised schedule".

Your action plan:

A customer has repeatedly expressed disappointment with your sales executive as she feels she is not receiving the service that she deserves. You know that you should solicit her views and resolve her concerns, but your salesman assures you that he is working on the relationship and you do not want to compromise the contract.

Your action plan:

Your eighteen year old son has a new friend that you and the rest of your family do not like as he comes from a broken home and appears to have a manipulative influence over your son, whose behaviour has been disappointing and out of character over the last few months. You know that your son has a strong allegiance to his friend but you are concerned about the peer influence.

Your action plan:

Share via e-mail or Facebook to level up. See OnBoarding for more info on how to do this.

There is also often the need to hold authentic **conversations with your boss** or other senior leadership impacting on your work responsibilities as a result of their leadership style, lack of strategic management or misaligned values. These are always more sensitive and require both courage and a professional and accomplished approach in addressing these delicate matters.

One of the interesting features that we utilise in facilitating **high performance team** workshops is during the latter stages in the session when we introduce the "dead cat" "metaphor and encourage the participants to surface the real issues from under the table and deal with them candidly "at the table". It is natural for a group of team members to tread warily around surfacing the critical issues for fear of clashing with sensitive feelings or damaging established personal relationships. The licence given to the team to list and work systematically through known irritants, constraints, derailing behaviours and dysfunctional dynamics acts as a stimulant to bring out "home truths" and commence a process of resolving real issues affecting high performance within the team.

One needs a similar candour, **boldness and accountability** to holding difficult and authentic conversations. It helps to understand how to prepare in advance for these conversations, develop the emotional awareness and conversation skills required, and then practice with a coach or learning partner using a **conversation guide and toolkit**. This is what we use in Leadership Programmes and we hope to share just a few highlights of these with you to help you on your learning and leadership journey.

8.4 TOWARDS A CULTURE OF HEALTHY CONFLICT

The rationale for holding authentic conversations has evolved from the myriad of modern business imperatives.

8.4.1 Strategic change management

We have always advocated that change is about difference and difference comes from different thinking. It is natural that with the exponential growth of change in our work environment as well as the variety of strategic change initiatives that are launched, the result is a multiplicity of different projects, ideas, expectations and timeframes that has the potential to heighten tensions and, pressure and increase conflict across management teams and structures.

8.4.2 Talent reviews or forums

The outcomes of organisation-wide talent reviews or forums necessitate comprehensive discussions regarding career management and succession planning proposals but also require candid feedback concerning each individual's strengths, development needs and weaknesses relating to performance and potential. Most talented individual's display good performance results and contributions to their teams that are commendable and need acknowledgement and reinforcement. But it is our experience that nearly everyone who befits the description of top talent also needs to be made aware of some aspects of their work – habits, thinking and behaviour that detract from high quality performance. It is through these authentic conversations that insights and action steps can be forged and initiated with win-win outcomes.

8.4.3 High-performance teams and collaboration

In today's world of work, we tend to work in multiple teams – strategic teams, functional teams, cross-functional teams, global workgroups, project teams, special assignments and so on …the list is endless! Teams and collaboration have emerged as the most important group phenomena in the organisation and have become the primary means for achieving the organisational goals. High performance teams demonstrate the following characteristics – clear purpose, informality, participation, listening, civilised disagreement, consensus in decision making, clear roles and assignment, shared leadership, open communication and self-assessment. Unfortunately these characteristics are not always displayed in team dynamics within a team. The need for authentic conversations with "offending" team members, collaboration partners or even the team as a collective will be one of the critical strategies to shape and achieve effective teamwork.

8.4.4 Personal mastery and self-empowerment

We have facilitated countless workshops in support of our best-selling publication, *I am Talent* which focuses on building awareness and perspective regarding the world of self – personality profiles, thinking and learning styles, emotional intelligence, coping and self-empowerment skills and how to differentiate yourself within a highly competitive world. It is fascinating to find how many people have responded so positively to learning and discovering more about themselves and how they can sharpen their "softer" skills and hone their personal effectiveness and impact. However, the field of personal mastery is also an extremely personal and private domain so any advice or suggestions regarding an individual's self-improvement will typically be met with defensive behaviour and rationalisations around the status quo. Apart from Executive coaches and managers who work professionally in this field, any other individual would need to apply the skills and process steps of holding effective authentic conversations in these kinds of interactions with diplomacy and empathy.

> *"How would your life be different if...you approached all relationships with authenticity and honesty? Let today be the day...you dedicate yourself to building relationships on the solid foundation of truth and authenticity." – Steve Maraboli, Life, the Truth, and Being Free*

8.5 THE LEARNING IMAGERY OF HOLDING AUTHENTIC CONVERSATIONS

We have found that authentic conversations are needed in three general zones of problems.

- **Relationship breakdowns** – often due to a breakdown of trust; often due to assumptions made and misunderstandings; often when relationship expectations are not met; when we feel let down, betrayed or disrespected; sometimes associated with feelings of loss – which provokes anger, fear or hurt
- **Performance or behavioural problems** – usually due to disengagement, lack of awareness or EQ, lack of skill in a new role, disappointment at work, inappropriate attitude, abusive behaviour or loss of respect from team members
- **Leadership style** – often when a leader's behaviour and attitude is in conflict with the organisational values, when the leadership style is autocratic, risk averse, non –communicative, too operational and indecisive

These conflictual issues, behaviours and attitudes require feedback, upward management and confrontation and there are real consequences that can evolve and spiral out of control, if left unattended. Ultimately it is affecting your performance as a leader.

One of the primary tips we teach that underpins the process of holding authentic conversations and helps people become unstuck is for you the leader, as the initiator, to visualise yourself in the conversation with the opposing person but also to stand back and take on a third party (observer) role. This imagery helps you act out a mediator function during the process, helps you filter the past perceptions and emotions associated with this relationship, and prevents you from losing control when you are participating in the actual session. It is always so easy to get into the infamous "I am right, you are wrong" mode, and sometimes you need to practise some lateral thinking or seek some middle ground to resolve a stalemate!

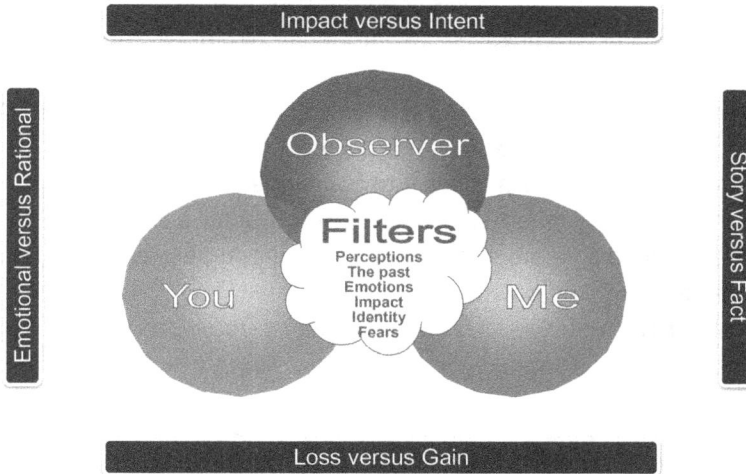

Figure 8.1: Perspectives for holding authentic conversations

There are also four perspectives that one needs to consider during the process of the conversation:

- **Impact versus intent** – distinguish between the motivations (intent) for the discussion against what actually happened. It is also helps to assume the best intention, but also be honest as the impact (on you and others) of the behaviour or action.
- **Story versus fact** – assess the facts of the situation under review against the distortion of perceptions and assumptions and "stories" we tell to create drama and gain attention.
- **Loss versus gain** – review the implications of concession and compromise – the need to lose the battle to win the war. Often a conflict arises when one party feels he/she has "lost" something while the other has gained credibility, time, money, and so on. It is useful to explore perceptions of loss and gain and acknowledge or reframe them to create a more realistic (and less personal) view of the situation.
- **Emotional versus rational** – keep control of your emotions and remain objective in contrast to being caught up in the "heat of the battle" and resorting to personal and subjective "blow-outs". A useful strategy is to let the other party express some of his/her feelings first and to respond with empathy and compassion before resorting to rational problem solving.

8.6 THE LEARNING PROCESS OF INITIATING AND HOLDING AUTHENTIC CONVERSATIONS

There are a number of distinct stages and sequences to master authentic conversations and we offer these steps for leadership to practise working through as shown below.

Purpose and initiation – The need for authentic conversations and tackling deep seated and difficult issues is not a daily occurrence, so the initiation of this event should be handled in a fairly formal manner, which also emphasises its significance to you. You need to consider the purpose and potential outcomes, weigh up the benefits versus the consequences, and decide when and where to have the conversation and how to set up the session.

With reference to the logistical arrangements, you need to invite the person for the conversation at a mutually suitable time, either in a written form or talking directly to him/her, and frame the high-level purpose and your desire to resolve any differences as a win–win outcome. It is also sometimes useful to hold the conversation away from the work environment at a neutral venue, removed from any disruptions and colleague or other staff interest.

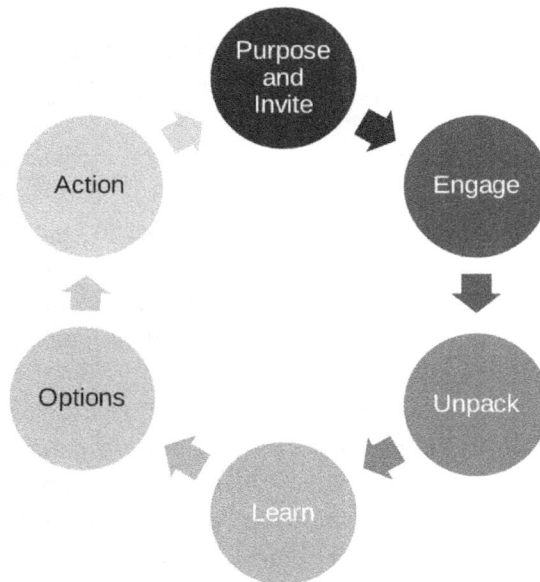

Figure 8.2: The learning process of initiating and holding authentic conversations

Engage – As is the case in any coaching or mentoring experience, the first step in the actual engagement is getting the conversation off to a good start by building rapport – showing interest or offering a view on a common area of work, family, leisure activity, and so on. It is also important to set the right tone, using eye contact and taking on a relaxed and informal conversational style. The opening is important – explaining what happened, how you felt about it, starting with all the facts as you set the scene. Always start with facts, not feelings, to avoid the issue spiralling out of control too early, before each person has been heard. Your feelings are the least factual and often the most controversial element. Remember the imagery of the observer watching over both of you, keep objective, keep your emotions in check, and respect the "taking of turns", and reciprocal exchange of dialogue. The greatest skill to apply at this stage is active listening, without any interruptions – listen in order to understand. Watch the other person intently for any cues and signals from which you can gain further clarification and build on. Show respect and real curiosity during this initial exchange and aim to discover what was going on behind what you experienced. Acknowledge whatever the position or defence is that is being presented by the other party. Remember that you need to be in control of this conversation.

Unpack – During this stage you need to move deeper into talking about feelings and allowing the space for both parties to express their interpretation on what happened, how you both responded, the influence it had on others in the team, and the impact on results. You need to unpack two of the process perspectives: what was lost in the altercation (loss versus gain) and what the original intention was compared to the impact of what actually happened (intent versus impact). The skill of dealing with multiple open-ended questions is paramount at this stage as you seek to build a clearer picture of the issue, incident, attitude or behaviour that precipitated the conflict or difference of opinion. It is extremely important to gauge and assess the other person's response to this unpacking process as it can provide significant information, viewpoints or rationalisation on which to focus. Again use the skills of empathy and acknowledgement to keep the conversational flow, integrity of approach and reciprocal exchange at a positive level. In a situation of poor performance or poor behaviour, where you are the manager, you need to have the courage to state that the performance or behaviour is inappropriate and not acceptable. Similarly, if this is in a personal or peer relationship, it takes assertiveness and courage to say that certain behaviours such as sexual harassment and disrespect are not acceptable.

Learn – Many clashes and conflicts occur as a result of different perceptions, assumptions, beliefs and past baggage that one brings to relationships. This stage requires discipline and flexibility and the ability of leaders to examine their own thinking, feelings and actions critically as a result of exploring the issue, and broadening their awareness and understanding during the process. Leaders need to evaluate their own judgement, reactions, self-image and emotional responses in the relationship. It is in essence the authentic conversation that you need to have with yourself as an after-action review. You need to take the wisdom and learning from the experience into your future. It is empowering to explore how both of you can learn from the experience and thereby improve the relationship going forward. We know that relationship issues are most often not just one-sided and that it takes two to tango.

Options – This is a critical stage at which to identify options and alternatives to resolving the problem or topic. The initiator needs to facilitate this stage skilfully and it is important that both parties enter into the spirit of conflict resolution, exploring the various options in an open manner and discussing the consequences that need to be considered. Some of the areas of investigation include what both parties can live with and a decision as to what you can let go of or sacrifice in order to move on. Obviously there can be a wide array of options across the continuum of consensus – from forgiving, forgetting and re-uniting, to slowly rebuilding trust, to agreeing to disagree and simply parting ways. Importantly, you need to strive for an acceptable outcome, and the philosophy of possibility thinking can facilitate some positive future plans. The use of empathy and reflection skills can add significant value and integrity to the conversation, as one of the parties may have to concede far more than the other in an effort to move on.

Actions – The final stage in the process of mastering authentic conversations is reaching agreement on specific actions to address the issue under review, as well as building trust and restoring the relationship. It is often useful to agree on the need to talk more and share expectations, which helps to heal some of the raw emotions that were central to the conflict. One of the commitments that can be entered into (in a case of misunderstanding or misperception) is to share thoughts and feelings earlier with each other and to extend an open invitation to ask questions in an effort to gain better understanding.

There can be a host of different actions, but one of these has to be the writing up of the rationale, overview, outcomes and commitments from the session, as notes for the record. There should also be an agreement reached on making time for coaching, performance reviews and regular feedback. The last feature of the conversation should be the initiator summarising the actions, accountabilities and timeframe before concluding the session with a positive or encouraging review of the spirit in which the discussion was held.

Brain Break: Do an emotional check – close your eyes, look within, and name what you feel.

8.6.1 "Real plays" – skills practice in holding authentic conversations

One of the ways to build skills and confidence in holding authentic conversations is to provide skills practice in a real-life challenging issue that can be worked through as a case example. Find a learning partner and give him/her a thumbnail sketch summarising what has transpired: the parties involved; their feelings about it; and the characteristics and typical responses of the "offending" person involved. Ask this person to "real play", that is, take on the personality and traits of the person involved by using his/her imagination, and then to practise responding and moving through the conversation steps. The learning partner can do his/her best to antagonise you, but practise staying calm and focusing on the conversation guidelines as outlined above. After the conversation, work through some feedback and tips. This can provide a "hands-on" immediate and dynamic learning experience.

Activity 2

Think about a difficult situation that you are facing at work or at home that needs an authentic conversation. Jot down a few ideas of how to approach this situation and set a time by which you will approach the person.

Share via e-mail or Facebook to level up. See OnBoarding for more info on how to do this.

8.7 CONCLUSION

Leaders are going to be faced with an increasing number of difficult and delicate situations, reactions and mind-sets in the future and cannot avoid or distance themselves from addressing and confronting derailing behaviours, sub-standard performance and inappropriate attitudes. They also cannot "shoot from the hip" and hope to have a professional outcome from a tough situation or emotive disagreement.

The progressive leader needs to master the art and practice of holding authentic conversations and take on future leadership challenges with confidence. We believe that our learning approach provides a real contribution in this quest.

PART 4

DESIGNING ACCELERATED LEARNING PROGRAMMES

Chapter 9: Learning architecture by *Debbie Craig*
9.1   Introduction
9.2   The challenge
9.3   A framework
9.4   Understand – the strategic priorities and capabilities
9.5   Design – the performance and competency standards
9.6   Analyse – the proficiency levels and the needs
9.7   Develop – organisational and individual plans
9.8   Conclusion

Chapter 10: Learning design by *Kerryn Kohl*
10.1 Introduction
10.2 Learning design for Accelerated Learning
10.3 Design in practice
10.4 Retention of learning
10.5 Steps in the design process
10.6 Methods and tools
10.7 Conclusion

Chapter 11: Gamification in learning by *Darryn van den Berg*
11.1 What is gamification?
11.2 Foundation principles driving the success of gamification
11.3 Building a gamification strategy
11.4 Gamification mechanics
11.5 Examples of gamification
11.6 Gamification lessons
11.7 So what does all of this mean, and how can you apply it?
11.8 Conclusion

Chapter 12: Learning assessment by *Kerryn Kohl*
12.1 Introduction
12.2 Levels of assessment
12.3 Strategic considerations in assessment decisions
12.4 Designing assessment to be incorporated into Accelerated Learning programmes
12.5 Assessment methods
12.6 Assessment dilemmas
12.7 Assessing the overall value of the ALP
12.8 Conclusion

CHAPTER 9

LEARNING ARCHITECTURE

By Debbie Craig

9.1 INTRODUCTION

*"… Managers will be judged on their ability to identify, cultivate, and
exploit the core competencies that make growth possible – indeed,
they'll have to rethink the concept of the corporation itself."*
– Hamel and Prahalad (1996)

To support a learning culture and build the leadership and technical competencies required to **compete and thrive in the VUCA world** of volatility, uncertainty, chaos and ambiguity, we need to craft a **foundation and an architecture** that allows navigation, mobility and accelerated growth toward expertise, mastery and high performance. Strategic alignment of learning interventions is critical to determine which competencies are core, distinctive and differentiating from competitors. We also need to know which competencies are critical now and in the future. Learning must be positioned to ensure that mission critical positions, key talent segments, key job families and scarce skills have the required competencies or learning support to accelerate bridging of the skills or succession gap.

Learning also plays a key role in **supporting change initiatives**. Never before has change been so pervasive, complex and persistent. Employees require the mind-sets and skills to adapt, respond, and learn faster and more effectively than our competitors. Every person in the organisation needs to be masters of change. Learning interventions and cultures can build these critical change and collaboration competencies to ensure high performance, adaptive and sustainable organisations.

In order to respond proactively, strategically and cost effectively to these needs, organisations need to know exactly **what competencies and capabilities** (knowledge, skills, behaviours, mind-sets) require development, why they are important, what the status quo is and the gap to future required competence and understand the most appropriate methodologies for the stage of organisational maturity, the culture, the learning support systems, and the current resources and skills.

The ultimate aim is to **build a learning organisation** that is naturally curious, hungry for learning, encouraged to collaborate and share, willing to take risks, and rewarded for enhancing overall organisational competence and performance.

9.2 THE CHALLENGE

Much has been published on learning architecture, competency management, the learning organisation, talent development and accelerated development. And yet the majority of organisations that we work with still struggle with knee-jerk "training" interventions, PDPs containing lists of courses instead of areas of competence and boring classroom power-point lectures. There is still a lack of alignment between strategic objectives, performance contracts and training plans, many of which miss the immediate need with long delays, plans and interventions – *the too little, too late syndrome*. We still see organisations training away a people-related "problem" instead of comprehensive diagnostics of the problem and a systemic approach to delivering measurable results.

Role profiling is done in the absence of performance and competency standards that are meant to set the standard at each level in the organisation to achieve stretch targets. Performance reviews are mostly a paper or tick box exercise, with little real investigation into **development needs**, apart from adding wish lists of training. Impact of training interventions are not tracked or measured, apart from the "happiness factor" immediately after the training which has little or no indication of impact on competence or performance. Organisations in South Africa that have a comprehensive long-term learning strategy and infrastructure to support it are still in the minority. Some of the complaints we hear continuously are as follows:

Table 9.1: Line manager and HR manager complaints

Line manager's complaints	HR manager's complaints
• Our organisation and mission are changing so rapidly, our people can't keep up with what they need to know to be successful. • We have high turnover in key areas – critical knowledge and expertise is walking out through the door.	• We don't get sufficient budget for training. • We are under-staffed and under-resourced (including technology). • Line managers don't follow-through on development discussions and plans.

Line manager's complaints	HR manager's complaints
• We can't get new people up to speed fast enough. • NetGeners who join our organisation expect to work in a collaborative Web 2.0 environment and require us to rethink how we engage employees. • We're understaffed and can't allocate time for our employees to take traditional training. • There's a big gap between our best performers and our worst performers -- there's no mechanism for sharing the knowledge and capabilities of our most experienced people. • We don't collaborate across organisational boundaries.	• We have poor attendance at training courses and people pull out halfway through. • We are excluded from key strategic discussions about competence and learning required.

Government and organisations lament the critical **skills gap** in the country, the lack of alignment of education and training to economic and business requirements, the unresolved complexity of the National Qualifications Framework (NQF) and Sector Education and Training Authority (SETA) processes and the lack of entrepreneurial skills and development in the country as a whole.

It is time that all executive managers, learning professionals, HR practitioners and OD consultants stood together and insist on the **professionalisation, modernisation and strategic positioning of the learning environment for real business impact** and results. We need to urgently transition and transform individual and organisational learning for the current and evolving world of work.

9.3 A FRAMEWORK

A framework is provided below that will be expanded upon in this chapter to describe the key building blocks of a learning architecture that will support the strategic objectives of an organisation and ensure optimal return of investment in learning (time, energy and money). It outlines the important phases of Understand, Design, and Analyse rather than rushing off and developing as a knee-jerk response to a crisis. C9 S3 W52

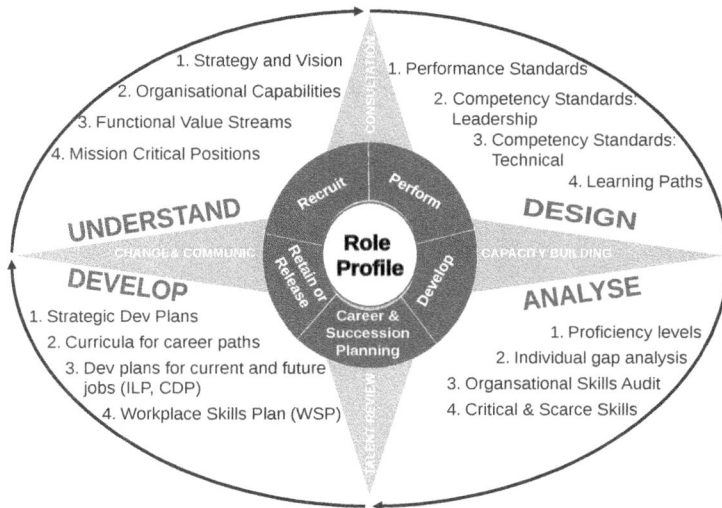

Figure 9.1: Competency management framework

Central to the framework are the **role profiles** which drive the people value chain of recruitment, performance, development, career and succession planning and retain or release. If the role profile accurately reflects the level of work, the outcomes required, the critical competencies and the minimum (and desired) requirements for the role, then you are more likely to recruit the right person; enable the person to perform at the right level; develop and enhance the skills required for exceptional performance or the next level role; and retain the person by matching needs and expectations from the outset.

Evolution of role profiles

While many organisations are still struggling to come to terms with effective role profiles and keeping them updated and benchmarked for remuneration, some organisations are moving to a more flexible approach to roles in keeping with the dynamic work environment where needs and roles change rapidly.

"Holacracy® **is a social technology or system of organizational governance in which authority and decision-making are distributed throughout** *through a fractal holarchy of self-organizing teams rather than being vested at the top of a hierarchy"* (Olivia Rud, 2009). With Holacracy, regular governance meetings structure and evolve how the work gets done – everyone leaves with clarity on who is accountable for what, with what authority, and what constraints. These change dynamically with every meeting, based on the real life tensions, challenges or insights sensed while doing the work. A structured process ensures the organisation's purpose is at the centre and everyone leaves with an explicit and light-weight role definition that is actually meaningful for the period at hand. (See Holacracy, 2006.)

The key phases of the framework are described as follows:

9.3.1 Understand

- Understand the vision, strategy, culture of the organisation and the opportunities for learning to play a role.
- Understand the core competencies and capabilities required by the organisation – both now and in the future.
- Understand the purpose and contribution of each function and its value chain.
- Understand and identify the mission critical positions without which the organisation would be at risk.

9.3.2 Design

- Design the performance standards required to achieve the strategy – at each significant level within the organisation.
- Design the functional career paths (role matrix) as well as the potential cross-over opportunities.
- Design the leadership (managerial) competency profile outlining the competencies required at each leadership level.
- Design the functional competency profile for each key role family/function outlining the technical and functional competencies required at each technical proficiency level.

9.3.3 Analyse

- Analyse the competency proficiency levels required for each role.
- Analyse the individual current level of proficiency in the role and establish potential learning needs.
- Analyse the consolidated proficiencies and learning needs and compile an organisational competence audit.
- Analyse functions and areas where critical and scarce skills are in short supply both internally and externally in the market place.

9.3.4 Develop

- Develop strategic learning plans to address strategic learning needs aligned to the strategy and informed by the competency audit and critical skills.
- Develop curricula for career paths/matrices with flexible and blended learning methodologies.

- Develop individual learning plans for current roles and career development plans for future roles aligned to the succession plan (and keeping retention in mind).
- Develop a consolidated view of all planned learning into a Workplace Skills Plan (WSP) to submit to the SETA and optimise learning investment and rebates.

Throughout the process it is important to communicate regularly, manage change proactively, consult with key stakeholders, build capacity with line managers, employees and HR specialists and integrate learning with talent review and management processes.

> This book will outline key elements of the framework. However, there is not sufficient space for all the examples and tools, so please feel free to find additional resources in the resource section of the Accelerated Learning site. Remember to opt in, on-board and join the journey for many additional resources, links and downloads. *www.accelerated.co.za*

9.4 UNDERSTAND – THE STRATEGIC PRIORITIES AND CAPABILITIES

9.4.1 Strategy and vision

All learning strategies and architecture start with understanding the vision and strategic direction of the organisation and how learning can play a role in achieving that vision. If you buy into the adage that for organisations to change people need to change, then you also by default agree that learning is the pathway to that change. It is not sufficient to read a strategy document and figure out the learning required. It is vital that the head of learning is an integral part of the strategic debate about what is possible, how fast can it be done and what capabilities exist in the company currently. Learning specialists need to be influencers of strategy and not just receivers of it.

For any organisation to succeed at achieving its vision and strategic goals, it is essential that every position in the company is filled with a fully performing and effective individual who is continually growing and enhancing his/her skills and required behaviours to excel in his/her functional, technical, managerial and leadership roles.

> **CASE STUDY**
>
> *For example, in a recently restructured, merged and globalised Agri-chemical business, the impediment to growth was seen to be lack of leadership skills, lack of depth of technical knowledge of sales staff and the skills required to streamline the procurement processes. These skills, among others such as multi-country accounting, virtual teams, optimising synergies and economies of scale, and aligning performance objectives with a whole new group of stakeholders all needed learning plans to address the needs in an accelerated way in order to make use of the global platform and new relationships before competitors could catch up.*

Another key aspect to understand is the culture of the organisation and the leadership's appetite for learning and change. As we learnt in Chapter 6, leadership style can impact culture by more than 70 per cent. Strategic change often requires leaders to adapt and learn new skills and approaches and in turn transfer these to their teams. Transforming culture has a large component of learning and desired behaviours need to be defined, learnt, reinforced and rewarded for the change to take place.

> **CASE STUDY**
>
> *For example, in a leading merchant bank, after a restructuring exercise, the largest component of a culture transformation journey was the leadership and learning stream, requiring every level of leadership to be involved in conversations and training sessions on a different way of leading, and every employee to have access to information and training on the new world of technology, data, insight, responsiveness, integrated services, and customer retention.*

9.4.2 Organisational capabilities

Learning architecture needs to take into account the core capabilities or competencies of an organisation in order to ensure these skills are maintained and enhanced faster than the competition.

Ulrich and Smallwood (2004) define the difference between competencies and capabilities as follows:

Table 9.2: Difference between competencies and capabilities

	The individual	The organisation
Technical	Technical or functional competencies (often called "hard skills")	Technical or business competencies (sometimes called "core competence")
Leadership and personal	Interpersonal or leadership competencies (often called "soft skills")	Organisation capabilities (often embodied in the culture)

Hamel and Prahalad (1996) describe core competencies as those capabilities that are critical to a business achieving competitive advantage.

"The starting point for analysing core competencies is recognising that competition between businesses is as much a race for competence mastery as it is for market position and market power. Senior management cannot focus on all activities of a business and the competencies required to undertake them. So the goal is for management to focus attention on competencies that really affect competitive advantage. It can be seen as a unique ability that a company acquires from its founders or develops and that cannot be easily imitated. Core competencies are what give a company one or more competitive advantage, in creating and delivering value to its customers in its chosen field".

CASE STUDY

For example, the reason that Dell has such a strong position in the personal computer market, is that they have three core competencies that are difficult for the competition to imitate:

- Online customer "bespoking" of each computer built
- Minimisation of working capital in the production process
- High manufacturing and distribution quality – reliable products at competitive prices.

(Jim Riley, 2012)

According to Hamel and Prahalad (1990), the three criteria to check whether the competence is core are the following:

- A core competence provides potential access to a wide variety of markets.
- A core competence should make a significant contribution to the perceived customer benefits of the end product.
- A core competence should be difficult for competitors to imitate.

However, in our experience there is also another aspect to core competence that can be added to the list and that is those core competencies that actually keep the business running effectively and efficiently. Many organisations fail to identify correctly those basic competencies that are the key inputs in allowing the organisation to achieve its stated intent.

For example, many manufacturing type operations will pride themselves on the quality of their product, and yet fail to identify clearly what the inherent competencies are which are required in the business to deliver a quality product. They may invest significantly in quality systems and a quality function and yet not address quality as being a core competence among the workforce, or possibly not even realise that the quality of a product is directly related to the ability to perform effective planned maintenance. Maintenance is often left in the hands of the Engineering department, with seldom any real input from production, where the impact of poor maintenance is always felt.

The learning function has the opportunity to influence this thinking with executives to ensure that learning and talent strategies focus on building or buying the competencies that will help them to retain or gain their competitive edge in the short and long term. It is also important to recognise the significant role that other organisational capabilities play, such as a long-term cohesive leadership team and a culture that really values people.

9.4.3 Functional value streams

Once we know what the core competencies and capabilities are, we need to understand the core functions of the business and how they add value to the business and in particular to the end customer. It is useful to start with a company-wide value chain, visually represented in Figure 9.2 below.

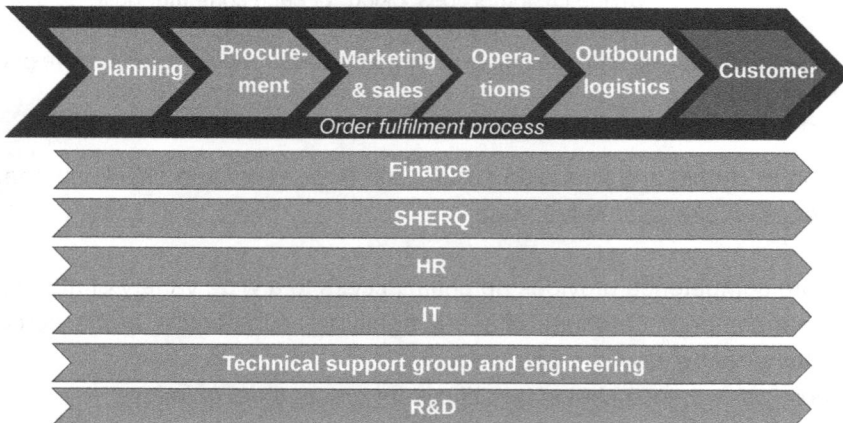

Figure 9.2: Company value chain

It is then useful to map out the value chains and associated key activities of each key function in the business. This can be facilitated with a group of functional heads with large sheets of brown paper and Post-it notes.

The process of reaching agreement on the key processes and activities assists with the identification of critical capabilities in each functional area. For example, if there have been problems in Procurement, together with Vendor Management, you can identify which particular activity requires a higher level of performance and therefore competence (knowledge, skills or behaviour). The functional heads can also identify which of the capabilities are critical now and which have the potential to build competitive advantage in the future.

9.4.4 Mission-critical positions

The next step in understanding the strategic learning priorities for a business is to identify the mission-critical positions (MCPs), which allows for a focused approach for developing future workforce plans.

Mission-critical positions are those positions that are critical to the ongoing sustainability and operations of the business, which impact substantially on productivity, delivery and cost. Mission-critical positions can occur at senior levels and at other levels in an organisation. They take into account those skills that are critical to the business and in short supply, either internally in the company or externally in the labour market.

MCPs can be identified using the matrix shown in Figure 9.3. Additional criteria can be added to risk impact.

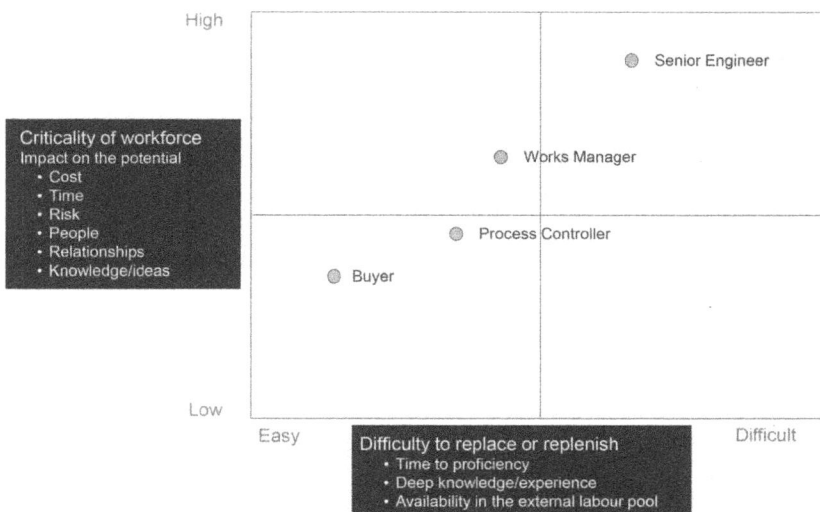

Figure 9.3: Mission-critical positions matrix

Managers can use the matrix to identify their suggested positions, which will then be validated at the annual talent forum or a special forum to review strategic resourcing requirements. The number of MCPs usually comprise less than 30 per cent of all positions, with the majority at more senior levels in the organisation.

> **CASE STUDY**
>
> While I was working with an oil refinery a few years ago, it was acknowledged that many executives were mission critical, but so were lower-level process engineers and some operators, without whom the refinery could grind to a halt or cause fires and explosions. A number of years ago, Transnet identified train drivers as mission-critical positions. They faced an ageing train driver population, and new entrants took up to four years to become qualified. Train derailments were a major risk and cost to the business.

If core competencies and capabilities are the backbone of the learning strategy, MCPs are the supporting ribs. It is critically important to ensure that both current and future MCPs (as per the strategic workforce plan) are filled with high-performing, talented and competent individuals AND that risk management plans are in place such as succession plans and retention initiatives.

9.5 DESIGN – THE PERFORMANCE AND COMPETENCY STANDARDS

To achieve success in each role at each level in an organisation, each person needs to understand the required performance and competency standards. These are described briefly below.

Table 9.3: Performance versus competence standards

How do I know I am successful in the role?	
Performance standards	**Competence standards**
The *level of performance required to be successful in the role (Outputs):* Tasks Activity Results Outputs/Deliverables	*The level of competence is required to reach performance standards (Inputs):* Knowledge Skills Behaviours Attitude/Value

Having user-friendly, relevant performance and competency standards at each level (and in each role) of an organisation ensures that every person knows what is expected of him/her and gives each person a line of sight to future career options. They are also the enablers to achieve the vision, strategy and desired culture. They provide the benchmark for equipping people with the insight, skills and behaviour to work with and lead others to achieve business results.

All too often during diagnostic interviews, prior to OD or leadership-development interventions, we hear the cries of lack of accountability, lack of engagement, poor performance, autocratic leadership style, lack of empowerment, and insufficient coaching and development to close skills gaps. The appropriate profiling and development planning will go a long way to addressing many of these issues (along with effective performance management and coaching), and enhance the attraction and retention of key talent.

Performance standards outline the level of performance required to be successful at each level in the organisation. These include the results and outputs required from the various tasks and activities that a role may require. There will be generic performance standards defining the standards required at a specific level: team level (managing others) or strategic level (managing a function). This will ensure consistency across functions and operations. These generic performance standards will be used as a basis for role profiles at each level, and can be customised for specific roles where unique standards are required.

Competency standards outline the skills and behaviours required to achieve the required standard of performance. In order to be an effective manager of others, you will need the ability to influence others and build effective teams. This includes the ability to demonstrate certain knowledge, skills, behaviours and values. There will be leadership competency standards with proficiency levels that will define the behaviour required at a specific level: team level (managing others) or strategic level (managing a function). This will ensure consistency across functions and operations. There will also be technical or functional competencies made up of knowledge, skills and behaviours. These standards will be used as a basis for role profiles at each level, and can be customised for specific roles where unique technical or non-technical skills and behaviours are required.

9.5.1 Performance standards

People need to know where they fit within the organisational structure or "family tree". One of the key factors of talent retention is having a clear career development path (or matrix) mapped out, including the support and opportunities to build the skills and experience to move through the matrix at a pace appropriate to the individual. A simple way of reflecting a leadership and technical career matrix is as shown below in Figure 9.4.

Leadership level	Criteria		Technical level	Criteria
L4 Executive Manage business (Business leadership)	Heads up an operation or a business comprising multiple operations		T4 Deep specialist Functional advice	No direct reports, experienced graduate and registered professional, deep specialist, many years, industry experience
L3 Strategic Manage function (Functional leadership)	Heads up a function comprising multiple departments		T3 Knowledge worker Technical/ professional advice	No direct reports, graduate and registered in terms of codes of practice
L2 Operational Manage managers (Results leadership)	Heads up a department. More than one layer of direct reports		T2 Skilled worker Technical application	No direct reports, some technical training required
L1 Team Manage others (Team leadership)	Heads up a team, with only one layer of direct reports.		T1 Operator/ administrator Task delivery	No direct reports, no formal training required

Figure 9.4: Career matrix with leadership and technical levels

Each of these levels has performance and competence standards against which we can assess and develop people. Transparency of the standards empowers individuals to develop their readiness to move along either technical or management career paths by understanding what is required at each level and which roles are potential options for career development. People can move across technical/ managerial career paths, as long as they have the required level of performance and competence. Each level in the organisation has a high-level description and a more detailed performance standard, examples of which are shown below.

Table 9.4: L2 detailed level description and performance standard

L2 Operational Manage managers (Results leadership)	OVERVIEW **Heads up a department. More than one layer of direct reports.** • Manages more than one team and more than one level • Secures people and financial resources • Coaches managers and technical specialists • Develops quarterly and annual budgets and plans
L2 Operational Manage managers (Results leadership	**DETAIL** **Financial** • Manages forecasting, budgeting, cash-flow management and reporting • Ensures wise spending for long-term sustainability • Improves profitability of the business, by reducing costs, improving efficiency and maximising productivity **People** • Clarifies and communicate vision, strategic goals, operational and departmental • Creates the environment to achieve high-performing teams • Manages coaching, mentoring and talent development for the team • Periodically and consistently recognises and rewards performance within the team • Lives the values • Recruits and retains talent to his/her pool **Business processes** • Participates in functional planning process with accountability for implementation in own areas • Forecasts and planns for capex • Manages operational plans, contracts and projects • Managing and maintains assets and achieves cost optimisation • Drives change, innovation and technology • Ensures compliance with all legislative and regulatory requirements **Customers** • Understands and manages customer relationships and expectations • Manages internal and external service providers

In addition to the expected outputs above, performance standards also contain role behaviours (how any given level should be spending their time) and warning signs for leading at the wrong level. These performance standards then form the basis of role profiles at each level, customised to the specific function and strategic phase. We recommend not more than two pages of a role profile for user-friendly reference and updating.

9.5.2 Competency profile: Leadership

While performance standards describe the **outputs** required for full performance, competency standards describe the **inputs** required at that level to be able to deliver the outputs.

The simple definition of a competency is the knowledge, skills and behaviours demonstrated to achieve an outcome. Competence is influenced by qualifications (knowledge), experience (skills) and values (behaviour). These in turn are affected by many other underlying (sometimes inherent) factors such as personality, aptitude, motives, self-esteem, and coping ability, among others.

Table 9.5: Knowledge, skills and behaviours

Competency		
Knowledge (What you need to know)	**Skills** (What you need to be able to do)	**Behaviour** (How you need to act)
Qualification (What formal qualification you need or RPL)	**Experience** (Type and years of experience and training you need)	**Values** (Underlying values and beliefs that determine behaviour)
Competency enablers (Attitudes, Aptitudes, Personality traits, Motives, Self-image, Team role, Energy, Style, Cognitive ability, EQ, Coping ability)		

In our experience, we have found that competency standards are most useful if focused on the skills and behaviour required to succeed in a role or a level. These can always be unpacked further to ascertain the underlying cause of the observable skill or behaviour: whether the lack of competence stems from a lack of knowledge, a value or belief system, a personality factor, or lack of experience.

> **CASE STUDY**
>
> We generally recommend that a competency profile, in order to be practical and actually used by managers, should contain no more than 25 competency areas, and not more than four to five behaviours in each cluster. You can imagine line managers being asked to give feedback on more than 100 behaviours, to more than a few staff or colleagues during a leadership programme. Less is more. It gives more focus, and should be about priority competencies (or meta-competencies) that drive other behaviours.

An example of our generic Catalyst Leadership Competency Profile is provided below, indicating 16 competency areas in four clusters.

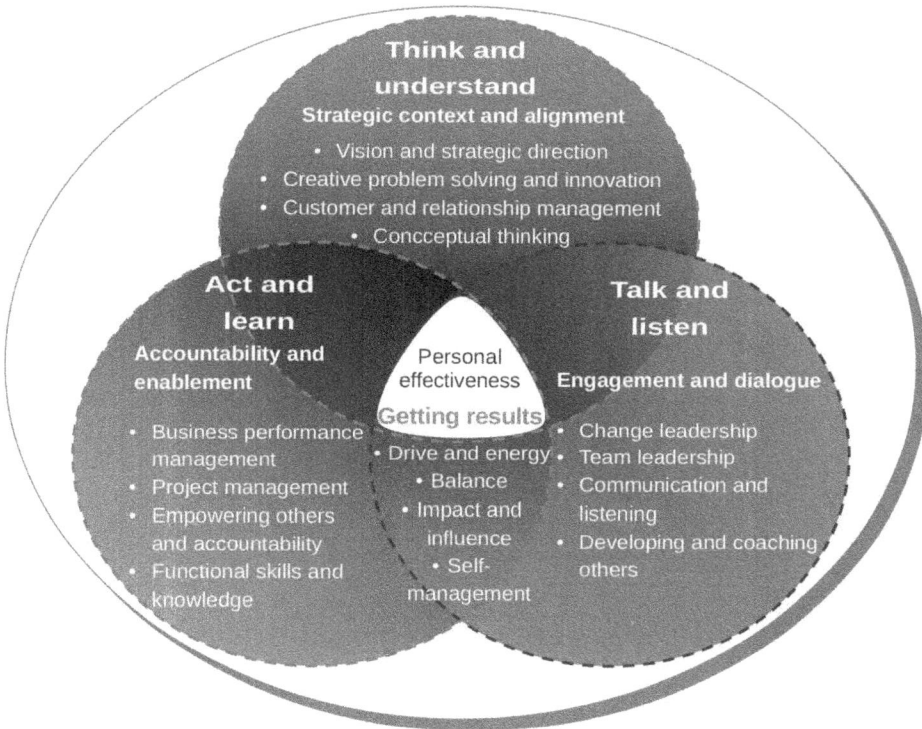

Figure 9.5: Catalyst leadership competency profile

Each competency area is further ascribed behaviours per competency area, as shown in the example below.

Change leadership	Initiates and plans change processes to realise the vision and strategy
	Facilitates change processes through clear change messages and interventions
	Deals with complexity and ambiguity
	Encourages others to overcome resistance to change and to embrace the change process

The generic competency profile can be further refined by level; with each competency area described with the behaviours applicable to that level: what change leadership looks like at team leader, operational leader, strategic leader, and executive leader level. Leadership feedback multi-raters can then be customised to the specific level.

> How sophisticated your competency profiling needs to be depends on the maturity of the organisation, and the exposure and skill of HR and OD practitioners and line managers. We recommend starting out with a generic leadership competency profile applied to everyone learning the language of leadership and competence and getting used to giving feedback. In time, the competency profile can evolve to be more specific to the level and role. Competency profiles also need to be reviewed every few years to ensure alignment with the strategic intent, core competencies, culture, and so on.

Leadership competency profiles can be exceptionally useful as part of a leadership development programme, in order for leaders to receive feedback on their skills and behaviours in comparison to their peer group and their own view of self. Feedback is critically important to build "self-regard" and "reality testing", two of the elements on the BarOn Emotional Intelligence Test.

Self-awareness = To be aware of and understand one's own thoughts, emotions and impact

Self-regard = To accurately perceive, understand and accept oneself

Reality testing = To objectively validate one's feelings and thinking with external reality.

Competency Profiles can also be very useful in ensuring role profiles fully describe the inputs required for the role, and thereby drive the recruitment and development process.

9.5.3 Competency profile: Technical

In the section above, we have described competency profiling from a leadership competence perspective, which in our experience is by far the most common application of competency profiles. The second major application for competency profiling is in the key functional areas or "job families" which describe the skills and behaviours which are more technical in nature.

Job family

A job family is a series of jobs involving work of the same nature, but requiring different levels of skill and responsibility. For example, it is quite common to find an accountant's job in a "finance" job family. An entry-level accountant would be one who has recently graduated from college, who has little experience, whose skills are being developed, and who would be given responsibilities at a lower level than those with experience. On the other hand, a senior-level accountant would be one with many years of experience whose skills and competencies are exemplary and who completes job duties of a high level. The value of an accountant therefore varies widely based on his/her experience, competencies, and the level of responsibility related to his/her key performance areas and tasks to be completed.

An example of a financial job family is shown below.

Financial job family		
Accounting	**Budgeting**	**Investment**
Staff accountant Project accountant	Senior budget officer Capital budget officer Financial planning officer	Investment account manager Investment analyst

In the South African context, it may be important to check the "organising framework for occupations" (OFO) and align the job families and role titles to these for future reporting purposes.

Similarly to the leadership competency recommendations, technical or functional profiles are most useful if they are clustered, have 25 or fewer competency areas, and not more than four to five behaviours per area. An example of an Engineering Competency profile with three clusters and 19 competency areas is shown below.

Engineering competency profile	
R&D, Planning and Design	**Managing engineering activities**
1. Long-term planning 2. Interprets and scopes design requirements 3. Develops engineering solutions 4. Identifies constraints on potential engineering solutions 5. Prepares concept proposal and seeks advice on latest technology 6. Implements planning and design process 7. Reviews the design to achieve acceptance 8. Prepares and maintains documentation during the design process 9. Validates design	10. Plans and develops operations and systems 11. Manages the processes within the operation/system 12. Manages the assets within the operation/system 13. Manages SHERQ performance 14. Measures and documents engineering operation/system 15. Contract management 16. Construction management
Professionalism	
17. Presents and develops a professional image 18. Pursues continuing professional development 19. Integrates engineering with other professional input	

Each of the competency areas is further broken down into specific observable criteria which can be assessed and strengths and gaps identified.

Implements planning and design process	Arranges design tasks to meet the agreed outcomes and cost structure
	Analyses and selects resources/processes/systems to develop the plan or design
	Develops and checks the design solution using the engineering specifications
	Creates (when appropriate) a demonstration model of the design

For another example of how to describe the competencies at different levels, see the one below from a private equity firm. This helps aspiring analysts and associates to develop their competencies and enable them to operate at higher levels and eventually become a partner.

Competency area	Analysts	Associates	Principals	Partners
Business understanding	Assists with sourcing and analysis of data on a target (or sector)	Sources, filters and analyses data on a target (or sector) and summarises findings clearly and concisely	Interprets target and sector findings in order to influence decisions and make investment recommendations	Evaluates recommendations and makes final investment recommendations for IC decisions

9.5.4 Functional learning paths

Once these technical and leadership competencies are in place, a functional learning path or matrix can be developed to show the learning required to reach higher level roles. These are particularly useful for entrants or staff interested in developing their skills toward higher level roles.

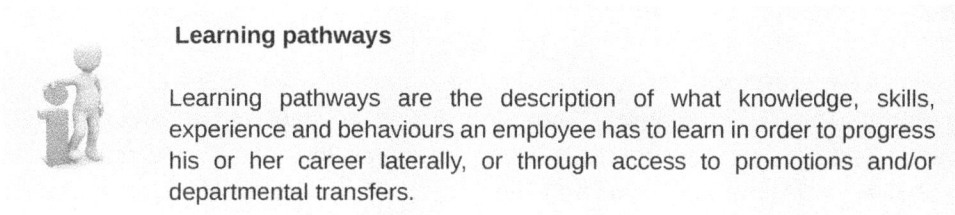

Learning pathways

Learning pathways are the description of what knowledge, skills, experience and behaviours an employee has to learn in order to progress his or her career laterally, or through access to promotions and/or departmental transfers.

Figure 9.6 shows a real-life example of an HR learning path across levels or types of work.

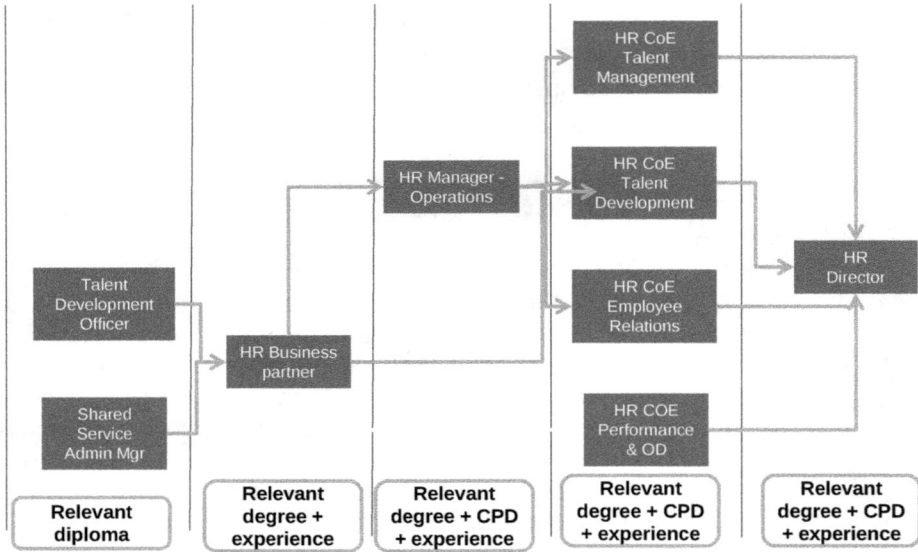

Figure 9.6: Example of a Learning Pathway

The benefits of developing competency profiles are numerous, as they drive many of the people processes in organisations.

9.6 ANALYSE – THE PROFICIENCY LEVELS AND THE NEEDS

9.6.1 Proficiency levels

We have **understood** the strategic learning priorities; we have **designed** the performance and competency standards for leadership and technical career paths; and we have incorporated these standards into role profile and career paths. Now it is time to **analyse** and find out how each individual stacks up against the standards, and where the opportunities for learning lie.

There are a number of mechanisms to do this, each of which has its complexities, challenges and benefits. We have found the most practical method is to use a system of proficiency levels. While it may not be the most accurate (behaviours are not described for every competency at every single level), it seems to have the best traction with managers. It is simple enough to use and can move the managers and organisation toward understanding the most important learning requirements, gaps and opportunities to achieve functional and strategic success. We also find it is much quicker and easier to implement and do a skills audit than the more detailed version.

The following is an example of a simple five-level proficiency scale (awareness, basic, intermediate, advanced and expert) which can be applied to each competency area. Proficiency levels can be further differentiated based on criteria such as level of skills and knowledge, problem-solving complexity, responsibility and supervision, communication ability, and coaching role. These criteria can be expanded further for a more detailed proficiency description.

Table 9.6: Proficiency levels

Level 1 Awareness	Level 2 Basic	Level 3 Intermediate	Level 4 Advanced	Level 5 Expert
• Individual has basic level of understanding but has not performed task before. • Too new in the role to determine competence	• Individual has performed task with help or has understanding and limited practical experience. • Has not yet demonstrated full competency	• Individual has intermediate understanding and consistently demonstrates ability to perform to required standard	• Individual has advanced knowledge and demonstrates an ability to solve complex problems and integrate results. Can train others	• Individual is considered an expert in the field, and continuously looks at ways of improving ways of working.
• Performs the activity with significant supervision and guidance Performs basic routines and predictable tasks • Little or no responsibility or autonomy	• Supervision is only required in more complex circumstances • Some individual responsibility or autonomy	• Significant responsibility and autonomy • Can oversee the work of others	• Performs the activity in a wide range of complex and non-routine contexts Substantial personal autonomy • Can develop others in the activity	• In-depth knowledge and experience. • Could mentor others. • Can take a strategic view • Applies a significant range of fundamental principles and complex techniques across a wide and often unpredictable variety of contexts • Wide scope of personal autonomy

These proficiency levels are used for two primary reasons:

- Defining the level of proficiency that **the role** requires, and
- Determining the current level of proficiency of **the individual** in the role.

Here is an example of an HR manager role, with required proficiency level, agreed actual proficiency level, and the resultant gap for development. The extent of the gap across different competencies (highlighted as red, orange or green or various shades of grey) can help to prioritise critical skills gaps across functions and the organisation as a whole.

Competency	HR Manager – required proficiency level	HR Manager – actual proficiency level	Gap for development
HR strategy	4	4	0
HR legislation	5	4	1
HR policies and procedures	5	3	2

9.6.2 Individual gap analysis

The gap between the required and actual proficiency level will form the basis of development discussions around strengths and opportunities for development. These discussions can be focused on the short or long term:

- Development discussion for current role.
- Career discussion for possible future role.

The outcome of these discussions will be an Individual Learning Plan (ILP) for the current role and/or a Career Development Plan (CDP) for future aspirational roles. The relevant sections of the learning plans can proactively be fed into the annual Workplace Skills Plan, to obtain maximum return on training spend. These plans can be validated and approved through various strategic planning and budget mechanisms including learning forums or committees, talent forums or executive HR committees.

There are many different methods to establish an individual's actual proficiency level, each with its own benefits and challenges.

There are two main forms of gap analysis:

- **Observational evidence-based** – using direct observation by manager, peers or subordinates.
- **Psychometric assessment-based** – using research and normative correlations.

Psychometrics can be expensive and may not be needed for all levels, but are useful where a finer level of discernment of future potential is required, for example, for future potential successors. Leaders should be taught to observe and record behaviours and results, which can be backed up with psychometrics assessments where investment is justified.

With **evidence-based assessment**, the main thing to look for is evidence of the competency descriptors or behaviours and then to apply the proficiency scales. Evidence can come in the form of observed behaviours or performance of a task, documents, reports, tests, portfolios of evidence, and direct feedback from others (not hearsay).

The methods for assessing an individual's level of proficiency and required development are summarised in the table below.

Table 9.7: Individual gap analysis

Method	Pros	Cons	Tips
Self-assessment	Easy to complete as each person does own assessment as pre-requisite to development discussion. No consensus required	Rater bias. May not have an accurate view of self in comparison to standards (either too high – ego issues – or too low – self-esteem issues)	Increase reality testing ability through regular feedback. Reduce threat by uncoupling competency assessment from performance incentives
Manager assessment	Easy to complete as each manager completes assessment as part of or development discussion organisation competence audit. No consensus required	Rater bias. May not have an accurate view of the person against standards conflict, performance issues or lack of understanding of competence and proficiencies	Increase objectivity through training on competency and proficiency assessment. Increase reality testing ability through regular feedback on variance to the norms

Method	Pros	Cons	Tips
Consensus between self and manager	Assists with establishing a more accurate view of competence and aligning expectations of future career options.	Takes longer as requires discussion and positioning of views and evidence. May not reach consensus. Requires good leadership skills.	Increase consensus building skills in both manager and employee through training and feedback. Keep the focus on evidence and not opinion.
Specialist focus group for a specific function (e.g. finance, engineering)	More objective – more heads are better than one. Specialists understand the competency requirements better.	Objectivity and confidentiality can be questioned, especially if group not credible.	Choose credible people to be in the focus group. Balance technical and learning specialists. Include multiple levels to work on all levels of the functional career path. Include a validation function with senior group.
Multi-rater online assessments	Holistic view of individual across multiple levels and roles. Automated for easy tracking and reporting. Creates great personal insight and reality testing ability to compare self-ratings to others and the norm group.	Rater bias and maturity. Raters may have personal or work issues with the ratee and "punish" them in the ratings. Time consuming if managers have to rate a number of people in a short time-period	Increase objectivity through training on competency assessment. Reduce threat by uncoupling competency assessment from performance incentives. Allow person to choose their own ratees. Schedule in advance and only necessary every few years or part of development programme.

Method	Pros	Cons	Tips
Psychometric Assessments	Considered valid and reliable and culturally fair. Quick and easy to administer – mostly online. Can be compared to local or international norms. Same test is administered to everyone equally. Can be used to validate or compare with evidence-based assessments	Some managers don't trust the "black-box" of psychometrics. Test anxiety or language barrier may skew the results. Expensive to administer and requires specialist skills. Only a set number of competencies available per provider	Use primarily for select talent segments or developmental programmes. Clarify the use of psychometrics and confidentiality aspects i.e. recruitment versus development and who will see the reports. Check against other forms evidence to build confidence in the tool

Assessments should never be used as the primary means of assessing and making decisions regarding an individual's career potential. All inputs need to be considered for an integrated view of potential.

To enhance the evidence-based approach, we encourage the use of a Portfolio of Evidence (PoE), a one-page summary, supported with additional documents or evidence where necessary. The PoE is used for career discussions in preparation for talent forums.

Each of the PoE areas can have weightings to focus behaviour accordingly; they can also be rated to result in a comparative score. The PoE can be completed by the individual and/or the employee in preparation for career discussions. The PoE encourages individual ownership of their development and careers. We often use this type of PoE in talent forums when selecting people for succession roles and accelerated development programmes. The manager presents their PoE for a potential successor, followed by robust debate and additional evidence until consensus is reached.

An example of a PoE at a recent client is as follows:

Evidence of performance	Wt	1–10	Total	Evidence of potential	Wt	1–10	Total
RESULTS Measures achieved as per Performance Contract (KPIs) e.g. project delivery (quantity, quality, time, cost), customer service, process efficiencies, financial results, people manage-ment	40%			**ABILITY** Cognitive processing ability (CPP), emotion-al intelligence (EQi), technical competence (proficiency rating)	30%		
ACCOMPLISHMENTS Awards, special achievements, going the extra mile, customer feedback, management recognition, special assignments	10%			**ATTRIBUTES** Energy, drive, positive attitude, passion, curiosity, fast learner, openness to change, resilience, willing to go the extra mile	10%		
RELATIONSHIPS Relationships built and maintained, networks developed, conflict resolved.	10%			**LEADERSHIP COMPETENCIES** As per leadership profile e.g. self-leadership, leadership of others, team player, relationship builder, influencer, communicator, innovator, problem solver	30%		
CONTRIBUTION Ideas, energy, commitment, delivery, support, accountability, ownership of projects	20%			**ASPIRATION** Desire for advancement and financial re-wards, ambition, sense of purpose	10%		
CULTURE Leadership brand, company values	20%			**ENGAGEMENT** Intent to stay, discretionary effort, enthusiasm, loyalty, responsive to change	20%		
TOTAL				**TOTAL**			

Figure 9.7: Example of Portfolio of Evidence

9.6.3 Organisational competence audit

An organisational competence audit becomes a simple and efficient process if the guidelines above have been followed and are supported with an IT system for integrated reporting. Captured ratings from individual learning assessments and plans can be rolled up into departments, functions, levels, EE categories, and so on, and form the base of the organisational competency audit. See below a visual representation of a small engineering department's competency result and priority needs.

Competency	Engineering Manager	Engineer	Technologist	Priority development need
Strategy	1	1	2	
Policies	0	0	1	
Analyse	2	2	2	
Design	1	1	1	
Implement	0	2	0	
Maintain	1	0	0	

9.6.4 Critical and scarce skills

The competency audit can further identify where gaps exist in the mission-critical position and scarce skills areas, allowing additional focus and investment to accelerate learning in these areas, or recruiting externally where needed.

Activity 1

Develop a competency profile for the top five competencies of your current or next level aspirational role and think about the proficiency levels you will need (required) versus what you think you have now (the actual proficiency level). Use the five proficiency levels above.

Share via e-mail or Facebook to level up.

Competency	Required proficiency level	Actual proficiency level	Gap for development

9.7 DEVELOP – ORGANISATIONAL AND INDIVIDUAL PLANS

9.7.1 Strategic development plans

Strategic development plans can now be the bridge between strategic priority learning needs (from core competencies, mission critical positions and scarce skills) and the organisational competency audit. It may be found that there are critical competencies required for the strategy, but at low proficiency level, for example, skills such as project management, strategic sourcing, change management, risk management, junior leadership, forecasting and budgeting. strategic development plans can be crafted per organisational level (L1–4 or T1–4) or per functional area.

There is potential for huge economies of scale and cost savings if learning interventions are planned proactively and strategically in this way. Many of them can cut across silos and encourage cross-functional learning experiences.

9.7.2 Curricula for learning paths

In large organisations, learning paths may also include specific curricula (programmes of outcomes and/or learning interventions) that a person may move through to develop the required competence. This would be applicable where a company has an internal Learning Academy or long-term contracts with specific learning providers such as training companies, business schools or technical colleges.

9.7.3 Development plans for current and future jobs

Development plans and priorities are usually determined based on a number of factors including: performance in the current role; future career plans and succession plans; business priorities; and budgets. We recommend that learning plans should be focused on building competence toward full performance in the current role, before spending time and resources on building readiness for future roles.

The quality of the development plan is critical to effective development. The tendency in the past has been to list training courses, conferences, and technical or management development programmes to develop someone. Research shows that the most effective development methodologies are:

- On-the job application and experience (70%)
- Coaching (20%)
- Formal interventions (10%).

While formal training is important, it is required primarily where a step change in knowledge or interaction is required or where experimenting in a safe environment is necessary.

Learning plans are best if they include a combination of development and deployment interventions and are aligned with individual career aspirations, lifestyle choices, learning preferences and organisational needs.

- **Development** includes the various development actions for individuals to build their competence in current and future potential roles. Development activities can include self-study, coaching and mentoring, differentiated development programmes for talent segments, and external management and leadership development programmes.
- **Deployment** includes the various on-the-job career opportunities for an individual to develop skills and experience for future roles. Many creative options are available including new appointments, stretch assignments, project roles, secondments, rotations, role exchanges, talent exposure programmes, or internships. Outside experiences are also important, including sabbaticals, time off from work to explore issues and return refreshed. and think tanks to orientate employees to new perspectives.

The most effective method of learning seems to be via new information or techniques gained through self-study or training programmes, combined with on-the-job or action learning. These methods allow leaders to apply and practise new techniques, and work with a coach to set realistic goals while offering regular feedback and opportunities for reflection. Action learning has become very popular in that it creates real-life business opportunities for learning, by combining learning sessions with project work. This is mutually beneficial for the organisation (assists with acquisition of problem solving) and the learners (new skills and knowledge).

Table 9.8 presents a summary of learning methods linked to their impact on behaviour change. We will delve more into different learning methods in a later chapter.

Table 9.8: Learning methods impact on behaviour change

Self-study	Formal Programmes	Group Learning	Coaching	Action Learning
Reading Reflection Internet/ e-learning Discovery/ Trial and error Assessment Soliciting feedback	Business school programmes Public courses Seminars Conferences Training programmes External supplier of programmes	Strategy sessions Team development Leadership programmes with peers Networking forums Just-in-time learning	External coach Mentor/Coach Manager Peers Setting goals, creating learning opportunities, sharing info, experience and tools Feedback	Special projects (full or part time) Secondment Job rotation Acting role Development programmes Talent programmes Leadership assignments
Behaviour change = lowest	Behaviour change = low	Behaviour change = medium	Behaviour change = high	Behaviour change = highest

Coaching and action learning are much more effective at changing behaviour than some of the formal programmes that we often hope will make the difference. They are also a low-cost option when budgets are limited. It is important to build a culture of abundant feedback and coaching and the skills to have effective coaching discussions. Managers should be encouraged to make time for regular discussions and coaching sessions to give feedback, solve problems and discuss options in order to gain experience and improve performance.

Activity 2

Write down three development activities you can embark on to start building competence for your current or next level role.

Share via e-mail or Facebook to level up.

9.7.4 Workplace Skills Plan (WSP)

The relevant sections of the individual and career learning plans can proactively be fed into the annual Workplace Skills Plan in order to obtain maximum return on training spend. These plans can be validated and approved through various strategic planning and budget mechanisms including learning forums or committees, talent forums or executive HR committees.

> *Brain Break:* Do a body scan and notice what you are feeling – release any tension you may feel.

9.8   CONCLUSION

It is important to underpin all learning with a clear understanding of the outcomes required. Performance and competency standards are an excellent way of facilitating this and communicating to people how they can develop themselves to high levels of performance, competence and organisational contributions. Although it may look complex and time consuming, just like the planning of a building, once built, it requires only ongoing maintenance and the occasional renovation to keep it current. The architecture should be reviewed at any time when there is major strategic organisational change, and should be a standard foundation for the capacity building of people.

CHAPTER 10

LEARNING DESIGN

By Kerryn Kohl

10.1 INTRODUCTION

"People ignore design that ignores people." – Frank Chimero

Designing learning for an accelerated learning programme or experience is not a complex process but it is one that needs consideration. In this day and age, and as we have seen previously in this book, the only constant that organisations are faced with is change. The only true competitive advantage an organisation has is its ability to respond to and predict future change. I firmly believe that the strongest weapon in an organisation's arsenal to meet the demands of this ever-changing environment is its learning function. The learning function should be used strategically to drive change.

When designing learning to support organisational change, we need to adopt a different lens through which we view this change. Suspend all judgement and for a moment accept the fact that, for a change programme to be successful, it requires a transformation, and for an organisation to transform, its **PEOPLE** have to **TRANSFORM**.

Very often we see organisations going to huge expense on transforming their systems, structures or capital investments. An example is the current trend in core banking transformation, whereby banks are trying to move off their legacy systems and onto enterprise-wide systems such as SAP. However, I am seeing one fundamentally flawed consistency. They are all spending money, time and thought on transforming their systems and yet are paying only a small amount of attention to the transformation of people and behaviour.

This approach is short-sighted. If the users of the system do not buy into the new system, or do not fully appreciate the context or how the system works together across the value chain, they will not use it to its full advantage. System change requires behaviour change. More often than not people will find brilliant ways to circumvent the system, lessening any hope of seeing a full return on investment.

When we see organisational change from this perspective we understand that people transformation requires us to engage people's hearts and minds (Kotter, 1995). Employee and leaders' thinking about the organisational change will drive how they feel and directly influence how they behave. Recent research on emotional contagion (Hatfield, Cacioppo & Rapson, 1994) demonstrates that the way leadership feels about something (a person, a process or a system), has a direct impact on the customer's experience.

Whether you are a learning specialist, designer, leader or coach, this view of change is an important consideration for designing learning experiences to accelerate the learning of individuals or groups. For the purpose of this book, the term "learning designer" applies to anyone involved in designing or planning learning experiences. These can include specialists, leaders, coaches and individuals on their personal journey of learning.

A primary consideration is the learning designer who, in shaping and moulding the learning plan will ultimately direct its outcome and influence the type of change that will be encouraged. For this reason, it is essential for the learning designer not only to understand the change required but also to buy fully into it.

Secondly, learning designers need to start with the end in mind. They have to understand what behaviours will be required to drive and sustain the change; have to connect these behaviours to how they want people to feel, think and act; and then have to design from this vantage point.

This chapter will focus on design principles for developing any Accelerated Learning programme and will cover the following:

- Learning design for Accelerated Learning – what it is and what it is influenced by.
- Design in practice – how to design an Accelerated Learning programme.
- Learning design methodology and tools.

Brain Break: Ask a small group of children what they have learnt this week about life, themselves, or others.

10.2 LEARNING DESIGN FOR ACCELERATED LEARNING

Accelerated learning is the name given to learning design that encompasses many different techniques, methodologies, and approaches that encourage whole brain learning (Heidenhain, 2014b). These include having music playing, using pod casts and video clips, artistic demonstrations, painting, collaging, using colour, playing games, doing group work, and so on. Research has shown that adults are best engaged when actively (physically and emotionally) immersed in a task. In an accelerated learning programme (ALP), often what looks like play is actually a technique used to engage adults actively in the stages of the Learning Cycle, as discussed in Chapter 5.

Definition: Accelerated learning (AL) is an integrated approach for speeding up and enhancing the learning processes for real business results. AL unlocks our potential for learning by tapping into our natural learning process, creating a positive, stimulating learning environment, accessing the whole brain, working with the whole person and balancing group needs with individual learning styles. AL engages, stimulates, motivates, inspires and encourages creating and collaborating during the learning experience. Lastly, AL is always contextualised in the real world of work with relevant and useful examples, access to organisational people and resources and application opportunities to build confidence and competence (Craig, 2014).

In order to understand how to design learning effectively for an Accelerated Learning programme, it is also important to understand the learning process. We know now that learning is a "whole brain process", otherwise referred to as "quantum learning" (Janzen, Perry & Edwards, 2012).

Worth reading: Article: Viewing Learning through a New Lens: The Quantum Perspective of Learning: www.scirp.org/journal/PaperInformation. aspx?PaperID=23343

As adults we have more practical, experiential and connected intellectual abilities to our advantage. We learn best by doing, experiencing, and associating; to enhance learning, it is therefore essential for learners to engage actively with the learning material in a variety of ways and incorporate a multi- sensory approach in their engagement. **Whole brain or quantum learning is learning in such a way that all of the neural pathways in your brain are activated**. When you are using all of your neural networks, you are able to assemble pieces of information in your own way, this means that you assign personally significant meaning to the information.

Watch this video on YouTube: **New Teaching strategies with Bobbi DePorter**
http://www.youtube.com/watch?v=9P787lS4qEY

What makes assigning personal meaning and the activation of all your neural pathways so important? When you use all of your neural pathways in dealing with new information, you link or associate the new information with your existing knowledge network. In doing so, you are giving it personal meaning, which makes it more relevant to you. When information becomes personally relevant, it becomes usable, and when information becomes usable, it becomes knowledge.

As learning designers, we can promote quantum learning by adopting a dialogic approach (Gravett, 2001).

The remainder of this chapter focuses on how we can use the principles underpinning the dialogic approach to enrich our designs for an accelerated learning programme. It also gives leaders a yardstick with which to measure how potentially effective a particular programme will be. The dialogic approach is a learning-centred approach.

The dialogic approach

There are three elements that I consider to be the most influential in this approach.

1. The formation of a learning relationship
2. Establishment and maintenance of a cooperative learning climate
3. Co-construction of knowledge through dialogue.

The formation of a learning relationship between facilitators, coaches, leaders and the learning environment and learners is characterised by "dynamic reciprocal unity", which encapsulates a co-operative learning climate. This learning climate surrounds the "learners, facilitators, coaches, leaders and the learning environment" in their "co-construction of knowledge" represented by the pyramid in figure 10.1 below.

This learning climate is also responsible for enabling and fostering the process of dialogue, which is the third and final core element that I have identified and is represented by the question mark between the learner's and the educator. Each of these elements will now be explored in terms of their interrelationships and their interdependence.

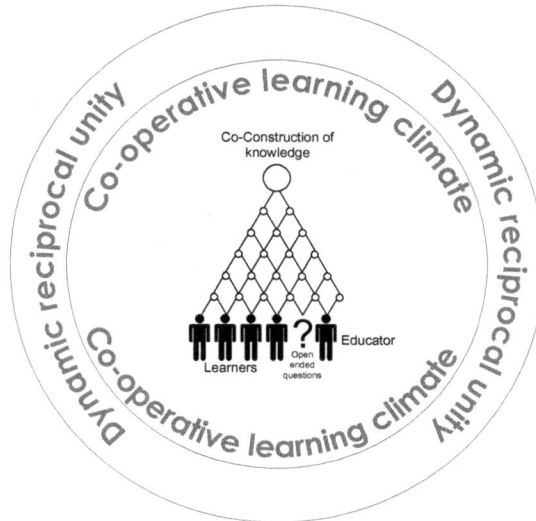

Figure 10.1: The dialogic approach to learning

This approach to learning describes the establishment of a unique relationship between the learning designer, the facilitator, the coach, the leader, the learner, and their peers for the purposes of knowledge construction and understanding. This relationship is characterised by mutual respect and mutual engagement of the participants in exploring, constructing and connecting knowledge.

Worth reading: Dialogic Learning from an Educational Concept to Daily Classroom Teaching.
http://www.ecswe.org/wren/documents/Article3GallinDialogicLearning.pdf

---

The learning process is largely determined by the learner's individual learning style and the learning climate. I believe that learning is enhanced when we design learning to include a variety of learning tasks or learning centred on questions. We need to use powerful questions as designers designing the learning, as facilitators when covering the content component, as coaches when supporting the ALP learners, and as leaders when assessing the performance of the learners. As we shall see, this ability to use questions to invite dialogue and evoke critical thinking is central to an accelerated learning programme. The ability to ask questions and invite dialogue is also central to the coaching process, as we saw in Chapter 7. Questions allow the learners to use their own learning style and give them the opportunity to engage in verbal thought, thereby allowing meaningful learning to occur.

Watch this video on YouTube: **Learning Styles**
http://www.youtube.com/watch?v=fQYW6vYSGXs

Another key consideration when designing learning is that learning should be seen as a pathway or a sequence of events rather than as a single training event. This sequence should be made up of mainly informal learning events. It is estimated that 80 per cent of our learning occurs informally, on the job, through observations, interactions and discussions with our peers, experts, or leaders. This should then be reflected in our learning budget, and most certainly in the way in which learning is designed. It is critical that the designer or leader has the knowledge and skill required to harness the power of informal learning opportunities and to design these into the ALP.

There are several models that influence the design of an ALP, and I like to use a combination of these. However, all of these have the following tenets in common:

1. Whole brain learning principles must be used.
2. The emotional state of learners will affect their learning.
3. The learning environment is crucial.
4. Learners must be engaged and intrinsically motivated to learn (through the learning environment).
5. Multiple intelligence, multi-generations and multiple learning styles must be catered for.

Point 5 is key for learning designers, facilitators and leaders alike. We always need to keep in mind that at present our organisations, our learning environments and our learning communities are made up of adult learners spanning four different generations. See Chapter 2 for more information on how generational theory affects the learning environment.

Designing learning for multi-generational adults

The learning community within any organisation is influenced by a host of factors including age, career, personal circumstances, social influences, education history, physiological differences, psychosocial influences, and so on. Most importantly, though, we need to understand that the base values defining each generation are also different. What is key about values is that they dictate the way in which we interpret and respond to what we are exposed to. For the most part and for the majority of the population, this happens unconsciously.

Watch this video on YouTube: **Learning Styles of the Net Generation**
http://www.youtube.com/watch?v=rzX21oQx94w

10.3 DESIGN IN PRACTICE

Several methods have been developed regarding designing for an accelerated learning programme.

Watch this video on YouTube: **Suggestopaedia – Georgi Lozanov**
http://www.youtube.com/watch?v=NRJG7fLpm1c

However, I like to use a combination of methods drawing from the theories of the "seven steps of program planning" (Gravett, 2001); the Accelerated Learning Cycle (Heidenhain, 2014a); and Gagne's nine levels of learning (Mind Tools, nd).

"Seven steps of program planning" forms a useful overarching framework and includes asking and answering seven key questions: Who, Why, When, Where, What, What for, and How. I find combining steps 2 and 6 (the why and the what for) to be of benefit in establishing clear learning objectives. Let's take a closer look at how to answer each of these questions when designing an accelerated programme.

10.3.1 Who?

Answering this question gives insight into who the learning audience is. As a designer it is imperative that you find out as much about your audience as possible. You need not only to consider the desired end state or competence that you want them to develop, but also to take their current levels of competence, their personal development plans, and their learning profile into account.

You also need to consider that your audience for any learning programme is bigger than just the end user. Your audience is made up of learners, leadership, facilitators, coaches, and the learning set or team.

Leadership: A key member of your learning audience should be the leadership. Your leaders also need to learn a new way of being in order for them to create the climate in which learning can take place and the change can be sustained.

The facilitator: Facilitators play an important part as catalysts for learning and it is critical that they are highly skilled and have keen powers of observation. They should be able to sense intuitively what the learners need and adjust their style accordingly. A great facilitator knows just when to step forward and direct the content and when to step back and facilitate a process of self-discovery. They know that their role is only to facilitate learning. They do this through creating a learning space that challenges learners' beliefs by asking powerful questions aimed at stimulating critical reflection (Mezirow, 1998) and dialogue.

The coach: The coaching relationship is a powerful learning space as it provides an opportunity for the learner to discuss and reflect on what has been learnt, or on feedback received. Learners are then able to explore ways of how to implement learnings or personal improvements, thereby increasing the opportunity for learning to become meaningful and integrated. The quality of the coach is very important. Like facilitators, they need not only to challenge the learning set as a group, but also to challenge and stretch each individual learner. Great coaches use methods of powerful questioning and keen observation to foster transformation.

Worth reading: The Chemistry of Accelerated Learning in Executive Coaching

http://coachworks.com/magento/pdfs/Formula7article.pdf

The learning set: An additional consideration when designing for accelerated learning is that learners will also be learning in groups. The designer must ensure that aspects of team formation and group dynamics are built into the design. When allocating people to groups, designers and facilitators must think about diversity, levels, personalities (introverts and extroverts), specialist skills and gender.

Questions need to be asked such as:

- What would the implications be if we ran groups for EE candidates only, or women only?
- How would senior high flyers feel working in mixed-level groups?
- Can the learners be taken out of the work environment – for how long at a time?
- How critical is their role?

Watch this video on YouTube: **Action Learning Professional Development**
http://www.youtube.com/watch?v=ZW9LCQ-3U2w

Other key players in an ALP include the mentors, line managers, input providers, designers, project managers, and others. You can develop a stakeholder plan to prioritise different groups and plan interaction with them, and to determine their exposure to previous learning.

10.3.2 Why?

Asking why helps the leader and the designer to identify the actual learning need or the pre-situation. For example, why do learners need to participate in this accelerated learning programme? Asking why also gives us a view of what the learners should be able to do differently after the accelerated learning programme, that is, the learning outcomes. As a designer you need to keep in mind that to change learners' behaviour, you need to change the way they think and feel.

An example of the why for an accelerated leadership programme could be the following:

Why: Pre-situation
- Organisation X needs to develop leadership capability in order to develop a comprehensive talent pool of leaders in order to ensure successful succession planning.

Why: Post-situation – Outcomes
- To understand different styles of leadership and their effectiveness in diverse situations.
- To develop a deeper level of self-awareness; self-regulation and self-motivation in order to improve relationship building and conflict management.

As we saw in Chapter 9 on learning architecture, it is useful to develop a set of core competencies that the ALP will address. You can have individual outcomes – behaviour, levels of performance, and so on – as well as organisational outcomes, such as reducing risk in the succession plan by identifying ready-now candidates for mission-critical positions. It is important to set clear pre- and post-programme measures so that you can track the benefit of the ALP and measure the learning that has taken place.

In Chapter 13 there is a Breakthrough Learning case study for potential successors. In this case study, you will see that in the design phase, a set of core competencies was developed and each learner was assessed against these competencies in an attempt to understand the extent of the change required. The learners were then assessed against these competencies after the programme and we were able to measure the progress each of the learners had made.

Asking **"What for?"** at this stage of the design helps us to define and articulate the "what" we expect the learners to have adopted or learnt by the end of the programme – these are our learning objectives. These objectives are known as achievement-based objectives and should be described using verbs that can be observed (action verbs), as illustrated in Bloom's Taxonomy. This will make the assessment of what has been learnt more effective.

HOT TIP

For a list of action verbs, see Bloom's Taxonomy – visit www.clemson. edu/.../Blooms%20Taxonomy%20Action%20Verbs.pdf

---

Watch this video on YouTube: **How to Set Learning Objectives** http://www.youtube.com/watch?v=dhzFDOKyXnI

10.3.3 When?

This question is aimed at establishing a time frame in which the learning event will take place. I find that often designers look at how much content has to be covered and then retrospectively fit this into a timeframe. A more effective approach is to look at the learning context and learner constraints systemically. Consider the timing from both a learner and a business perspective. Think about how much "learning" needs to take place by when and how much the learner can absorb and integrate in that time – not how much content should be covered. Also consider urgent business priorities, the role the learner fulfils in the organisation, and what is possible regarding off-the-job and on-the-job activities.

The learning power of an ALP is that there is not just a single training event, but a sequence of learning events using both formal and informal opportunities.

Additional questions to ask at this stage are: *Will learning be face to face or virtual? How much time off the job is required? Is there opportunity to practise skills on the job? How long do you have before learning has to be applied? Can the person do the learning individually or only with a group? Are there any other programmes or business events (such as year-end) that will have an impact on people's ability to attend training?*

10.3.4 Where?

This refers to the actual sites or locations in which learning will take place over the period of the programme, including both formal and informal aspects of the programme. We highly recommend intensive learning sessions to be held off-site to avoid the distractions of the office and to get into a different headspace for learning. If there are constraints, and learning sessions have to be held in-house, then you will need to work harder as a facilitator in order to contract with the learners on their mind-sets and behaviours, and avoid the distractions. Coaching sessions are best held in a quiet, neutral venue away from prying eyes and interruptions.

The way in which the corporate classroom and other learning environments are set up is crucial and needs to cater for highly interactive and informal learning. The space must allow for natural light and air, and enough space for movement, activities and games. Seating must be arranged for effortless movement into group activities. Wall space is very important as colourful visual stimuli such as charts and posters are of key importance in accelerated learning. Multi-media technology support is also vital to ensure that we can engage multiple senses through videos, music and movement and thereby stimulate the learning process.

Watch this video on YouTube: **Turning Your Classroom into a Quantum Learning Environment** http://www.youtube.com/watch?v=X4WhQRnCK0I

Plan ahead for learning that requires group collaboration and learning through electronic platforms and social networks.

Example: Online coaching programme

I recently completed an online learning programme – *Foundations of Corporate Coaching* – hosted through Get Smarter for the University of Cape Town. It was amazing to see how seamlessly they blended technological tools to create a fantastic and engaging learning experience. Learning modules were posted online for us to access. These were made up of a combination of video lectures, course notes and podcasts, and additional reading was provided through a collection of articles. To ensure that we practised our coaching skills, we were assigned a partner at the beginning of the programme and we would "coach" each other using the skill we had been introduced to that week over Skype. To assist us throughout the programme, various discussion forums were held and we had access to the course co-ordinators through various electronic means.

Methods like this can be used effectively to foster collaborative learning in global companies where people are globally or regionally dispersed. Consider the cost of people travelling versus the risk of the learning not taking place. When deciding on using "technology-intensive" learning methods, ensure that you check the basics – as simple as that may sound. You need to ensure that your learners will have connectivity through access to computers and mobile devices. They must be able to access the Internet and not be hindered by firewalls or slow connections.

Worth reading: E-Learning No How
http://www.astd.org/Publications/Magazines/TD/TD-Archive/2009/01/E-Learning-No-How

---

10.3.5 What?

The "What" question helps us as leaders and designers to determine what content needs to be covered – and the level at which learners need to be familiar with it. Then look at the blended learning methods available to you and determine which "chunks "of content would suit that method best. Design accordingly. The trend is to provide content electronically so that people arrive at sessions with the knowledge, and then spend time exploring, discussing, understanding and reviewing it. By using various methods to present the content, you give learners a choice with regard to how they would prefer to get to grips with it, whether through books, articles, video, podcasts, blogs, or other means. People love choice and it allows them to work with their preferred learning styles and unique personalities.

10.3.6 How?

This is the meat of the design process. In this step it is important for us to see learning as a sequence of events or a learning chain (Buning, 2010). A learning chain links knowledge nuggets/training interventions in a continuous and sustainable way. For example, a compulsory e-learning module could form the core link, strengthened by the inclusion of several others presenting the information in different ways, such as a variety of articles or presentations and an opportunity to engage in dialogue through the use of blogs and other social network tools.

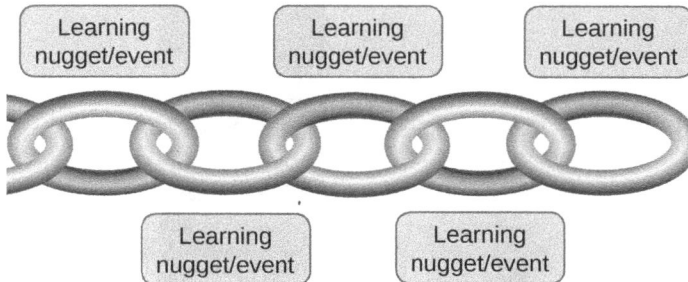

Figure 10.1: Learning chains

Worth reading:: Sustainable Learning through Learning Chains
http://www.slideshare.net/mindrom/sustainable-learning-through-learning-chains-norbert-buning-global-hr-forum-2010pdf-seoul-korea

Learning chains allow us to integrate formal and informal learning. By developing this chain, the designer ensures that learning is sustainable by linking learning nuggets or links. These nuggets or links allow for the introduction, **repetition, reinforcement, review and recall** of information. A learning chain also allows us to do interval-based learning which is key to retention. We know that if learning is presented in a single event, we will forget up to 90 per cent of this over time and usually before we have had a chance to integrate the learning.

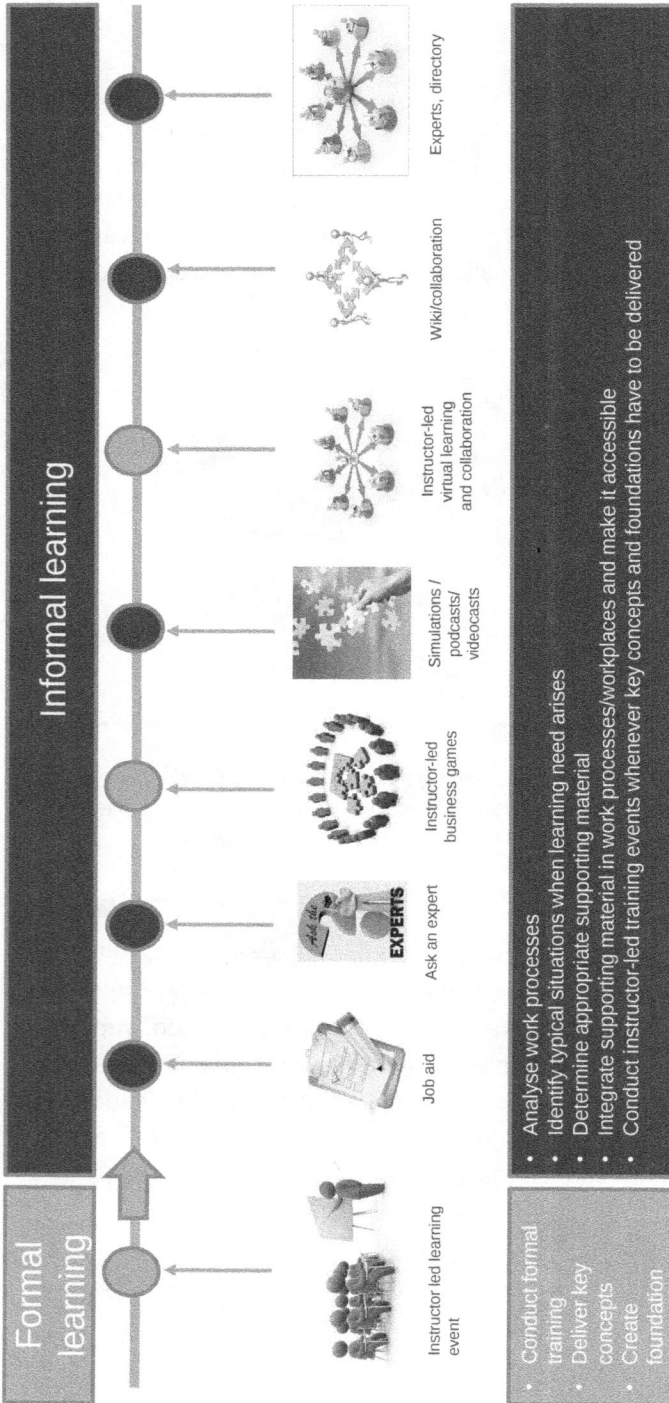

Figure 10.2: Learning chain (© Accenture Adapted from Buning, 2010)

By designing a learning chain, we are working with our neurobiological process of memory. Certain links are focused on putting information in or encoding it; some others should be focused on consolidating knowledge or the storage of information; and finally, others should be concerned with getting the information out again or developing recall ability. We need to keep in mind that these processes of memory are inextricably linked. The way in which we encode information has a direct impact on how it is stored and how it is accessed or recalled. This is why, when developing an accelerated learning programme either for yourself or your organisation, or even as a leader evaluating an ALP, you need to ensure that it incorporates whole brain learning principles as outlined in Chapter 5.

The ALP should also cater for rhythmic repetition. A learning chain that links learning nuggets allows for this rhythm to be set.

As we see in the next section, delivering learning via a learning chain greatly enhances knowledge retention.

10.4 RETENTION OF LEARNING

It is a well-known fact that the retention of learning and the ability to apply it successfully decreases rapidly over time, particularly if the material is covered in the classic single-session classroom-based approach. Many years ago Hermann Ebbinghaus established the "forgetting curve" (Stahl et al, 2010).

This trend has been confirmed many times through the ages and emphasises the need to find different ways to learn which include repetition, recall,

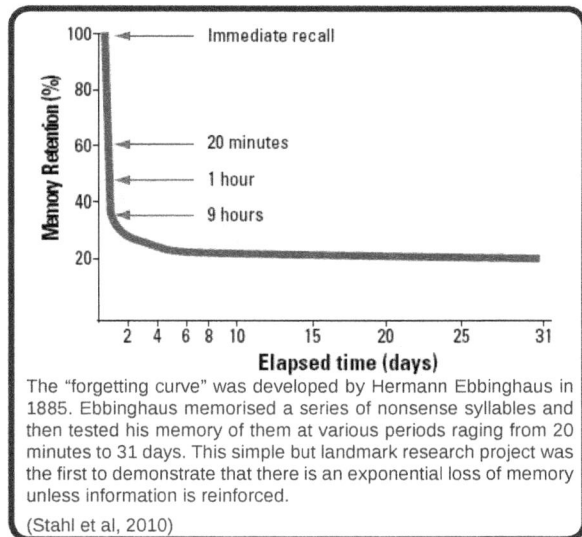

The "forgetting curve" was developed by Hermann Ebbinghaus in 1885. Ebbinghaus memorised a series of nonsense syllables and then tested his memory of them at various periods raging from 20 minutes to 31 days. This simple but landmark research project was the first to demonstrate that there is an exponential loss of memory unless information is reinforced.

(Stahl et al, 2010)

Figure 10.3:The forgetting curve

review and reinforcement in order to accelerate and enhance long-term memory and the embedding of new neural pathways.

> **CASE STUDY**
>
> "A modern example of this loss of knowledge without repetition is a study of cardiopulmonary resuscitation (CPR) skills that demonstrated rapid decay in the year following training. By three years post-training only 2.4 per cent were able to perform CPR successfully.
>
> Another recent study of physicians taking a tutorial they rated as very good or excellent showed mean knowledge scores increasing from 50 per cent before the tutorial to 76 per cent immediately afterward. However, score gains were only half as great 3–8 days later and incredibly, there was no significant knowledge retention measurable at all at 55 days." (Stahl et al, 2010)

The ability to retain knowledge and skills is becoming ever more challenging. We are constantly bombarded with an ever-increasing volume of information from many different sources, and we can retain only so much. Our brains become overloaded, and in order to "survive" we undergo a process of filtering, prioritising, categorising and encoding to retain what we can, but our brain ends up dumping most of it to create room for new data (information). Only through repetition, recall, review and reinforcement can we create permanent neural pathways that will kick in when required.

Unfortunately many schools, universities and businesses are still stuck in the old paradigm of transferring knowledge through bombarding our brains with more and more information through lectures, reading, presentations or workshops. These techniques are easiest for the designers and teachers, reach the widest audience in a short time, and are the most cost effective. However, these benefits are wasted if not much is retained in the long term to enhance competence and performance.

> "First world countries have not seen any increases in standardised test scores for literacy, numeracy and science since the mid-1960s, primarily because we have actually reached the upper limit of efficiency and effectiveness of the first paradigm shift to text-based episodic (rote/ knowledge) learning. Regardless of how many billions of dollars we spend on education we will not see any significant changes in these levels of success until we adopt the second paradigm and leverage these new effectiveness and efficiency gains to improve the learning that takes place in our schooling systems. More testing is not the answer; the answer is to adopt a new paradigm around teaching and learning and prepare our learners for the richness and vibrancy of learning in a collaborative, multimedia-rich environment." (Treadwell, 2013)

In order to accelerate learning and the retention and successful application of learning, we need to build in live practice of skills and immediate use of knowledge in the work environment with feedback, coaching and group discussions. Retention of learning in memory improves significantly as we move up the ladder of learning as illustrated below in Stahl's article, *Play it again* (2010).

We need to see the learning content over a period of time, in bite-sized chunks, with regular revision.

In addition, we need to build in reinforcement within the first two days, for example, a follow-up survey on key learnings and work impact; and after the first two weeks, for example, on-the-job observation; and again after the

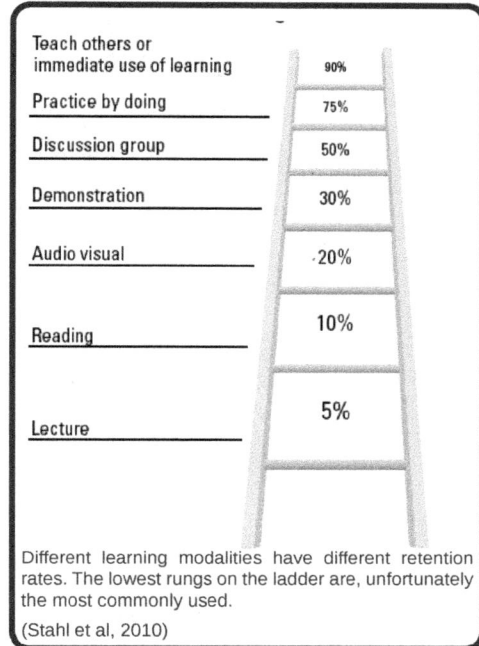

Teach others or immediate use of learning	90%
Practice by doing	75%
Discussion group	50%
Demonstration	30%
Audio visual	20%
Reading	10%
Lecture	5%

Different learning modalities have different retention rates. The lowest rungs on the ladder are, unfortunately the most commonly used.
(Stahl et al, 2010)

Figure 10.4: The ladder of learning

first two months, for example, a group discussion or Q&A. This approach is known as "interval learning" or "spaced learning", and can be built into "learning chains" as we saw above by utilising the many Internet-based digital learning platforms and applications available blended with important face-to-face engagement and discussion time. Learning shows best long-term retention and results when it offers choice; is relevant to the current role; is time efficient and flexible; links new knowledge to old knowledge; is interactive; engages the learner; and uses creative and stimulating ways to revise, recall and test proficiency.

10.5 STEPS IN THE DESIGN PROCESS

When designing each nugget or link, I like to draw on Gagne's 9 levels of learning (Mind Tools, nd) and the Accelerated Learning Cycle (Heidenhain, 2014a) to guide me. These two theories provide the framework within which the sequence of learning events or the learning chain should be designed.

| Level 9: Enhancing retention and transfer (Generalisation) |
| Level 8: Assessing performance (Retrieval) |
| Level 7: Providing feedback (Reinforcement) |
| Level 6: Eliciting performance (Responding) |
| Level 5: Providing learning guidance (Semantic encoding) |
| Level 4: Presenting the stimulus (Selective perception) |
| Level 3: Stimulating recall of prior learning (Retrieval) |
| Level 2: Informing learners of the objective (Expectancy) |
| Level 1: Gaining attention (Reception) |

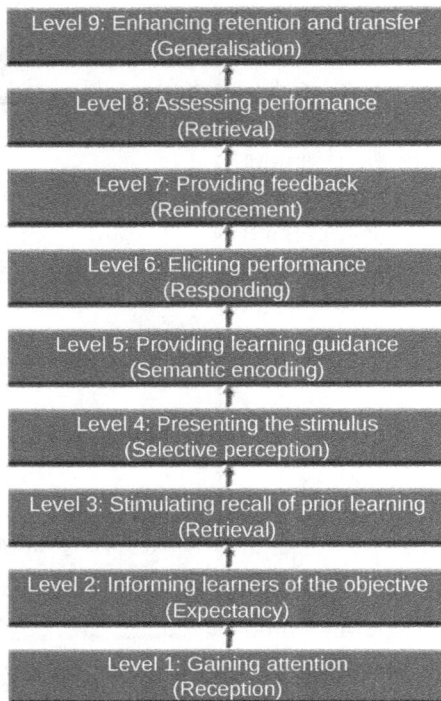

Figure 10.5: Gagne's nine levels of instruction (Mind Tools, nd)

10.5.1 Level 1: Gaining attention (reception)

For the learning process to begin and to help our learners to prepare for learning, it is very important that we gain the attention of our audience. As ALP designers, we can ask learners to complete pre-work ahead of attending a workshop or an instructor-led event. This pre-work can take the form of:

- Pre-reading
- Joining discussion forums, or
- Having them engage with SMEs.

This preparation phase is important as it builds enthusiasm and sets the tone for team work and collaboration.

As facilitators we also need to prepare the learning environment. We need to ensure that the room is set up to accommodate group work and that there is plenty of space to allow for activities and games, set up and test our audiovisual equipment, and so on. We also need to find ways in which to present the content that will grip the learners.

Attention grabbers

Some great examples that can be used are asking profound questions; telling a story; presenting shocking statistics; discussing fascinating photographs; or using an ice-breaker to encourage teamwork. I have in the past removed all tables from the room and placed the chairs randomly throughout the room. This gets the learners' attention and is a great way to observe how they respond. Feed these observations back to them later as part of the learning experience.

Worth reading: Ice Breakers Easing Group Contribution
http://www.mindtools.com/pages/article/newLDR_76

10.5.2 Level 2: Informing learners of the objective (expectancy)

It is always valuable to start the session by stating the learning objective upfront as we defined it in the "what" question. It is also important to link this to the broader context of the "what for" question which we answered earlier on. This is usually done in pre-workshop communication. It is always a good idea to ask learners why they think they are doing this learning and reaffirm this with the objectives in all material. Keep referring to the objectives as you complete one of them (if appropriate), as this also helps the learners to mark their progress.

Example: Learning journey chart

It is sometimes useful to use a visual learning journey wall chart and update it with the learners at the end of each section. The learners can add their own quotes and diagrams on the chart as a record of their learning. The chart can be recorded with a photograph at the end of the session and sent to all learners.

10.5.3 Level 3: Stimulating recall of prior learning (retrieval)

It is important when working with adults that you link what they are learning to any prior knowledge they may have about the topic. It is also important to find out what they have been exposed to before. This level also gives us an opportunity to connect with the learner. Engaging learners physically and emotionally is a distinguishing factor of an ALP. To make this connection, learners could be asked to use visual imagery, for example, tell the group about a leader who has inspired them; or ask them to draw something that represents good leadership to them and explain it to the rest of the group.

Also, when using a learning chain, it is important to review the previous learning in the teams before we proceed. This helps to cement the learners' thinking and provides an opportunity to clarify any misconceptions they may have. It is also important to ask people about their previous experiences relating to the topic and to allow them the opportunity to engage in dialogue around this. The role of the facilitator here is to link and connect what the learners discuss regarding their previous learning with what they are currently learning. You need to balance the needs within a group context as you will always get some people who have had more exposure than others. Ask them to share their experiences and help others with understanding.

CASE STUDY

Recall examples

A good way to do this is to ask each learning set to construct a mind-map of everything they know about a particular topic. In this way everyone is able to contribute regardless of his/her level of experience, but it also allows for those with the most experience to remain engaged.

The World Café technique is a very efficient way of sharing previous knowledge and team conversations as groups move around to different tables, while the host remains and shares previous highlights, insights and outcomes.

10.5.4 Level 4: Presenting the stimulus (selective perception)

When designing learning, organise the information into chunks to help with memory retrieval. Present the content in a way that is stimulating, easy to understand, builds on what the learners already know, and engages the whole brain through visual cues, verbal instruction and group dialogue.

In a classroom situation, be discerning when using PowerPoint presentations as learners generally switch off, especially if the facilitator is reading the slides. PowerPoint should be used only to highlight or reinforce key themes and ideas and should be as simple and as visual as possible. PowerPoint is not about putting a book on a slide.

With on-line learning, content should be provided in a user-friendly, colourful and engaging way, with choices as to how to engage with the content. Include articles, slide summaries, mind-maps, video-clips, a quiz, and even games (see Chapter 11 on *Gamification in learning*).

It is also useful to schedule learning pods and send these out to learners so they can work through content on their mobile devices in their own time.

With on-the-job learning, include activities such as interviews with SMEs, site visits, Internet searches, and observation of masters of their craft.

CASE STUDY

Framework example

A visual framework can be useful to outline the key elements of a topic, for example, a talent management framework. As each aspect is covered, it can be summarised and linked back to the visual framework.

10.5.5 Level 5: Providing learning guidance (semantic encoding)

Semantic encoding is the processing and encoding of sensory input that has particular meaning or can be applied to a specific context. The learning process needs to assist learners in integrating new information with existing knowledge or experiences (that is, to make it become meaningful) and encoding the information into their long-term memory so that they are able to recall it and apply it to a variety of contexts. (Information is held in short-term memory for about 20 to 30 seconds unless rehearsed.)

Following on from the principles of quantum or whole brain learning and those of neuroscience, as seen in Chapter 5, we know that it is important to present the information in as many different ways, using as many connections to it as possible. This will help the learner to build and strengthen the neural pathway to the information.

CASE STUDY

Semantic encoding examples

This can be done using many different methods. Chunking, visual images, symbols, mnemonics, and summaries are very effective. Other options include real-life examples, case studies, analogies, personal anecdotes, and story-telling. It is important for learners to have an opportunity to put the content "into their own words" through discussions or teaching others.

10.5.6 Level 6: Eliciting performance (responding)

This is one of the great benefits of adopting an accelerated approach. Because the programme involves a variety of learning methods and many points of contact with the learners, including close and intimate contact through the coaching process, we can immediately assess the learners' grasp of the information and their ability to use what they are learning. In addition, we are also quickly able to assess and address areas in which they are struggling and provide them with the support they need, either through the facilitator or through their team. By using activities such as role play or case studies, or by playing games or using a simulation, we are immediately able to determine the learners' level of competence and infer their ability to apply what they are learning in a real-world context. Another way we use is on-the-job observation.

Examples of eliciting performance

CASE STUDY

One of the ways in which we elicited performance on the Breakthrough Learning (BL) project (see the case study in Chapter 14) was through getting each learning set to present to the executive team. Prior to their presentations they did a dry-run presentation to their project team for feedback and tips for improvement.

10.5.7 Level 7: Providing feedback (reinforcement)

Immediate and continuous feedback is an important catalyst for learning. Learning should always be reinforced with a discussion in which the learner receives and provides immediate feedback regarding what has been observed and how this relates to the bigger context. A key consideration when designing a learning event is to ensure that you have included ample time for discussion, feedback and reflection, as it is here that knowledge is cemented. The most effective feedback is that which is specific, relevant, honest, and received immediately.

Example of feedback

CASE STUDY

A great example of this was the Foundations of Corporate Coaching online programme – hosted through Get Smarter for the University of Cape Town. Throughout this programme the learners were required to submit recordings of their practice coaching sessions each week which would then be made available to the other participants, who would later be invited to review and give feedback. This provided a great cycle of learning, not only through the feedback being received, but also through the insight gained in listening to how others completed the same assignment.

Table 10.1: Some feedback methods

Some feedback methods	
360° review	This is an opportunity to get feedback from your peers, the level above and the level below. Participants in an ALP would include: Leaders; facilitators, coaches, team members and yourself. Each 360° **review** should be based on a set of pre-defined questions or should concern rating performance based on set criteria and competencies.
Postbox	Each learner in the ALP has a folder in which he/she receives feedback from the group during each facilitated session. The learners are then given an opportunity at the end of the session to read through the feedback they have received and discuss this with their coach.
Observation-based	During the facilitated sessions and throughout the ALP, coaches observe the learners and provide them with feedback as immediately as possible.
Traffic light	Learners green-light (using a green highlighter) the work of their peers to indicate where the success criteria have been achieved, or amber-light (using a yellow highlighter) where improvement is needed. This strategy is best used on a work-in-progress, although it could also be used, with coloured sticky notes, to provide feedback on a final piece of work.

Giving feedback

- Make this a positive process.
- Do it as immediately as possible.
- Do it as regularly as possible.
- Back up with observed examples.
- Do not generalise.
- Do not criticise.
- Use an "I" statement.
- Provide alternatives that would teach the person a new skill: "I noticed in that situation that you did not make eye contact. Eye contact is very important to customers as it's a way of connecting with them. Do you think that next time you could try to make eye contact with your customers and hold their gaze for at least 5 seconds?"
- Be careful of sandwiching the constructive feedback as this may get lost.
- Give the person an opportunity to respond.

10.5.8 Level 8: Assessing performance (retrieval)

Assessment of learning is a complex and highly debated component of the learning journey and we have dedicated the entire next chapter to this. For us to say that learning has occurred, there must be a way in which we can measure this and ultimately assess whether learning has resulted in enhanced performance.

In an ALP it is very important that we continuously assess learning and build these assessment points into the learning chain. For example, we can use case studies or role play to gain an understanding of how well learners have understood and integrated the knowledge. We can then immediately give them feedback on this, which is seen as another form of assessment.

We can also use surveys, knowledge tests, competency assessments, observation and assignments. Assessment is so important that we have dedicated an entire chapter to this – see Chapter 12.

10.5.9 Level 9: Enhancing retention and transfer (generalisation)

For learning to be sustained and for the true benefit to be realised, learners must be able to apply what they have learnt too many different situations, particularly to the workplace (on the job). Transfer of learning is greatly enhanced through the use of coaching to support the learners and provide feedback during the application of their knowledge.

Retention is also enhanced through the use of a learning chain, as this encourages frequent revision, reinforcement, and assessment of learning.

CASE STUDY

Examples for learning transfer and retention

A variety of methods can be used here that are simple, quick and fun. You can ask learners to write a reflective blog or use a game that requires them to summarise the key information and how to apply this in a real-world context. You can send learners short articles or links to video-clips to remind them of what they have learnt. You can also provide them with a pocket-book or laminated card with key notes and diagrams. You can develop a friendly competition for learners to practise a new skill. Visual aids, such as screen savers, posters and desk gadgets, are also important.

At one company we rewarded each person who committed to the jointly-developed Leadership Principles a Bonsai tree. The analogy was made between leading people and nurturing a Bonsai. Bonsai trees are often very old and require daily watering and the right temperature to thrive – just as staff need daily attention, recognition and a culture conducive to learning and growth.

To increase motivation and engagement, remember to reward learners for their efforts. This could be as simple as giving them a mini prize – anything from a chocolate to a certificate. If you are a leader reading this, please remember to provide a generous budget for this!

Activity 1

Use the seven steps of programme planning to design a current learning experience (for an individual or group of learners):

Who?
Why?
When?
Where?
What?
What for?
How?

Share via e-mail or Facebook to level up.

Activity 2

Use the nine levels of programme design to outline how you will design a current learning experience (for an individual or group of learners).

Gain attention:
Inform of objective:
Stimulate recall:
Present stimulus:
Provide learning guidance:
Elicit performance:
Provide feedback:
Assess performance:
Enhance retention and transfer:

Share via e-mail or Facebook to level up.

10.6 METHODS AND TOOLS

Learning methods fall into three broad categories: formal learning, informal learning, and social learning. Much has already been written about these methods and it is not necessary to recap on these here. Instead, I would like to focus on how to draw from these methods and combine them to compile an effective ALP.

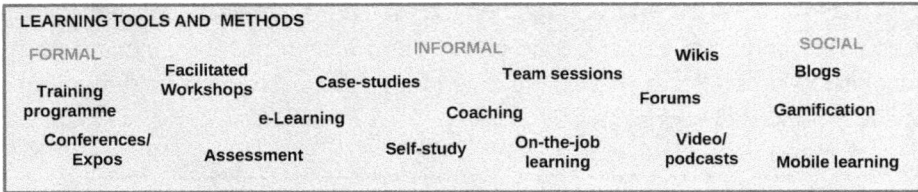

LEARNING TOOLS AND METHODS

| FORMAL | | INFORMAL | | | SOCIAL |

FORMAL

Training programme
Facilitated Workshops
Case-studies
Team sessions
Wikis
Blogs

e-Learning
Coaching
Forums
Gamification

Conferences/ Expos
Assessment
Self-study
On-the-job learning
Video/ podcasts
Mobile learning

Figure 10.6: Learning framework

A design combination for an accelerated learning programme should look something like this:

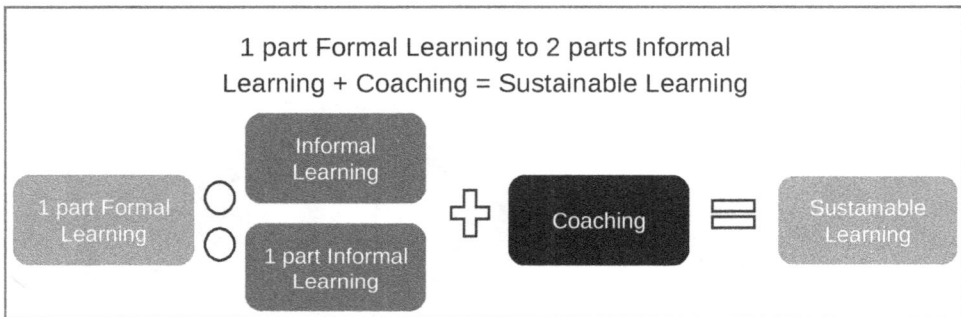

1 part Formal Learning to 2 parts Informal Learning + Coaching = Sustainable Learning

1 part Formal Learning

Informal Learning

1 part Informal Learning

Coaching

Sustainable Learning

Figure 10.7: Design combination for an accelerated learning programme

10.6.1 Formal learning

A formal learning component (learning that takes place within a facilitated or instructor-led manner) is essential for introducing learners to the content and helping them to understand what they should be able to do after the learning. In other words, it outlines the learning objectives and introduces the learners to the content. This component of the accelerated learning programme formula could be either replaced by or supplemented with a self-paced e-learning component. An e-learning component provides many benefits, the biggest being increased numbers at a reduced cost.

Some other methods include classroom training, facilitated workshops, conference presentations, and assessments.

10.6.2 Informal learning

Informal learning occurs through the experience of day-to-day situations and through our interactions with one another. Organisations often fail to pay attention to the importance of the role it plays and thereby do not realise, enable, or use this to its full potential. It is this informal learning component that sets an ALP apart.

Two key tools for this informal component are the Learning Set or group of learners and what is referred to as Learning 2.0 or Web 2.0.

Additional methods of informal learning that can be used are self-study, coaching, on-the-job, team sessions, community of practice, and so on.

Watch this video on YouTube: **What is informal learning?**
http://www.youtube.com/watch?v=qgVd0R2-O4E

The learning set

The word "set" refers to the group of learners who have been grouped together for the purpose of solving a real business challenge within a realistic timeframe. Throughout this group's life span, they come together formally to learn content that will enable them to generate better solutions to the business problems they are trying to solve.

The learning that takes place is highly social and informal in nature, as members of the group interact with one another and with experts external to the group. Learners are able to draw on and learn from one another's prior experience and are automatically engaged in whole brain learning. It is through this level of social engagement and engrossment in problem solving that real learning takes place. Each member of this learning set is important and must commit to the group. They are there to support each other, make equal contributions, and hold each other accountable. It is through this level of social engagement and engrossment in problem solving (repetition) that real learning takes place.

10.6.3 Social learning or Web 2.0

Social learning refers to the use of Web 2.0 technologies in the learning process to promote collaboration or "social" learning. Examples of this include wikis, forums, podcasts, blogs, mobile learning, user-generated content, and, of course, the latest method, gamification, as covered in Chapter 11.

Web 2.0

Web 2.0 is a vehicle that can be used to drive informal learning. It refers to a collection of technologies that enable users to generate content, interact with this content, and collaborate with each other. Although this may still seem a new and foreign way of interacting to older generations within the workplace, younger generations cannot imagine a world without such interactions. They learn in this way, anyway. Their mobile devices are seen as extensions of themselves.

One key way in which Web 2.0 can enable learning is through the establishment of social networks. Social networking refers to individuals forming online learning communities in order to collaborate, network and co-create. Being part of a social network organised around a particular topic provides learners with the opportunity to discuss, critique and share information on the particular learning topic. It also provides a platform for them to engage with others at varying levels of experience, allows them direct access to knowledge experts, and provides a support forum in cases where they are struggling.

Web 2.0 methods also allow the learners to tap into subject matter experts. SMEs could post blogs or podcasts to share their knowledge and experience of a particular topic. Learners could then comment, ask follow-up questions, and start discussion groups or forums. Another way in which we could encourage learning and sharing of information is to get our key SMEs to have "public" (blog, podcast, and so on) discussions with each other. You can also set up group blogs among the learners themselves as a great tool for them to share tips, tricks, and live experiences. As learning practitioners or leaders, we could initiate discussions on particular topics by using our blogs to drive conversations. ASTD (ATD) provides excellent examples of this. They host several blogs spanning a number of topics, providing a platform for experts and newcomers to collaborate and discuss various topics.

Worth reading: Blending Web 2.0 Technologies with Traditional Formal Learning
http://www.trainingindustry.com/media/2122678/element%20k%20-%20blending%20web%2020%20technologies%20with%20traditional%20formal%20learning.pdfforum

Watch this video on YouTube: **Informal Learning in a Web 2.0 World: Making Social Media Work**
http://www.youtube.com/watch?v=Gi5RXjtvPW8

10.6.4 New trends in learning methods and tools

There are a number of newer methods becoming more popular in the learning space to accelerate personal insight and change, group-based learning, and organisational learning and transformation.

There is definitely a trend towards organisations realising that change starts with individuals and that in order for people to change, they need a deeper level of self-awareness and self-insight as well as support for discovering more about their purpose and passions, what motivates them, what their strengths are, and connecting with their impact on and contribution to others and the organisation. While these very personal aspects of life were often left for individuals to explore in their own time and at their own cost, it is becoming more common for organisations to encourage (sometimes coerce) their staff to participate in personal and leadership development initiatives that create the space for self-discovery and self-actualisation. Some of the methods and tools we have witnessed include self-reflection and journalling; mindfulness practices; neuroscience of leadership; strengths identification; wheel of life; purpose discovery activities; building personal brand; psychometric assessments; feedback activities; life coaching; NLP techniques; gratitude journaling; and wellness optimisation, among others.

Another trend we see is the acknowledgement that people are social beings and are both influenced by and influence the social interaction and energy of the "group". More and more we see organisations investing in team-development or team-alignment sessions, which have moved away from the superficial team-building activities of the past towards more meaningful conversations. There is a greater appetite for reviewing team effectiveness, constructive individual and team feedback, sharing personal aspirations and pet peeves, telling life and leadership stories, and unpacking the elements of high-performance, high-engagement teams with an attitude of continuous improvement. Some of the methods and tools we have witnessed include team-purpose activities; team-effectiveness surveys; individual and team strengths-sharing and implications; team personality and roles; team authentic conversations (dead-cat topics); individual and feedback activities; team coaching; affirmative inquiry in teams; and energy optimisation strategies, among others.

At an organisational level, there is also a trend towards deeper and more meaningful engagement with staff, recognising them as individuals with a voice, and encouraging participation in various transformation programmes such as culture transformation or strategy, structure or systems change. More positive, systemic and whole-person approaches are being used for engagement. Some of the methods and tools we have witnessed include organisational effectiveness surveys; organisation purpose; alignment of personal, team and organisational values; affirmative inquiry; World Café sessions; rewriting the narrative of our past, present and future stories; social blogging and forums; deep democracy; executive visioning sessions; and staff energy and wellness strategies

For more information on some of these methods and tools, see Table 10.2 below.

Table 10.2: New trends in learning methods

Method	Description	Link
Strengths approach	• Strengths are our natural repetitive patterns of thoughts, feelings, or behaviours that we can harness to improve our productivity. • In order to help people uncover their talents, Gallup introduced the StrengthsFinder online assessment. • The Centre for Applied Positive Psychology (CAPP) has a great strengths tool, Realise2, which is available online. • There are also plenty of free strength tests – see the link in the next column.	https://www.gallup-strengthscenter.com/?g-clid=CO6hw6K1p78CFe-jHtAod6QMARg http://www.cappeu.com/realise2.aspx **Free test:** http://freestrengthstest.workuno.com/free-strengths-test.html
Appreciative inquiry	This is an approach to problem solving that requires a shift to a positive perspective, to look at the things that are working, and then build on them. Focusing on what is working in the present situation allows us to discover what strengths we can use to effect positive changes. A good summary and application techniques are available through Mind Tools – see the link in the next column.	http://www.mindtools.com/pages/article/newTMC_85.htm

Method	Description	Link
World Café	**World Café** is a process whereby groups enter into structured conversations. Different topics are covered by each table and people move from table to table to hold structured conversations around each topic. Each table is hosted by a table host who is responsible for introducing the topic and providing the conversation structure.	http://www.theworldcafe.com/method.html
Deep democracy	This is a method of facilitation for groups that allows for every voice to be heard but at a level deeper than just the exchange of ideas. The methodology brings to the surface individual emotions and values, and uses this to enrich the group process.	http://deep-democracy.net/
The U process	This method is a leadership development method aimed at reconnecting leaders to the inner source from which they operate to help them re-imagine the future. The process consists of five movements: • CO-INITIATING: Build common intent. Stop and listen to others and to what life calls you to do. • CO-SENSING: Observe, observe, observe. Go to the places of most potential and listen with your mind and heart wide open. • PRESENCING: Connect to the source of inspiration, and you will go to the place of silence and allow the inner knowing to emerge. • CO-CREATING: Make a prototype of what is new in living examples o that you can explore the future by doing. • CO-EVOLVING: Embody the new in ecosystems that facilitate seeing and acting from the whole.	http://www.ottoscharmer.com/publications/summaries.php

Method	Description	Link
Gestalt	From the Gestalt perspective, learning is placed at the centre of life and all learning is seen to be experiential. Followers of Gestalt adopt an existentialist viewpoint, promoting learner self-direction and autonomy. This view of the learner as autonomous and self-directed should influence learning design. Therefore, learning must be designed to give the learners choices around what they want to learn, where they will learn it, what method suits them best, and so on.	http://www.mgestaltc. force9.co.uk/a_gestalt_approach_to_learning.htm
The narrative method	This is an interpretative approach to learning and involves using storytelling methodology. The story becomes a vehicle to understand the way in which our learners experience the world, and contextualise what they have learnt within this world.	http://usablelearning.com/about/presentations/narrative-techniques-for-learning/
Reflective practice	This is a process in which learners engage in analysis of what they have learnt, how they have applied it, what they could do to improve, or what else they still need to learn about a particular topic. This level of critical analysis helps learners to generate new knowledge and ideas and is a powerful way to change behaviour.	http://www.csp.org.uk/faqs/cpd/what-reflective-practice-how-do-i-do-it

10.7 CONCLUSION

In summary, as learning practitioners in this day and age, we have many tools and methods at our disposal, and by using the principles of ALP designing, learning design can be a fun-filled, creative process able to yield great returns on investment. This is especially true if you involve leaders and learners in the process.

CHAPTER 11

GAMIFICATION IN LEARNING

By Darryn van den Berg

11.1 WHAT IS GAMIFICATION?

"In ev'ry job that must be done
There is an element of fun
You find the fun ... and Snap!
The job's a game." – Mary Poppins

"Gamification" is the latest "buzz word" that is taking the corporate world by storm – and it is here to stay!

The word "gamification" was coined in 2002 by Nick Pelling (2014) – although it really started to gain momentum only in 2007, after Rajat Paharia (predominantly recognised as the father of gamification) created the "gamification industry" (Paharia, 2014).

UK Department for Work and Pensions

James Gardner, who was chief technology officer for the UK Department for Work and Pensions (DWP), saved up to $41 million by letting employees send and discuss ideas to improve their work environments

Through a virtual trading platform, British civil servants could buy and sell stock in new ideas with a virtual currency. Civil servants turned ideation into real cost savings. Those who posted comments and helped execute change could accrue more points, and were even rewarded through promotions.

In less than nine months, the DWP incurred about $41 million in hard savings by innovating its business processes, Gardner says. "The [employees] found motivation through games we were playing to submit new ideas for change and actually execute new ideas, and the money just added up over time".

(Gardner, 2010)

There are MANY definitions for "gamification". However, we define gamification as follows:

> *"Gamification uses the stuff that makes play fun and irresistible and applies these measurably into non-game contexts. Engaging 'players' through Feedback, FUN and Friends." – www.p4d.co.za*

So gamification is NOT a game – and has to do with the lessons learned from game designers, totally underwritten by game design principles, and of course is still used in game design. It has now leaked into the business, medical, ecological, health, and learning and development worlds.

What our definition means is that the mechanics, dynamic, elements and foundations of games have been studied and measured, and are now applied across different industries and strategies to increase engagement, change behaviour or simply enhance solutions through people. Gamification should be viewed as an overlay to enhance a current strategy or process. It is not a standalone tool for business or pleasure.

Aspects of gamification have been around for many years and some of the principles originate from long-established practices. The military have had the concept of badges, rank and medals to show progress or achievement for thousands of years. The Boy Scouts, while not as old as the military, have a similar concept. The original concept of the artisanal trades embodied progression through ranking as a means to encourage continuously developing skills from apprentice, to journeyman, to master.

Gamification brings these aspects of measuring progress and achievement into everyday learning and business practices.

> *"If the Game you play becomes boring, it needs Gamification to overlay it to make it more engaging." – Morgan Tinline*

11.2 FOUNDATION PRINCIPLES DRIVING THE SUCCESS OF GAMIFICATION

Some of the psychology and research underpinning gamification comes from theories such as FLOW or the psychology of optimal experience: what motivates us, how we are conditioned through rewards, and the benefits of play. These are described below.

11.2.1 Flow

Flow is the Psychology of Optimal Experience derived by Csíkszentmihályi (2008). He suggests that people are happiest when they are in a state of "flow" concentration or complete absorption with the activity with which they are involved. "It is a state in which people are so involved in an activity that nothing else seems to matter." The Millennials (also known as Gen Y or those born from about 1980 to 2000) tend to say *"in the zone"* or *"catching my groove".* This state *of "intrinsic motivation"* is where people do whatever they choose, with no other reason than they totally want to – what they are "doing" IS the reward. If you can achieve a continued "flow" experience during learning and development initiatives, change management projects, or any other activity (personal and business), you can expect to experience optimised absorption, engagement, fulfilment, and skill, which in and of itself will accelerate learning.

"Flow" can be achieved only during the engagement of "active" activities. Passive activities, such as taking a bath or watching TV, usually **do not** elicit flow experiences, as individuals are not actively involved from a whole person perspective" (Csíkszentmihályi, 2008).

I believe that in the near future, "Flow" will be achieved watching TV through a greater opportunity to engage while watching. Research conducted by Yahoo shows that already 41 percent of people reported posting on Facebook while watching TV (Gaming admin, 2012). In the recent MTNAPPAWARDS (2014), we saw that the DSTV application that allows you to review, learn, engage and watch the sport that is being shown live on air enables the consumer to be more engaged in the game.

In learning, adapting the Csíkszentmihályi model, we build on the three conditions that have to be met to achieve a "flow state":

1. Learners must be involved in an activity with a clear set of goals and progress. The direction will add structure to the task, whatever it may be, and provide an opportunity for the learner to find their own method of achieving.
2. The task at hand must have clear and immediate feedback. This will enable the learners to negotiate any changing demands immediately, consider the feedback and then adjust their performance accordingly to remain in the state of flow.
3. Learners must have a good balance between the perceived challenges of the task at hand and their own perceived skills. This is most simply achieved through a simple assessment of some kind. They must have confidence in their ability to complete the task at hand.

In a recent accelerated learning experience, we provided feedback to the learners on a fun and engaging task. What we experienced was that the feedback we provided to the learners achieved what we were trying to achieve, but did not align to the feedback they were expecting to receive. This caused many of them to move OUT of a state of flow. The missing ingredient was more effective on-boarding to clarify the set of goals.

So what does "Staying in the state of FLOW" look like? Figure 11.1 is an adaptation of Csíkszentmihályi's "eight flow states", and is a simple visual depiction of what Flow is. The challenge to be mastered (*y*-axis), as set by the company, must be proportionately challenging to the *x*-axis which shows the skills or ability of the learner to remain engaged at completing the specific task.

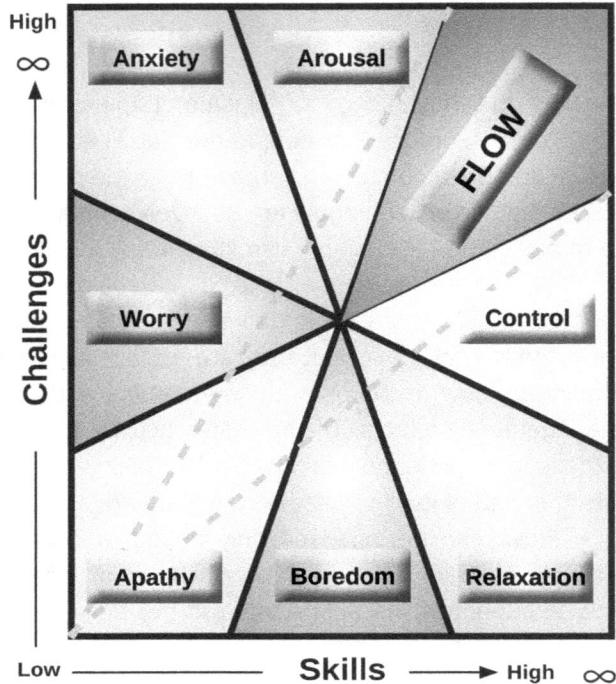

Figure 11.1 FLOW: The eight flow states (adapted from Csíkszentmihályi)

As the "challenge" increases in difficulty/complexity, so provision must be made for the learner to develop skills and abilities.

This is a foundation required to successfully achieve Accelerated Learning. Increased Fluid Intelligence, (which we define as: *the ability to identify patterns and relationships to novel and complex challenges, then find or access information from many different sources, assimilate that information and the apply it to achieve innovative solutions)* of the learners, progressing at their own pace, in their own way for their own reasons, is most often the result of a well-designed FLOW process.

Each of the eight different states demonstrated in Figure 11.1 is caused when either the skills or abilities progress too quickly for the challenge, *or* the challenge is too difficult for the current skills and abilities. The goal is to remain within the two orange dashed lines – in our experience this yields the most effective performance and direction for coaches or mentors to work with the learner in achieving their career/training programme goals. Gamification optimises the FLOW experience through the process of levelling up, and by gradually increasing the difficulty of the task as the skill level increases. When building a gamification strategy, elements such as on-boarding, different levels, and choice to play is so important, as it takes flow into consideration.

"We believe that a person can remain in a state of 'flow' from the first engagement with your specific challenge – if you design well, with forward thinking" (Zichermann & Linder, 2013).

Activity 1: Where are you in the flow?

The purpose of this activity is to practise ascertaining where you are in relation to the flow. Once you know this, you will be able to decide whether to get back into the Flow or remain in the Flow.

Take any activity that you are currently engaged in (workplace project, sports game, video game). Read through the "Flow Measures" and their descriptions in the table below.

1. "Challenge": After reading through the descriptors, select the one you feel best describes the *current* challenge of the activity.
2. "Skills factor": After reading through the descriptors, select the one you feel best describes your *current* skills in regard to the challenge.
3. Using the numbers that you rated yourself, plot yourself in the FLOW table below (as a grid) and then see where you are placed.

For example, if you rated yourself a 3 for challenge and a 9 for skills, you will plot yourself in the "Green Relaxation" diamond.

The optimum place to be is between the dashed lines. That shows you are in "FLOW". If you are outside these lines, see what you can do to up the challenge or the skills level. If you need some help with ideas, join the Gamification journey and get access to chat to the authors: visit http://goo.gl/YGwOFH

Share via e-mail or Facebook to level up.

Flow measure	0–3	3–6	6–9	9–up
Challenge	I mastered this long ago, and there is no growth in sight.	The challenge is not bad, but I already have the solutions and now I just need time to complete.	The challenge is great. It is causing me to think, and I am still pondering solutions.	The challenge is HUGE. I have NO idea at the moment where to start.
Skills factor	I have never been able to do this, and I have NO clue where to start.	I have done something similar to this before a while ago. I think I can hack this one.	This is great – I've done it before and I can get the task done quickly. I'm really good at this.	This is SO do-able, and if I get stuck I know where to look or who to call without a challenge.

Example of flow

When conducting a 4-day training programme for a public group, Passion4Development ensured that all the learners were mapping their "Flow" positioning for each outcome. Based on the results from previous courses, the productivity of the learners during the training increased 10-fold measured against the learner completing different self-tasks and learning application results.

When any of the learners were moving out of their "flow" they started to pair up or form groups *during* the facilitation. Those whose skills were exceeding the challenge started to assist those who were becoming anxious.

What was unexpected was the successful increase in post-course work, as people left the training on day 4 in their "flow".

(Passion4Development: http://www.p4d.co.za)

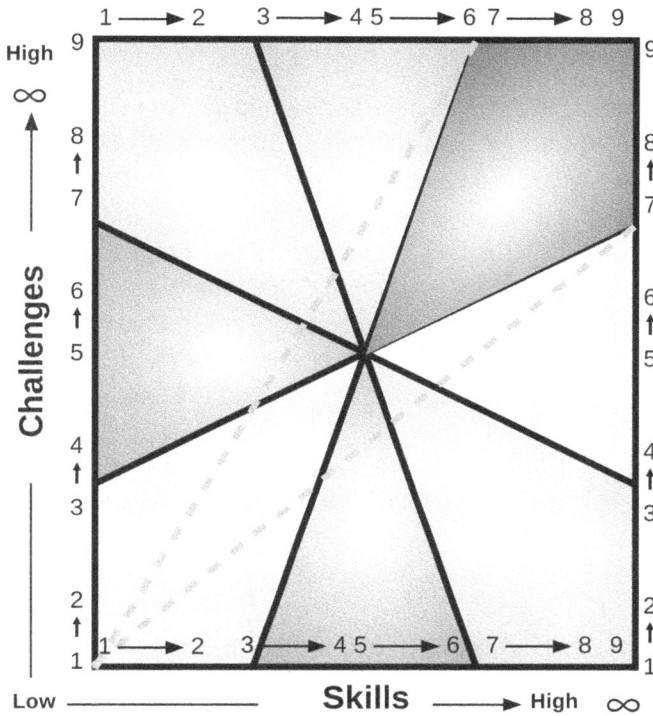

Figure 11.2: Where you "flow"

11.2.2 Motivation

To build on the foundation of WHY to use gamification, there is a need to discuss motivation. In his book *The Surprising Truth about What Motivates Us: Drive*, Daniel Pink (2011) defines motivation as "the driving force that causes the flux from desire to will in life". The fundamental underlying reason for building or applying gamification strategies should be to increase the motivation of your target population (what we call players) to willingly change a behaviour and engage with you. "We have found the following combination of **key factors** are what contribute to motivation and ultimately lead to engagement and change in behaviour" (Paharia, 2013; Pink, 2011).

1. **Autonomy**: I get to choose – to "opt in"
2. **Challenge**: Progression – the experience, feelings, and overall well-being as a result of challenging successes
3. **Mastery:** Overall success in an individual
4. **Achievement**: Progression in work orientation, endurance, cognitive structure, order, play, and low impulsivity

5. **Purpose**: Being a part of a bigger picture – or something that is larger than me.

Of course, the more these key factors are applied in the building or application of a gamification strategy, the greater the chance of motivational increase and success in behaviour change you will have.

There are MANY motivational theories that all give great insight and guidance on what motivation is. We have elected to talk through the "self-determination theory" (SDT), devised by Deci and Ryan (1995), as this is linked more closely to the level and progressive nature of gamification. This theory focuses on the degree to which an individual's behaviour is self-motivated and self-determined. SDT identifies three innate needs that must be satisfied to experience optimal function:

1. **Competence** – Knowledge + understanding, skills and desire
2. **Relatedness** – What I am doing relates my state of being and enhances my desires
3. **Autonomy** – I get to choose when and how I can do what I WANT to do

Positive consequences are experienced with the satisfaction of these needs, such as well-being and growth. These typically increase people's motivation to learn, and apply their abilities to the different tasks. This theory suggests that we are inherently proactive with the potential and desire to master our drive and emotions, that we have an in-built tendency to improvement, grow, and integrate development and community-based functioning.

Figure 11.3, illustrating Self-determination Theory, shows the relationship between autonomy and motivation through the lenses of extrinsic (external) or intrinsic (internal) motivation. Intrinsic motivation is the natural, inherent drive to seek out challenges and new possibilities and associates with cognitive and social development. To move people to Intrinsic towards your "quest" (or task set) in your gamification strategy is the optimum success to achieve. Extrinsic motivation, has varying degrees of autonomy, from externally regulated behaviour such as: "I do it because my boss told me to" to integrated regulation: "I WANT to do it, but I need a push to keep the task alive, such as a gym buddy."

As learning specialists and leaders, we are primarily interested in how to build intrinsic motivation opportunities into learning as well as the work place, as it is more sustainable (and less costly) over time. This then leads to the question: "HOW should we alter the current learning offerings to enable an accelerated approach?" The key focus is to enable the access to correct information at just the right time for the correct reason, and to achieve the most desired result.

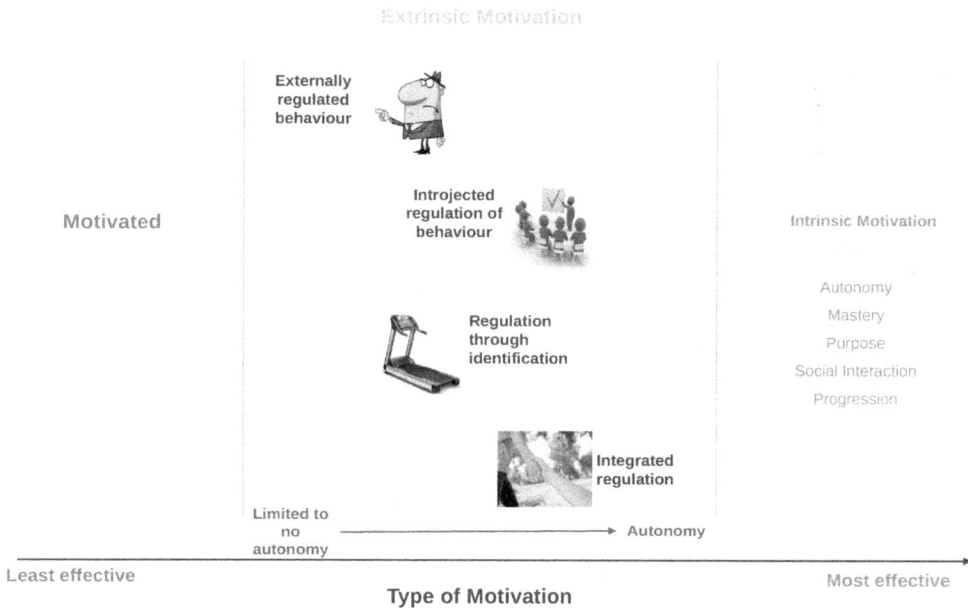

Figure 11.3: Self-determination Theory

When we applied accelerated learning methodologies with a gamification overlay in a recent workshop, there were two surprising outcomes:

1. The learners accelerated their learning in a direction that was not expected.
2. The accelerated learning self-driven opportunity increased anxiety with the learners, as the rules and direction to learning was not stringent but the engagement was what we wanted to achieve.

Gamification focuses on optimising the motivational elements of autonomy, mastery, purpose, social interaction and progression to engage learners over the course of the learning programme.

11.2.3 Operant conditioning

BF Skinner (1938) coined the term "operant conditioning" which, roughly translated, means the changing of behaviour by the use of reinforcement, given after the desired response is achieved. The principle for learning is that an individual's behaviour can be influenced and modified by both rewarding or unpleasant experiences and potential consequences. Skinner identified three types of responses or operant conditions that can follow behaviour, as shown in Table 11.1.

Table 11.1: Operant conditioning (adapted from Skinner, 1938)

Neutral	Responses from the environment that neither increase nor decrease the probability of a behaviour being repeated
Reinforcers	Responses from the environment that increase the probability of a behaviour being repeated. Reinforcers can be either positive or negative
Punishers	Responses from the environment that decrease the likelihood of a behaviour being repeated. Punishment weakens behaviour

These responses can be incorporated into the design of learning programmes and gamification strategies in order to influence learners into practising new behaviours or skills. Designers must be aware that the effectiveness of the rewards/consequences will depend on the schedule of response as well as the variable nature of the response.

Table 11.2 below gives examples of different approaches and their impact on engagement.

Table 11.2: Approach impacts on engagement (adapted from Skinner, 1938)

Type of interval	Defined	Impact on engagement	Example
Fixed interval	Every X minutes, reward the user with the same reward (or similar)	High impact at the beginning. Quickly becomes predictable and ultimately boring. Disengagement ensues.	1 loyalty point for every ZAR 10.00 I spend every time I go and buy from the shop.
Variable interval	Randomly reward the user with the same reward (to make it "fair"), but with an average interval of X minutes	Impact and sustainability increases slightly on the fixed interval. However, if the reward remains predictable, it leads to boredom and ultimately disengaging behaviour is experienced.	The reward is always a bag of oranges. These are given to the 13th, 19th, and 29th consumers.

Type of interval	Defined	Impact on engagement	Example
Fixed ratio	After every X responses from the user, reward him/her	This is great to encourage community engagement and enhance team interaction. It can also assist in encouraging respondents to complete surveys. If the reward is not altered sufficiently, the fixed ratio schedule will lose the critical mass.	When applying a company culture survey, every time the department increases their completion of survey by 20% they are rewarded.
Variable ratio	Randomly reward the user, with an average of X responses to trigger the reward	The ultimate addictive behaviour schedule. I know I am going to win!! I just don't know WHEN or WHAT. The challenge with this is that if the reward does not change – that is, it is always money- or commodity-based – you will engage fewer players.	Slot machine and casino tables.

A number of factors will impact on the decision of when to reinforce a behaviour. In cases where you are specifically trying to teach a new behaviour, it is important to consider a **continuous schedule**. Once the behaviour has been learnt, switching to a partial schedule is often preferable.

Realistically, reinforcing behaviour every single time it occurs is difficult, and a well-designed engagement system will be necessary. These are often expensive to design or subscribe to. Partial schedules tend to lead to behaviour that is more resistant to extinction as well as reducing the risk of satisfaction and leading to boredom. If the reinforcer being used is no longer desired or rewarding, the players tend to stop performing as desired. (Consider the 13th cheque and pay raise scenario. Just before these are provided, productivity increases; just after, many people resign and productivity decreases again.)

Think about the current loyalty programme of your company (or any other loyalty programme of which you may be a member). Which of the operant condition intervals do YOU offer and what are the results?

Gamification utilises the power of operant conditioning by combining the above strategies to engage learners' attention and keep them coming back for more with a combination of regular, random and surprise rewards and unpleasant consequences for failure.

11.2.4 Play and fun

Play is as important to the brain as sleep in terms of creativity, memory and productivity. Michael Shore in his discussion on What Is Fun? (2010) defines ten expressions relating to fun (the things that people would say when they encounter fun). From the research, these are defined in order of what people rated as important:

1. **I'm free:** Liberation (unstructured voluntary activity, limited constraints and living in the moment)
2. **I dream:** Imagination and pretending. Possibilities and make-believe. Great for strategy and ideation
3. **I'm special:** I have just received the most insanely brilliant new (thing) and I am SO lucky!! (For example, I won the lottery.)
4. **I belong:** I am part of a bigger purpose – I'm not alone. This ties into the "Purpose" motivation
5. **I'm wacky:** I create delight for myself and others – and sometimes look a little … out there
6. **I know:** I am a learner and have taught this to myself! I have gained mastery and a sense of control and accomplishment
7. **I'm cosy:** Kicking back, relaxing, sitting around – letting my brain rest and rejuvenate
8. **I'm proud:** I have a feeling of beneficence – I have done well, I have achieved, I am the best performer, or have beaten my best achievement
9. **I stand out:** Theatrical play, self-expression, performing, creative, customisation, passion
10. **I dare:** This is where we show our bravery to the group, gaining acceptance and being seen as leaders – this is often how innovation happens, because we are breaking the rules!

Gamification weaves many elements of play and fun into the learning experience through a combination of choice, imagination, creativity, story-telling, social interaction, scoring and prizes, public status, challenge levels, and pride.

Brain Break: Take a break and play a game on your mobile, such as Angry Birds or Sniper S.

11.3 BUILDING A GAMIFICATION STRATEGY

So how do we apply gamification in order to accelerate learning? Gamification is not a learning strategy *per se*, but an enhancement to the learning experience for greater engagement and retention of learning. It is ultimately about enhancing the business strategy or increasing productivity or empowering learners to increase their competence in any way they see as having an impact on them.

The above discussions on the different motivation patterns and psychology are vital to understand when building your gamification strategy. As discussed in Chapter 10, you first need to understand **who** the learners (players) are, **what** and **why** they need to learn (skill or behaviour change), and then to decide IF a gamification will enhance the **how** of your design. Gamification is often associated with technology. However, many low-tech gamification techniques have added massive value to learning programmes over the years. (See the Monica Cornetti Pirate Game later in this chapter.)

A good gamification strategy will enhance what Martin Seligman coined as PERMA (2012):

P – positive emotion
E – engagement/flow
R – relationship
M – meaning
A – accomplishment.

When you achieve PERMA, you will find that gamification is not only about having fun, but about experiencing positive emotions, such as enhancing the feeling of discovery, or enhancing the feeling of security and safety.

As part of experiencing positive emotion, there is a need for "engagement loops". These are actions that occur in response to an action that a "player" has made.

They encourage further engagement through providing feedback to HOW the activity has been achieved, prompting the next

Microsoft

CASE STUDY

Microsoft obtained 16 times more feedback through its Communicate Hope gamified system, which aided the development of Microsoft's Office Communicator (now known as Lync). The goal was to get users to provide feedback on the product design and usability and to submit bugs.

The leader board was linked to five charities, and Microsoft's contributions to those charities was tied to the game results. Microsoft got 16 times more feedback from people playing the game than from those not playing the game, and tens of thousands of dollars went to the charities.

Communicate Hope worked at both ends of the testing process, as it had a second component that rewarded the test team members if they responded quickly to feedback (taking them away from their usual focus of recording and fixing bugs).

(Microsoft, 2010)

step as the level up occurs or an "unlock" is achieved. One of the keys to your successful gamification implementation is the application of engagement loops – remember:

"If the players do not see it, it did not happen." – Amy Jo Kim (2012)

11.3.1 Player types

For whom, then, are you actually building your gamification strategy? We call them your players (Bartle, 1996), also referred to as stakeholders.

Figure 11.4, below, is a quadrant that helps to define the different types of players who will engage with your gamification strategy, and more importantly, explains HOW they will most likely engage with your strategy.

The quadrant is an adaptation from the Amy Jo Kim player types model (2012) and is built on the *x*-axis of Acting and Interacting, and the *y*-axis of Content and People.

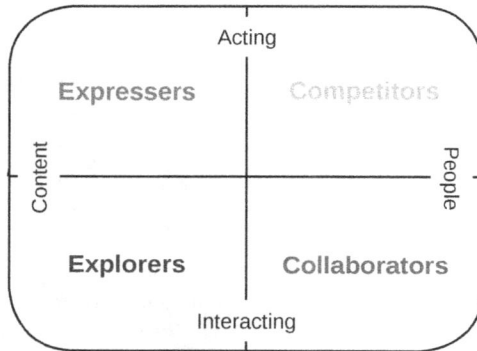

Figure 11.4: Player types (adapted from Kim, 2012)

Sun International SA

CASE STUDY

Colin Carmody, the training manager of Boardwalk Casino in Port Elizabeth in South Africa, started by including three gamification mechanics in his induction programme for scheduling.

Colin says: "Being responsible for ensuring that all SI employees as well as contractor staff attend our combined induction has been challenging. On average we were struggling to get 20 people per month onto an induction course.

"After we had applied the three mechanics, we had five hundred applications in the first 10 days. We are now rolling out the induction and measuring the increased impact and engagement, thanks to gamification".

(Carmody, 2014)

Basic descriptions of the players are shown in Table 11.3, below.

Table 11.3: Descriptions of the player types (adapted from Kim, 2012)

Expressers	These are people who enjoy acting on content. They enjoy expressing themselves through writing or commenting on content, drawing pictures, changing the look and feel of a page, being in control of what they want the world to see them as.
Competitors	The players are engaged by acting on people. They like to win – and they do not just want to win, but to be seen winning by all their friends and social groups.
Explorers	These are players who enjoy interacting on content. They want to research and explore different thinking, ideas, papers. They are not really fussed about connecting with people, as long as they feel safe and are finding out new information.
Collaborators	These players NEED people. They want to have friends around them, platforms for boasting, sharing, chatting, bouncing ideas of. They interact with people. They really enjoy the time spent engaging with others to improve themselves or just to have fun

We can individually be any of the four player types depending on the environment, culture, and mood we are in. However, research suggests that we will predominantly lean toward or express one of these types more frequently (and with more passion) than the others.

Activity 2: What type of a player are you?

From the list below tick the word/s that speak to you the most and total up the number of words ticked in each row.

Place the number from Row one into the Competitor Square of the quadrant.
Place the number from Row two into the Collaborator Square of the quadrant.
Place the number from Row one into the Explorer Square of the quadrant.
Place the number from Row one into the Expresser Square of the quadrant.

The quadrant with the highest number will give you a high-level indication of what type of player you are, or you may have a balanced spread across the different types.

Share via e-mail or Facebook to level up.

1	Win, beat, brag, World of Warcraft, taunt, challenge, monopoly, fight, poke, pass, grand theft auto, rankings
2	Join, Facebook, share, help, gift, greet, exchange, Twitter, trade, WhatsApp, chat, like, visit, crowd, hi five
3	View, read, research, collect, Slide share, curate, complete, LinkedIn, delve, unpack, review, treasure hunters
4	Choose, Pinterest, customer, design, layout, Instagram, dress up, show off, scrapbooking

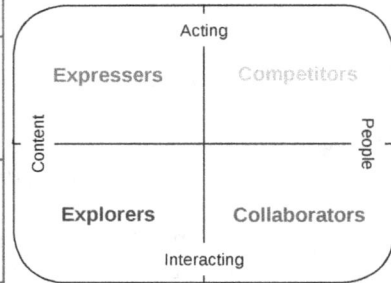

When designing your gamification strategy for learning, make sure you create activities and options for each of the four types to ensure that you engage them all.

11.3.2 Engagement

The key concepts to focus on to increase and sustain engagement are feedback, friends and fun.

Feedback: Applied as engagement loops, this is a response to how the "player" is achieving the standard – and is received in a VERY short amount of time. It is vital that feedback happens immediately (or as close to immediately) after the event has occurred. Think about what happens if you draw cash from an ATM: you receive an immediate short message (SMS). If the "player" does not receive immediate feedback on their performance of the task at hand, they will soon disengage from the strategy, and boredom with your product will set in (they will move out of the "flow"). When you build your engagement strategy, research and explore as many different feedback mechanics as possible.

When we conduct our gamification workshops, one of the feedback mechanisms that we use is Skype. It makes a "whoop" beep every time someone posts. This tells them that they have posted as well as reminding others to post on Skype.

Friends: We live in a social revolution that has fundamentally changed the way in which we interact with friends and "strangers". People want to be seen, to feel they belong, and to be part of something bigger than they are. Here are some of the staggering statistics in terms of *what happens in an Inter-+net minute (Intel)*:

- 204 million emails are sent.
- 100 new LinkedIn accounts are created.

- 20 million photos are viewed on flickr; 3 000 photos are uploaded.
- 320 new Twitter accounts are created; 100 000 new tweets are sent.
- 277 000 Facebook logins; 6 million Facebook views.
- 72 hours of video are uploaded to YouTube; 1.3 million videos are viewed.

(Domo, nd).

These statistics reflect the fundamental human need for friends and connections. People do what others are doing, and will engage where others are engaging. It is one of the reasons Facebook continues to do so well. In your process or strategy, if people start to drop off and disengage, it is time to review and change – and quickly. What others get wind of in terms of trending, they will follow suit. It is important to see the "popular kids" liking what you are doing. Most of history's revolutions, democracies and best places to stay were achieved when a group of like-minded "friends" came together with a common cause.

Fun: Zichermann and Linder (2010) say: "Fun is the new power metric! Increasingly consumers care about FUN." Fun is the enticing factor which value is growing as a currency which consumers expect in their product and services. A fun place to work is not just for the employees of an organisation; it's for the people running the organisation as well. It is no longer an option for a business to ignore fun. A business that believes that "work is for work" and "play is for play" and that the two cannot mix, will not survive the next fifteen years. A large amount of research shows that it is fun to lower stress levels both in the office and at home; it's well worth the effort. The stress of running a business doesn't go away, but it does change. We all know that happy employees increase production (Amabile & Kramer, 2010), and as a business owner, you will find other intrinsic and unexpected benefits that employees having fun will bring.

"Fun is often induced through play," says Ross Smith (2012). Clair Mellenthin (2011) says: "Play relieves stress and boredom, connects people in a positive way, stimulates creative thinking and exploration, regulates emotions and boosts confidence. Play boosts learning and development, and sustains memory."

Gamification is very effective for combining all three of these elements of feedback (through immediate comments, points or level-ups), friends (through interactive elements of sharing information, finding passwords, or chatting on- and off-line) and fun (stories, prizes, choices and colourful, visual interfaces).

Worth reading: Importance of Play
http://www.slideshare.net/jinjin14/importance-of-play

"Remember that 'happy employees don't leave', and FUN always leads to happiness." – Susan Adams (2012)

Foldit

Foldit gamers have solved a 15-year AIDS Virus Protein problem within 10 days.

Foldit is a multiplayer online game in which players compete to find well-folded protein structures. In Foldit, protein structures are posted online as puzzles, accessible for fixed periods, usually one week, during which players compete to achieve the highest scoring solution structures. Players interact with the protein in a variety of ways:

1. They can pull on it directly, place bands in position to pull it indirectly, and freeze pieces to prevent them from moving.
2. They can also launch optimisations, called *shakes* and *wiggles,* that will computationally improve their protein.

The score of the player's solution is updated in real-time. Foldit is organised as a competition, and a leader board of all other players and their scores is displayed. Players can form groups which can work together and share their solutions. Groups compete on a separate group leader board.

(Cooper *et al*, 2011)

11.3.3 Rewards

Gamification is all about rewards. It is about people being told how well they are doing and then being rewarded for doing it. If your reaction at this point is "that is what our performance management system, or loyalty programme, is for", read on. The most effective rewards are not stuff. **So *how* do we reward in the right way?**

We recommend that you leverage off the best-practice reward acronym of SAPS or **S**tatus, **A**ccess, **P**ower and **S**tuff.

Status: Most humans have a need for status, recognition, fame, prestige, attention and, ultimately, the esteem and respect of others. People need to engage themselves in activities to gain this esteem, though. All elements of game mechanics drive these dynamics, with levelling-up (such as getting a gold or platinum credit card) being one of the primary motivators. This is the most effective reward that most often requires the least cost and is the most sustainable and effective reward option. "Employees want to use their skills to be 'recognised' in the workplace (status), but they need to feel empowered and safe in their jobs" (Bunchball, 2012).

Status drives loyalty! Not redemption stuff. Zichermann and Cunningham (2011) state: "You cannot exract $1 from Farmville/Cityville; it is all money in and

NOTHING out. No real-world redemptions." Virtual loyalty programmes are the flavour of the day and companies are more and more applying them. Through these (and other big data initiatives) our individual status is becoming more public. Thanks to the "Internet of things" it is becoming more challenging to hide. People are now being seen at the level at which they perform. This is driving huge engagement and excitement (and in some cases fear).

Access: These types of rewards give users the opportunity to interact in a private, more detailed or special way with your company, service, clients or person. For example, an access reward may be to provide "players" with a dinner with your company's C-suite managerial staff, or for your providers could be a tour of your offices. Another example is to give social shopping "achievers" a five-minute head start on deals on your website. The option with client within South African, we encouraged the employees to improve on their OWN service targets. The employee with the top increase (based on OWN targets) won access to a C-level manager for about 25 minutes – either at the employee's desk or in the canteen – the choice was for the executive to sit through and listen to a customer call (and impress them), or just to chat about anything – or both. As a reward option, this is more expensive than status, and is sustainable for a shorter period (if you consider the Operant Conditioning model discussed above): when I've seen the entire executive team, then what?

Power: This reward offering specifically entitles players to "be above" others (manager for a day, promotion to supervisor). A funny video to watch on this can be found on YouTube http://goo.gl/wmZoMF, where Nev, a call centre manager, offers a promotion to an employee to become a supervisor if the employee wins an arm-wrestling challenge. However, there is a consequence for losing. The challenge with this as a reward offering is that once the power is received as a reward, the real life of responsibility kicks in.

By applying the "Gartner Hype Cycle" to this scenario, the "technological trigger" to the process is receiving the power as a reward. However, as the realisation kicks in, when the reward of **power** decreases because of the increased responsibility (that was not expected or wanted), the learner will slip down into the "trough of disillusionment". At this point, if the reward is not managed well it will cause unnecessary cost to your business and does not encourage a sustained performance. This type of reward creates the expectation of more power, and can "sink" a learner who is not prepared to handle the power correctly.

GMAT

Beat the GMAT: Learners increase their time spent on site by 370% through a gamified system.

Beat the GMAT dramatically increased social sharing and incentivised user participation. In fact, they witnessed an increase of 1 500 comments within their social community and more than 900 community members "followed" their favourite schools during each month following the implementation of Gamification techniques such as Badgeville's Social Fabric platform. With Badgeville, Beat the GMAT was also able to increase pages-per-visit by 195% and time users spent on site by 370%.

Visit http://www.fastcompany.com/1840235/gamification-and-power-influence

Stuff: This is what we give people or what they can redeem and take with them. Examples are toasters, air miles, extra petrol, 13th cheques, and salary increases. This is by far the most ineffective reward schedule that can be offered, the most expensive, and definitely the least sustainable. Yet it is these rewards which we in South Africa are predominantly offering to everyone all the time, and expecting a different type of engagement.

Consider for a moment what might happen if the talent, remuneration and rewards department got together and shifted the focus away from standard remuneration and rewards. You could offer more frequent feedback opportunities, learning opportunities, status opportunities, time off for goal achievement, and less "stuff" rewards. The shift in behaviour would be surprising.

Gamification allows for short-term, random and scheduled rewards that can stimulate someone's need for Status, Access, Power and Stuff. The flexibility of gamification is that people can often choose the rewards that make the most impact for them.

11.4 GAMIFICATION MECHANICS

Gamification loop: This is another loop that it is important to consider when building your gamification strategy. In their book *Gamification by Design* (2011), Zichermann and Cunningham explain that: "If your gamification strategy is built around a good points system, you will undoubtedly achieve a better uptake quickly. Just ensure that the points and badges are able to be earned for the different player types."

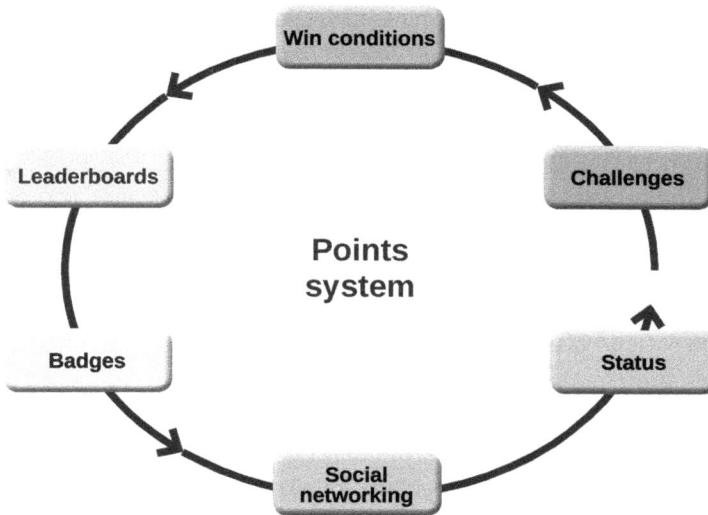

Figure 11.5: Gamification loop (Zichermann & Cunningham, 2011)

There are over 35 different gamification mechanics in the building of gamification strategies. These are the five simplest to use in your first attempts. (See Figure 11.5 above.)

11.4.1 Leader boards

The most successful and sustainable games created implement "high-score tables" and great scoring systems. They bring aspiration, and they "put your name in lights" – Status. They indicate "How am I doing?" and enable you to measure yourself against:

a. Yourself
b. Friends, and
c. Everybody else.

In the context of gamification, leader boards are used to track and display the behaviours that you want to reward. If you want to use competition to drive valuable behaviour, remember that the best leader board does not show too much information about ALL who are in the game. They show YOU in the middle, the two players who are directly beating you and what you need to do to catch them; and the two players directly below you.

In the leader board screen somewhere are the top 3 to 5 players *without* their scores. If their scores are too high, this will demotivate the other players from playing and will push them away. (Think about you would consider competing in an initial game where the winning player already has 124 987 points!)

11.4.2 Avatars

An avatar is the representation of the player or the player's alter ego or character. It may take either a three-dimensional form, as in games or virtual worlds, or a two-dimensional form, as an icon in Internet forums and other online communities. It is an object representing the player. The reason for an avatar is that it provides Individualism – I can dress my avatar, or change my avatar as often as I wish. It also provides the platform for "fitting in". If all my connections have hats on their avatars, I can put one on mine, making me still individual as I have my *own* hat – I am still fitting in because, like all my friends, I am wearing a hat.

An avatar is a great way to reward an expresser, as they achieve different goals, and they can dress their avatar with new fashion items.

Lloyds TSB (2008)

CASE STUDY

The goal of the whole process (gamification strategy), after all, was To encourage Lloyds employees to work together more efficiently and develop creative ideas for innovation, and asked them to submit and rate ideas.

Highest rated ideas were placed in a virtual stock market allowing others to buy into or cash out of an idea using a virtual currency call Bank Beanz. The Beanz could then be traded in at an innovation store.

Because they created an internal market for ideas, they were experiencing all the standard market behaviours you usually experience externally. Firstly, they had hyperinflation and had to put special controls in place to avoid what was essentially a system that just printed money.

Then, they had insider trading in ideas. However, they realised in this instance that insider trading can be a good thing. It makes people want to be on the inside so that they can speculate successfully. And how do you get on the inside? You have to work on the team making the idea happen.

Werbach (2012)

11.4.3 Guilds/Groups/Communities

Given that we are in a social revolution, the importance of guilds/groups/communities is key to the success of your strategy. People need to feel the autonomy to create their own groups for their own reasons. These groups need to have a pivotal rewards structure. From these groups they will often create new parts to the "world" in which your gamification overlay is positioned.

11.4.4 Trading systems

Hackenberg (2009) says: "The token economy is a system in which targeted behaviours are reinforced with tokens (secondary reinforcers) and are later exchanged for rewards (primary reinforcers)." Tokens can also be badges, currency, stickers, or any tradeable items. While rewards can range anywhere from snacks to privileges/activities, our experience is that players can become over-reliant on the tokens for motivation – which remain in extrinsic motivation and defeat the objective of altering behaviour from intrinsic desire. People enjoy trading, and if designed correctly, you could create the move towards your employees creating and managing their own trading system, and perhaps you too can experience the "hyperinflation" that Lloyds of London experienced.

11.4.5 Tutorials

Have you ever started something and wondered, "What on earth am I doing?" Tutorials/on-boarding and packs/course norms are vital for every step of your gamification strategy. They are an instruction manual, and a reason for the next level. The reason that most tutorials, online training and other on-boarding concepts fail so badly is that they are mostly *boring*! There is no excitement or reason to read them, and the players are more excited to fail trying to achieve the unknown, than to read the "rules and regulations". Have you noticed that most products purchased these days no longer have the instructions *in the box*? They are now accessible online if you want them. Remember, at each step of the way, you *must* provide an interactive and exciting tutorial of what is expected and *how to use it correctly*.

Using these five simple mechanics in developing a gamification strategy for a specific learning outcome should support an accelerated learning approach and introduce fun into the learning activities, as learners will be more engaged, both with the content as well as having an emotional engagement with the process. Each of these mechanics will appeal to the different player types as well as encourage the correct learning behaviour.

These mechanics will help accelerated learning in that setting outcomes/goals will require access to tutorials and on-boarding "packs". The more effective the on-boarding is at each level in the learning experience, the more engagement you will experience from your learners.

When your players are able to express themselves through their avatars, it provides a platform of escapism into their virtual world – imagination. And, of course, if they can make use of a powerful trading system where the players are in control of the currency, they can trade for ideas, coaching, mentorship and online learning, among others. Access to articles helps to achieve the outcomes, and you may then even experience the players forming guilds to create different items of clothing for the avatars, which can then also be traded.

Accelerated learning is the foundation, with a process in place that can be made engaging and super successful, if the strategy designed is simple and effective.

In the previous chapter, we discussed the importance of assessment. Yet, as important as assessment is, it is not gaining the success that is required by the people who design and want the models implemented. A simple model to apply gamification to is the Kirkpatrick/Phillips model. There is a defined process in place; the steps define the different behaviours for each level; and then you are shown how to build a player journey for the desired behaviours.

Gamification has the potential for you to apply the entire ROI model in your business through to management – engaging with changing behaviours, seeing and impact on business – and then demonstrating ROI per cent and ROI ratios to the board. For a simple example of ROI application, see Passion4Development at http:// p4dinternational.wordpress.com/2014/06/27/return-on-investment-in-learning/.

11.5 EXAMPLES OF GAMIFICATION

There are numerous examples of where gamification is being used specifically to accelerate learning. Here are a few examples.

Monica Cornetti from the United States, a top 25 Gamification Guru (as recognised by UK-based Leaderboard) uses low-tech Gamification very successfully in learning sessions and at large conferences to build engagement, have fun, and maintain interest throughout the learning experience. She uses a Pirate-themed game board and brings in numerous props such as pirate hats, hooks, flags, maps, and so on for the participants to play with and be able to score points throughout the session. There is a leader board which is completed by the teams on an honesty system; avatars are selected (for example, hats and props); groups move through the learning together (guilds); and there is a trading economy as groups can share and swap points and rewards. There are five levels, so that people can level up and attain additional status and rewards. There is plenty of information available both in the room and online if required (http://www. entreprenowonline.com/).

Below is an example of the game board for a learning process of developing and implementing a gamification strategy.

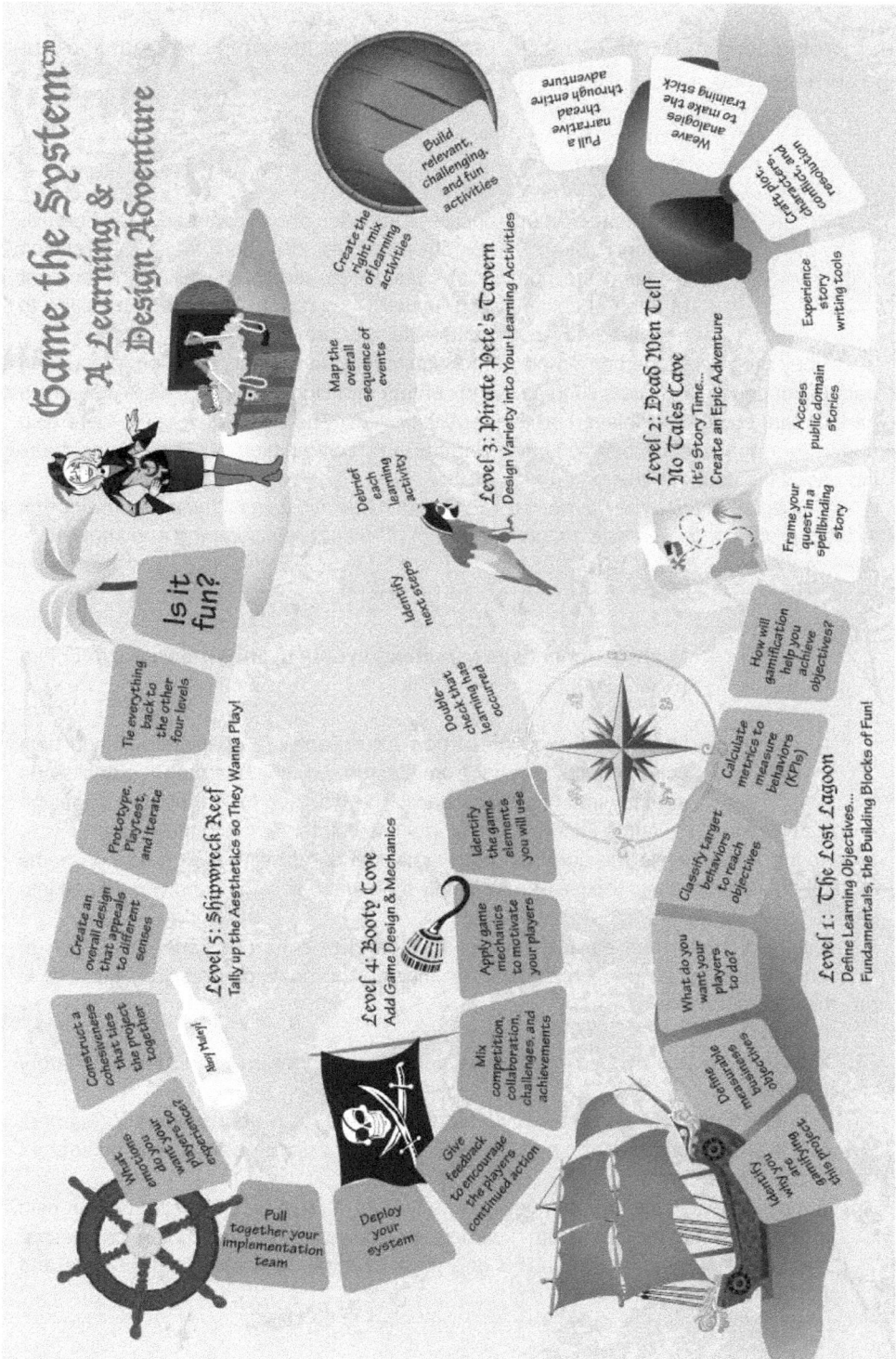

Game the System™
A Learning & Design Adventure

Level 1: The Lost Lagoon
Define Learning Objectives...
Fundamentals, the Building Blocks of Fun!

- Identify why you are gamifying this project
- Define measurable objectives
- What do you want your players to do?
- Classify target behaviors to reach objectives
- Calculate metrics to measure behaviors (KPIs)
- How will gamification help you achieve objectives?

Level 2: Dead Men Tell No Tales Cave
It's Story Time...
Create an Epic Adventure

- Frame your quest in a spellbinding story
- Access public domain stories
- Experience story writing tools
- Craft plot, characters, conflict, and resolution
- Weave analogies to make the training stick
- Pull a narrative thread through entire adventure

Level 3: Pirate Pete's Tavern
Design Variety into Your Learning Activities

- Build relevant, challenging, and fun activities
- Create the right mix of learning activities
- Map the overall sequence of events
- Debrief each learning activity
- Identify next steps
- Double-check that learning has occurred

Level 4: Booty Cove
Add Game Design & Mechanics

- Identify the game elements you will use
- Apply game mechanics to motivate your players
- Mix competition, collaboration, challenges, and achievements
- Give feedback to encourage the players continued action
- Deploy your system
- Pull together your implementation team

Level 5: Shipwreck Reef
Tally up the Aesthetics so They Wanna Play!

- What emotions do you want your players to experience?
- Construct a cohesiveness that ties the project together
- Create an overall design that appeals to different senses
- Prototype, Playtest, and iterate
- Tie everything back to the other four levels

Is it fun?

Almost there!

Other examples from the top 25 best examples of gamification in business (visit (http://blogs.clicksoftware.com/clickipedia/top-25-best-examples-of-gamification-in-business/) are as follows.

Accenture

Accenture wanted to increase adoption of their social and collaborative platform (SharePoint). They noticed that there was a correlation between the number of customised user profiles and the amount of internal collaboration. Initially they ran an internal competition to encourage users to customise their profiles.

They then developed an employee recognition system that gave users points and badges for certain activities, such as rating content and blogging. Users were also given badges that could be displayed on their public profiles. The top 100 bloggers were also added to a public leaderboard. They found that this combination of Gamification ideas increased the usage of their internal systems.

The accelerated learning that was achieved in this initiative is that in order for them to blog, grow, complete and engage came from different areas learning and knowledge platforms (Altrup, 2012).

Maths teacher uses gamification to help at-risk learners succeed (Ross, 2006)

Here is an example of how Kate Fanelli (a special-education high school maths teacher from Canton, MI) implemented a gamification strategy into her maths class. The first step for Fanelli was to design an organisational structure for the curriculum. The "MathLand" structure is premised on gaming levels, while the common core state standards for the high-school maths curriculum are sorted into topics. Fanelli simply took the topics and subdivided them into levels.

Learners could then earn credits for mastering a level. (The current version of MathLand has 20 levels (Motivation factors = mastery, purpose, progression). Each level has three components:

1. A lesson with step-by-step instructions, necessary information, and a few mandatory exercises.
2. A practice problem section, completed by learners on a **needs basis**. If learners feel they are competent on a given topic, they can skip this section and go straight to the mastery test.
3. A mastery test is the final component of any level. It must be completed without help in a quiet part of the classroom. Learners are allowed to use their notes, calculators, manipulatives, or computers. (This is a clear example of accelerated learning and fluid intelligence.)

<table>
<tr>
<td>CASE STUDY</td>
<td>Maths teacher uses gamification to help at-risk learners succeed (Ross, 2006) (Continued)

4. However, they are not allowed to talk to other learners or ask the instructor for help. Learners tell the instructor when they feel they are ready to take the test. If they do not pass, they are welcome to redo the test until they do succeed, or go back and try some practice problems.</td>
</tr>
</table>

"Points are awarded only for successfully completing the mastery test," says Fanelli. She continues by saying: "I tell the kids, the lesson and practice are for learning, the mastery test is for showing you've learnt it. That's what they earn points for: actually demonstrating they've learnt something."

Another key component of MathLand is a visual tracking system/AKA Mathboard (leader board). Each learner creates an pretty basic avatar on the first day of school. "The avatars are pretty basic at first," says Fanelli. "That's intentional."

The avatars evolve as learners level up in maths learning. The avatars begin to move up the board and gain coloured dots as badges of accomplishment each time they level up. At certain thresholds of accomplishment, learners are allowed to replace their basic avatars with ones that are fancier.

The purpose of the Avatar Board is to tell a story without a lot of bells and whistles which nevertheless engages the learners, as they love to watch their avatars moving up the board.

What is the secret of MathLand's success?

In its first year, MathLand led learners to a 17 per cent improvement in state-wide assessment performance. Attendance increased 13 per cent in the first two years. Standardised test results continued to move upwards – by 22 per cent at the end of year three. "I don't think [my learners] would be intimidated by a college maths course," says Fanelli. "And some will feel that they can handle a career that requires maths."

Treehouse is a **virtual training academy** (http://teamtreehouse.com) for learning code, app development, and business skills, used by beginners to learn valuable career skills and experienced professionals for career advancement. Learners choose from various tracks for defined outcomes, and earn badges and points as they work through the library of courses to show off their achievements and impress potential employers. Tracks are broken into manageable chunks, and a tracker shows your progress as you work towards your goals. The more points you earn, the higher your potential salary.

Kaplan University implemented **Badgeville solutions** to enhance its curriculum by encouraging more engaged participation. By incorporating challenges and badges, Kaplan saw results such as higher learner grades and decreased rates of learners failing to complete courses and programmes, and they conducted behaviour analysis to differentiate what distinguishes the most successful learners from the rest in order to derive gamification processes that would foster the same practices across the learner population, according to InformationWeek. Visit http://blogs.clicksoftware.com/clickipedia/top-25-best-examples-of-gamification-in-business/

Deloitte Leadership Academy

An executive training programme **increased by 46.6%** the number of users who returned daily to their platform by embedding gamification mechanics into it.

The Deloitte Leadership Academy is an executive training programme that Deloitte has rolled out to more than 50 000 executives. Their business challenge was to encourage busy executives to take the time to go through the training available. They have used the Badgeville platform to embed gamification mechanics into the whole of the website. Using things such as missions, rewards, rank, status and more. they have been able to have a significant impact on usage of the site.

Facts taken from the case study are as follows:

Increased User Retention

a.   46.6% increase in the number of users that return to DLA daily.
b.   36.3% increase in the number of users that return to DLA weekly.

Active User Engagement and Adoption

a.   An average of three achievements unlocked per active user.
b.   Top users have earned as many as 30 achievements already.

Deloitte Leadership Academy (nd)

11.6 GAMIFICATION LESSONS

Through applying gamification to different industries and different areas, we have learnt the following valuable lessons that you should consider when applying this to your projects:

- **Time frame:** Build for 3 to 6 months at maximum. Your strategy is most effective when it is short term, and you can receive a lot of feedback and re-direct quickly and effectively.
- **Make it measurable:** Design only if you are able to measure the success. Look for different metrics and measurable tangible opportunities. Just be aware that more elaborate the reward strategy, the more complex the design of the system.

- **Player types:** Build your first iteration for one or a maximum of two player types. Too big, too soon will cause unnecessary pain. In their predictions for 2020 around gamification, Gartner (a leading research group that provides technology research to global technology business leaders to make informed decisions on key initiatives) predicts that 80 per cent of gamification strategies will fail by 2016. This is because there is a lack of understanding of gamification as well as trying to build too big the first time round. See http://www.growthengineering.co.uk/future-of-gamification-gartner/
- **Find a partner:** Although there are limited gamification providers in South Africa (many are game designers claiming to be gamification experts), research thoroughly, and use those that have expertise and a few scars. There is no perfect gamification partner, only those who make your quest exciting and those who want to offer *another* game.
- **Use the players:** Monica Cornetti (http://www.entreprenowonline.com/) allows her players to score themselves on a "trust" platform. This is working wonders for the gamification "board game" she has designed. What she explains is that based on this testing she is finding innovative, *low-tech* ways of building gamification strategies.

Most importantly: Always have fun!!

11.7 SO WHAT DOES ALL OF THIS MEAN, AND HOW CAN YOU APPLY IT?

The application of gamification will be successful only when a focused strategy is in place and is applied. Gamification is a great "middleware for motivation", and needs to be used in both the low-tech as well as the high-tech opportunities.

Remember that you need to decide on the longevity of your gamification strategy. Most games have a start and an end to them. They are designed for you to "clock" the level and beat the "big boss". At this point, big dopamine mechanics are experienced (fireworks on the screen and a huge "Well done!" is shown), and the player feels a sense of achievement and mastery. However, when your strategy needs to be designed to be more long term (six months to a year), the entire structure and the feedback loops need to be reviewed.

These are some of the recent projects in which gamification (not games) is being applied in South Africa:

- **SAAB:** Currently testing gamification strategy in an eLearning programme.
- **Capitec Bank:** Gamification strategy has started to increase sales in the branches.

- **Sasol:** Gamification of a four-day training programme has shown a 92 per cent increase in pre-course work completion and 120 per cent increase in engagement *during* classroom training.
- **PE Boardwalk Casino:** Gamification has increased the number of people entering the induction programme from 20 to 300 people per month.
- **Sasol HR Academy:** There has been a 94 per cent increase in behaviour change with Sasol Train as the trainer and 240 per cent ROI implementation.

Other projects under way include:

- Designing a low tech "induction programme" gamification strategy for a shared services department.
- Gamification strategy to align SMEs with training linked to roles, competencies, learning curriculum and assessments.
- Gamification strategy for the launching of events.
- Gamification of the assessment process for conducting a situational needs analysis on performance for employees.

> Watch this video on TED: **Jane McGonigal: Gaming can make a better world**
> http://www.ted.com/talks/jane_mcgonigal_gaming_can_make_a_better_world

11.8 CONCLUSION

While gamification is still the "new kid on the block" from a learning tools and approach perspective and is still very much in its infancy in the South African context, we believe that when it is planned and used effectively in the development of accelerated learning programmes and interventions, it can clearly support learner buy-in and engagement with the learning process and therefore the learning that takes place will be improved.

The additional aspect of autonomy of learning further supports intrinsic motivation as highlighted throughout the chapter, and gamification also provides opportunities to introduce flexibility of learning through encompassing and integrating different learning techniques and methodologies that are already mature and well entrenched among learning providers.

Gamification is only as effective as the team that is driving the strategy. Only the best platform or system will reveal how good (or poor) the gamification strategy is. Paharia sums this up most successfully in his book *Loyalty 3.0* (2013). Gamification is best used when building loyalty and increasing fun. It will achieve the required effect only when combined with two other elements. Evidence of all three elements is required for the desired impact to be achieved in increasing and sustaining behaviour change and engagement.

Motivation + Big Data + Gamification = Loyalty 3.0 (Paharia, 2013).

Gamification is NOT a game, nor the playing of a game. Mostly games are short lived and have fairly short shelf lives. The games that have been around for years (for example, World of WarCraft) have great gamification engagement strategies that overlay them: continued co-operation, opt-in, group and guild engagement, individual *and* combined rewards, and increased experience in purpose, mastery, autonomy, progress and social interaction.

Good luck as you apply this awesome new tool in accelerating your learning.

CHAPTER 12

LEARNING ASSESSMENT

By Kerryn Kohl

12.1 INTRODUCTION

"Those people who develop the ability to continuously acquire new and better forms of knowledge that they can apply to their work and to their lives will be the movers and shakers in our society for the indefinite future." – Brian Tracy

Assessment of learning is a contentious topic. The reality is that very few organisations go beyond the learner's happiness rating of a training session or a short knowledge assessment after an e-learning module. Leaders talk about the strategic importance of skills development and culture change at strategy sessions and talent forums, and yet very little of this talk gets translated into actions, measures and accountabilities. As consultants we are often asked to implement a learning solution toward leadership development, talent management or a system change, but are given very little scope, budget or time to design programmes using Accelerated Learning principles, and almost none for the full assessment value chain.

Businesses think about volumes, productivity and cost without taking into consideration the long-term impact of superficial change (not building the mindsets and behaviours for sustainable change). A quick 10 question knowledge assessment is provided for the learner to progress through the modules, the checklist is ticked for the stakeholders, and learners are then deemed competent and released back into the real world – only to find that they are unable to perform and require a significant amount of coaching, correcting and cajoling (never mind the cost of errors and customer service glitches). So this begs the question – **why, then, do we assess if it is merely a tick box exercise?**

According to ASTD's *Value of Evaluation* report: "Only about one-quarter of respondents agreed that their organisation got solid 'bang for the buck' from its training evaluation efforts. With the tough economic demands, business leaders have to scrutinize costs even more, to find greater efficiencies. This highlights the need for the true value of evaluating learning to be realized and for current practices to adapt to increased efficiency and effectiveness demands" (ASTD Staff, 2009).

The time has come for learning to prove its worth. Organisations and learning functions must build the right knowledge, skills and processes to implement assessment methods that can discern the true value of learning. However, the choice of method must be carefully considered in order to balance the costs of assessment versus the benefits of having the proof.

This chapter will explore some of the foundations of assessment and some of the dilemmas the learning and HR practitioners face in making learning assessment decisions. We will also cover some critical strategic questions to consider and give some examples of assessment in practice. For more information on specific assessment frameworks and methodologies, please refer to the recommended reading.

12.2 LEVELS OF ASSESSMENT

The Kirkpatrick/ Phillips Assessment Model is the golden standard for learning assessment and categorises five levels of training assessment. The levels are outlined in Figure 12.1.

While 92 per cent of respondents of the above mentioned report are measuring Level 1 (reactions of participants) (Bailey, 2003), less than 18 per cent are measuring at Level 5 (ROI). The startling facts are that 75 per cent of the respondents found value only when training was measured at Level 3 (evaluation of behaviour) and Level 4 (evaluation of results).

Table 12.1, which starts below Figure 12.1 on the next page, indicates some of the methods we have been exposed to at each level of the Kirkpatrick model. Each of these methods has some benefits and key considerations.

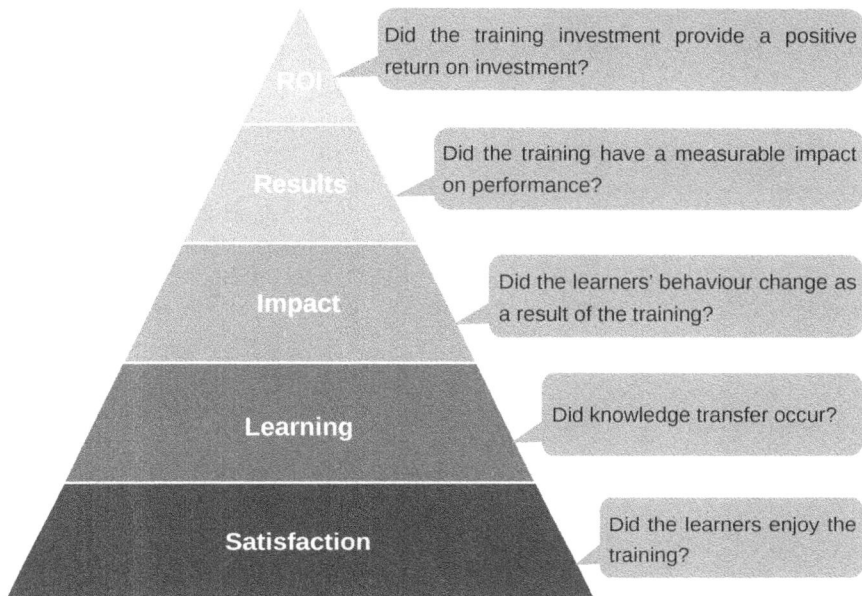

Figure 12.1: Five levels of assessment

Table 12.1: Assessment methods and key considerations

Level	Methods	Considerations
Satisfaction Has there been a favourable participant reaction – similar to measuring customer satisfaction?	• Post-workshop evaluation (form or online survey) • Anecdotal participant or leader feedback	*Benefits* • Immediate indication of satisfaction and perception of learning • Mechanism to get feedback on learning providers, methods and venues *Considerations* • Participant reactions don't necessarily translate into behaviour change or job impact

Level	Methods	Considerations
Learning Have the learning objectives been attained, and has there been a transfer of knowledge, skills or behaviour?	• Knowledge assessment • Online test or game • Self-assessment • Peer review of behaviour change • Skills observation and feedback • Psychometrics e.g. EQi assessment centre	*Benefits* • Encourages commitment to learning if participants know that they will be evaluated • Can be quick and fun to develop and complete • The feedback process can further enhance self-awareness, continuous improvement, and embedding the learning *Considerations* • Need to gain participant commitment to complete the survey – may require administrative follow-up • Observation requires time and expertise • Feedback can be subjective • Accurate results require a pre- and post-assessment
Impact Has there been a job impact on training – an observable change in the way the job is done (skills or behaviours)?	• Self-assessment of job impact • 360° competency assessment (self, manager, peers) • Learner interviews • Manager or coach feedback on learning impact • Peer review of behaviour change • Portfolio of Evidence e.g. reports, presentations, customer feedback	*Benefits* • Encourages commitment to learning if participants know that they need to demonstrate job impact post-learning • The feedback process can further enhance self-awareness, continuous improvement, and embedding the learning • Involves the manager in the learning process *Considerations* • Issues with peer reviews • Accurate results require a control group and pre- and post-assessment

Level	Methods	Considerations
Impact (continued)	• Learners teaching others • Performance review by manager (pre- and post-) • Case study using pre- and post- metrics	• Feedback can be subjective • Need to gain participant, observers and feedback providers' commitment to complete the job impact process and submit to learning • May require administrative co-ordination and follow-up • Observation and feedback requires time and expertise – assessment certification • Case studies require setting up of metrics prior to the learning
Results Have business results such as those listed below improved as a result of the training? • Employee retention • Production volumes or quality • Productivity • Employee morale • Reduced waste • Increased sales • Customer satisfaction • Fewer staff complaints	• Employee engagement survey results • Staff retention of key talent segments • Production or productivity reports • Quality versus waste reports • Sales reports • Customer satisfaction surveys • Number of staff complaints	*Benefits* • Gives an indication of the types of job impacts occurring (cost, quality, time, productivity) • Helps build the case for the positive impact of learning • Involves the business in understanding the learning process *Considerations* • Takes time for changes to take place • Can be expensive and time consuming • Need to involve many people – time away from their work • Accurate results require a control group and pre- and post-assessment • Measures immediately post the intervention may not be sustainable • Many other factors can influence these results other than learning e.g. economy, strategic initiatives, new employees, payment of bonuses • Requires administrative co-ordination and follow-up

Level	Methods	Considerations
ROI Has there been a financial benefit to the organisation as a result of the training?	• Financial evaluation e.g. ROI calculation: ROI = benefits – costs/ costs x 100	*Benefits* • Provides an unequivocal financial business case • Can influence future investment of training • Enhances credibility of the learning function • Involves the business in understanding the learning impact *Considerations* • Accurate metrics need to be set up and agreed in advance and built into the full value chain • Assumptions need to established and managed • Accurate tracking of metrics • Can be expensive and time consuming • Need to involve many people – time away from their work • Timing of the measures can influence the results • Many other factors can influence these results • Requires administrative co-ordination and follow-up

If these assessment models exist and add value, why are they not being implemented fully in organisations? Businesses require detailed business cases and ROIs on large capital investments, and dedicate resources to this. Why not with significant human capital investment?

The usual complaint is shortage of time, resources and money. Assessment takes time and is not always perceived to be a value- making exercise. Rather, it is perceived as a time-consuming bureaucratic process that is keeping us away from the coalface where real learning occurs. Perhaps that is the case. Let's explore how we can find the right balance between learning and assessment to build credibility of the learning profession and the case for investment in learning, but not at the expense of quality time spent with learners and leaders.

Worth reading: Kirkpatrick/Phillips model
The Value of Evaluation: Usage and Value of Kirkpatrick/Phillips model. *ASTD – Learning and Development Blog* (ASTD Staff, 2009)

Brain Break: Put on some high energy music and do a crazy dance with no co-ordinated movements.

12.3 STRATEGIC CONSIDERATIONS IN ASSESSMENT DECISIONS

Before embarking on an assessment approach, a number of critical strategic questions can be useful. These include:

- Why assess learning?
- What are we assessing?
- Who should conduct the assessment?
- When should we assess?
- Who should we assess?
- How should we assess?

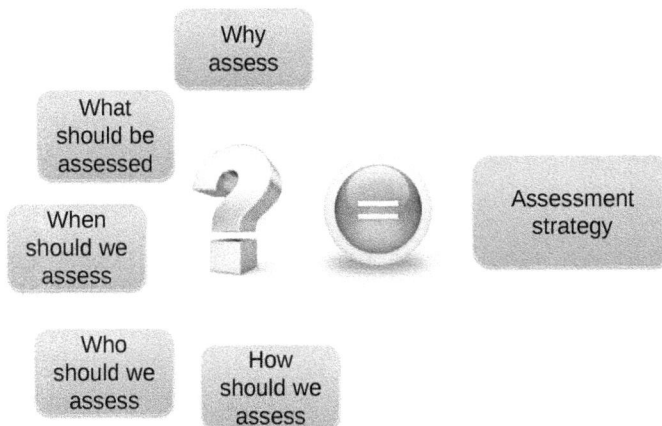

Figure 12.2: Strategic assessment questions

12.3.1 Why assess learning?

This is the most critical question. Think about whether you are assessing in order to:

- Support the learner in building awareness of improvement.
- Achieve a recognised qualification or competence that may affect your career options or income.
- Build credibility of the learning function in order to convince business of the value.
- Determine whether a pilot is successful in order to make a significant investment in the future.
- Determine readiness to sign off a system for a client.
- Determine talent pool readiness on a succession plan and therefore organisational risk.

Or are you assessing for other reasons?

Assessment to support learning

Assessment can be a core part of ensuring that learners remain engaged in learning activities and are provided with feedback which they are able to use to tweak their performance. Feedback is critical to the learning process and helps learner's assess where they are currently in the learning process and what they need to do to improve. This must be given regularly to drive continuous improvement and not only at the end of the process.

Feedback has the most impact when combined with coaching. Feedback in isolation results in the learners not knowing what to do with the information or how to modify their behaviour. Coaching allows the learners the time and space to digest the feedback received and to explore ways to implement personal improvements. It also provides an opportunity to explore and discuss these critically and practise the new skill or behaviour in a safe space. Learning can thereby become more meaningful and integrated.

The answers to these questions will indicate at which level you need to assess, and will help you to justify the additional resources required for impact and results based assessment.

12.3.2 What are we assessing?

Whatever level we are choosing to assess at, we know upfront what we are measuring. Are we measuring:

- Learning or course outcomes?
- Specific knowledge, skills or behaviour?
- Qualification standards?
- Competence standards for talent readiness?
- Transfer of knowledge to job performance?
- Business impact?

The answers to these questions will indicate which methods you will use and the timing of them. The higher the level of assessment, and the greater the focus on performance improvement, the more you need to move away from knowledge-based assessments to performance- and observation-based assessments.

From this perspective we see that the practice of designing a uniform assessment is obsolete – people do not apply learning or perform in a uniform way. Accelerated learning principles suggest that we allow learners to use what they have learnt in their own way, and then assess their overall performance in the real world. This may raise a debate of fairness versus subjectivity. Yes, assessments need to be fair, but organisations and leaders are the ones that have an idea of the level of performance and behaviours required. They are therefore in the best position to observe these and give them a value.

For example, can these learners apply critical reasoning to solving complex problems and apply their knowledge and ability to doing so in real-world contexts?

Depending on the experience, expertise and personality preferences of an assessor, we may get differing views. Assessor objectivity and skill is another contentious issue that needs to be debated in organisations in order to find the best way to manage this paradox. It is best if the knowledge, skills and behaviour standards required on the job are clearly defined during the design phase and agreed by the leaders and learners. See more on defining competencies in Chapter 9.

Also, the higher you go, the more cost, time and resources are usually required. Some executives believe strongly in investing in people, so they don't need to be convinced. Others, perhaps with a more technical, analytical or financial focus, need the facts to help them to make investment decisions.

> *Worth reading: Knowing is Not the Same as Understanding: What is Understanding? http://www.cdtl.nus.edu.sg/success/sl20.htm*

12.3.3 Who should conduct the assessment?

Assessors can comprise a combination of the following:

- **The Learner** – the assessment criteria should be so transparent that learners are able to determine continually if they are measuring up or where they need to improve. Self-assessment involves learners judging their own performance. However, there is one caveat when it comes to self-assessment. Learners usually judge themselves on what they intended to achieve rather than on what they actually achieved. The level of Emotional Intelligence (specifically self-awareness, self-regard and reality testing) will affect the maturity and accuracy of self-assessment.
- **The coach** – the coach (or manager as coach) is critical for providing feedback and helping people to internalise the feedback. For more on the role of the coach or to recap on this role please refer to Chapter 7.
- **Peers** – one of the best ways to teach learners to assess their own work more objectively is to get them to assess each other's work by means of a peer evaluation. The peer review process allows learners the opportunity to engage critically and analyse the topic or information, and also gives them the opportunity to practise giving and receiving feedback. This kind of feedback requires a certain level of relationship and team maturity and needs to be set up under the right conditions.
- **Line manager/leaders** – leaders are in the best position to observe and evaluate performance. Leaders also require the knowledge and skills for understanding performance standards, assessing competence and giving feedback in a constructive way.
- **Technical or qualified assessors** – where learning outcomes are directly related to a qualification or unit standard that is part of a larger system of education, such as the NQF in South Africa, a degree, and so on, a qualified assessor is usually required to do the assessment. Some organisations train some of their line managers and technical experts in assessment in order to optimise both the accuracy of the evaluation and the practical ability to observe the person on the job.

Watch this video on YouTube: **Assessment for Learning in 5 m.wmv** http://www.youtube.com/watch?v=5OEBTtm5yG0

12.3.4 When should we assess?

Assessment is a continuous cycle of learning, coaching, assessment, feedback, with key events scheduled to indicate progress or attainment.

As noted in Chapter 10, when designing learning for an ALP, the formula is:

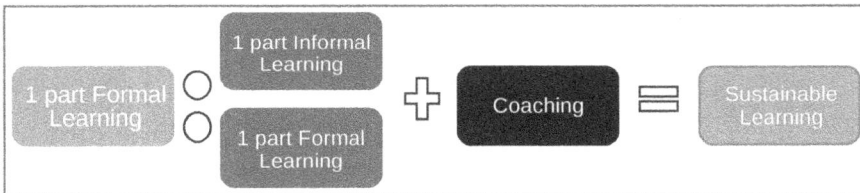

Figure 12.3: Design combination for an accelerated learning programme

This formula can be interpreted as:

> **1 part Formal Learning to 2 parts Informal Learning + Coaching**
> **= Sustainable Learning**

In this way we encourage behaviour integration. See the ALP value chain below for an example of building assessment and feedback into an ALP.

12.3.5 How should we assess?

The methods you choose will depend on the reasons for assessment, level of assessment required, what you are assessing, experience and skills of assessors, and availability of the technology to support certain methods. As you will have seen in the Levels of Assessment section, there are benefits and considerations for each method. We will outline some of these in more detail later in this chapter.

Assessment in the South African NQF context

CASE STUDY

With the establishment of the South African Qualifications Authority (SAQA) and the National Qualifications Framework (NQF) back in the mid-1990s, assessment became a real focus area for South African companies and organisations. There was a drive to formalise achievement of credits towards qualifications through learning programmes and demonstration of learning on the job.

In order for learners to achieve credits, they have to be assessed as being competent, based on the NQF level of the qualification that they wish to attain.

In the South African context assessment can be defined as:

The process of forming judgement about performance based on evidence provided against agreed criteria. Assessments measure whether the identified outcomes – knowledge, skills and attitudes of learning (formal or informal) – have been transferred with consistency to the workplace.

This is particularly relevant to apprentices, interns, graduates in training, or any other employee wishing to attain a professional qualification aligned to the NQF.

Within this context there are a number of principles that need to be considered:

- **Appropriateness:** The method of assessment is suited to the performance being assessed.
- **Fairness:** The method of assessment does not present any barriers to achievements, which are not related to the evidence.
- **Manageability:** The methods used help to ensure that assessments are easy to understand, cost effective, and do not interfere unduly with working.
- **Integration into work and learning:** Evidence collection is integrated into the work and learning process, where it is appropriate and feasible.
- **Validity:** The assessment is fit for purpose.
- **Direct:** The activities in the assessment mirror the conditions of actual performance as closely as possible.
- **Authenticity:** The Assessor is satisfied that the work being assessed is attributable to the person being assessed.
- **Sufficient:** The evidence collected reasonably establishes that all criteria have been met and that performance to the required standard (formal or informal) can be repeated consistently.
- **Systematic:** Planning and recording is sufficiently rigorous to ensure that the assessment is fair.
- **Open:** Those being assessed can contribute to the planning and accumulation of evidence. They understand the assessment process and the criteria that apply.
- **Consistent:** The same assessor would make the same judgement again in similar circumstances, or the judgement made is similar to the judgement that would be made by another assessor.

However, while the focus has been on assessment of learning at lower levels of the organisation, there still appears to be a sense in some organisations that there is little need for assessment at higher levels.

Assessment in the South African NQF context (continued)

Here lies a great opportunity for assessment, especially when we look at the cost of training for senior and executive level management (the costs of internationally recognised MBA programmes, as an example, are well documented). All too often L&D practitioners don't calculate or quantify the expected ROI from these training or development initiatives. We hope that the rest of this chapter will provide some insight in this regard.

12.4 DESIGNING ASSESSMENT TO BE INCORPORATED INTO ACCELERATED LEARNING PROGRAMMES

To assist organisations in moving beyond level 1 and 2 assessments, particularly in ALPs, where the investment is significant, it is useful to build an assessment value chain. This allows you to provide a true measure of the learner's ability to apply knowledge and skills back in the workplace and enhance performance and results.

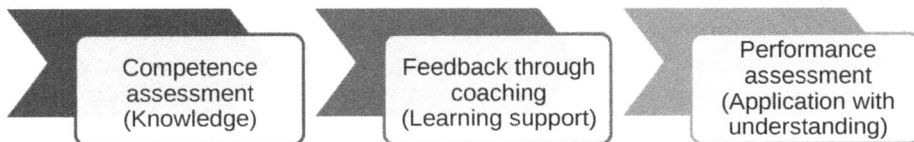

Competence assessment (Knowledge) → Feedback through coaching (Learning support) → Performance assessment (Application with understanding)

Figure 12.4: The assessment value chain

There are 3 broad phases of assessment within the value chain:

- The **competence assessment** – this is conducted by means of a knowledge-, skills- or behaviour-based assessment once the learner has completed a learning event in the learning chain. This is a level 2 assessment and can include methods such as a knowledge assessment, online test or game, self-assessment, peer review, skills observation or assessment centre.
- The **feedback or coaching phase** – between the learning events of an ALP, the learner should receive support by means of feedback and coaching. As we have seen in Chapter 5, coaching plays a critical role in learning process and feedback is necessary to enhance self-insight and reality testing and get an accurate view of competency and performance. This phase encourages continuous improvement in the application of new skills. This is the first part of a level 3 assessment and can include methods such as manager or coach feedback on learning impact, peer review of behaviour change or learners teaching others.

- The **performance assessment** – this is usually conducted at the end of the ALP. It is based on how the learners have performed throughout the programme as well as observation of how well the learners apply what they have learnt to enhance their performance on the job. This is the second part of a level 3 assessment and can include methods such as manager's assessment of job impact, 360° competency assessment (self, manager, peers) or a portfolio of evidence, for example, reports, presentations, customer feedback.

What I call the assessment value chain takes into account both formative and summative assessment.

"Formative assessment provides feedback and information during the instructional process, while learning is taking place, and while learning is occurring. Formative assessment measures progress ... **Summative assessment** takes place after the learning has been completed and provides information and feedback that sum up the teaching and learning process" (Northern Illinois University, Faculty Development and Instructional Design Center, nd).

Watch this video on YouTube: **Take Your Level 2s Up a Notch Presented** by **Ken Phillips for CCASTDStyles**
http://www.youtube.com/watch?v=74wxr4rZjK8

When designing the assessment value chain for the ALP you can use the following questions to guide you. If you are a leader or learner, trying to assess the effectiveness of an assessment make sure it addresses the following questions:

- Does the assessment include a **written and visual instrument**?

  A written as well as a visual component provides learners with the opportunity to reflect on and synthesise their knowledge. Tools can include a journal, blog, report, portfolio or presentation. Combinations of these allow us to assess innovation, synthesis of knowledge, oral skills and presentation ability.

Presentations can include the learners' views of their learning, which will indicate self-awareness and feedback. Presentations of team project work can also assess their ability to work as a team and apply their knowledge, skills, and ability in a real-world context.

- Is the **"speed"** at which they perform a task of importance?

  If so, ensure that the relevant assessment task has a time constraint allocated.

- How has the "**learning set**" been encouraged to complete the assessment as a group?

  Group assessments should include some pre-coaching so that the group can be observed while they discuss, debate, problem solve and work together. The coach can then give feedback to the group and see how they incorporate the feedback into improvements.

- Has each learner set up a **learning contract**?

  This contract can be set up between the learners and the coach and/or manager. It provides an opportunity for the learners to focus on their individual learning needs and outlines the KPIs against which they will be assessed.

- Has the **line manager** been set up to assess performance after a period of time?

A good example of the assessment value chain is the Breakthrough Learning programme for a talent pool, which is explained in more detail in Chapter 13. See the visual value chain and description below in Figure 12.5.

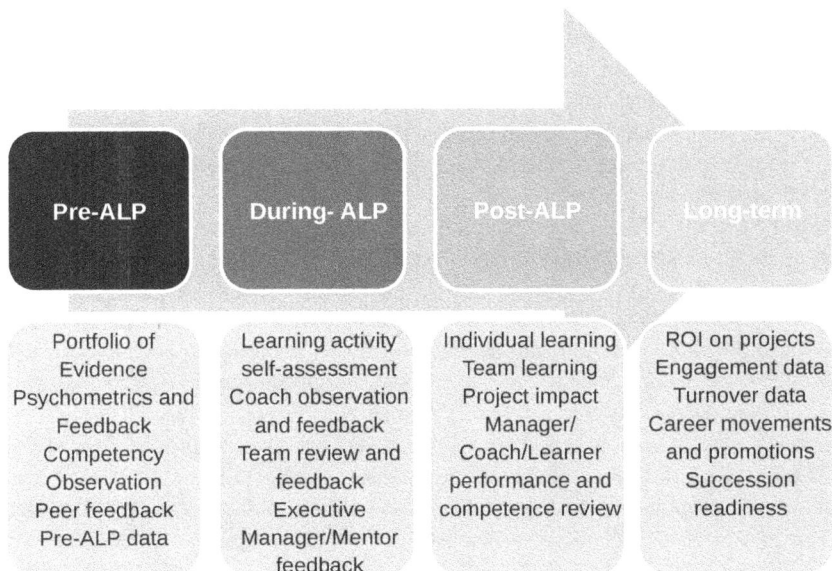

Pre-ALP	During-ALP	Post-ALP	Long-term
Portfolio of Evidence	Learning activity self-assessment	Individual learning	ROI on projects
Psychometrics and Feedback	Coach observation and feedback	Team learning	Engagement data
Competency Observation	Team review and feedback	Project impact	Turnover data
Peer feedback	Executive Manager/Mentor feedback	Manager/ Coach/Learner performance and competence review	Career movements and promotions
Pre-ALP data			Succession readiness

Figure 12.5: Breakthrough Learning programme

Example: Breakthrough Learning programme assessment value chain

Throughout the nine months of the Breakthrough Learning programme, facilitators, peers, coaches and line managers had numerous opportunities to view and give feedback on the behaviour and performance of the participants. Some of these opportunities are described below:

Pre-programme and launch

Portfolio of Evidence and career discussion – each potential participant had the opportunity for a career discussion with their manager and jointly put together a portfolio of evidence and review the development plan (performance and potential – as described in Chapter 10). The Portfolio of Evidence was presented to the Exco, the BL project team, and the coaches for a good overview of current performance, competence and development needs.

Psychometrics – as part of the selection process, all participants underwent psychometric assessments to determine their strengths and areas of development in comparison to the norm groups as well as the performance and competency standards expected in future next level roles. Each of them received an integrated report with suggested development areas and a full debrief with a psychometric coach.

Peer feedback – the 3-day launch process included a feedback post-box for each participant. ACT feedback cards were used to capture Actions/Consequences/Try this, and were looked at and debriefed on the last day of the launch workshop.

Coach observation and feedback – the 3-day launch workshop was set up with a number of assessment centre-type of activities, including project activities such as negotiating which project to work on and preparing project charters and presentation. Coaches and additional observers were set up with competency observation forms to capture examples of behaviours (influence, strategic thinking, initiative, teamwork, and so on), which were then summarised and fed back to the participants individually.

Data – were collected for the participant group for level 4 results, including engagement survey results, performance ratings, and turnover rates, among others.

During programme

Self-assessment and reflection activities – activities such as self-reflection, self-assessment, team reviews and team feedback were built into each facilitated leadership session.

Coach observation and feedback – coaches were involved in all the facilitated leadership sessions. Each individual received up to 5 coaching sessions to discuss observations, reflections, insights and development opportunities.

Team reviews – learning sets got together at the end of every facilitated session with their coaches to review team dynamics and assess their progress.

Executive feedback – teams presented at Executive forums and project prioritisation committees and received feedback on their project approach and their presentations.

Manager/Mentor/Project owner feedback – managers, mentors and project owners were encouraged to give on-going feedback and suggestions to their direct reports or mentees.

Example: Breakthrough Learning programme assessment value chain (continued)

Post-programme

Project and team evaluation – each team was evaluated against both learning criteria and project criteria.

    Manager/Coach pre- and post-competence review – tri-partite discussions with the learner, manager and coach were held after the ALP to determine improvements in behaviour and performance, using the same competence assessment template that was used in the initial launch workshop.

Long-term measures

Project ROI – projects results are being tracked via the project office and business owners for long-term business impact.

    Data tracking – other measures being tracked with regard to the learners include engagement scores on surveys, turnover statistics, performance scores, and career movements/promotions.

Activity 1

Using the Strategic Assessment Questions, develop your own assessment value chain based on the learning experience you designed as part of your activity in Chapter 10.

- Why assess:
- What to assess:
- When to assess:
- Who to assess:
- How to assess:

Share via e-mail or Facebook to level up.

12.5 ASSESSMENT METHODS

Some of the generic assessment methods have been mentioned so far. We have included some of the common methods of assessment that we use for ALPs and some of their merits and uses in the table below.

Table 12.2: Examples of assessment methods

Assessment method	Merits	Best used
Written reflections	Encourage reflection and synthesis of knowledge	At the end of a presentation, lecture, discussion or learning activity, ask learners to write down in one minute what the most important thing is that they have learnt that day, for example, or what they feel they still need clarity on. A creative option is for learning groups to draw pictures or symbols of key learning at the end of a day or as a review at the beginning of the next day.
The pause effect	Provides a check point for understanding. This gives learners a moment to pause, take in what they are learning and assess if they are understanding. This allows for in-the-moment clarification and ensures that the learners are following.	At certain points during the presentation lecture or discussion or learning activity, learners are asked to reflect on what they have just heard. During the presentation, the facilitator could say to the learners something like: "Let's take a moment here to reflect on what we have just heard."
Group project	The ALP learning sets are allocated or choose a real-world project to work on during the programme. This directly allows all those involved in the assessment value chain to observe and measure each person's contribution, growth and ability directly in order to apply their knowledge, skills, and abilities to solving business challenges.	A project should be assigned to or chosen by the learning set at the beginning of the ALP. The projects must be relevant, at the appropriate level of challenge, and meaningful to both the participant and the organisation in order to maintain interest.

Assessment method	Merits	Best used
Group presentations	Each learning set can present their particular project. This provides them with an opportunity to synthesise their knowledge, reflect on what they have learnt, and understand what value their project has achieved. Keep in mind that these may be difficult to assess. It needs to be made clear what is being assessed – content, presentation skills, impact, and so on.	Presentations can be made at start-up or scoping phase to get approval and prioritisation, at project planning phase to get input, at pilot/project results phase, and at the end of the ALP, for final evaluation.
Individual presentations	ALP participants can be asked to present in their individual capacity. Their presentations could provide a way for them to articulate what they have learnt and provide a tool for learner self-assessment and deep reflection.	As above
Peer assessment and feedback	A peer-review process helps participants learn how to give and receive feedback as well as how to assess themselves.	These should be scheduled at regular intervals throughout the ALP and supported through coaching and debriefing to ensure healthy feedback and insight.
Reflective (online) journals	Learners can keep a journal in which they summarise their key learnings, perceptions and reflections. Written communication is an important skill; it gives learners the opportunity to explain succinctly what they have learnt.	This can be daily, weekly or monthly, depending on the amount of reflection the designer or leader would like built in.

Assessment method	Merits	Best used
Simulations	Simulations require the learners to apply their knowledge and skills in a "simulated" or imitated" environment. This provides the learners with the "feel" of a real-world challenge and is a great way to observe their ability to solve problems practically, or allow them to self-assess their ability.	Simulations are helpful when applying knowledge in a real-world context is not possible, for example, military training operations, or changing details on a customer's bank account.
Case studies	Learners can be asked to apply their knowledge in solving problems contextualised within a case study. Case studies can range in complexity.	Used to assess learner ability to apply their knowledge. Case studies are best used as formative evaluations. There are often several right answers, and the level of detail they contain must be balanced. If they have too much detail they can be confusing. However, if they have too little detail, they may be unchallenging, or insufficient detail may be provided for the learner to answer the question.
Direct observation	Learners are observed applying their skills either through role play or within a real-world context.	This assessment method is specific to demonstrable application of practical skill, and the assessment criteria must be clear.

12.6 ASSESSMENT DILEMMAS

The assessment process can be fraught with challenges and frustrations as a result of complexity; role confusion; resistance to feedback; time involved; skills required; and many other reasons. Some of the dilemmas we face as learning practitioners in setting up an assessment value chain and reaching agreement with key stakeholders and learners include the following:

- At which level are we going to assess, and is the time spent in assessing worth the cost?
- How do we get senior managers to agree to an assumption of learning impact on business results?

- How do we ensure that learners are fairly and accurately assessed if there is rater bias?
- Do we need to have qualified assessors or technical experts to do the assessment?
- How can we design uniform assessments when everyone's work environment is different?
- Is assessment of learning HR's role or the line manager's role?
- Whose KPIs should be assessed and evaluated?
- What responsibility does the learner have to prove competence?
- Should we give certificates for attendance, knowledge assessments, or proof of competence (performance and results)?
- How do we hold assessors in the value chain accountable for their role if they say they don't believe in doing something or don't have time?
- How do we manage to prevent people from manipulating 360° feedback to exaggerate results for their friends or downplay results for colleagues with whom they don't get on?

To avoid some of these issues and challenges, it is a good idea to raise these issues and agree in principle at the beginning of a learning project, document the principles and align the design of the assessment value chain to the principles. There must be clarity on purpose and level of assessment required, understanding and buy-in from stakeholders/budget holders as to the resources required for pre-, during and post-intervention assessment and role clarity on who is responsible for what within which timeframes. Include the outputs of these discussion in performance or learning contracts or talent forum outputs, where they can be reviewed and accountability issues addressed. All pre-intervention data must also be agreed on and signed off prior to the start of the programme. This includes pre- and post-data sources and assumptions for levels 3 to 5 assessments.

Whose role is it? The new trend is for the learners to drive the "proof of competence" process, and they will receive the relevant qualification or certification or "role" only once this has been done. It helps to have some kind of positive recognition or reward to encourage this process, as well as clear consequences of not completing assessment assignments. While this is ideal, there is still a power dynamic between the learners and their manager or assessor, so a support structure is required that can intervene where necessary.

There is always a trade-off with assessor skill and objectivity. While some organisations invest in training assessors, technical specialists and line managers in competence assessment, many others cannot afford this, and resort to trusting the professional judgement of their line managers or training providers. There are benefits and risks with both approaches. With peer feedback there will always be some level of rater bias and manipulation. This can be reduced through good training, communication and oversight (such as a validation committee), but you can also argue that any feedback is good feedback and will raise the level of self-awareness over time. Development in emotional intelligence is a good start towards raising the level of feedback maturity in an organisation and making feedback a regular part of the culture through team review sessions, monthly coaching or performance discussions, and skip-level meetings.

To build in an element of individually relevant assessment, set performance and competence standards per level of work (see Chapter 9) that can be applied in multiple environments and then allow learners and managers to agree how they will provide sufficient evidence while not compromising work outputs and productivity.

Ultimately the assessment process requires a robust project and change management approach. Potential stakeholder, risks and barriers need to be identified, engaged and addressed proactively to facilitate a smooth process and avoid the derailers of assessment.

> Watch this video on YouTube: **Evaluation: Accountability and Learning**
> http://www.youtube.com/watch?v=UkzlKrJvpCA

Activity 2

What are your two biggest dilemmas that you face as an organisation in assessing learning?

1
2

Share via e-mail or Facebook to level up.

12.7 ASSESSING THE OVERALL VALUE OF THE ALP

As noted at the beginning of this chapter, less than 18 per cent of organisations are measuring the Kirkpatrick/Phillips model at level 5 (return on investment). Too many stop at level 2 of measurement. This is not sufficient to prove the worth of the ALP to either the participants or the executives who are funding the ALP.

Measuring ROI need not be that complicated, and there are a number of methods that one can use depending on the purpose, available resources and culture.

12.7.1 Expectation Method (Tobin, 2010)

This is a basic method is to measure whether the following expectations have been met:

- **Expectation 1:** Through a comprehensive set of learning events focused on key competencies, you will help participants to develop the business acumen and execution skills they will need. If you planned your ALP with input from company executives and participants, you will have met this expectation.
- **Expectation 2:** You will retain some of your top talent. Employees who see that the organisation is investing in them will be more likely to stay. This will be evident from the number of participants who are still with the organisation at the end of the ALP.
- **Expectation 3:** Through the ALP some long-standing challenges may be solved that might otherwise never have been addressed. Again, whether this expectation is met is self-evident. There is a caveat here, though, and that is that even if the project was not successful, it does not mean that significant learning did not take place.
- **Expectation 4:** You will see participants improve their performance in their current roles as a result of learning gained through the ALP. The best judges of this expectation are the participants' direct managers.

12.7.2 Brinkerhoff's Success Case Method (SCM) (Brinkerhof, 2005)

Brinkerhoff (2005) goes beyond training evaluation to include the systemic factors that can impact on learning and performance and suggests that any evaluation can answer the following questions:

- How well is an organisation using learning to improve performance?
- What organisational processes/resources are in place to support performance improvement? What needs to be improved?
- What organisational barriers stand in the way of performance improvement?

The Success Case Method (SCM) "combines the ancient craft of storytelling with more current evaluation approaches of naturalistic inquiry and case study" (Brinkerhoff, 2005). Essentially, when you apply SCM, you ask:

- What groups/individuals have been successful in applying a learning opportunity to achieve a business result? Why have they been successful?
- What groups have been unsuccessful? Why have they been unsuccessful?

There are a number of steps involved in SCM.

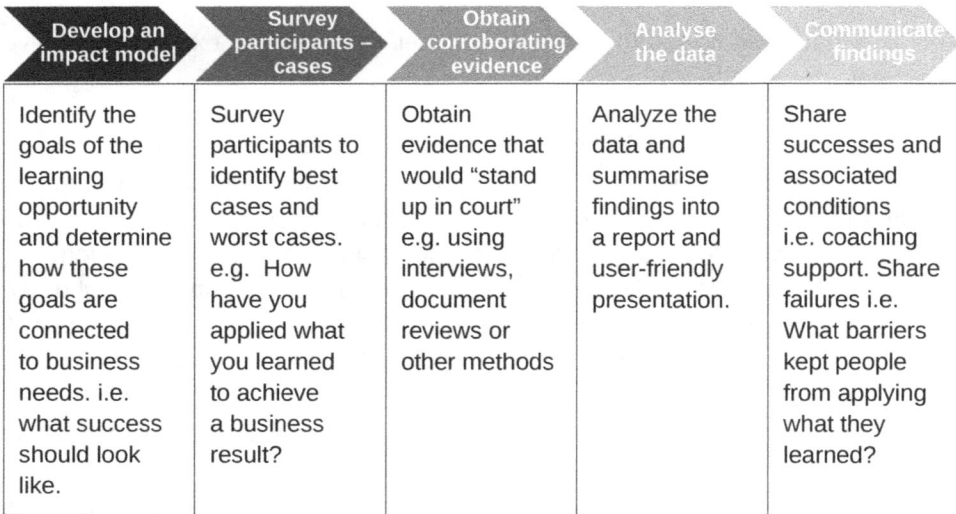

Develop an impact model	Survey participants – cases	Obtain corroborating evidence	Analyse the data	Communicate findings
Identify the goals of the learning opportunity and determine how these goals are connected to business needs. i.e. what success should look like.	Survey participants to identify best cases and worst cases. e.g. How have you applied what you learned to achieve a business result?	Obtain evidence that would "stand up in court" e.g. using interviews, document reviews or other methods	Analyze the data and summarise findings into a report and user-friendly presentation.	Share successes and associated conditions i.e. coaching support. Share failures i.e. What barriers kept people from applying what they learned?

Figure 12.6: Success case method (SCM) (Brinkerhoff, 2005)

Among the benefits of Brinkerhoff's SCM have been noted that it is more user-friendly and cost-effective; it uses relevant stories that can be shared; and it uncovers emergent success factors and unexpected business results. It covers potential survey bias with corroborating evidence and is a positive way of engaging stakeholder in dialogue about continuous improvement and the link to learning.

12.7.3 Kirkpatrick–Phillips level 5 ROI assessment

If you want to do a full ROI, this must be planned from the beginning and follow a robust process. See Figure 12.7 below.

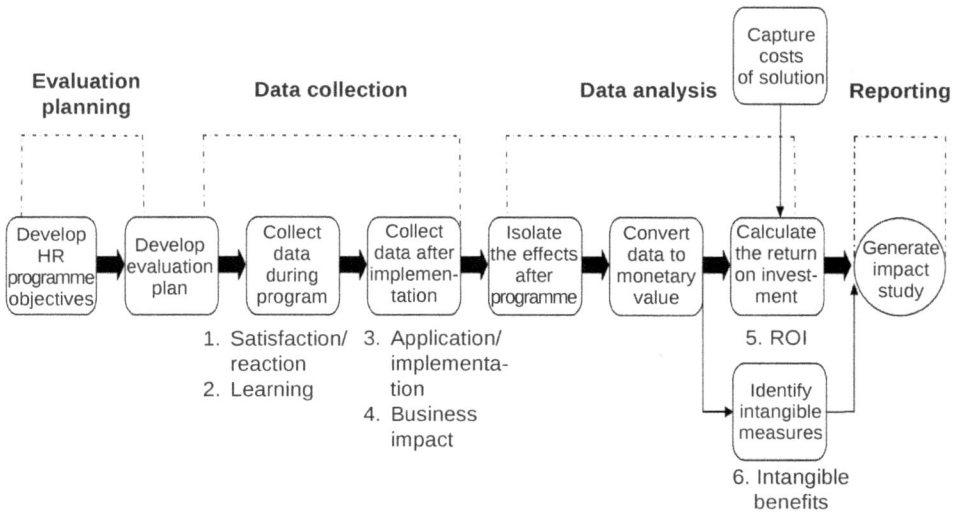

Figure 12.7: Measuring ROI (Phillips, 2002)

- **Evaluation planning** – the assessment process and metrics must be planned up-front and the right stakeholders engaged, for example, executives, financial team, HR team.
- **Data collection** – both hard data and soft data need to be collected pre- and post-programme, and once sufficient time has passed to be able to assess the impact on the job and the results.
- **Isolate the effects of the programme** – you need to determine the amount of output or performance directly related to the programme, as there are many factors that will influence performance data. At the least, agree with stakeholders on key estimates and assumptions and the percentage of impact.
- **Convert data to monetary values** – it is best to use expert estimates (research studies, best practice examples, standard models).
- **Tabulate costs of the programme** – capture all related costs of the programme. You need to decide whether you are including both direct and indirect costs such as the salaries of learning staff.
- **Calculate the ROI** – use the formula: ROI = (benefits – costs/costs) x 100
- **Identify intangibles** – these are the benefits which may not be easily convertible into monetary terms but may still have a positive impact on the organisation.

Worth reading: Leadership Development: Return on Investment
http://www.ddiworld.com/DDIWorld/media/client-results/leadershipdevelop-mentroi_rr_ddi.pdf?ext=.pdf

---

HOT TIP — **Ten Tips for Measuring ROI (Bennington & Laffoley, 2012)**

Bennington & Laffoley in their article, *Beyond Smiley Sheets: Measuring the ROI of Learning and Development* (2012), suggest the following 10 tips in measuring ROI:

1. *Don't go overboard.*

   ROI need only demonstrate value beyond a reasonable doubt. Find out what the executive sponsor identifies as success and stick to that.

2. *Shift from a quality to a results mindset.*

   When designing L&D programmes, it's all about delivering a quality experience that encourages learning. When evaluating, it's about results. When calculating ROI, focus less on the quality of the experience and more on the effect of learning.

3. *Calculate ROI continuously.*

   Always know how the L&D programme is performing so that adjustments can be made. This not only helps to improve the programme, but can justify how income is being spent at any time.

4. *Build a step-by-step case for ROI.*

   Analyse organisational needs and develop strategic learning plans, prioritise them, and present them with sound justification – based on anticipated ROI – about why senior leaders should support them.

5. *Gather data beyond the programme delivery and don't forget data that are already available.*

   Evaluation and feedback should come from as many sources as feasibly possible – from participants, their supervisors, their peers and senior leaders.

6. *ROI isn't just about money.*

   When analysing results, consider such learning measurements as quality, effectiveness, job impact and business results.

7. *Be conservative in ROI calculations.*

   To compensate for bias, self-reported ROI should be factored down and follow-up evaluations should be weighed more than evaluations reported immediately after the programme.

8. *Represent the money outlay as a per participant ratio.*

   Personalise it. Show the per participant cost (versus a total cost) to make the investment more palatable (for example, for this target population, we are looking at a R7 000 investment in learning for an employee responsible for, on average, R1million worth of business).

9. *Communicate the story behind the numbers.*

   This is where using anecdotal information can be helpful in confirming the numbers. It never hurts to highlight data with meaningful examples.

10. *If the ROI numbers are low, don't be discouraged.*

    ROI is intended to assess what is working and what should be shelved or revamped.

Watch this video on YouTube: **How to Measure Learning ROI** by **VP of Learning at ShoreTel, Heather Bennett** http://www.youtube.com/watch?v=FVwx6tLuotg

12.8 CONCLUSION

In summary, assessment of learning is critical to the on-going credibility and effectiveness of accelerated learning as a core organisational competence, culture and practice. Assessment helps us to measure the level of understanding and competence developed through the ALP. It is a way of supporting and enhancing learning, and demonstrates the value of the ALP to the organisation.

PART 5

MAKING IT REAL – CASE STUDIES OF ACCELERATED LEARNING

Chapter 13: How to guide – learning to accelerate change by *Kerryn Kohl*
13.1 Introduction
13.2 A new perspective
13.3 The learning landscape and audience
13.4 The learning design
13.5 Alignment with learning design principles
13.6 Conclusion

Chapter 14: Case Study: Breakthrough Learning for talent pools by *Debbie Craig*
14.1 Introduction
14.2 What is Breakthrough Learning?
14.3 Why Breakthrough Learning?
14.4 Setting up the programme
14.5 High-level design
14.6 Programme outline
14.7 Selection of programme participants
14.8 Assessments
14.9 BL launch workshop
14.10 BL learning modules
14.11 BL project work
14.12 Learning portal
14.13 Final presentation and celebration dinner
14.14 Final wrap-up – ensuring results and sustainability
14.15 Conclusion

Chapter 15: Case Study: Creating a culture of effective decision management by
John Gatherer and *Debbie Craig*
15.1 Introduction
15.2 Context and rationale for effective decision management
15.3 Background to the case study
15.4 The company business case for decision management
15.5 The learning themes and outcomes
15.6 A robust process for WISE decisions
15.7 Accelerated Learning principles
15.8 Conclusion: Quo vadis?

CHAPTER 13

HOW TO GUIDE – LEARNING TO ACCELERATE CHANGE

By Kerryn Khol

13.1 INTRODUCTION

"Any fool can know. The point is to understand." – Albert Einstein

In this chapter what I would like to focus on is how an Accelerated Learning Program (ALP) could be applied in a real-world context. Using a banking example, let's suppose that a major bank identified the need for transformation in order to get closer to their customers and harness the benefits (financial and non-financial) of implementing Customer Relationship Management (CRM) systems and processes.

In order to develop a training strategy for such an implementation, the ultimate outcomes of the CRM strategy and system would need to be clearly understood. After understanding these outcomes, which could be to adopt a new approach to customer intimacy, insight and engagement, it quickly becomes clear that a standard training approach would be insufficient to harness the benefits of such an implementation. In order to derive true realisation of benefit, a shift in perspective would be required from training to a systemic learning approach; that is, focus not just on system skills but on supporting employees through a culture transformation towards true customer relationship management, supported by the CRM system.

13.2 A NEW PERSPECTIVE

To attain competitive advantage in a highly competitive, complex business environment, organisations need both **systems** (technology enabled capability) AND **people** (customer centricity) to win. We needed leaders at all levels to understand that.

The point of view I put forward at the Core Banking Transformation Conference in 2013 (Trade Conference international) was:

To transform core banking systems successfully –
our PEOPLE have to TRANSFORM.

This is quite a challenge, as most stakeholders will still hold the old paradigm of skills training. In order to transform, they need to acknowledge that what they are asking their people to do when asking them to "adopt the change" actually means that they are asking them to **transform** their perspective. The learning strategy developed therefore needs a foundation firmly rooted in transformational learning. People using the system need to engage with both hearts AND minds and think, feel and behave differently for the change to take effect and deliver the benefits.

To guide the development of the learning strategy I would suggest using the following premise (Kotter, 1995):

> What we THINK drives ... What we FEEL, which drives ... How we BEHAVE.

The learning strategy should include a clear definition of the following in relation to the system and their interactions with customers:

- How people should behave.
- How people should feel.
- How people should think.

This perspective should inform the bigger "frame" in which learning should be positioned, and the design of each learning event.

Learning versus training

The learning function has high value to add if treated as a strategic partner. Strategic partners understand the learning architecture and how to describe the transition from current competencies to future desired competencies required to drive the business forward – into the "new world".

A key difference between a learning versus a training perspective is that learning approaches a complex change from a strategic and systemic point of view. Training, on the other hand, results in organisations trying to develop skills retrospectively to fit the "new world". The end result here is that organisations are continually trying to develop competence as opposed to having that competence in place and ready to drive further innovation.

13.3 THE LEARNING LANDSCAPE AND AUDIENCE

Using the principles of Accelerated Learning Programmes (as outlined in Chapters 5 and 10) transformational learning can be driven throughout the key layers of the learning landscape across the different audiences.

13.3.1 The landscape

The learning landscape describes and integrates the **climate** elements required for CRM (or any other implementation for that matter) and the individual and team **behaviours** required, as well as the **system and process** skills to enable effective and efficient performance. These aspects are outlined in Figure 14.1 below.

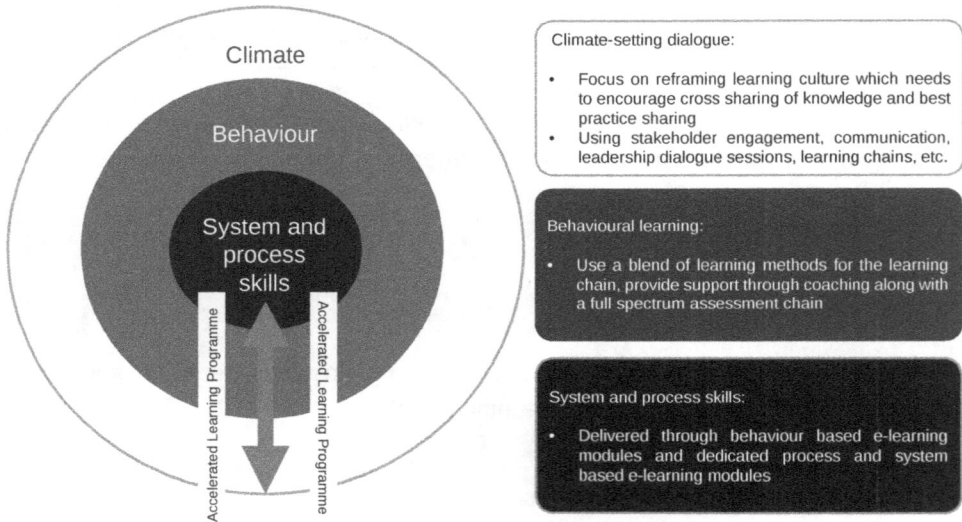

Figure 13.1: Learning landscape

Questions to consider when analysing the landscape and the audience could be as follows:

System and process skills

- What system and process skills are required?
- What level(s) are the current knowledge and skills?
- Can the current staff learn the new skills and processes?

Behaviour

- What behaviours are required to drive the system and execute the process?
- How do these behaviours differ from current behaviours?
- What are the underlying beliefs and mind-sets needed to drive the new behaviour?

Climate

- How can we create a culture/climate that will be able to nurture and sustain the transformation?
- What is the degree of transformation required?
- How can we incorporate both an outside-in and an inside-out perspective?

The climate is important in ensuring that the transformation can take hold and be sustained. In other words, it must be a climate that understands that the implementation is usually greater than a system; it is rather a deep-seated philosophy, as we see in the case of most CRM implementations.

13.3.2 The audience

The learning audience should be mapped by following a cascading approach:

- **Leadership** must be tasked with accountability for creating the correct climate for change in which end-users would be empowered to act and think differently.
- **Line managers and team lead roles** should go through the leadership learning as well as the end-user learning (to a greater or lesser extent, depending on how much real-time system support they would need to provide).
- **End-user learning** should focus on contextualising the strategy and system as a mind-set shift and on the behaviour that is needed to execute the processes and drive the system.

These audiences are reflected in Figure 14.2.

Behaviour coaches should be used as an important part of the strategy to assist with the behavioural change aspect of the learning. Coaching can be both a cost-effective and a high-touch solution, and this role should be catered for in the learning strategy.

What needs to be kept in mind is that each of these audiences, as well as the individual learners in each group, learns differently, and needs to apply learning in different ways. This means that a blanket approach to learning events is largely ineffectual. However, the need to balance a "learner-centric" approach with achieving economies of scale associated with blanket learning methods such as e-learning remains a driving force. This poses a significant challenge, which can be addressed through harnessing the power of accelerated learning.

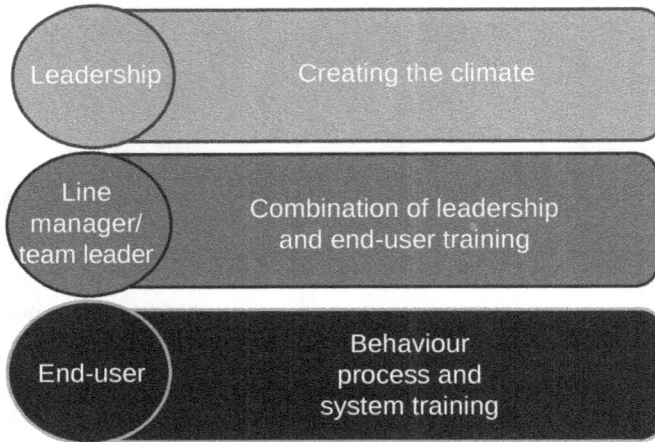

Figure 13.2: Learning audience

13.4 THE LEARNING DESIGN

The challenge of driving transformation needs to be driven from both a top-down and a bottom-up perspective. You cannot simply focus on the end-users and train them to behave in a certain way and interact with the systems in a particular way. This is not sustainable.

Three key design principles should be used as a guide:

1. **Leaders** need to be engaged and given the tools they will need to drive the transformation.
2. **Learners** need "high-touch" support through behavioural coaching.
3. **Learning events** need to grab the learners' attention, foster transformation, and reinforce learning.

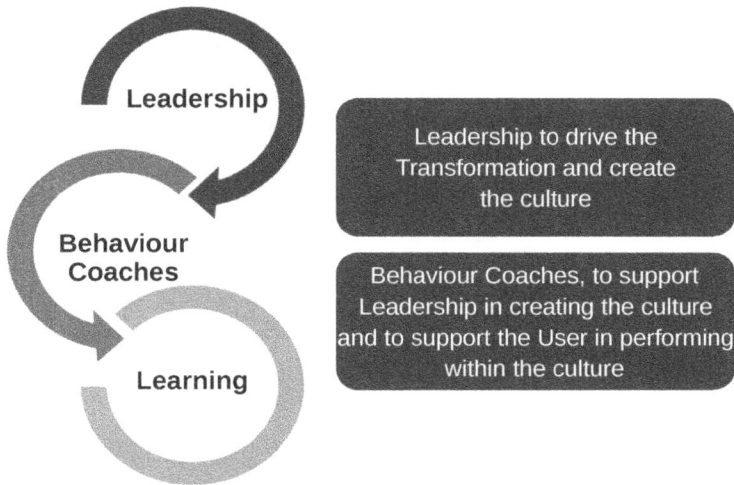

Figure 13.3: Design principles

13.4.1 Leaders

An Accelerated Learning programme for leaders should aim to get them on board and equipped to lead the transformation quickly. The learning programme should be based on both dialogic and accelerated learning principles as described in Chapter 10. These are both key components of transformational learning.

Points that need to be agreed on are the following:

- To drive transformation, you need to start with the leaders.
- Leaders should remain acutely aware that people will always "do what they do and not what they say".
- Leaders need to be exposed to new ways of thinking.
- Leaders need an opportunity to engage in "critical dialogue".

Leadership behaviours should also be clearly defined. In order to lead the change, the organisation needs leaders who understand and can communicate the sense of urgency for transformation. They also need leaders who have vision, can communicate, walk the talk, and remove obstacles for people. Lastly, they need leaders who are aligned, committed, and can take action.

Aim to incorporate through the learning design the following adult learning principles or, when evaluating a design, check that these principles have been included. These are especially true for those in leadership positions:

- Adults learn best through story telling.
- Adults enjoy being exposed to provocative content which they can debate.
- Adults need to feel a sense of autonomy.
- Adults rise to the occasion if an element of competition is introduced.

Leaders should be exposed to powerful **knowledge-sharing sessions** with credible SMEs and given the opportunity to engage with them in dialogue regarding their experience and "war stories". Leaders should then be given the opportunity to develop their own plans and risk mitigations.

13.4.2 The behaviour coaches

The behaviour coach role takes learning facilitation to a new level – by taking learning to the learners in their own environment. This allows the learners to transfer and apply their knowledge and skill easily on the job. The behaviour coach is also able to provide real-time support and immediate feedback. They provide hands-on, high-touch support to the learners on their journey to competence.

Behaviour coaches add the following value:

- Create ownership and involvement throughout all layers.
- Enable awareness and understanding of the change required.
- Provide real-time feedback.
- Reduce change resistance by forming strong relationships based on trust.
- Create a climate in which support is valued and demonstrated.
- Break the changes and learning required into manageable chunks that are easier to understand.
- Promote and advocate bottom-up dialogue.

13.4.3 The learners (including leaders and coaches)

The learners should be exposed to a variety of learning nuggets as part of a learning chain (see Chapter 10), using a blended approach of e-learning; coaching; communities of practice; social media tools; and classroom sessions.

An assessment value chain can be superimposed on the learning chain to track and enable the achievement of competence. See Figure 14.4 below.

Brain Break: Stand up and do a yoga salute to the sun (look it up if you're not sure what it is).

Learning chain

| Learning nugget/event | Learning nugget/event | Learning nugget/event |

| Learning nugget/event | Learning nugget/event |

Action learning	**Learner self-service**	**Performance support**
Components include: • Simulations • Case Studies • Application Driven through a combination of an e-learning platform, other learning technologies, and classroom training.	• Online help • Blog • Community of practice • Ask the expert	• Social media-focused learning applications • Hand outs • Quick reference guides • Other – as required

Assessment value chain

| Competence assessment (Knowledge) | Feedback through coaching/learning support | Performance assessment (Application with understanding) |

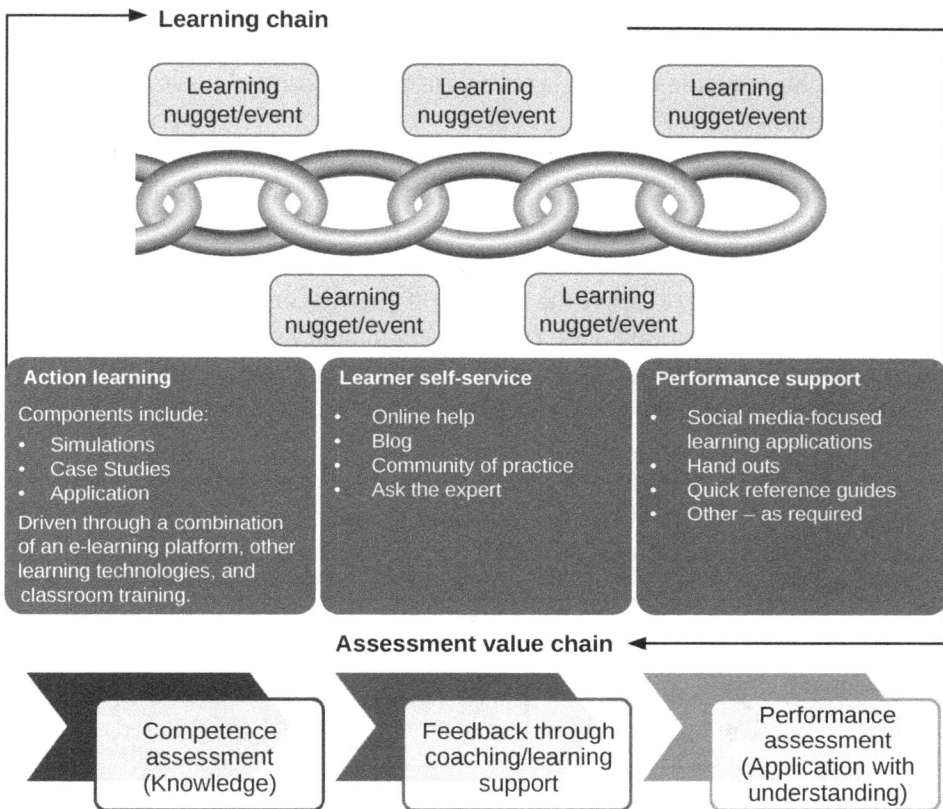

Figure 13.4: Learning design

The power of a learning chain lies in being able to harness the potential of the informal learning opportunities already present in the environment. The formal learning nuggets should be planned to integrate with informal learning opportunities in order to create a highly individualised learning experience and to cater to the different needs and ambitions of the audience. The learning chain links knowledge nuggets or training events in a continuous and sustainable way. For example, a compulsory e-learning module could still form the core link, but could be strengthened by the inclusion of several other links presenting the information in different ways, such as articles, dialogue sessions, blogs, or other social network tools. This learning framework is designed for scalability, flexibility and integration, and can be modularised, thereby making it easy to keep up to date.

13.4.4 Assessment value chain

To increase the robustness of the learning strategy, incorporate a way to measure the effectiveness of the learning and the competence of the learners. As learning professionals we can only create the opportunity for learning; we cannot be held accountable for ensuring that an individual has learnt. Traditionally, most organisations measure their training only at a level 2, or at a knowledge level which assumes that programme attendance and a light knowledge test automatically translates into the ability to apply the learning in the work environment. As we learnt in Chapter 10, this is not true. Line managers continually complain with frustration that they are not competent and struggle to transfer what they have learnt to their job. They either return to their old ways of working or find new, creative ways around the system.

This requires a mental shift for most organisations, and the change must be navigated and managed carefully to avoid too much resistance. Apply the full assessment value chain to achieve this.

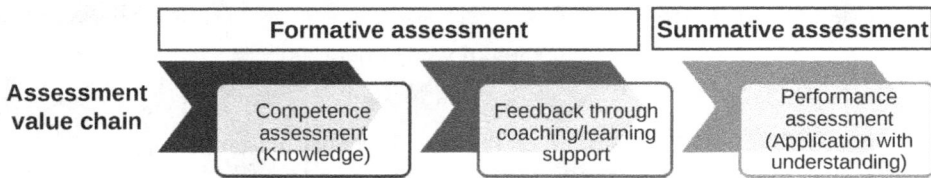

Figure 13.5: Assessment value chain

Through the use of this assessment chain, learners are exposed to the information they need to know and are assessed by means of a knowledge assessment or a scenario-based assessment. The learning strategy should then make provision for a period of time in which the learners apply their knowledge in a real-world context with support by the behaviour coaches. After this period of supported application, their competence (based on their performance) can be assessed. This provides a true measure of their ability to apply what we wanted them to know in the manner in which we intend it to be applied.

13.5 ALIGNMENT WITH LEARNING DESIGN PRINCIPLES

To show how this design aligns with Gravett's *Seven Steps of Program Planning* (Gravett, 2001), as discussed in Chapter 10, the CRM learning strategy is summarised into the seven steps below.

Table 13.1: Seven steps of programme planning

Who?	• **Leadership:** To lead this change we need to create an **engine to drive the** change, not simply control it. Leaders will therefore need to understand the change and be able to lead the transformation. • **Learners:** This group isJu made up of the line managers and the end-users. • **The coach:** Use e-learning supported by face-to-face coaching for behaviour change. The coach role can thus be used both to revise content and to reinforce it through on-the-job observation and immediate feedback. • **Other key players:** The SMEs, e-learning providers, designers, project managers, and change team are key stakeholders. Meet with them often to ensure that they understand what you are trying to achieve and that they support it. Remember that this is a learning journey for them, too.
Why/What for?	• **Leadership:** Leaders need to learn how to lead the transformation and create a culture in which learning can be sustained • **Learners:** Users must be able to drive the system and execute the processes competently. In addition, they must change behaviours with regard to how they interact with customers and each other in order to maximise the benefits of the system. • **The coach:** Observe behaviour and provide support and feedback sessions in order to support behaviour change.
When?	• Learning chains are used to allow for learning and reinforcement as a continuous learning cycle. • Learners are continuously supported by the coaches. • Learning assessment is built into the learning chain to ensure competence. • There should be on-going engagement for leaders and other key stakeholders.
Where?	• Learning throughout the learning cycle should be delivered in several ways. • Online learning is used primarily to keep costs low and includes e-learning modules, learning links, and articles. • Face-to-face learning could include instructor-led sessions, dialogue sessions and coaching. • On-the-job learning includes coaching and performance assessments by the line managers.

What?	• **Leadership:** Ability to understand customer, for example, the CRM implementation holistically through engagement with experts. • **Coach:** Ability to coach learners on how to apply the learning in their learning environments and build competence. • **End-user:** Ability to use the systems and processes as well as soft skills behaviour training such as how to use the various systems and processes most effectively.
How?	• Use a combination of Gagne's 9 levels of instruction and ALP principles to guide our design of the learning cycle and the assessment value chain.

13.6 CONCLUSION

This is a good example of how to develop a learning strategy, landscape and design for a project (in this case we used a CRM implementation example) using an accelerated learning framework and applying this to work challenges. Different learner groups are identified and learning is customised to their unique needs. Learning chains are used which will allow you to optimise both formal and informal learning opportunities with a good blend of learning methods. Learners should be given the opportunity to apply their knowledge and receive feedback in their work environment for continuous improvement and ultimately enhanced performance. The learning needs to be embedded through a continuous cycle of repetition, recall, review and reinforcement in order to ensure sustained learning.

CHAPTER 14

CASE STUDY: BREAKTHROUGH LEARNING FOR TALENT POOLS

By Debbie Craig

14.1 INTRODUCTION

With the increasing economic uncertainty, growing complexity and need to respond proactively and rapidly to changing conditions, never before has the competition for exceptional talent been so fierce. The financial services industry is faced with fierce global competition, market consolidation, expansion into new markets, technology and innovation challenges and the need for significant productivity improvement and cost optimisation to attract and retain very "sticky" customers. To operate and be better than your competitors in this environment requires strategic and collaborative leadership; an ability to respond rapidly and lead others through change; and continual development of leading edge technical skills applied to develop innovative, integrated, team-based solutions. In the operations and technology space, there is a legacy of promoting good technical people into leadership positions, resulting in less than effective leadership styles, experience and understanding of the true role required to lead the company and its people into the evolving future world.

Within this context we were asked to assist a key client with the accelerated development of potential technology and operations successors (future leaders and technical specialists) that would play this important role. A key challenge was ensuring that the chosen participants would continue delivering results in their current roles, while simultaneously learning and working on innovative strategic projects with their learning teams. So we partnered with the company's talent and learning team to customise a pilot "Breakthrough Learning" programme with a view to its full implementation as an annual programme. This chapter outlines the key aspects of this case study including design principles, project management, selection, change management, challenges, examples, and lessons learnt.

14.2 WHAT IS BREAKTHROUGH LEARNING?

Breakthrough Learning (BL) is our tried-and-tested, customised approach to business-driven action learning, as described in Yury Boshyk's book, *Business Driven Action Learning: Global Best Practice* (2000). This is an accelerated learning intervention based on the two key elements of ACTION and LEARNING. The key elements of business-driven action learning are visually depicted below and include personal and organisational learning through focused, team-based projects aimed at generating solutions to real business challenges or opportunities.

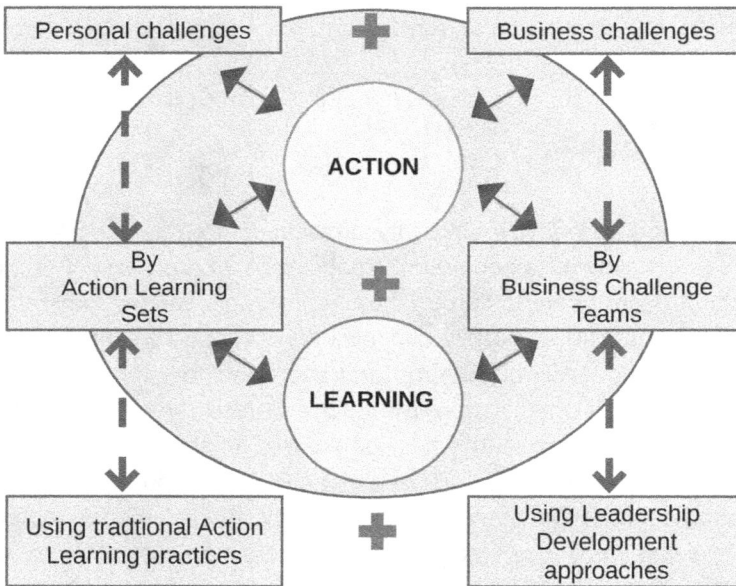

Figure 14.1: Key elements of business-driven action learning (adapted from Boshyk, 2000)

The key features of Breakthrough Learning (typically facilitated over 9 to 12 months) are a blend of the following:

- **Individualised personal growth options** – These consist of external coaching, internal mentoring, assessment centres, learning sessions on leadership and technical competencies, self-study, interactions with thought leaders and organisational role models and feedback from managers and peers. Competency areas are carefully selected to ensure participants get feedback on critical leadership and technical skills required for future successor roles.

- **Team development and collaboration opportunities** – These entail the development of high-performance teams and associated processes of team interaction, feedback and learning. The ideal team has four to eight diverse cross-functional and cross-cultural members, who can bring a variety of perspectives and viewpoints to the tasks and learning at hand. There are regular team coaching and feedback sessions to build feedback fitness and to develop and address areas of team effectiveness proactively. The different teams also interact monthly to share knowledge and learn from each other and explore additional opportunities for co-ordination or collaboration with key stakeholders or technical expertise.
- **Breakthrough Learning projects** – These are executive-sponsored strategic business projects (opportunity and/or problem based) specifically selected for the programme, exposing the individuals and teams to new learning, thinking, skills and behaviours. The projects test the formulation of ideas and solutions, realistic scoping, organisation-wide stakeholder engagement, and presentation of project proposals and progress to the sponsors and executive managers.
- **Outside-in approach** – A key element in the learning process is to encourage outside-in thinking and exposure, in order to bring 'outside the box' solutions to strategic challenges. This can take the form of select benchmark visits or virtual connections to industries and organisations that do things differently, exposure to thought leaders, best practice research and testing ideas with a variety of people from all walks of life.

14.2.1 Key design elements for Breakthrough Learning

In order to ensure a successful programme, it is important to work alongside key organisational stakeholders, to understand the business intimately, and to *customise the design which will optimise learning and results*. There is a need to interrogate the business strategy, the culture, current challenges, competencies required, past and current learning programmes, and current and future roles required. It is also important to identify and customise the most effective processes for *selection of participants, coaches, mentors, teams, project sponsors, and strategic projects*. All of these factors can make or break an intensive, demanding, extended programme that has to happen alongside business as usual.

Talented individuals are by nature and nurture bright, fast learners, well-read, exposed to many learning opportunities, busy people and quite concerned (and fussy) with value for time spent. So it was quite a challenge to design something that would be *perceived as excellent value*, a career-enhancing experience which delivered on exposure to top leaders and influencers and was interactive and experiential in order to make the learning meaningful and fun. Gone are the days where a high flyer is willing to sit in a classroom environment and watch PowerPoint presentations or just listen to plain knowledge or opinion sharing.

The learning environment needs to be stimulating, with a good **blend of learning methodologies and technology** and with the right level of input; and should include knowledge sharing, teamwork, collaboration and practice sessions to test understanding and application and to encourage self-awareness and insight. Many talented individuals have an overly-developed ego (bordering on arrogance) that can prevent an appreciation of personal impact and opportunities for improvement. Individual and group feedback and guided reflection activities are critical for self-insight, boosted with coaches who are able to observe behaviour and give immediate feedback and support.

The **selection process** was also carefully thought through, with tools and training provided to the senior managers and a full talent review process implemented. We needed to consider the appropriate level of candidates with regard both to diversity and EE talent; what to do about emerging talent; reporting lines; and a balance of functions, specialists and generalist leaders in the mix. Other key considerations were career stage; time available (potential candidates were excluded if completing an MBA or were involved in any other intensive long-term learning programme); length of time in the role; and capacity to take on the stress and challenge of more late nights and diary shuffling in order to deliver to multiple stakeholders.

14.3 WHY BREAKTHROUGH LEARNING?

When strategic succession planning identifies the need to develop successors sooner rather than later, or when skills audits identify critical skills gaps in the short term, a faster, more intensive, higher impact process is required to accelerate learning and tap into potential in the fastest possible time.

There are many studies demonstrating that on-the-job or applied learning (with coaching) is the most effective for sustainable adoption of new competencies. Breakthrough Learning offers this aspect in a dual manner through work on strategic projects with diverse, multi-functional teams AND through the need to continue delivering in the current role in less time and with more pressure. In addition, the participants in a BL programme are supported with coaches, mentors, project owners and various inputs to enhance their knowledge, awareness, behaviour and impact.

Breakthrough Learning also offers two additional benefits. Having a group of high-potential, talented individuals working on strategic projects that keep executives awake at night results in innovative ideas being brought into the business AND accelerated project delivery, thereby producing real business value and return on investment (excluding the advantage of having "ready now" successors, and addressing the skills gap, which is very costly to the business in terms of productivity, risk, employee engagement and morale).

The participants in the programme are also exposed to more aspects of the business that may expand their career options, more senior people who may be able to utilise their skills in the future, and more colleagues in other functions whom they can call on for knowledge sharing and collaboration opportunities.

BL Objectives and Business Case

The Breakthrough Learning Programme for high-potential, high-performing talent is designed to unleash exponential possibilities through accelerated learning opportunities in both leadership and specialist skills over a 9-month period through:

- Exposure to world-class thinking and knowledge
- Stimulating team based project work
- Internal and external coaching, mentoring and feedback
- High level sponsorship and recognition
- Longer-term career development planning.

The O&T (Operations and Technology) division is looking for talent that thinks strategically, innovates, unleashes efficiencies and synergies, builds relationships, develops people, and delivers results as a strategic business partner to the front office. Leaders and specialists of the future need to go beyond routine administrative and implementation roles to delivering exceptional value to internal and external customers together as one team with one purpose.

Measures

- Talent attraction through high-quality development.
- Bench strength of succession plan.
- Increase engagement scores of participants.
- Retention of key talent segments and reduction in replacement cost.
- Raised level of competence in relevant technical and leadership areas.
- Positive participant and stakeholder feedback and pilot approved for full implementation.

The biggest challenge to BL programmes is the time and energy commitment required for a successful programme. BL programmes needs a core design-and-implementation team and co-ordination and logistics management to manage the many parties involved including participants, managers, coaches, mentors, project owners, sponsors, consultants, assessment providers, faculty, guest speakers and facilitators. The resources required to manage the programme over 9 to 12 months are significant. While the resources and budget may be off-putting at first, there is conclusive evidence showing exceptional ROI time and time again, and a long-term, strategic view is necessary for the organisation to be able to see the potential results.

The other challenge is perception management of the successful and unsuccessful candidates. That is why the selection process is so important and why it needs to be transparent, objective and credible. If the selection process loses credibility, the programme loses its value and high flyer status.

14.4 SETTING UP THE PROGRAMME

As with any strategic programme or project, the **business imperative and business case** must be clearly documented, communicated, understood and bought into by the key stakeholders. Whether you are an internal or external consultant, it is important to identify the critical strategic levers that will drive executive decisions related to the BL programme.

It is important before embarking on a programme of this nature that there is full **commitment and understanding** of the time, support and effort required from each of the key stakeholders in the programme. It is not just about signing off the budget and tracking the progress. It is about commitment to meeting agenda items, one-on-one influencing sessions, signing off communiqués, attendance at key events, and standing in as mentors or in project owner roles and suchlike. These must be explicit at the beginning of the process in order to prevent resistance at a later stage.

The BL programme was set up with the key roles shown in Table 13.1 in order to apply effective **project governance**.

Table 14.1: Key roles in project governance

Roles	Description
Sponsors	Ensure executive accountability; achieve organisational objectives: and act as change champions
Steercom	Ensure that project meets organisational needs, drives results, makes critical decisions and gives final approval
Project owner	Primary content and context advisor and decision maker; manage provider relationship, integration and stakeholder management; and drive project delivery in partnership with project manager
Project manager	Advise and govern applying project management principles and processes to ensure delivery of project within time, cost and agreed deliverables in partnership with business owner and provider
Project team members	Preparation and participation at project meetings and implementation of agreed processes and actions. Drive change management plan
Key stakeholders	Be kept informed and consulted where appropriate on the project

The **budgets and resources** were identified early to ensure these were part of the business case and that executives knew what they were committing to. There is always a discussion regarding internal versus external resources. In this case, for two years, the internal team had been trying to get the programme started, but had been unsuccessful. Business school programmes had also been investigated, but were found to be too generic for the specific technical nature of this business. It was therefore decided to partner with us as external consultants to customise and project manage the programme with a view to building internal capacity for the internal talent/learning team to take over the process in the future.

This company had a well-developed **project management** office with clear procedures for project management and documentation. Project plans were developed by the core team and submitted to the project management officer (PMO), who allocated a project manager to the core team. Project plans and meeting schedules were shared, updated and monitored. With the sponsors' help, we were able to secure a monthly spot on the O&T Exco meeting for updates and decisions.

The core team developed a **change management** plan identifying all the key stakeholders, their needs, communication channels, events, and timing; and allocated tasks to each core team member. Important stakeholders included the sponsors, the Steercom, the O&T Exco members, the Group management board, the core team members, the Group human capital business partners, the learning academy, the transformation manager (for equity issues), and managers of the participants.

14.5 HIGH-LEVEL DESIGN

When designing a programme of this nature, there are a number of aspects to consider which need to be agreed to in principle before detailed design can begin. There are so many options to choose from, each of which carries advantages, disadvantages, cost, and resource implications. We made a list of the key decisions to be made and then discussed and agreed the design principle with the core team. We were also given input and approval by the Steering Committee (Steercom).

Table 14.2: Design principles and considerations

Principle	Considerations
Number of participants	24 participants were decided on as optimal for one group, with 2 o facilitators and 4 coaches. There is always some fall-out as a result of family or health-issues, promotions, studies or work overload, so it is best to identify 4 to 6 additional candidates who can be invited before the launch of the programme.

Principle	Considerations
Levels of participants	There is a choice between people of the same level or a cross level to build cross-generational learning. We selected people of a similar level and to target the input sessions and projects to address specific next-level learning needs in that group. The programme was also pitched as a prestigious one, so we didn't want a higher level person to feel that they were on a course that was not relevant to them. Cross-level programmes can be useful to build leadership competencies of diversity, optimising team resources, working with others and finding solutions to operational issues requiring all levels of input and experience.
Leadership or technical specialist focus	This being a back-office function with an operational and technology focus, it was important that successors were being developed for both leadership and technical specialist roles. We therefore designed the programme with a 60/40 split, with slightly more focus on leadership, because the technical specialists also require leadership skills in order to be effective in their specialist roles – often leading a small team, or working collaboratively in project teams. The challenge was to ensure that the sessions were mostly relevant to both types of people. We considered splitting the input sessions with options to attend different sessions, but it was finally agreed that both types needed a clear understanding of leadership and technical issues in the industry and company, and could then dig deeper into the areas of speciality through other learning mechanisms.
Within or across functions	We chose a cross-functional approach to build awareness of and networks across different functions. This became a key highlight of the programme for the participants. Same-function groups can be useful when working on solving function-specific problems and building deep functional skills.
Competency profile	To ensure clear measurement of the learning, we selected 10 leadership and 10 technical competencies relevant to most of the candidates and undertook both pre- and post-reviews of the competency level to identify areas of greatest growth. The competencies were derived from a combination of role profiles, performance and competence standards for the level. A combination of psychometrics, assessment centre activities and manager feedback was used to determine growth areas during the programme and learning priorities post-programme.
Length of programme	An action learning programme can be anywhere from 3 months to 2 years in duration. We have found that the ideal timing is 9 to 12 months for a part-time programme. Longer than that, and there are often too many changes in positions, priorities, line managers, and so on to continue effectively. Shorter than that, the learning may become superficial and unsustainable.

Principle	Considerations
Length of programme (continued)	Also, it is very difficult to get a strategic project off the ground and find solutions in a shorter time. We chose 9 months (based on the time it takes to bring a child into the world). This included the December/January period. In hindsight, it is better to build in some extra time if going over the year-end period, as it created some unnecessary stress and pressure at a time when people are tired and need a holiday.
Full-time versus part-time programme	It is an option to take people out of their normal roles for the period of the programme and let them work full time on strategic projects and the learning journey. In our context, it was more important for the business to keep these relatively senior people in their roles, and additionally to stretch them to manage 2 important roles simultaneously, thereby learning how to prioritise, delegate, empower, and manage their time and stress. It was made very clear during the invitation stage that it would be a tough process in this regard.
Percentage of time required from participants	We estimated that the participants would be spending approximately 10% of their time on the programme, that is, half a day a week. This included the one day a month input sessions and coaching. In reality, the participants probably spent about 15% because of the nature of the strategic projects and the culture of the company, which required consultation with many stakeholders before decisions could be made. Most of the participants, despite the additional challenge, did really well in their "day jobs" as well and were glad to be forced to learn to prioritise, delegate and empower in more creative ways. It is critically important to get senior executive and line manager buy-in to this principle, so that they can assist the person in their prioritising, and not just expect to spend 100% of the time in their day jobs.
Selection process	You can nominate people, ask for volunteers, or undergo a rigorous selection process. We opted to enhance the organisation's talent review process, train the managers, and hold a special selection forum. It was important as a result of past issues with the credibility of selection and the programmes that the selection was seen to be objective, credible and fair. The whole level that was eligible received communication about the programme and the selection criteria and process, and interested individuals were then required to put together a portfolio of evidence to submit to the forum.
Employment equity	This issue became a hot topic, as it does. There were arguments for both a target approach and for the "by merit only" approach. The organisation was behind on its EE targets, particularly at the senior levels, and some executives wanted to include some up-and-coming talent to accelerate their learning. Others suggested that this would dilute the programme's prestigious nature, and that some senior leaders would not want to attend once they realised this. The selection forum categorised the candidates as A-, B- or C-level candidates. Ultimately, it was decided to include a few EE candidates from the B category, on the condition that they would cope with the pressure and their role in the project teams without its leading to confidence issues.

Principle	Considerations
Psychometric assessments	There was a big debate around using assessments for filtering versus development. There is always a cost and time challenge around assessments. Do you offer every candidate who enters the process the opportunity of assessments (which may be many), or do you select the participants first on performance and behavioural evidence, and then do the assessments to validate the selection and to develop them further? It was agreed to complete a full battery of assessments that would be used primarily as a development tool, and only as an exception to filter out candidates who were not going to make the grade.
Team selection for projects	Participants can choose their own teams or be allocated to teams in advance. We chose to allocate people to teams to ensure a mix of function, gender, leadership versus specialist role, and race. We also considered personalities to ensure that the teams were well-balanced. We kept the option open for swaps but only if this was requested directly.
Competition versus collaboration	We spent a lot of time talking about the advantages and disadvantages of working in competing teams versus having joint collaborative projects. Collaboration and consultation are key skills in the new world of work. We opted for separate projects for each team for logistical purposes, but encouraged collaborative learning through sharing tips and contacts and building relationships at the monthly input session.
Breakthrough learning projects	The identification and selection of BL projects took a significant amount of time and energy. We set criteria for the projects, and then asked the executive team to put projects forward for consideration. Ultimately, the choice is between strategic or operational projects and between functional or cross-functional projects. We also had to consider willing business owners, complexity, availability of resources, outside-in thinking, cost, timeframes, and so on.
Choice of projects	Many learning programmes allocate projects to the groups. We believe it is always good to give choices to learners for their buy-in and motivation. In this case we chose a short-list of possible BL projects and developed an activity for the launch workshop in which the teams had to choose and negotiate for their preferred project. This worked really well as we got buy-in and we were able to observe the behaviours of the participants and give them feedback on their approach and skills in this type of typical business requirement.
Roles in strategic projects	To ensure success of the projects, we worked with the executive team and relevant business managers to find both sponsors (senior executives on the board) and business owners (who would drive the project to completion post-BL programme). We also identified possible subject matter experts (SMEs) as resources in specialist areas.

Principle	Considerations
PMO link of strategic projects	The choice was to run the project as a pure learning project outside business-as-usual processes or to run the projects as official business projects. We chose the latter, which created opportunities for the participants to learn the process of business case development, stakeholder buy-in, presenting for prioritisation, budget allocation, and ultimately proving the return on investment (ROI). There were very rigorous processes, and although tough, the candidates appreciated the learning curve.
Support roles – coaches/ mentors	The choice here was to have internal or external coaches and/or mentors. While there was some internal capacity for coaching, it was decided to utilise external coaches/facilitators who would have many opportunities to observe the candidates in action in the various learning sessions, and could be very objective and confidential. It was decided to allocate each team an internal mentor to assist with internal culture issues, networks, problem solving, stakeholder influencing and support where required. Each team was allocated an external coach who worked with the team on effectiveness and dynamics. Each candidate was offered 3 one-on-one coaching sessions during the programme, one post-programme review session with the line manager, and an additional session for integration as required after the session.
Line manager roles	Line managers were included in the initial communications about the programme and in the selection process, and engaged with on their role and support required for their report on the programme. It is important that they are kept up to speed on the programme, projects, and so on. It is also important to request the manager to observe behaviour and skills for the post-programme review.
Input provider roles/faculty	There are so many choices to get great input into a learning programme. The key choice was the balance of interna, company-specific input from SMEs in the company and external options from business schools or guest speakers that could create new insight into topics. International options were also considered, but became quite cost prohibitive for a small group. It was decided to use about 50/50 internal and external providers (with international experience). Internal and external providers were briefed and sessions customised to the needs of the group. As the programme evolved, we were able to secure top company and group leaders for fireside chats and additional input sessions which were highlights in the programme.

Principle	Considerations
Outside-in learning	Some programmes build in budgets to send their teams for best practice visits abroad. This was considered, but based on the nature of the strategic projects, it was felt that much of the information required could be found in the company or group of companies and through specialists in the country. International best practice research was, however, encouraged, including contacting other researchers or organisations to share ideas, interviews and surveys. We also invited a provider early on in the programme to review research approaches and tips.
Executive roles	To ensure that the programme and BL projects were taken seriously, the executive team was identified as a key stakeholder. With the sponsors help, we were able to secure a monthly agenda item to work through the initial design principles, selection process and strategic project decisions. We also were able to train the execs on the refined talent management process and specifically the selection forum role, because they were members of the forum. As the projects progressed, the team presented at the executive meetings on their progress and were given additional ideas, critique and support at these sessions. At the final presentation, the executives were on the evaluation panel and judged the outcomes. This level of involvement ensured the success of the programme and project and it was a key benefit to the participants to receive this level of exposure.

14.6 PROGRAMME OUTLINE

Once the key design elements had been agreed, it was possible to develop a high-level programme plan. An overview of the nine-month programme is visually depicted below, with the groups getting together every six weeks for learning modules, team coaching and knowledge sharing.

The introductory session and the final presentation were the start and finish of the programme. The three-day launch workshop was a fundamental design element in the programme. The morning sessions were earmarked for interactive leadership modules, while the afternoon sessions were spent with internal or external guest speakers on practical "how to make it happen" sessions on industry- and business-specific topics. At the end of each day, the teams would get together with their team coaches, and debrief the key insights from the day, talk about project progress, team dynamics and effectiveness (using a variety of team tools), and plan for the next six weeks. Most of the teams met in their work environment weekly for two to three hours to keep the momentum going.

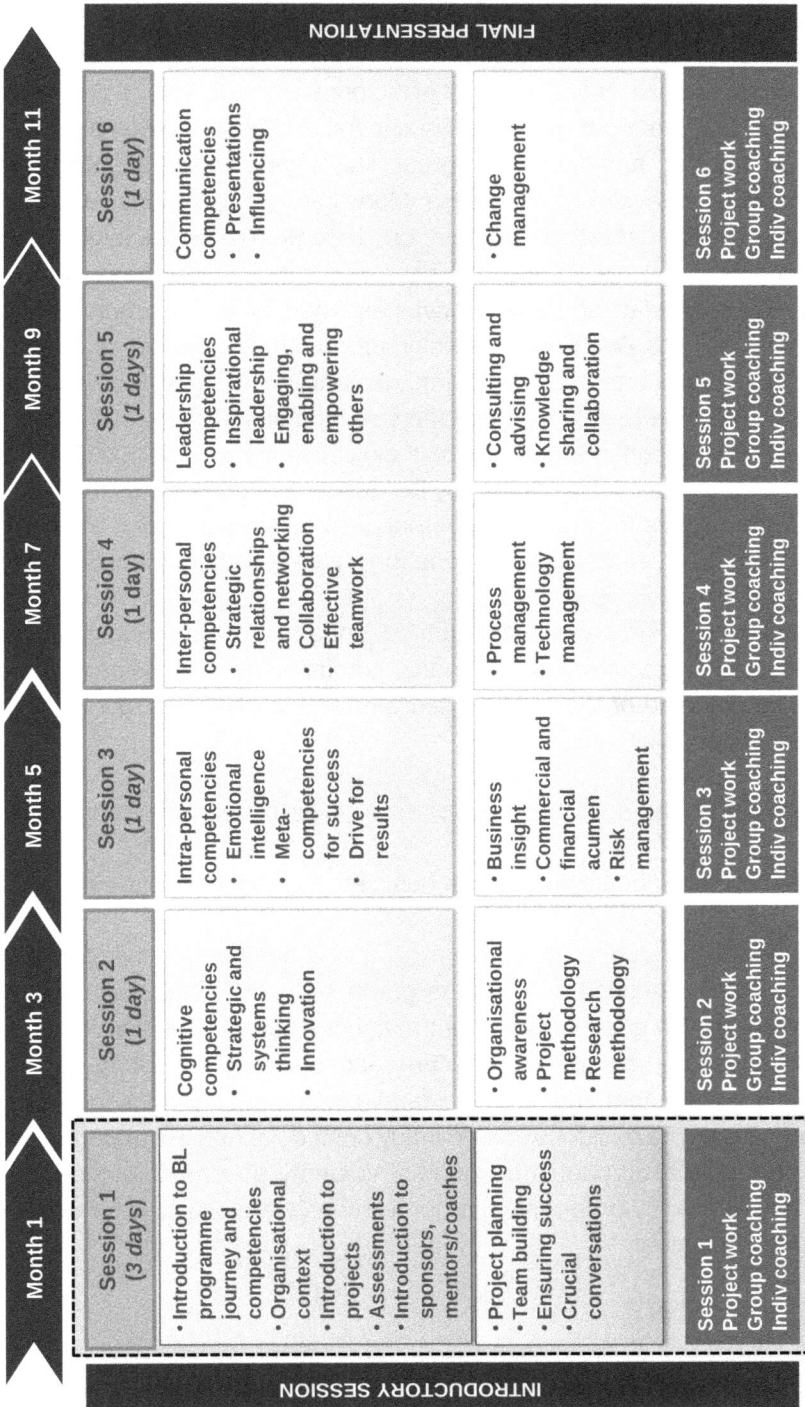

INTRODUCTORY SESSION ... **FINAL PRESENTATION**

	Month 1	Month 3	Month 5	Month 7	Month 9	Month 11
	Session 1 (3 days)	Session 2 (1 day)	Session 3 (1 day)	Session 4 (1 day)	Session 5 (2 days)	Session 6 (1 day)
	• Introduction to BL programme journey and competencies • Organisational context • Introduction to projects • Assessments • Introduction to sponsors, mentors/coaches	Cognitive competencies • Strategic and systems thinking • Innovation	Intra-personal competencies • Emotional intelligence • Meta-competencies for success • Drive for results	Inter-personal competencies • Strategic relationships and networking • Collaboration • Effective teamwork	Leadership competencies • Inspirational leadership • Engaging, enabling and empowering others	Communication competencies • Presentations • Influencing
	• Project planning • Team building • Ensuring success • Crucial conversations	• Organisational awareness • Project methodology • Research methodology	• Business insight • Commercial and financial acumen • Risk management	• Process management • Technology management	• Consulting and advising • Knowledge sharing and collaboration	• Change management
	Session 1 Project work Group coaching Indiv coaching	Session 2 Project work Group coaching Indiv coaching	Session 3 Project work Group coaching Indiv coaching	Session 4 Project work Group coaching Indiv coaching	Session 5 Project work Group coaching Indiv coaching	Session 6 Project work Group coaching Indiv coaching

Figure 14.2: Sample BL programme outline

14.7 SELECTION OF PROGRAMME PARTICIPANTS

The selection process was a critical element of the programme to ensure credibility, transparency and that the "right" people were chosen. Although the company had a reputation for choosing and developing great talent, there wasn't an integrated talent identification and development process. Many career discussions happened in an *ad hoc* way or as an afterthought to performance discussions. Development was largely left up to the individual's manager and local HR business partner. Talent forums were a relatively new concept and had been launched only in some departments. The Breakthrough Learning programme was seen as an ideal opportunity to launch an integrated Talent Management Process and Toolkit across the business, and use the results to inform the selection of the BL participants.

A **special talent forum** consisting of the O&T executive committee (Exco) and a few key HR specialists was set up especially for selection of participants for the BL programme. Prerequisites for presenting potential candidates included attending the training, having a career discussion, preparing a career development plan, and producing a portfolio of evidence.

The **career discussion** was important to understand career aspirations, learning plans, support required, and personal commitment to participate in the programme. The outcome of the career discussion was a **portfolio of evidence** which included evidence of:

* **Performance:** Results, accomplishment, relationships, project/team contribution, culture.
* **Potential:** ability, attributes, leadership qualities, aspiration, engagement.

This robust process (although time consuming) had a number of advantages. It gave managers the information and tools to get to know their staff much better. It gave the O&T Exco an overview of all of the talent existing at middle to senior levels in the business and the risk areas where readiness was still a long way off. It helped to build a consistent and fair process across the business for identifying and developing talent. The business offered many other development opportunities and learning programmes through the Learning Academy, so even if an individual was not selected for the BL programme, other avenues were explored for optimal exposure and development.

14.8 ASSESSMENTS

The use of psychometric assessments is often a hotly debated topic in talent and learning environments. Some managers argue that they are best placed to observe performance and behaviours and therefore have the evidence to make good development or placement decisions. Specialist HR professionals argue that managers may be biased or less skilled at competency or potential assessment and therefore should leave these decisions to the professionals. In this project, it was decided to use the best of both worlds and compare and consider the results of managers' views with the result of a battery of psychometric assessments. These included assessments for Emotional Intelligence (EQi), Cognitive Processing Potential (CPP), Personality (OPQ), Derailers (Hogan), and Competence

Each of the participants received a one-on-one feedback session with the assessment specialist, in order to understand their results and what it meant for them on the programme, and to help them to prioritise development needs. The participants were also encouraged to discuss their results with their coaches and develop a detailed PDP for the programme (although this was voluntary owing to the confidential nature of the assessments). Most participants chose to share their full report with their coaches, which indicated a high level of trust in the process and the coaches.

A complete pre- and post-assessment process was outlined to ensure progress was tracked.

14.9 BL LAUNCH WORKSHOP

It was important at an early stage in the process to set the context for the entire nine-month programme, demonstrate the senior leadership commitment to the programme, build the necessary relationships within the programme, and ensure that the choice and scoping of the learning projects were optimal. The other very important part of the launch programme was to observe the participants tackling a variety of tasks, and undertaking an initial behavioural assessment of each person linked to the overall programme competencies.

The purpose and objectives of the launch workshop were set as follows:

* To create the strategic context for the BL programme.
* To ensure that the BL programme commitments, deliverables and outcomes were clarified.
* To introduce the coaches, mentors and sponsors to the participants.
* To build the team-effectiveness of the project teams.
* To prepare participants and teams for success.
* To encourage personal insight through feedback and coaching.
* To develop and refine draft project charters for the action learning projects.

A blended learning approach was adopted in the design, utilising information sharing, guest speakers, pre-reading, facilitators, coaches, observers, experiential learning, self-reflection, team discussions, feedback processes, music, visual charts, an online learning portal, and many others.

One of the powerful processes we use regularly is the concept of feedback post-boxes. Each participant is encouraged to observe the behaviour of their team members and other participants and give them caring, constructive, coaching-style feedback in the form of ACT cards (Action, Consequence, Try this). The intent is to catch people behaving as effective leaders and to notice where people could be more effective if they adjusted their approach or style. The ACT cards are then posted into the post-box of the feedback receiver, who then collects and reflects on his/her feedback on the last day with an opportunity for a debriefing with a colleague and after the workshop, with their coach.

After the workshop, all of the participants received feedback from their coaches (who were all behavioural observers at the session), linking their observed behaviour to their post-box feedback received, their personal view of self, and their assessments, to get a holistic view of strengths and areas requiring some attention or ways of minimising exposure, for example, by delegating or partnering.

14.10 BL LEARNING MODULES

The next step of the process was the detailed design of the learning module objectives, **choosing guest speakers or facilitators**, and working with them to ensure that the learning experience met all the criteria of a prestigious high flyer programme. It was important that the guest speakers were knowledgeable about the subject, would incorporate the global context and cutting edge thinking, were well respected in their industries and peers, were effective and engaging facilitators (rather than academic lecturers), could bring a practical case study element to the session, and were relevant to the level, industry and work functions of the participants.

Another important factor to consider in the design of such a programme is to determine whether the learning sessions will be **focused on knowledge, skills, behaviours** or **mind-sets**. Developing a technical or leadership skill takes time, practice and repetition, and each of the competency sets would take a minimum of two days plus practice for skill building. It was therefore decided that, because of the diverse nature of the group, we would design the sessions as knowledge and mind-set sessions, introduce the skill areas, and encourage the participants to include areas of interest or requirements on their PDPs and work with their coaches and line managers to continue the learning journey toward skill and ultimate competence for the next level role.

The **feedback f**rom the participants after the programme indicated that they found all of the sessions valuable (all rated over 80 **per cent**), with the exception of two which were found to be too theoretical and dry. The greatest impact was the fireside chats with senior leaders set up in a coffee lounge environment (with armchairs and real cappuccinos and lattes) and the ability to connect with senior management, listen to their leadership stories and see their human side.

14.11 BL PROJECT WORK

The choice and management of the learning projects is the trickiest part of the whole programme and has the potential to make or break the experience for the participants and stakeholders.

Typical complaints we heard from previous action learning programmes are as follows:

*   The projects were either too basic or too complex and time consuming.
*   Senior managers didn't take them seriously as they were not involved in the selection.
*   Participants didn't see the relevance of them to their work.
*   The projects didn't reach implementation phase and were seen as a waste of time.
*   It was difficult for the participants to get together to complete the projects.
*   Many of the projects were individual projects which didn't test teamwork.

Taking these issues into consideration, the core team spent a lot of time testing criteria with the senior stakeholders and then rating the learning project options against these.

The criteria set were as follows:

*   Specialist and leadership exposure
*   Feasible time frame (8 to 9 months)
*   Links to strategic objective
*   High probability of implementation
*   Brings 'new' knowledge to company
*   Cross-business unit applicability
*   Suited to a team of approximately 5 to 6 people
*   High-level committed sponsor in place
*   Highly relevant to programme participants.

These criteria were put into a decision matrix with the final seven projects, making a short-list for the participants to choose from. These included projects across the spectrum such as implementing knowledge management systems, integrating

HR systems, developing new technology applications, streamlining spreadsheet systems, single view of client data, and even building capacity for emerging entrepreneurs as a CSI initiative.

The teams had an opportunity to consult with the project sponsors owners during the launch workshop in order to select their project and complete the high-level scope and plan. It really worked to have senior leaders as part of the selection process. Not only were the participants exposed to critical strategic issues in the company, but the senior leaders were really interested in the learning team's findings and recommendations.

The **highlights** of the project work from the participant's perspective were being exposed to senior leaders across business units; getting to know and network with colleagues in other business units; and gaining insight into strategic challenges and the difficulties in overcoming them.

The **biggest challenge** was finding the time to work together as teams, scheduling senior leadership sessions with busy people, for joint analysis and problem solving and learning how to balance priorities across work and learning project deliverables and deadlines

Our **key learning** from the learning projects was to carefully manage the scope of the projects within the 10 **per cent** of time available over the nine months, bearing in mind that all the participants already had full-time important roles in the organisation. Some of the teams managed their scope and timing really well, while some of the teams were a little over-ambitious and underestimated the complexity of the task and the number of sessions required with multiple stakeholders to find an agreed approach going forward. We would recommend breaking large complex projects up into the phases of analysis, design, testing, and implementation, which could potentially be followed through with different learning teams over a longer period of time or handed over to business project teams.

The learning projects would have been exceptionally difficult to complete without the support of some key people, notably their mentor, coaches, sponsors and business owners. The support roles were clearly defined, and each of the possible players identified and engaged with around their roles. The internal mentors were also given some refresher training on mentoring skills.

14.12 LEARNING PORTAL

To support virtual learning, knowledge sharing and collaboration in between sessions, a BL portal was developed by internal IT developers. The learning portal was designed to support the following:

Programme section (for all participants) for getting to know you, photo uploads, chat, programme schedule, programme pre-reading and material, additional articles or references.

Team sections (colour coded) for team chat, document sharing, calendar of events, timelines, uploads, and so on, specific to the learning team projects.

Open access for sponsors, mentors and input providers to engage online with the group.

Each learning team identified a portal champion and was responsible for ensuring use of the portal and regular updating of documents. In the initial stages, we had to spend some time reinforcing the importance of virtual spaces and online knowledge management, as for many it was a new mind-set; but by the end of the programme, it had become the way of working and is a critical skill for the future world of work.

14.13   FINAL PRESENTATION AND CELEBRATION DINNER

There were two parts to the finale of the programme, the final presentation and evaluation, and the celebratory dinner.

The final presentation session was arranged as a high-profile event to create a sense of Great Opportunity and Great Risk. The judges were the O&T Exco members. Additional invited guests to presentations (but not eligible to judge) included the sponsors, owners, mentors, coaches, and HR business partners. There was also a film crew video-interviewing the teams pre- and post- their presentations and talking to the judges. All the judges were briefed on the criteria and the judging process, and were supported with spreadsheets to calculate the quantitative and qualitative aspects of the final results.

The final evaluation criteria included both Learning aspects and Delivery aspects, each counting for 50 **per cent** of the total.

Table 14.3: Evaluation criteria

Learning criteria (50%)	Project criteria (50%)
Individual and team learning	Business improvement
Organisational learning	Operationalisation
Innovation/outside-in thinking	Final presentation/document

There was much nervousness and excitement as well as a good dose of anticipation by the various stakeholders. As a fitting end to an intensive, challenging and exciting year of learning, we held a celebratory dinner at an upmarket venue, with the usual speeches, photos, joker prizes, and final prize-giving and thank-yous.

All in all it was considered a resounding success by all involved, with some significant benefits for the participants and for the company.

14.14 FINAL WRAP-UP: ENSURING RESULTS AND SUSTAINABILITY

Many projects lose their initial focus once key milestones have been achieved. People lose interest, momentum is lost, and all the hard work does not create sustainable value. A number of mechanisms to address this tendency were built into the project, including tri-partite pre- and post-competency reviews, integration coaching and development planning, project handover to owners for implementation, and tracking through the PMO.

The tracking process is still under way. However, it was unanimously agreed by the O&T Exco that they will continue the BL programme as a standard developmental programme within the company.

14.15 CONCLUSION

Overall, the participants and executives perceived the programme as a very valuable process with an excellent ROI, and recommended it as an annual learning programme going forward. There was measurable competence improvement, and many of the participants have moved into more senior roles or clarified their career expectations through the process. The biggest benefit participants felt was exposure to senior managers and leaders in different functions and across the group and in building networks with peers across the business, leading to expanded career opportunities and options and a better understanding of the business overall. Another key benefit was the realisation of leadership requirements (technical or people leadership) and what the participants personally needed to practise to become leaders of the future. We also observed a marked improvement in confidence and inter-personal relating, presenting, and influence in the group as a whole. The PMO and talent team will continue to track longer-term benefits of the strategic project and talent metrics.

Advocates of BDAL emphasise that "action without learning is unlikely to provide fruitful longer term results, and learning without action does not facilitate change in the organization. So, whether balanced or not, there is still a need to have both." – Cho, 2013

Brain Break: Take 5 bright Post-it notes and write down an affirmation on each of them regarding something you want to learn or change. Stick them up where you will see them every day.

CHAPTER 15

CASE STUDY: CREATING A CULTURE OF EFFECTIVE DECISION MANAGEMENT

By John Gatherer and Debbie Craig

15.1 INTRODUCTION

Decision making is one of the most important business skills, but few people have actually been trained in the art and practice of effective and consistent decision making. Most people find it difficult to make decisions, but the reality is that we all have to make them and some decisions have extremely important consequences! Some people put off having to make decisions by endlessly searching for more information, while other people would prefer someone else to offer advice or make the recommendation on the quandary regarding which they need to make a decision.

We have recently had an exciting opportunity to apply an integrative learning solution and upskilling approach in decision management that incorporates critical thinking and effective decision making across a "critical mass" of managers within the business units of one of our key global clients. This chapter provides the context and imperative for the design and development of this capability-development project as well as an overview of the critical features of our accelerated learning product.

15.2 CONTEXT AND RATIONALE FOR EFFECTIVE DECISION MANAGEMENT

"How many of you here have been on a training programme or read a book about decision making?" This was a question posed by a presenter on leadership impact at a business breakfast in Durban's International Conference Centre to an impressive audience of over 500 people. The few hands that appeared in the huge auditorium prompted her to exclaim incredulously, "I have had that same poor response from all the audiences in which I have asked that question… and yet it is the single biggest requirement of management!"

It appears to be one of the modern paradoxes that in spite of our lack of competence and confidence in making decisions, we continue to make them anyway! And the results are haphazard. Research indicates that up to 60 per cent of executives say that their business decision making has a 50 per cent success rate. It is common knowledge that up to 83 per cent of mergers and acquisitions fail to create value for shareholders. How do we explain why 40 per cent of senior managers are pushed out, fail or quit within 18 months? On a personal front, why do we struggle to choose the right relationships or continue to get work-life balance so wrong? Is it not amazing that the majority of us are happy to continue making decisions in everything we do without a thorough understanding of the complexities of decision making and the impact of our own personal influences and behavioural traps on the quality of decision making!

In the face of the difficult demands in the changing business world over the last twenty years, there has been a growing focus on management development and leadership effectiveness through business school programmes, training workshops, management education publications and online links. But for some strange reason, we digest everything else about the art and practice of leadership but ignore one of our critical competencies – decision making. The irony is that our hit rate and track record in decision management is distinctly ordinary and many organisations report a crisis of confidence in their managements' decision-making ability.

In this turbulent and complex world where change and uncertainty are bombarding us daily, never before has the need for swift, effective and collaborative decision management been more critical.

A company with true decision competency …

- Routinely makes high quality decisions and frames decisions appropriately.
- Relishes coping with difficult and complex questions.
- Confronts high-conflict issues.
- Makes what seem like courageous acts become habit and an integral part of their organisational culture.
- Views decisions as a critical step toward effective action – rather than as a bureaucratic process.
- Ensures that their decision makers understand their roles – they "walk their talk".
- Has a common language and a broad array of tools, techniques, and processes that are used appropriately.
- Understands the behavioural traps inherent in natural decision making and knows how to compensate for them;
- Continually endeavours to learn and improve its decision competency.

(Adapted from Spetzler, 2007)

15.3 BACKGROUND TO THE CASE STUDY

Our journey in building a learning solution in decision management capability started with a-fascinating trigger. Over eighteen months ago we had an interesting meeting with two MDs from one of our biggest global clients, with whom we had been working closely over the previous six years in implementing strategic change management, leadership development and talent management throughout their organisation.

They were expressing their concerns and exasperations regarding the general quality and variability of decision making throughout their business units. There was a tendency to defer decisions upwards and to avoid collaborating where required, or to make reactive decisions which then had to be damage controlled! Although each of them looked after different regions in the world (Africa/Europe and South East Asia/China), their anecdotes and experiences had an uncanny similarity. The result of this conversation and further sharing of ideas on decision management was the establishment of a joint design team to develop a programme to bridge the gap in their company in critical thinking and decision making. While the original brief seemed simple – "fast track our managers through a training programme in effective decision making" – the complexity of the subject provoked us to design a learning approach that would address the following key questions:

- How does one create a culture of effective decision management within an organisation?
- How do we instil in people the discipline of critical thinking and questioning?
- What clear framework, skills sets and mindset shifts will enhance the quality of decision making?
- How can we heighten people's awareness regarding their personal influences on decision making – biases, emotions, over-confidence, narrow framing, and so on?
- How can we promote a collaborative approach to decision management that ensures greater engagement, involvement and synergies of the process, and ownership of the outcome?

The design was an iterative and collaborative process using our research, consulting and design expertise with their internal knowledge of their business realities, decision challenges and their people. We also had regular review sessions with the two MDs.

Some of the key influences affecting the design included the following:

- A Stanford decision-making workshop that one of the MDs had attended.
- John Adair's book, *Decision Making and Problem Solving (Creating Success)*, covering concepts such as how the mind works, how to sharpen critical and creative thinking skills, and how to develop a framework for decision making.
- Chip Heath and Dan Heath's bestselling book, *Decisive: How to Make Better Choices in Life and Work*, which tackles the thorny problem of how to overcome our natural biases and irrational thinking to make better decisions about our work, lives and careers.
- Daniel Kahneman's international bestseller, *Thinking, Fast and Slow*, which explores a ground-breaking tour of the mind and explains the two systems that drive the way we think and make decisions.
- Numerous articles and research studies including:
  o The Corporate Executive Board's 2013 executive guidance,*Breakthrough Performance in the New Environment*, which provides an excellent context to the new high performer who needs to adapt to change, work collaboratively, and apply judgement and insight.
  o An article by David Rock in the *NeuroLeadership Journal*, (2008), entitled "SCARF: a brain-based model for collaborating with and influencing others".
- External and internal case studies reflecting the dynamics of decision making in a complex, globally-connected business world.

The final programme was piloted with a select group of 26 senior managers who raved about the programme and gave us additional ideas on how we could further enhance the learning experience. Feedback to the Global Leadership Group in Memphis resulted in keen interest from across the many divisional executives and the Global CEO. This interest has resulted in the launch of a facilitator training process, to build capacity of selected line managers from each global division in order to cascade the learning experience throughout the international structures.

15.4 THE COMPANY BUSINESS CASE FOR DECISION MANAGEMENT

It actually is a "no brainer"! The quest to improve the quality of decision management has a pivotal rationale in that many of the decisions that we make on a daily basis have important consequences and strategic implications. Providing people with better knowledge and skills as well as a collaborative, dialogue-orientated approach relating to critical thinking and decision making will result in a dramatic impact on their performance and effectiveness. Decision making pervades all aspects of managers' daily lives and work – their ideas, thinking and contributions to projects and teams, their business and personal goals, and the breadth and effectiveness of their relationships.

This investment in up-skilling the "critical mass" of line management in tools in analysis and critical thinking and creating awareness of the dangers of subjective habits and tendencies will lead to a significant benefit to the business. I am sure that it is safe to say that most of us have had experiences with managers who make bad decisions, impulsive decisions, or even worse, the manager who is hesitant about making any decision! This dysfunctionalism detracts from bottom-line profits, increases incalculable risk and creates delays, frustration and demotivation, which can often compromise the future sustainability of a business.

The stated need

The MD sent us a note of what he wanted to achieve through the Accelerated Decision Management programme. His objectives were to:

- **Outline levels and types of decision making:** We have issues where decisions are being made at lower levels that have a strategic impact on the company while in some cases we have the opposite where senior management is focusing operational/transactional decisions. This comes down to partly culture of the company, poor job descriptions/accountability and poor/non-existent processes.

The stated need (continued)

- **Identify when a decision has to be made:** Sounds basic, but I have often come across where things are just accepted as they are and the manager does not realise that he/she actually has to make a decision in order to change the outcome of the given situation.
- **Improve collaborative decision making:** We still have issues where managers make decisions in a vacuum that have consequences on the entire organisation. We therefore need a clear, simple process to help inculcate this into our culture.
- **Improve the quality of the actual decisions:** Being aware of our own biases and those of others, looking at objective information, and ultimately making the best decision for the company.
- **Build a sustainable company with strong decision-making competency:** That will help direct and shape our destiny as a high-performance company and not one of chance or luck.

15.5 THE LEARNING THEMES AND OUTCOMES

Our next step was to cluster the learning segments into three or four major themes and objectives. The three key elements to effective decision management that the collaborative design team chose were:

- Understand how our minds work and understand our own decision-making style, preferences and derailers.
- Engage and collaborate with others to ensure that decisions are thoroughly considered, accepted and implemented effectively.
- How to use an agreed process and tools to avoid the typical traps of poor decision making.

Our decision-making profile: Daniel Kahneman (2011) explains that our intuitive, feelings-based, thinking system (which is automatic and unconscious) has a significant impact on our decision-making ability. We can easily be derailed by erroneous assumptions, short-term emotions, over-confidence or confirmation bias. We need to understand how to become aware of these automatic programmes and our personal decision-making style and to override them with more effective processes and the use of our decision-making processing centre or pre-frontal cortex. Here, we offered mini-self-assessments on decision-making style, personality, brain dominance and SCARF motivators or fears, resulting in a Personal Decision-making Profile and a Team Decision-making Profile.

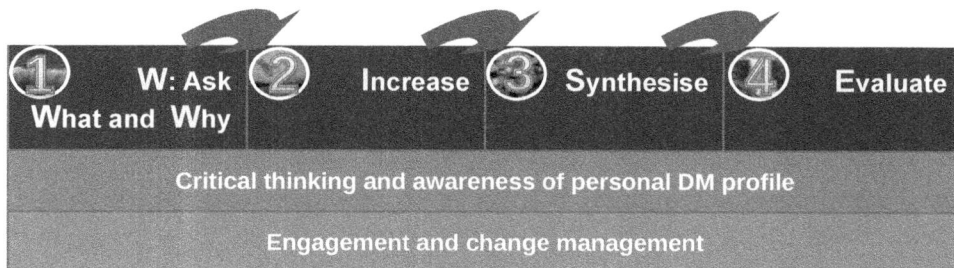

A robust process: Process breeds rigour and confidence. A study by the University of Sydney and McKinsey tracked 1 048 important strategic business decisions over 5 years, for example, whether to launch a new product or not, to restructure, to enter a new country. or acquire another firm, among others (Lovallo & Sibony, 2013). While most conducted rigorous analysis, the differentiator was the extent to which they followed a rigorous process. The process needed to include robust discussions about uncertainties and assumptions, consideration of contradictory ideas, and eliciting participation from a wide range of different people in an attempt to get different views. The result is that the process mattered **six times** more than analysis. A really good decision process substantially improves the results of the decisions, as well as the financial returns associated with them. We used a customised **WISE Decision-making Process Guide** with key considerations, steps, critical thinking tips and tools. This was used as the foundation of the case study that progressed through these steps and tools over the course of the learning experience. The process guide is described in more detail below.

Engagement and collaboration: Diverse people and ideas are critical to effective decision making. Knowing when and how to involve key stakeholders in the decision making process should be a major consideration. Collaboration with colleagues or team members builds on the dynamics of synergies – diverse views, ideas and expertise, broad exposure of information with typically a better outcome, than just doing your "own thing."

All too often, executives delegate key issues to project teams, but then get to see only a high-level PowerPoint version of the recommendations before being forced by deadlines to make a decision. We need to build in the space and make time for regular "two-way" reciprocal sessions to share and test ideas with executives, different functions, or external stakeholders. This must include those who will be involved in implementing the decision down the line.

To bring this aspect to life in the learning experience, we designed the case studies in such a way that certain critical information was missing and became available only on **consultation** with the "mock" **Decision Committee** which was set up at the back of the training room during each case study activity. The Decision Committee (part of the facilitation team), was also briefed to ask critical questions throughout the process to challenge thinking and encourage broader perspectives. Lastly, a section of the programme emphasised the importance of **project and change management principles** throughout the decision-making process, particularly in the period post-decision, where the decision had to be implemented and stakeholders engaged to make it happen for sustainable results.

15.6 A ROBUST PROCESS FOR WISE DECISIONS

We developed a decision management framework and process to assist with this important aspect and to introduce certain tools and critical questions at each step. The learning methodology, built on action-learning principles, featured a pre-selected set of business case studies allocated to small groups in the workshop. As each of the participant groups was exposed to the steps and tools associated within the framework, they were able to experience the value of working collaboratively on the applicable tools and questions relating to each step. The framework is visually depicted in Figure 15.1, with the steps described below the diagram.

15.6.1 Step 1: Ask What and Why

This step is about identifying and analysing the decision to be made by asking "what" and "why" questions. We need to understand fully the real issue and analyse the situation before launching into solutions. Using critical questioning, clarify the benefits and business case, the business context, the affected parties involved, the impact and complexity of the decision, and the deadline or specific time-line. It is a thorough and systemic sourcing and analysis of all information.

15.6.2 Step 2: Increase

The second step requires increasing and expanding one's thinking, ideas and options in order to bring fresh perspectives to the decision alternatives. This step could involve creative ideation tools, mind-maps, cause-and-effect diagrams, storyboarding, and brainstorming. It is also important to challenge mind-sets and assumptions and be aware of narrow framing and personal influences.

15.6.3 Step 3: Synthesise

The third step is to process the available information that can help to guide the decision. It involves shortlisting and prioritising the useful options and playing a devil's advocate role, which could involve experimenting with and piloting feasible choices. Choose the few critical options and test them against organisational goals and values, current business realities, and strategic priorities.

15.6.4 Step 4: Evaluate

The final step is to determine whether the decision is appropriate. Use questioning, robust thinking, and a critical examination of your judgement process to consider all aspects. Evaluate each option using both quantitative and qualitative dialogue. Ascertain the decision's potential up-sides and down-sides and associated consequences. Summarise benefits and concerns, and anticipate problems and transition challenges.

15.6.5 Decision-making tools

In addition to the steps above, each stage includes a set of tools and techniques such as mind-mapping, visual story-boards, Six Thinking Hats, the Devil's Advocate, the Discerning Voice, and prioritisation matrices, among others

15.6.6 Implementation issues

It is always imperative to consider the implementation of any decision that affects other stakeholders using effective change management, project management, and clear decision-management guidelines. The pivotal focus on collaboration and engagement all the way through decision management reinforces a progressive leadership and management practice which is universally supported and entrenched in successful organisations across the world. In the end it is also a simple truth – that it is always best to consult, engage and collaborate with everyone concerned to achieve a high quality and sustainable decision!

① W: Ask What and Why	② Increase	③ Synthesise	④ Evaluate
• Business context • Statement of the challenge/ opportunity • Benefits or business case? • Systemic sourcing and analysis of relevant information • Impact and complexity of decision • Stakeholder impact and involvement	• Increase, widen and expand options • Reframe – see it from different perspectives • Paradigm busting to challenge mind-sets and assumptions • Creative brainstorming • Examine alternative industries or methodologies • Ask ... What if?	• Criteria for prioritising • Financial implications and risks • Values and strategic priorities • Immediate eliminations? • Experiment and pilot • Stay alert for confirmation bias • Encourage devil's advocate role • Choose critical few options	• Weight each criteria • Evaluate each option against criteria • Ask critical questions? • Test confirmation bias and "status quo bias" • Summarise benefits and concerns • Anticipate problems, assess probability, test scenarios • Transition challenges?
Critical thinking and awareness of personal DM profile			
Engagement and change management			

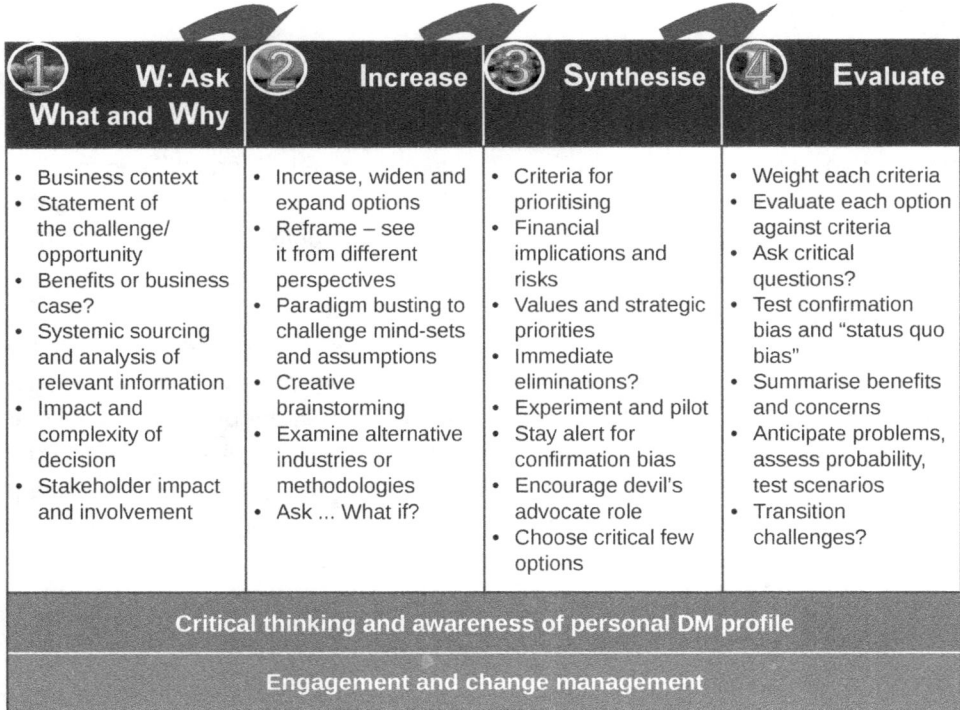

Figure 15.1: The Catalyst WISE Decision Management framework

15.7 ACCELERATED LEARNING PRINCIPLES

Our *WISE Decision Management programme* takes participants through each of these three important aspects using interactive, accelerated learning and whole brain techniques to hone competence and confidence. Managers are provided with insights and understanding of the challenges and pitfalls of decision making as well as understanding their own decision-making profile. Throughout the workshop, there is a strong emphasis on mindfulness (thinking about thinking), and the managers are encouraged and coached to explore a rigorous questioning technique and critical thinking competency that results in a much richer array of data, ideas, options and choices.

In line with Accelerated Learning principles, the learning experience is **practical**, **relevant**, and **highly interactive**. The focus is on sustainable change in mind-set, skills and behaviours. There is a good blend of information sharing with personal reflection, assessments, practice sessions, **case studies**, and identification of application opportunities in both the work and life experience.

There is a **daily reflection** session to recall, remind and review information and progress from the previous day. We also create time for the case study teams to **review** the **effectiveness of their team** work and how the combinations of personal profiles are impacting the dynamics and results.

After the workshop, participants are given an option to choose a team and work through a **30-day problem or opportunity** in their workplace that requires a significant decision. They are allocated a mentor from the facilitator team which consists of highly respected line managers. They are encouraged to collaborate and consult with their team members, their managers and the mentor, who also signs off their **project charter** in the first week. The final **decision process** has been completed and documented and submitted to the Managing Director ... to keep the pressure just right, and the strategic focus aligned.

In the background, the original design team of senior managers is **tracking** these projects and other strategic and operational decisions with regard to the organisation, in order to determine the value to the business.

The **feedback** from the participants is that their real value from the learning experience lies in practising and applying the concepts, tools and techniques to real, relevant business issues which reflect real life.

The power of collaboration

The highlight of this whole process of learning design, piloting, training facilitators and implementation was the realisation of the power of collaboration. What started as a need developed into an idea and a plan and was discussed and debated widely, both internally and externally, and the information-gathering process began. It was a magical mix of internal motivation coupled with knowing the people and the business were working in tandem with external design expertise and understanding the psychology of people and learning AND our combined ability to research the topic at hand. The design team of four client leaders and three Catalyst consultants continued to stretch each other, challenge thinking, put creative options on the table for vigorous debate, and collaborate as a dynamic virtual team to deliver an exceptional programme. The pilot programme allowed us to test and gain input from our target audience. Right up to the last day of the facilitator training we were tweaking content, case studies and post-programme actions to ensure real, accelerated learning and application for performance improvement.

15.8 CONCLUSION: QUO VADIS?

When it comes to making decisions, it is fascinating to witness the paradoxical influences and interplays of simplicity and complexity. Our "new work environment", aptly referred to as the VUCA world (where **v**olatility, **u**ncertainty, **c**omplexity and **a**mbiguity ratchet up life's difficulties and business challenges), demands intelligent, responsive and realistic decision management which will become a critical competence for leaders in the future – the winning formula for success! We look forward to contributing to and influencing management practice and debate through sharing our experience, insights and new thinking in this area and through building capacity in critical thinking and effective decision making.

CHAPTER 16

CASE STUDY: MEASURING THE IMPACT OF LEADERSHIP DEVELOPMENT PROGRAMMES AND PRACTICES AT ESKOM

By the Eskom Leadership Institute (ELI)

16.1 INTRODUCTION

In striving towards becoming a high-performance organisation and ultimately being recognised as a top-performing utility, strong and visible leadership is critical. To facilitate this, the Eskom Leadership Strategy was prioritised in 2010 as a key enabler to realise Eskom's aim of shifting performance and growing sustainability in order to become a top 5 global performing utility.

To this end, the Eskom Leadership Strategy has four key focus areas which aim to:

- Build leadership capacity to execute the strategy effectively.
- Build the transformational leadership mind-set to embrace the new organisation and the associated leadership brand, with a specific emphasis on demonstrated performance and genuine accountability.
- Build a comprehensive leadership pipeline across all leadership segments in order to ensure the strengthening of the Eskom leadership bench.
- Intensify the development outcomes of leadership assessments.

To ensure that the above key focus areas are purposefully driven and implemented, it was necessary to develop a comprehensive measurement framework in order to provide Eskom with a sound methodology, process and system to assess the organisational impact of leadership development programmes and processes effectively. This comprehensive measurement tool is known as the Eskom Leadership Scorecard.

The Leadership Scorecard and related reports were developed at all levels of measurement (strategic, tactical, operational and quality) and linked to the impact assessment system for Supervisory, Senior Management, Middle Management and Executive Leadership development programmes.

The Eskom Leadership Scorecard accepts that investment in leadership excellence must lead to demonstrable business benefits. In order for this investment to do so, the Eskom Leadership Institute (ELI) have to ensure that specific deliverables are achieved. This means that all leadership assessment and development practices must be relevant to Eskom's intent with leadership, which is ultimately to build leadership capacity in order to execute the organisational strategy effectively.

Given the preceding, a framework for the Eskom Leadership Scorecard was designed, as shown in Figure 16.1. It consists of four dimensions with three elements each.

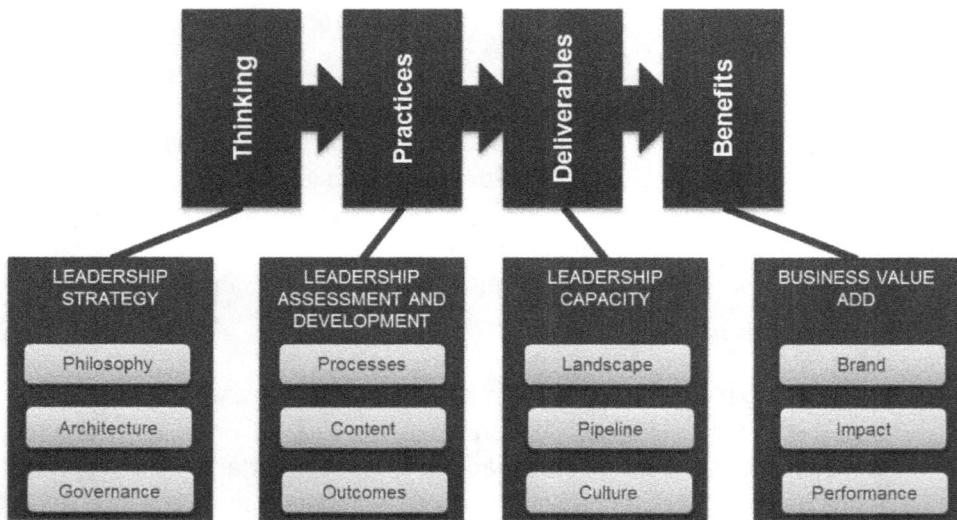

Figure 16.1: Framework for the Eskom Leadership Scorecard

The key measurement objective for each dimension is as follow:

- **Leadership strategy:** To ensure the high-level plan of action designed to drive the achievement of the long-term aspirations for the organisation through effective leadership, this strategy is clearly defined in order to identify and develop talent and to ensure that Eskom has a clear set of roles and accountabilities in place for leaders.

- **Leadership assessment and development:** To ensure the required processes, content and outcomes to create leadership capacity within Eskom, leadership assessment and development are clearly defined and deliberately linked to Eskom's leadership strategy so that the leadership development processes lead to a perceivable improvement in leadership behaviour.
- **Leadership capacity:** The dimension of leadership capacity refers to the leadership landscape, organisational culture and leadership pipeline which will drive ultimate business value add. It is imperative to ensure that the Eskom leadership landscape enables leadership to be effective as a collective and reflects high levels of trust and collaboration. In addition, it has adequate cover, now and in the future, for leadership in all key and high-risk roles. Lastly, the Eskom leadership brand is lived consistently internally.
- **Business value add:** This refers to the longer-term benefit realisation of leadership brand, leadership impact or effectiveness, and business performance. This measurement determines to what extent the Eskom leadership philosophy is lived consistently externally; whether leaders have the competence and capability to be effective in their roles; and how well leaders are aligned to the overall business and leadership strategy for successful execution.

At the time of writing, the Eskom Leadership Scorecard has four dimensions (as described above), 12 elements, and currently consists of 27 leadership measures and metrics (KPIs). On a quarterly basis, a mapping exercise is performed between the 27 KPIs and scorecard elements which relate to each of the four dimensions. The quarterly results are therefore based on the KPI results applicable for that specific quarter. Evidence is gathered from various stakeholders across the organisation.

Going forward, the ELI wishes to create awareness across the organisation with regard to the Leadership Scorecard in order to provide organisational members with insight on how Eskom is faring in building leadership capacity to execute business strategy successfully.

Figure 16.2 depicts an example of overall leadership scorecard results in a quarter.

Eskom Leadership Scorecard – An Example

EXCO | Board

Generation | Transmission | Distribution | Customer | Human Resources | Finance | Group Capital | Technology | Commercial | Sustainability | Enterprise Dev | Office of the CE

Leadership Strategy

	Unit	Trend	YTD	Target	Actual vs Target
Leadership Philosophy	Rating		3.2	3.8	
Leadership Architecture	Rating		4.0	4.0	
Governance	%		87.9%	100%	

Leadership Assessment & Development

	Unit	Trend	YTD	Target	Actual vs Target
Process	%		47.5%	86%	
Content	Rating		3.6	3.8	
Outcome	Rating		3.4	3.8	

Leadership Capacity

	Unit	Trend	YTD	Target	Actual vs Target
Leadership Landscape	Rating		3.7	4.0	
Culture	Rating		3.7	4.0	
Leadership Pipeline	%		53%	60%	

Business Value Add

	Unit	Trend	YTD	Target	Actual vs Target
Leadership Brand	%		42.6%	60%	
Leadership Impact	%	Future versions	21%	74%	
Business Results	%		73.5%	80%	

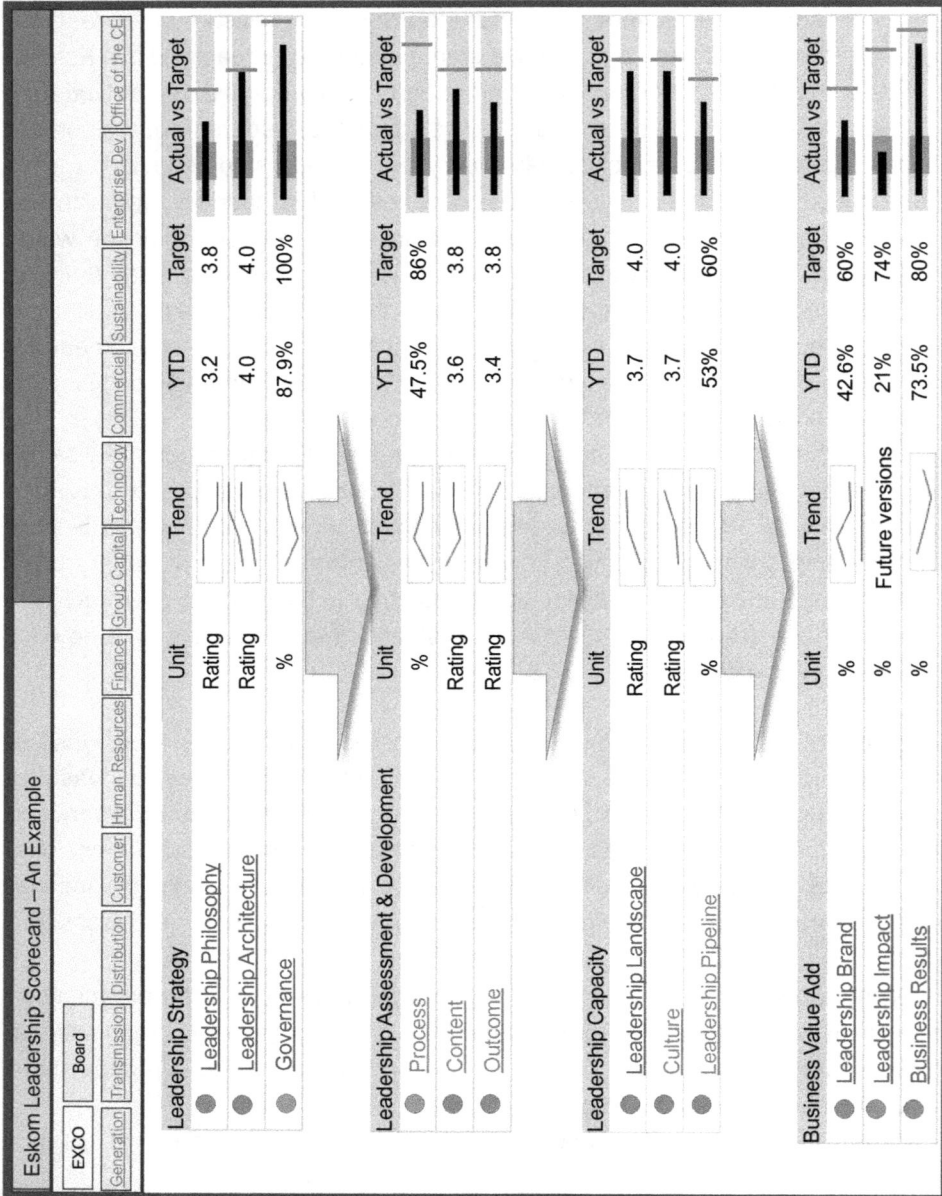

Figure 16.2: Example of overall leadership scorecard results

Behind each of these 12 elements sit the detailed results of the 27 KPIs relating to each of the four dimensions. As development programmes and practices changes in future, measurement KPIs pertaining to the scorecard will be reviewed and amended in order to ensure a consistent and valid measure of the impact on the organisation of leadership development programmes and practices.

REFERENCES AND BIBLIOGRAPHY

CHAPTER 1

Corporate Executive Board. 2013. *Breakthrough Performance in the New Environment. Executive Guidance*. 8. [Online]. Available: http://www.executiveboard.com/exbd-resources/pdf/executive-guidance/eg2013-annual-final.pdf. [Accessed 24 September 2014].

Deloitte Consulting. 2014. *Global Human Capital Trends: Engaging the 21st-century Workforce*. A report by LLP & Bersin. [Online]. Available: http://www2.deloitte.com/global/en/pages/human-capital/articles/human-capital-trends-2014.html. [Accessed 24 September 2014].

Heath, C & Heath, D. 2013. *Decisive: How to Make Better Choices in Life and Work*. New York (NY): Crown Business, an imprint of Crown Publishing Group, a division of Random House, Inc.

Kahneman, D. 2011. *Thinking, Fast and Slow*. New York (NY): Farrar, Straus and Giroux.

Manpower Group. 2013. *Talent Shortage Survey Research Results*. [Online]. Available: http://www.manpowergroup.com/wps/wcm/connect/manpowergroup-en/home/thought-leadership/research-insights/talent-sources/2013-talent-shortage#.U6AHVSjm55E. [Accessed 24 September 2014].

Sloane Centre on Aging & Work. *South Africa – Country Workforce Profile 2009*. [Online]. Available: http://www.bc.edu/content/bc/research/agingandwork/archive_pubs/CP11.html. [Accessed 24 September 2014].

Stahl, SM, Davis, RL, Kim, DH, Lowe Gellings, N, Carlson, RE Jnr, Fountain, K & Grady MM. 2010. Play it Again: The Master Psychopharmacology Program as an Example of Interval Learning in Bite-Sized Portions. *CNS Spectrums*, 15(8):491–504. [Online]. Available: http://www.cnsspectrums.com/aspx/articledetail.aspx?articleid=2783. [Accessed 24 September 2014].

Stout-Rostron, S, Cunningham, N & Crous, W. 2013. *The 2013 Leadership Development Survey*. Randburg: Knowledge Resources Publishing.

Treadwell, M. 2013. *The Paradigm Shift*. [Online]. Available: http://www.marktreadwell.com/. [Accessed 24 September 2014].

CHAPTER 2

Ambient Insight. 2013, *The 2012–2017 Worldwide Mobile Learning Market*. [Online]. Available: www.ambientinsight.com. [Accessed 26 June 2014].

Bullas, J. 2013. *GlobalWebIndex Sudy*. [Online]. Available: http://www.jeffbullas.com/2013/09/20/12-awesome-social-media-facts-and-statistics-for-2013/#CUHDue6biOM8hlo0.99. [Accessed 26 June 2014].

Canalys. 2013., *Mobile Device Market to Reach 2.6 Billion Units by 2016*. 22 February. Press release 2013/056. [Online]. Available: http://www.canalys.com/newsroom/mobile-device-market-reach-26-billion-units-2016. [Accessed 26 June 2014].

Cipolla, C. 2013. e-Learning Trends. *Knowledgeone Blog*, July. [Online]. Available: http://knowledgeone.ca/blog/post/2013-e-learning-trends.aspx. [Accessed 27 June 2014].

Defence Centres of Excellence. *Learning Style, Defence Centres of Excellence*. [Online]. Available: http://www.dcoe.mil/Training/Educator_Resources.aspx. [Accessed 26 June 2014].

Enders, BJ. 2013. *Manager's Guide to Mobile Learning* (Briefcase Books Series) (Ch 1). New York (NY): McGraw-Hill. 1.

Fourie, S. 2012. Understanding Learning Organisations in a South African Context. *Human Capital Review*, [Online]. Available: http://www.humancapitalreview.org/content/default.asp?Article_ID=1227. [Accessed 27 June 2014].

Hart, J. 2008. Understanding today's learner. *Learning Solutions*, September. [Online]. Available: http://www.learningsolutionsmag.com/articles/80/. [Accessed 27 June 2014].

Hart, J. 2011. *Learning in the Social Workplace.*

Heick, T. 2013. *Shift Learning: The 7 Most Powerful Ideas Shifts in Learning Today*. [Online]. Available: http://www.teachthought.com/trends/shift-learning-the-7-most-powerful-ideas-shifts-in-learning-today/ . [Accessed 26 June 2014].

Imber, J. 2014. The History (and Future) of MOOCs. *Shift Learning*. [Online]. Available: http://www.shift-learning.co.uk/sites/default/files/MOOC%20White%20Paper.pdf. [Accessed 28 June 2014].

Kapp, K. 2013. *The Gamification of Instruction and Learning*. [Online]. Available: http://karlkapp.com/. [Accessed 28 June 2014].

Kearney , AT. 2013. *The Mobile Economy. (Research)*. 4, 9. [Online]. Available: http://www.atkearney.de/documents/856314/1214748/BIP_The_Mobile_Economy_2013.pdf/. [Accessed 26 June 2014].

Laal, M. 2011. *Collaborative Learning: What Is It?* [Online]. Available: http://www.sciencedirect.com/science/article/pii/S1877042811030217. cessed 28 June 2014].

Maritz Institute. 2010. *White Paper: The Neuroscience of Learning: A New Paradigm for Corporate Education The Neuroscience of Learning: A New Paradigm for Corporate Education*, May, [Online]. Available: http://www.themaritzinstitute.com/Perspectives/~/media/Files/MaritzInstitute/White-Papers/The-Neuroscience-of-Learning-The-Maritz-Institute.pdf. [Accessed 28 June 2014].

Massive Open Online Course. [Online]. Available: http://en.wikipedia.org/wiki/Massive_open_online_course. [Accessed 1 May 2014].

Prensky, M. 2001. Digital Natives, Digital Immigrants. *On the Horizon*, 9(5):1–6. [Online]. Available: http://www.marcprensky.com/writing/Prensky%20-%20Digital%20Natives,%20Digital%20Immigrants%20-%20Part1.pdf. [Accessed 15 July 2014].

Senge, P. 1990. *The Fifth Discipline: The Art and Practice of the Learning Organization*. New York (NY): Currency/Doubleday.

  [See also Senge, P. 2006. *The Fifth Discipline: The Art and Practice of the Learning Organization*. (Rev. & updated ed.) New York (NY): Doubleday, a division of Random House, Inc.]

Senge, P. 2012. *What is Systems Thinking?* [Online]. Available: http://www.mutualresponsibility.org/science/what-is-systems-thinking-peter-senge-explains-systems-thinking-approach-and-principles. [Accessed 15 July 2014].

Stahl, SM, Davis, RL, Kim, DH, Lowe Gellings, N, Carlson, RE Jnr, Fountain, K & Grady MM. 2010. Play it Again: The Master Psychopharmacology Program as an Example of Interval Learning in Bite-Sized Portions. *CNS Spectrums*, 15(8):491–504. [Online]. Available: http://www.cnsspectrums.com/aspx/articledetail.aspx?articleid=2783. [Accessed 24 September 2014].

Stout-Rostron, S, Cunningham, N & Crous, W. 2013. *The 2013 Leadership Development Survey*. Randburg: Knowledge Resources Publishing.

Tanis, DJ. 2012. Exploring Play/Playfulness and Learning. In DJ Tanis (ed). *The Adult And Higher Education Classroom. A Dissertation in Adult Education*, [Online]. Available: https://etda.libraries.psu.edu/paper/16086/13127. [Accessed 30 April 2014].

Treadwell, M. 2013. *The Paradigm Shift*. [Online]. Available: http://www.marktreadwell.com/. [Accessed 24 September 2014].

CHAPTER 3

Plater, M. 2014. *Chief Learning Officer: Three Trends Shaping Learning*. [Online]. Available: http://www. clomedia.com/articles/5644-three-trends-shaping-learning. [Accessed 12 August 2014].

CHAPTER 4

Bharwaney , G, Bar-On , R & MacKinlay, A. 2007, 2011. *EQ and the Bottom Line: Emotional Intelligence Increases Individual Occupational Performance, Leadership and Organisational Productivity*. [Online]. Available: http://www.eiconsortium.org/pdf/Bharwaney_BarOn_MacKinlay_EQ_and_ Bottom_Line.pdf. [Accessed 5 May 2014].

Cantrell, S & Smith D. 2013. *Trends Reshaping the Future of HR – Managing Your People as a Workforce of One*. Accenture Institute for High Performance. [Online]. Available: http://www. accenture.com/SiteCollectionDocuments/PDF/Accenture-Trends-Reshaping-HR-Workforce-One. pdf [Accessed 30 May 2014].

Csíkszentmihályi, M. 2008. *Flow: The Psychology of Optimal Experience*. New York (NY): Harper Perennial Modern Classics.

Honey, P & Mumford, A. 2000. *The Learning Styles Helper's Guide.* Maidenhead (Berks, UK): Peter Honey Publications Ltd.

Kahneman, D. 2011. *Thinking, Fast and Slow*. New York (NY): Farrar, Straus and Giroux.

Mobbs, R. 2003. *How to Be an e-Tutor*. University of Leicester. http://www2.le.ac.uk/departments/ gradschool/training/eresources/teaching/theories/honey-mumford. [Accessed 5 May 2014].

Herrmann, N. 1996. *The Whole Brain Business Book*. New York (NY): McGraw-Hill.

Prinsloo, M. 2010. *Cognitive Process Profile: Cognitive Assessment in the Corporate Context*. Cognadev Ltd. [Online]. Available: http://www.cognadev.com. [Accessed 5 May 2014].

Rock, D. 2008. Adapted from SCARF: A Brain-Based Model for Collaborating with and Influencing Others. *NeuroLeadership Journal*. [Online]. Available: http://www.your-brain-at-work.com/files/ NLJ_SCARFUS.pdf. [Accessed 4 November 2013].

CHAPTER 5

Baumeister, RF, Schmeichel, R & Vohs, B. 2003. K Self-regulation and the Executive Function: The Self as Controlling Agent. In AW Kruglanski & ET Higgins (eds). *Social Psychology: Handbook of Basic Principles*. (2nd ed.) New York (NY): Guilford Press.

Bechara, A, Tranel, D, Damasio, H, Adolphs, R, Rockland, C & Damasio, AR. 1995. Double dissociation of conditioning and declarative knowledge relative to the amygdala and hippocampus in humans. *Science*, 269(5227):1115–1118, 25 August.

Bjork, RA & Linn, MC. 2006. The Science of Learning and the Learning of science: Introducing Desirable Difficulties. *American Psychological Society Observer*, 19:29–39, March.

Boyatzis, R. 2011. Coaching with Compassion: Inspiring Desired Sustained Change. Unpublished paper. Executive Coaching Conference: Meeting the Leadership Needs in the Changing Landscape of Business. 29–30 March. New York (NY): Conference Board.

Boyatzis, R. 2013. When Pulling the Negative Emotional Attractor Is Too Much or Not Enough to Inspire and Sustain Outstanding Leadership. In R Burke, C Cooper & G Woods (eds). *The fulfilling Workplace: The Organisation's Role in Achieving Individual and Organisational Health*. London: Gower Publishing.

Brainfacts.org. 2014. *What is Neuroscience?* Society for Neuroscience. [Online]. Available: http://www.brainfacts.org/about-neuroscience/what-is-neuroscience/. [Accessed 20 June 2014].

Chapman, SB, Aslan, S, Spence, JS, DeFina, LS, Keeble, MW, Didehbani, N & Lu, H. 2013. *Shorter Term Aerobic Exercise Improves Brain, Cognition, and Cardiovascular Fitness in Aging*. [Online]. Available: http://journal.frontiersin.org/Journal/10.3389/fnagi.2013.00075/abstract. [Accessed 5 July 2014].

Cozolino, L. 2006. *The neuroscience of human relationships: Attachment and the developing social brain*. New York (NY): WW Norton & Company.

Cunningham, N. 2014. *Rethink: Growth and learning Through Coaching and Organisational Development*. Johannesburg: Knowres Publishing.

Damasio, AR, Grabowski, TJ, Bechara, A, Damasio, H, Ponto, LLB, Parvizi, J & Hichwa, RD. 2000. Subcortical and cortical brain activity during the feeling of self-generated emotions. *Nature Neuroscience*, 3(10):1049–1056. doi:10.1038/79871.

Davidson, R, Kabat-Zinn, J , Schumacher,.J, Rosenkranz, M, Muller, D, Santorelli, SF, Urbanowski, F, Harrington, A, Bonus, K & Sheridan, JF. 2003. Alterations in Brain and Immune Function Produced by Mindfulness Meditation. *Psychosomatic Medicine*, 65(4):564–570, July.

Division of Sleep Medicine (Harvard Medical School). 2007. *Sleep, Performance, and Public Safety*. [Online]. Available: http://healthysleep.med.harvard.edu/healthy/matters/consequences/sleep-performance-and-public-safety. [Accessed 22 September 2014].

Eisenberger, NI, Lieberman, MD & Williams, KD. 2003. Does Rejection Hurt? An fMRI Study Of Social Exclusion. *Science*, 302(5643):290–292, 10 October.

Hendel-Giller, R in collaboration with C Hollenbach, D Marshall, K Oughton, T Pickthorn, M Schilling & G Versiglia. 2010. *The Maritz Institute White Paper: The Neuroscience of Learning: A New Paradigm For Corporate Education*, May.

Honey, P & Mumford, A. 2000. *The Learning Styles Helper's Guide*. Maidenhead (Berks, UK): Peter Honey Publications Ltd.

Huffington, A, 2014. *Thrive: The Third Metric to Redefining Success and Creating a Life of Well-Being, Wisdom, and Wonder*. New York (NY): Harmony Books, an imprint of the Crown Publishing Group, a division of Random House LLC, a Penguin Random House Company.

Jack., AI, Dawson, AJ, Begany, KL, Leckie, RL, Barry, KP, Ciccia, AH & Snyder, AZ. 2012. fMRI Reveals Reciprocal Inhibition Between Social and Physical Cognitive Domains. *Neuroimage*, 66C:385–401, October.

Kabat-Zinn, J. 2003. Mindfulness Based Interventions in Context: Past, Present and Future. *Clinical Psychology: Science and Practice*, 10(2):144–156.

Kolb, DA. 1984. *Experiential Learning: Experience as the Source of Learning and Development*. Englewood Cliffs (NJ): Prentice Hall.

LeDoux, J. 2000. Emotion Circuits in the Brain. *Annual Review of Neuroscience*, 23:155–184, March. doi: 10.1146/annurev.neuro.23.1.155.

Lieberman, ND & Eisenberger, NI, 2008. The Pains and Pleasures of Social Life. *NeuroLeadership Journal*, 1:38–43.

McClure, SM, Laibson, DI, Loewenstein, G & Cohen, JD. 2004. Separate Neural Systems Value Immediate and Delayed Monetary Rewards. *Science,* 306:503–507.

McGonigal, J. 2011. *Reality is Broken: Why Games Make Us Better and How They Can Change the World*. New York (NY): Penguin Press. 400.

Meltzoff, AN & Prinz, W. 2002. *The imitative Mind: Development, Evolution and Brain Bases*. Cambridge (UK): Cambridge University Press.

Organisation for Economic Co-operation and Development (OECD). 2007. *Understanding the Brain: The Birth of a Learning Science* (Vol 2). OECD Publishing.

Richland, LE, Bjork, RA, Finley, JR & Linn, MC. 2005. Linking Cognitive Science to Education: Generation and Interleaving Effects. In BG Bara, L Barsalou & M Bucciarelli (eds). *Proceedings of the Twenty-Seventh Annual Conference of the Cognitive Science Society*. Mahwah (NJ): Lawrence Erlbaum.

Rizzolati, G & Craighero, L. 2004. The Mirror Neuron System. *Annual Review of Neuroscience*, 27:169–192.

Rock, D. 2008. Adapted from SCARF: A Brain-Based Model for Collaborating with and Influencing Others. *NeuroLeadership Journal*. [Online]. Available: http://www.your-brain-at-work.com/files/NLJ_SCARFUS.pdf. [Accessed 4 November 2013].

Rock, D. 2009. *Your Brain at Work*. New York (NY): Harper Collins.

Schwartz, J & Begley, S. 2002. *The Mind and the Brain: Neuroplasticity and the Power of Mental Force*. New York (NY): Regan Books.

Schwartz, J & Gladding, R. 2011. *You Are Not Your Brain: The 4-step Solution for Changing Bad Habits, Ending Unhealthy Thinking and Taking Control of Your Brain*. London (UK): Avery Publishing, a book publishing imprint of the Penguin Group.

Siegel, DJ. 2006. An Interpersonal Neurobiology Approach to Psychotherapy: Awareness, Mirror Neurons and Neural Plasticity in the Development of Well-being. *Psychiatric Annals*, 36(4):248–258, April/May.

Siegel, DJ. 2007. *The Mindful Brain: Reflection and Attunement in the Cultivation of Well-being*. New York (NY): WW Norton & Company.

Society for Neuroscience – The Society for Neuroscience is the world's largest organisation of scientists and physicians devoted to understanding the brain and nervous system. The non-profit organisation, founded in 1969, now has nearly 40 000 members in more than 90 countries and 130 chapters worldwide. [Online]. Available: http://www.sfn.org/. [Accessed 20 June 2014].

Standing, L, Conezio, J & Haber, RN. 1970. Perception and memory for pictures: Single-trial learning of 2500 visual stimuli. *Psychonomic Science*, 19(2):73–74.

Stone, L. 2008. *Continuous Partial Attention: Not the Same as Multi-tasking*. [Online]. Available: http://www.businessweek.com/business_at_work/time_management/archives/2008/07/continuous_part.html. [Accessed 20 June 2014].

Wright, RD & Ward, LM. 2008. *Orienting of Attention*. New York (NY): Oxford University Press.

Zull, JE. 2002. *The Art of Changing the Brain: Enriching the Practice of Teaching by Exploring the Bology of Learning*. Sterling (VA): Stylus Publishing, LLC.

Zull, JE. 2006. Key Aspects of How the Brain Learns. *New Directions for Adult and Continuing Education* (special issue), 110:3–9, Summer.

CHAPTER 6

Collins, J. 1996. *Looking out for Number One*. [Online]. Available: www.jimcollins.com/article_topics/articles/looking-out.html. [Accessed 23 September 2014].

Craig, E, Pham, CT & Bobulsky, S. 2008. *Accenture Research Report 2008: Rethinking Retention: If you Want Your Best Executives to Stay, Equip Them to Leave*. Accenture.

Gatherer, J & Craig, D. 2009. Talent Management – an Integrated Approach. *Human Capital Review*. June. Bryanston: Knowledge Resources. Knowledge Resources. [Online]. Available to subscribers only: http://www.humancapitalreview.org/content/default.asp?Article_ID=509. [Accessed 2 October 2014].

Gatherer, J; Craig, D. 2010a. Leading and Building High Performance Teams; *Human Capital Review*. Bryanston. Knowledge Resources. [Online]. Available: http://www.catalystconsulting.co.za/downloads/articles/High%20Performance%20Teams.pdf. [Accessed 16 October 2014].

Gatherer, J; Craig, D. 2010b. Strategic Change Journey to High Performance: From Resistance to Resilience. *Human Capital Review*. May. Bryanston: Knowledge Resources. [Online]. Available to subscribers only: http://www.humancapitalreview.org/content/default.asp?Article_ID=809. [Accessed 2 October 2014].

Gatherer, J. 2011. The "X" Factor of Talent in Business - Build and Promote Your Personal Brand. *Human Capital Review*. November. Bryanston: Knowledge Resources. [Online]. Available to subscribers only: http://www.humancapitalreview.org/content/default.asp?Article_ID=1061&ArticlePage_ID=2137&TxtSearch=I am Talent. [Accessed 2 October 2014].

Heath, C & Heath, D. 2013. *Decisive: How to Make Better Choices in Life and Work*. New York (NY): Crown Business, an imprint of Crown Publishing Group, a division of Random House, Inc.

Lesser, R. 2011. *Are Knowledge Workers Being Replaced by "Insight Workers"?* [Online]. Available: http://www.huffingtonpost.com/rich-lesser/post_1664_b_817400.html. [Accessed 23 September 2014].

Mind Tools. nd. *Johari Window*. [Online]. Available: http://www.mindtools.com/CommSkll/JohariWindow.htm. [Accessed 23 September 2014].

Partners for Possibility. [Online]. Available: http://www.pfp4sa.org. [Accessed 23 September 2014].

Prosci® ADKAR® Model for Change. 1999. [Online]. Available: http://www.prosci.com/adkar-model/overview-3/. [Accessed 23 September 2014].

Semler, R. 2004. *The Seven-Day Weekend: A Better Way to Work in the 21st Century*. New York (NY): Penguin Group.

Senge, P. 2006. *The Fifth Discipline: The Art and Practice of the Learning Organization*. (Rev. & updated ed.) New York (NY): Doubleday, a division of Random House, Inc.

CHAPTER 7

Cavanagh, M. 2014. *New Models for Coaching in the 21st Century – Staying Ahead of the Curve in Uncertain Times*. Extract from conference proceedings: *Coaching Conference*. 17–20 March 2014, Hyatt Hotel, Rosebank. South Africa.

International Coaching Federation. [Online]. Available: http://www.coachfederation.org/. [Accessed 20 June 2014].

Kiefer, C & Constable, M. 2013. *The Art of Insight: How to Have More Aha! Moments*. San Francisco (CA): Berrett-Koehler Publishers, Inc.

Landsberg, M. 2003. *Tao of Coaching: Boost your Effectiveness at Work by Inspiring and Developing Those Around You*. London (UK): Profile Books Limited.

McLean, P. 2012. *The Completely Revised Handbook of Coaching: A Developmental Approach*. San Francisco (CA): Jossey Bass, a Wiley imprint.

Michael Hall, L & Duval, M. 2005. *Coaching Conversations for Transformational Change*. New York (NY): Crown House Publishing.

Rock, D. 2007. *Quiet Leadership – Six Steps to Transforming Performance at the Workplace*. New York (NY): HarperCollins.

Starr, J. 2003. *The Coaching Manual: The Definitive Guide to the Process, Principles and Skills of Personal Coaching*. Harlow (UK): Pearson Education Limited.

Stout-Rostron, S. 2009. *Business Coaching Wisdom and Practice: Unlocking the Secrets of Business Coaching*. Johannesburg: Knowledge Resources.

Stout-Rostron, S, Cunningham, N & Crous, W. 2013. *The 2013 Leadership Development Survey*. Randburg: Knowledge Resources Publishing.

Theeboom, T, Beersma, B & van Vianen, AEM. 2014. Does Coaching Work? A Meta-analysis on the Effects of Coaching on Individual Level Outcomes in an Organizational Context. *Journal of Positive Psychology*, 9(1):1–18.

Worldwide Association of Business Coaches (WABC). [Online]. Available: http://www.wabccoaches.com/. [Accessed 20 June 2014].

CHAPTER 8

Patterson, K, Grenny, J, McMillan, R & Switzler, A. 2004. *Crucial Confrontations – Tools for Talking about Broken Promises, Violated Expectations, and Bad Behavior*. New York (NY): McGraw-Hill.

Patterson, K, Grenny J, McMillan, R & Switzler, A. 2011. *Crucial Conversations – Tools for Talking when Stakes are High*. 2nd ed. New York (NY): McGraw-Hill.

Stone, D, Patton, B & Heen, S. 2010. *Difficult Conversations – How to Discuss What Matters Most*. 10th anniversary ed). New York (NY): Penguin Putnam Inc.

Teversham, L. 2013. *No Problem – the Upside of Saying No*. Rondebosch (RSA): Kima Global Publishers.

CHAPTER 9

Hamel, G & Prahalad, CK. 1990. The Core Competence of the Corporation. *Harvard Business Review*, 68(3):79–91, May–June.

Hamel, G & Prahalad, CK. 1996. *Competing for the Future*. Boston (MA): Harvard Business Review Press.

Holacracy: How it Works. 2006. [Online]. Available: http://holacracy.org/how-it-works. [Accessed 23 September 2014].

Riley, J. 2012. *Core Competencies*. Nottingham (UK): UK Essays. [Online]. Available: http://tutor2u.net/business/strategy/core_competencies.htm. [Accessed 23 September 2014].

Rud, OP. 2009. *Business Intelligence Success Factors: Tools for Aligning Your Business in the Global Economy*. Hoboken (NJ): John Wiley & Sons.

Ulrich, D & Smallwood, N. 2004. Capitalizing on Capabilities. *Harvard Business Review*, 82(6):119–127, June.

CHAPTER 10

Blooms Taxonomy. [Online]. Available: http://www.clemson.edu/.../Blooms%20Taxonomy%20Action%20Verbs.pdf. [Accessed 19 March 2014].

Buning, N. 2010. *Global HR Forum: Sustainable Learning Through Learning Chains*. [Online]. Available: http://www.slideshare.net/mindrom/sustainable-learning-through-learning-chains-norbert-buning-global-hr-forum-2010pdf-seoul-korea. [Accessed 18 June 2014].

Gravett, S. 2001. *Adult Learning: Designing and Implementing Learning Events, A Dialogic Approach*. Pretoria: Van Schaik Publishers.

Hatfield, E, Cacioppo, J & Rapson, R. 1994. *Emotional Contagion: Studies in Emotion and Social Interaction*. Cambridge (MA): Cambridge University Press.

Heidenhain, G. 2014a. The Accelerated Learning Cycle – A Design Template. *ASTD Learning and Development Blog*, 22 April. ASTD.

Heidenhain, G. 2014b. The Pillars Of Accelerated Learning Design. *ASTD Learning and Development Blog*, 15 April. ASTD. [Online]. Available: http://www.astd.org/Publications/Blogs/L-and-D-Blog/2014/04/The-Pillars-of-Accelerated-Learning-Design. [Accessed 22 June 2014].

Janzen, KJ, Perry, B & Edwards, M. 2012. Viewing Learning Through a New Lens: The Quantum. *Scientific Research*, October. [Online]. Available: http://www.SciRP.org/journal/ce; http://dx.doi.org/10.4236/ce.2012.36106. [Accessed 30 June 2014].

Kotter, J. 1995. Leading Change: Why Transformation Efforts Fail. *Harvard Business Review OnPoint*, 1–10, March–April.

Lozanov, G. 1978. *Suggestology and Outlines of Suggestopedy*. Philadelphia (PA): Gordon & Breach Science Publishers Inc.

Mezirow, J. 1998. On critical reflection. *Adult Education Quarterly*, 48(3):185–198.

Mind Tools. nd. *Gagne's Nine Levels of Learning: Training Your Team Effectively*. [Online]. Available: http://www.mindtools.com/pages/article/gagne.htm. [Accessed 10 August 2014].

Stahl, SM, Davis, RL, Kim, DH, Lowe Gellings, N, Carlson, RE Jnr, Fountain, K & Grady MM. 2010. Play it Again: The Master Psychopharmacology Program as an Example of Interval Learning in Bite-Sized Portions. *CNS Spectrums*, 15(8):491–504. [Online]. Available: http://www.cnsspectrums.com/aspx/articledetail.aspx?articleid=2783. [Accessed 24 September 2014].

Treadwell, M. 2013. *The Paradigm Shift*. [Online]. Available: http://www.marktreadwell.com/. [Accessed 24 September 2014].

CHAPTER 11

Acabado , RJ. 2011. *Importance of Play*. Presentation, September. [Online]. Available: http://www.slideshare.net/jinjin14/importance-of-play. [Accessed 24 September 2014].

Altrup, T. 2012. Enterprise Gamification. New Marketing International Congress 2012, Badgeville_. [Online]. Available: http://www.slideshare.net/taltrup/gamification-keynote-new-marketing-international-congress-2012. [Accessed 24 Septembre 2014].

Amabile, TM & Kramer, SJ. 2010. *The HBR Lst: Breakthrough Ideas for 2010*. [Online]. Available: http://hbr.org/2010/01/the-hbr-list-breakthrough-ideas-for-2010/ar/1. [Accessed 23 September 2014].

Bartle, R. 1996. Hearts, Clubs, Diamonds, Spades: Players Who Suit MUDS. *Journal of Virtual Environments*, 1(1). Colchester, Essex (UK): MUSE Ltd. [Online]. Available: http://mud.co.uk/richard/hcds.htm. [Accessed 23 September 2014].

Bunchball. 2012. *Gamification 101: An introduction to game dynamics*. © Bunchball, Inc., 2012.

Carmody, C. 2014. *Training Induction Experiment*. (Colin Carmody is the training manager of Boardwalk Casino, PE, South Africa.)

Cooper, S, Khatib, F, Makedon, I, Lu, H, Barbero, J, Baker, D, Fogarty, J & Popovi, Z. 2011. *Analysis of Social Gameplay Macros in the Foldit Cookbook*. Center for Game Science, Department of Computer Science & Engineering, University of Washington. [Online]. Available: http://grail.cs.washington.edu/projects/protein-game/foldit-fdg11.pdf. [Accessed 24 September 2014].

Csíkszentmihályi, M. 2008. *Flow: The Psychology of Optimal Experience*. New York (NY): Harper Perennial Modern Classics.

Deci, EL & Ryan, RM. 2002. *The Handbook of Self-determination Research*. Rochester (NY): University of Rochester Press. Research paper: [Online]. Available: http://mofetinternational.macam.ac.il/jtec/Documents/Self-Determination%20Theory%20and%20the%20Facilitation%20of%20Intrinsic%20Motivation,%20Social%20Development,%20and%20Well-Being.pdf. [Accessed 23 September 2014].

Deloitte Leadership Academy. nd. [Online]. Available: http://badgeville.com/sites/default/files/library/pdf/Case_Study_Deloitte_Leadership_Academy.pdf?form=85. [Accessed 24 September 2014].

Domo. nd. DATA Never Sleeps 2.0. [Online]. Available: http://rack.3.mshcdn.com/media/ZgkyMD-E0LzA0LzIyLzZjL0RhdGFOZXZlclNsLjA4MjI4LmpwZwpwCXRodW1iCTEyMDB4OTYwMD4/efa67779/9e5/DataNeverSleeps_2.jpg. [Accessed January 2014].

Gaming admin. 2012. FANGO Delivers on Social TV. 11 February.

Gardner, J. 2010. *Innovation Squared: The Department for Work and Pensions Turns Innovation Into a Game*. (Gardner: Case Study: 23 November 2010. ID Number: G00208615).

GMAT. [Online]. Available: http://www.fastcompany.com/1840235/gamification-and-power-influence.

Hackenberg, T. 2009. Token Reinforcement: A Review and Analysis. *Journal of the Experimental Analysis of Behaviour*, 91:257–286.

Intel. nd. [Online]. Available: http://www.intel.co.za/content/www/za/en/communications/internet-minute-infographic.html. [Accessed 24 September 2014].

Kim, AJ. 2012. *Social Engagement: Who's Playing? How Do They Like to Engage?* 19 September. [Online]. Available: http://amyjokim.com/2012/09/19/social-engagement-whos-playing-how-do-they-like-to-engage, https://www.youtube.com/watch?feature=player_embedded&v=ZIzLbE-93nc. [Accessed 23 September 2014].

Marczewski, A. 2012. *Gamification: A Simple Introduction*. Amazon Digital Services Inc.

Mellenthin, C. 2011. *What is Play Therapy and Why Does It Work?* [Online]. Available: http://clairmellenthin.com/play-therapy. [Accessed 25 September 2014].

Microsoft. 2010. *Score One for Quality! Using Games to Improve Product Quality*, [Online]. Available: http://www.42projects.org/docs/GTAC_LQG.PDF. [Accessed 23 September 2014].

Paharia, R. 2013. *Loyalty 3.0: How Big Data and Gamification are Revolutionizing Customer and Employee Engagement*. New York (NY): McGraw-Hill. [Online]. Available: http://www.loyalty30.com/. [Accessed 23 September 2014].

Passion4Development. [Online]. Available: http://www.p4d.co.za. [Accessed 23 September 2014].

Pelling, N. 2014. Personal Web Page. [Online]. Available: http://www.nickpelling.com/. [Accessed 23 September 2014].

Pink, DH. 2011. The Surprising Truth About What Motivates Us: Drive. New York (NY): Riverhead Books (a division of Penguin Group (USA)).

Ross, P. 2006. *Math teacher Uses Gamification to Help At-Risk Students Succeed*. [Online]. Available: http://www.goventureoasis.com/resources/pdf/5111201034254.pdf . [Accessed 24 September 2014].

Seligman, MEP 2012. *Flourish: A Visionary New Understanding of Happiness And Well-Being*. [Online]. Available: http://positivepsychologymelbourne.com.au/PERMA-model. [Accessed 23 September 2014].

Shore, M. 2010. What is Fun? TEDxManhattanBeach. [Online]. Available: http://tedxtalks.ted.com/video/TEDxManhattanBeach-Michael-Shore. [Accessed 23 September 2014].

Skinner, BF. 1938. *The Behavior of Organisms: An Experimental Analysis*. New York (NY): Appleton-Century. See also Operant conditioning [ONLINE]. Available: https://www.youtube.com/watch?feature=player_embedded&v=I_ctJqjlrHA, [Accessed 23 September 2014]; Reinforcement theory [ONLINE]. Available: https://www.youtube.com/watch?feature=player_embedded&v=YIEt6TrjJXw [Accessed 23 September 2014].

Smith, R. 2012. *How Play and Games Transform the Culture of Work*. [Online]. Available: http://www.journalofplay.org/sites/www.journalofplay.org/files/pdf-articles/5-1-interview-how-play-and-games-transform-the-culture-of-work.pdf. [Accessed 23 September 2014].

Werbach, K. 2012. *For the Win*. Wharton Digital Press. Article on Lloyds. [Online]. Available: http://www.finextra.com/news/fullstory.aspx?newsitemid=19430. [Accessed 24 September 2014].

Zichermann, G & Cunningham, C. 2011. *Gamification by Design: Implementing Game Mechanics in Web and Mobile Apps*. Sebastopol (CA): O'Reilly Media.

Zichermann, G & Linder, J. 2010. *Game-based Marketing: Inspire Customer Loyalty through Rewards, Challenges, and Contests*. Hoboken (NJ): Wiley & Sons, Inc.

Zichermann, G & Linder, J. 2013. *The Gamification Revolution: How leaders Leverage Game Mechanics to Cush the Competition*. New York (NY): McGraw-Hill.

CHAPTER 12

ASTD Staff. (2009, October 29). *The Value of Evaluation: Usage and Value of Kirkpatrick/Phillips model.* ASTD - Learning and Developemnt Blog. [Online]. Available: http://www.astd.org/Publications/ Blogs/ASTD-Blog/2009/10/The-Value-of-Evaluation-Usage-and-Value-of-KirkpatrickPhillips-Model?

Bailey, A. 2003. *The Kirkpatrick/Phillips Model for Evaluating Human Resource Development and Training.* Learning Designs Online .

Bennington, K., & Laffoley, T. 2012. *Beyond Smiley Sheets: Measuring the ROI of Learning and Development.* [Online]. Available: www.execdev.unc.edu: www.kenan-flagler.unc.edu/~/... development/beyond-smiley-sheets.pdf

Ip, YK. 2003. Knowing is Not the Same as Understanding: What is Understanding? *Successful Learning.* Centre for Development and teaching of Learning, [Online]. Available: http://www.cdtl. nus.edu.sg/success/sl20.htm. [Accessed 22 September 2014].

Northern Illinois University, Faculty Development and Instructional Design Center . (nd). facdev@niu. edu. [Online]. Available: http://facdev.niu.edu, 815.753.0595 .

QOTFC. The Clinical Educator's Resource Kit. *The Feedback Process.* [Online]. Available: http:// www.qotfc.edu.au/resource/index.html?page=65380. [Accessed 22 September 2014]. *(Crago & Pickering, 1987; Ende, 1983; Ovando, 1994; Watts, 1990, as cited in Clinical Placement Advisory Committee [CPAC]' 1997)*

Tobin, DR. 2010). *Feeding Your Leadership Pipeline: How to Develop the Next Generation of Leaders in Small to Mid-Sized Companies.* San Francisco (CA): ASTD Press & Berrett-Koehler.

CHAPTER 13

Bailey, A. 2003. *The Kirkpatrick/Phillips Model for Evaluating Human Resource Development and Training* . Learning Designs Online .

Buning, N. 2010. *Global HR Forum: Sustainable Learning Through Learning Chains.* [Online]. Available: http://www.slideshare.net/mindrom/sustainable-learning-through-learning-chains-norbert-buning-global-hr-forum-2010pdf-seoul-korea. [Accessed 18 June 2014].

Gravett, S. 2001. *Adult Learning: Designing and Implementing Learning Events, A Dialogic Approach.* Pretoria: Van Schaik Publishers.

Heidenhain, G. 2014. The Accelerated Learning Cycle – A Design Template. *ASTD Learning and Development Blog*, 22 April. ASTD.

Kotter, J. 1995. Leading Change: Why Transformation Efforts Fail. *Harvard Business Review OnPoint*, 1–10, March–April.

CHAPTER 14

Boshyk, Y. 2000. Business Driven Action Learning: Global Best Practices. New York (NY): Palgrave Macmillan.

Cho, Y. 2013. What is Action Learning? Components, Types, Processes, Issues, and Research Agendas. *Learning and Performance Quarterly*, 1(4). Indiana University.

Cho, Y & Egan, TM. 2009. Action Learning Research: A Systematic Review And Conceptual Framework. *Human Resource Development Review*, 8(4):431–462. doi:10.1177/1534484309345656.

Cho, Y & Egan, TM. 2010. The State of the Art of Action Learning Research. *Advances in Developing Human Resources*, 12(2):163–180. doi: 10.1177/1523422310367881.

CHAPTER 15

Adair, JE. 2013. Decision Making and Problem Solving (Creating Success). *Sunday Times*.

Adamson, B, Dickson, M & Toman, N. 2013. Dismantling the sales machine. *Harvard Business Review*, 102–109, November.

Corporate Executive Board. 2013. Breakthrough Performance in the New Environment. *Executive Guidance*. [Online]. Available: http://www.executiveboard.com/exbd-resources/pdf/executive-guidance/eg2013-annual-final.pdf. [Accessed 30 August 2014].

de Bono, E. 2009. *Six Thinking Hats*. London (UK): Penguin Books Ltd.

Heath, C & Heath, D. 2013. *Decisive: How to Make Better Choices in Life and Work*. New York (NY): Crown Business, an imprint of Crown Publishing Group, a division of Random House, Inc.

Herrmann, E. *Brain dominance*.

Kahneman, D. 2011. *Thinking, Fast and Slow*. New York (NY): Farrar, Straus and Giroux.

Lovallo, D & Sibony, 2013. Early-stage Research on Decision-making Styles. *McKinsey Quarterly*, April.

Paul, R & Elder, L. 2006. *The Miniature Guide to Critical Thinking Concepts and Tools*. 2nd ed. Dillon Beach (CA): The Foundation for Critical Thinking.

Rock, D. 2008. Adapted from SCARF: A Brain-Based Model for Collaborating with and Influencing Others. *NeuroLeadership Journal*. [Online]. Available: http://www.your-brain-at-work.com/files/NLJ_SCARFUS.pdf. [Accessed 4 November 2013].

Spetzler, CS. 2007. Building Decision Competency in Organizations. In W Edwards, RF Miles & D von Winterfeldt (eds). *Advances in decision analysis: From foundations to applications*. New York (NY): Cambridge University Press.

INDEX

A

ability, 4, 5, 10, 30, 31, 79, 111, 114, 115, 131, 140, 141, 189, 245, 246, 289, 292, 294, 312, 314, 315
  coping, 192
  decision-making, 336, 340
  learner's, 287
  testing, 201, 202
Accelerated Learning Cycle, 217, 227
Accelerated Learning in South African organisations, 1, 13
accelerated learning programme. *See* ALP
accelerated learning programme formula, 236
accelerated learning programmes, 32, 45, 49, 50, 127, 134, 211, 213–215, 217, 219, 225, 236, 272, 285, 287, 306
accountability, 55, 120, 124, 132, 134, 143, 146, 155, 168, 174, 189, 191, 193, 204, 275
action learning, 32, 48, 50, 207–208, 311, 316
Action-learning coach, 51
action learning programmes, 322, 331
action learning projects, 49, 53, 121, 138, 329
action plan, 128, 167
actual proficiency level, 200, 201, 205, 206
adoption rates, 34, 45–47
adults, 33, 104, 213, 229, 310
affirmative inquiry, 48, 239, 240
ages, 4, 21–22, 24, 67, 84, 85, 102, 103, 131, 211, 216, 225, 242
alignment, 44, 45, 50, 124, 133, 145, 179, 180, 193, 194, 239, 303, 312
ALP (accelerated learning programme), 13, 14, 41, 49–52, 177, 211–217, 219, 220, 225, 233, 234, 236, 285, 287–288, 291–293, 296–297, 301, 306
application, 12, 30, 31, 34, 35, 50, 51, 55, 126, 130, 136, 227, 234, 250, 256, 287, 311, 312, 318
  practical, 49, 51, 71, 73, 75, 76, 157

assessment, 138, 201, 203, 234, 236, 266, 272, 276, 277, 280–289, 291, 295, 296, 301, 303, 324, 327–330
  individual learning, 205
  level of, 283, 285, 295
  psychometric, 129, 203, 239, 290, 328, 329
  summative, 288, 312
assessment decisions, 177, 281
assessment methods, 127, 177, 276, 277, 286, 291–294
assessment process, 272, 286, 294, 296, 299
assessment value chain, 275, 287–292, 294, 295, 310–312, 314
assessors, 283–286, 295
assumptions, 37, 62, 64, 73, 114, 148, 162–163, 170, 171, 173, 280, 294, 295, 299, 341, 342, 344
attention, 14, 20, 38, 39, 59, 60, 65, 66, 70, 72, 89, 93, 94, 102–106, 113, 166, 171, 228, 229, 235, 236
  continuous partial, 102, 107
  shifting, 105
attention density, 104
attention management strategies, 107
authentic conversations, 14, 119, 165–166, 168–170, 172, 173, 175
autonomy, 34, 82, 83, 96, 97, 132, 199, 242, 249–251, 264, 272, 273, 310
  personal, 199
avatars, 264–266, 269

B

Baby Boomers, 19–20, 22, 26, 27
barriers, 8, 18, 83, 85, 93, 159, 160, 286, 296, 298
behavioural change aspect, 307
Behavioural learning, 306
behaviour change, 129, 208, 211, 250, 255, 272, 277–278, 287, 313
  sustaining, 273

behaviour change skills, 152

behaviour coaches, 307, 309, 310, 312

behaviours, 34–36, 61–65, 110–112, 121–122, 127–129, 137, 138, 140, 162–163, 169–171, 189, 192, 251–253, 265–266, 282–283, 306–307

   changing, 162, 208, 266

   changing external, 103

   correct learning, 265

   current, 64, 307

   defensive, 166, 170

   derailing, 114, 122, 152, 168, 175

   five, 37, 192, 195

   individual's, 250, 251

   leader's, 170

   new, 64, 147, 252, 253, 307

   observed, 201, 330

   required, 145, 183

   social, 81, 96, 111

beliefs, 2, 3, 10, 48, 55, 61, 64, 67–69, 80, 86, 99, 128, 153, 159, 162–163, 173

biases, rater, 201, 202, 295, 296

Big Hairy Audacious Goals (BHAGs), 122

BL. *See* Breakthrough Learning

blended learning approach, 49, 329

blogs, 22, 24, 25, 28, 222, 223, 236–238, 268, 288, 311

boredom, 87, 99, 252, 253, 258, 259

brain, 13, 16, 27, 30, 35, 59, 89–96, 98–100, 102–105, 107, 108, 110, 112–117, 148, 213, 226

   emotional, 94, 96

   social, 59, 94, 107, 110

Brain Break, 9, 36, 50, 85, 90, 142, 149, 174, 209, 212, 254, 281, 310, 334

Brainfacts.org, 89

brain learning, 28, 35, 212, 231, 237

brain learning principles, 216, 225

brain messages, deceptive, 111–114

brain networks, 82

brain research, 69, 89

brain's ability, 35, 89, 103

Brain Thinking, 35, 74

Breakthrough Learning (BL), 14, 232, 289–291, 303, 316–318, 328

Breakthrough Learning Programme, 315, 319

budgets, 124, 130, 206, 208, 275, 319–321, 326

Building Coaching Cultures in Organisations, 164

building learning organisations, 36

business, 42–44, 46–49, 54–57, 133, 134, 185–188, 190, 191, 244, 245, 259, 266, 270, 279, 280, 298–300, 316–319, 327, 328, 339

   high-level, 5

business case, 319, 320, 342, 344

business challenges, 49, 316, 346

business coaching, 145–146, 157

business context, 54, 342, 344

business leaders, 51, 276

   global technology, 271

business objectives, 145, 146

business owners, 259, 291, 320, 324, 332

business result, 297, 298

business schools, 51, 52, 114, 206, 325

business units, 42, 332, 335, 337

business world, changing, 336

buy-in, 124, 126, 295, 324

C

candidates, 44, 45, 318, 322–325

capabilities, 4, 95, 177, 178, 180, 182–188

   core learning, 37

capacity, 35, 37, 42, 54, 66, 68, 89, 101, 103, 104, 120, 128, 135, 147, 183, 318

CAPP (Centre for Applied Positive Psychology), 240

career, 3, 19, 20, 38, 53, 123, 132–134, 181, 197, 203, 216, 246, 269, 328, 338

Career Development Plan (CDP), 181, 183, 200, 319, 328

career discussion, 200, 290, 328

case studies, 14, 57, 60, 71, 73, 76, 231, 232, 234, 279, 294, 303, 315, 335, 337, 344, 345

CDP. *See* Career Development Plan

Central Nervous System (CNS), 95

Centre for Applied Positive Psychology (CAPP), 240

challenges, 42, 45, 148, 149, 198, 201, 246–250, 253, 258, 261, 292, 294, 295, 315, 317–320, 322, 344

   common, 42

change, 1–6, 8–10, 27, 28, 35, 37, 59–64, 103, 120, 121, 123–125, 140–141, 183–184, 211–212, 239, 303–305, 312, 313

brains, 84
 significant, 47, 61, 84, 134
 sustainable, 275, 344
 system, 211, 275
change agents, 23, 43
change behaviours, 242, 244, 313
change champions, 41, 320
change cycle, 144, 152
change leadership, 193, 194
change learn, 25
change learners, 219
change management, 43, 47, 54, 55, 126, 129,
 130, 140, 206, 315, 327, 341, 344
 implementing strategic, 337
change management projects, 245
change process, 3, 14, 121, 193
change resilience, 130
Changing organisational culture, 139
Chemistry of Accelerated Learning in Executive
 Coaching, 218
Chief Learning Officer. See CLO
children, 20, 38, 85, 104, 148, 212
chunks, 101, 104–105, 222, 230, 269, 310
CL (Collaborative learning), 32–34, 46, 222, 324
classroom, 27, 31–33, 42, 43, 57, 61, 106, 150,
 221, 268
clients, 15, 25, 43, 143, 145, 147, 148, 203, 261,
 282
climate, 161, 217, 306–308, 310
CLO (Chief Learning Officer), 55, 126
clusters, 192, 193, 195, 340
CNS (Central Nervous System), 95
coachees, 144, 146–149, 151, 155, 161–164
coaches, 31, 32, 48, 49, 136, 137, 143, 144,
 148–152, 156–160, 162–164, 214–215, 217,
 218, 233, 284, 289–291, 313, 314, 317–319,
 329–330
 accredited, 143
 external, 32, 49, 149, 325
coach feedback, 278, 287
coaching, 31, 32, 48, 49, 51, 119, 121, 122, 137–
 139, 143–150, 152, 156–160, 164, 207–208,
 236, 237, 285, 287, 310–313
 group, 327
 in-the-moment, 158, 160
coaching conversations, 137, 145, 148, 150,
 158, 162, 164

coaching mode, 139
coaching principles, 163
coaching process, 32, 144–147, 156–158, 215,
 232
coaching relationship, 32, 146, 149, 150, 156–
 158, 163, 164, 218
Coaching roles, 48, 144, 149, 151, 199
coaching sessions, 138, 139, 157, 158, 208, 221,
 290, 325
coaching skills, 48, 143, 144, 150, 152, 222
coach observation, 289, 290
cognition, 66, 107, 108
Cognitive Process Profile. See CPP
collaboration, 47, 51, 55, 56, 99, 103, 129–131,
 169, 224, 228, 317, 318, 324, 327, 332, 341,
 343
 power of, 9, 130, 345
collaborative learning, 32, 33, 46, 222
Collaborative learning. See CL
Collaborators, 41, 256–258
commitment, 37, 42, 121, 123, 124, 126, 134,
 139, 163, 174, 204, 278, 279, 320
communities, 8–10, 13, 26, 28, 29, 130, 135,
 237, 264, 310, 311
companies, 5, 6, 45–49, 53, 54, 119–124, 130,
 135, 136, 149, 150, 183, 185, 321–323, 325,
 326, 331, 332, 334, 337, 339, 340
competence, 7, 9, 12, 31, 131, 132, 179, 180,
 185, 187, 190, 192, 201, 202, 217, 305, 310,
 312–314
 core, 9, 130, 132, 185–186
 level of, 124, 188, 232
competence assessment, 12, 287, 295, 311, 312
competence standards, 188, 190, 283, 296, 322
competencies, 4, 10, 132, 133, 178, 182, 184–
 186, 192, 195, 197–201, 203, 205, 206, 220,
 317, 327, 329
 functional, 182, 185, 189
competency areas, 192–197, 199, 316
competency assessment, uncoupling, 201, 202
competency management, 123, 179
competency profiles, 182, 192, 194, 205, 322
competency profiling, 194
competency standards, 12, 14, 177, 179, 181,
 188, 192, 198, 209, 290
competition, 2, 31, 33, 37, 60, 66, 68, 76, 133,
 184, 185, 260, 263, 310, 315, 324

competitive advantage, 31, 185, 187, 211, 304

competitors, 2, 31, 131, 135, 178, 184, 185, 256–258, 315

complaints, line manager's, 179, 180

complexity, 31, 36, 54, 55, 57, 73, 77, 193, 198, 294, 324, 332, 336, 337, 342, 344, 346

concepts, 17, 36, 38, 71, 76, 99, 116, 178, 244, 330, 338, 345

conflict, 166, 168, 170, 171, 173, 174, 204

connect, 24, 25, 71, 73, 83, 103, 212, 230, 241, 331

consensus, 169, 174, 201–203

considerations, 277–280, 321–326

consultants, 52, 136, 138, 275, 319

contact sessions, 51, 52

content, 24–27, 29, 31, 43, 45, 46, 100, 101, 104, 218, 220, 222, 228, 230–231, 236–238, 256–258, 265

context, 40, 42, 43, 91, 93, 116, 119, 145, 150, 161, 165, 229, 231, 323, 329, 335, 336

real-world, 232, 234, 283, 289, 294, 304, 312

continuum, 69, 174

contract, 157–158, 167, 191, 221, 289

contracting, 151, 157

control, 56, 83, 95–97, 106, 109, 112, 116, 145, 159, 170, 171, 173, 254, 257, 265, 313

control group, 278, 279

conversations, 9, 15, 53, 54, 57, 109, 123, 128, 153, 154, 157, 161, 164, 165, 167, 168, 170–175, 184, 327

structured, 145, 241

conversation skills, 152, 168

core competencies, 125, 178, 182, 185–186, 188, 194, 206, 219, 220

courage, 68, 96, 156, 157, 166, 168, 173

CPD, 198

CPP (Cognitive Process Profile), 77, 78, 204, 329

creation, 99–102, 126

creativity, 19, 38, 68, 90, 100, 115, 116, 137, 254

credibility, 7, 67, 97, 171, 280, 282, 301, 320, 323, 328

CRM (Customer Relationship Management), 304, 306

Cross-functional learning projects, 134

cross-functional teams, 49, 134, 169

Cross-functional team sessions, 133, 134

Cross-level programmes, 322

culture, 42, 44, 56, 57, 119–125, 127–130, 136, 140, 141, 178, 179, 184–186, 189, 204, 296, 307, 309, 339, 340

culture transformation journey, 119, 139–141, 184

curricula, 181, 182, 206

Customer Relationship Management (CRM), 304, 306

customers, 60, 122, 130, 135, 136, 166, 167, 185, 186, 191, 193, 233, 258, 304, 305, 313, 314

customise, 56, 60, 268, 315, 317, 321

D

Decision Committee, 342

decision competency, 337

decision-making style, 340

decision management, 303, 335–339, 343, 346

culture of effective, 14, 303, 338

decisions, 3, 4, 43, 45, 65, 68, 70, 71, 82, 84, 105, 121, 124, 129, 130, 321, 323, 335–344

better, 2, 3, 338

effective, 335, 337, 341, 346

good, 97

making, 203, 336, 346

Defence Centres of Excellence, 21

Deloitte Leadership Academy, 270

Department for Work and Pensions (DWP), 243

description, 19–21, 25, 51–53, 69, 72, 80–82, 169, 197, 240–242, 247, 257, 289, 320

design, 46, 48, 60, 177, 182, 196, 211, 212, 216–218, 235, 270, 295, 314, 317, 329, 330, 337, 338

design combination, 236, 285

designers, 212, 215–220, 222, 223, 226, 252, 293, 313

design learning experiences, 25, 104

design principles, 212, 309, 315, 321

design process, 106, 177, 196, 223, 227

design programmes, 98, 275

design team, 345

development, 43, 45, 53, 54, 123, 124, 126, 127, 144, 149, 150, 178–181, 200, 203, 206, 207, 255, 259, 290, 328

development areas, 77, 79, 129

development discussion organisation
  competence audit, 201
Development plans, 206, 207, 290
  strategic, 206
dialogic approach, 214, 215
dialogue, 9, 12, 37, 46–48, 129, 140, 155, 173,
  193, 214–215, 218, 223, 230, 298, 310
Didata, 42, 46, 48, 52, 54, 56
difference, 41, 50, 68, 92, 105, 123, 166, 168,
  172, 173, 184, 185, 208
digital immigrants, 23–27
digital language of computers, 21, 23, 24
dimensions, 37, 74, 77–81
direction, 68, 161, 245, 246, 251
downsides, 149, 150
drive, 126, 128, 132, 192–194, 198, 212, 249,
  250, 282, 286, 305, 307–309, 313, 320, 324,
  327
drive change management plan, 320
DWP (Department for Work and Pensions), 243

E

economies, 6, 7, 85, 122, 124, 184, 206, 279,
  308
education, 6, 7, 17, 19–21, 38, 56, 126, 180, 226,
  284
educators, 28, 30, 40, 95, 98, 131, 214, 215
effective decision management, 14, 303, 335,
  336, 338, 340
effectiveness, 12, 27, 28, 69, 133, 164, 219, 226,
  252, 288, 300, 301, 312, 325, 326, 339, 345
effort, 25, 34, 36, 48, 62, 65, 66, 68, 102, 174,
  235, 259, 320
e-learning, 32, 33, 46, 222, 236, 308, 310
eLearning, 22, 34
e-learning modules, 47, 275, 313
  based, 306
  compulsory, 223, 311
e-learning platform, 46, 311
emotional intelligence, 9, 32, 53, 54, 61, 67, 79,
  86, 132, 152, 169, 284, 296, 327, 329
emotions, 3, 74, 79, 80, 89, 93, 105–108, 111,
  112, 114, 166, 170, 171, 173, 194, 204, 250,
  259
  positive, 38, 71, 96, 98, 108, 255
empathy, 5, 9, 39, 62, 80, 105, 111, 152, 159,
  161, 170, 171, 173, 174
employees, 6, 8, 129–133, 135, 140, 141, 144,
  178, 180, 183, 184, 202, 203, 243, 259–261,
  265, 297, 300
employers, 131
encoding, 225, 226, 231
energy, 37, 103–105, 152, 165, 180, 192, 193,
  204, 239, 324
engagement, 24, 35, 55, 56, 239, 244, 245, 249,
  251–253, 255, 256, 258, 261, 262, 265, 266,
  272, 273, 313, 314, 341, 343, 344
engagement loops, 255, 256, 258
engagement type, 24, 25, 27
entrants, new, 44, 48, 52, 188
environment, 9, 23, 24, 35, 36, 42, 49, 77, 82, 84,
  95, 128, 138, 252, 257, 310, 311, 315
Eskom, 41, 43, 48, 50, 51
evaluation, 275, 276, 281, 284, 296, 297, 299,
  300, 333
events, 12, 21, 31, 40, 81, 83, 126, 128, 155,
  172, 221, 223, 224, 258, 311, 321
evidence, 29, 30, 85, 108, 112, 201–204, 273,
  286, 290, 298, 319, 328
  portfolio of, 8, 288, 290, 323, 328
Examples of Accelerated Learning programmes,
  1, 50
excellence, 21, 22, 68, 74, 149
exchanges, 166, 241, 258
  reciprocal, 166, 173
executive leader level, 194
executives, 42, 120, 133, 186, 188, 270, 283,
  296, 299, 321, 323, 326, 334, 336, 341
executive team, 121, 123, 124, 232, 261, 324,
  326
exercise, 114–116, 155
experience, 4, 5, 29, 30, 43, 60, 61, 135, 149–
  151, 192, 194, 195, 197–199, 207–208, 230,
  231, 238, 245, 246, 249–251, 264–266
experiential learning cycle, 98
experiment, 30, 35, 39, 49, 71, 73, 76, 82, 83,
  100, 147, 152, 344
expertise, 4, 5, 7, 68, 102, 131, 150, 151, 165,
  178, 179, 271, 278, 279, 283, 341
  technical, 4, 51, 57, 317
experts, 10, 19, 27, 28, 31, 34, 56, 101, 163, 199,
  216, 237, 238, 311, 314
exploration, 27, 30, 31, 78, 259

explorer, 124, 256–258

exposure, 51–53, 67, 82, 83, 85, 105, 194, 219, 230, 317, 319, 326, 334, 341

expresser, 256–258, 264

extension, 18, 20, 21, 238

eye contact, 153, 233

F

Facebook, 15–17, 34, 62, 67, 102, 104, 106, 162, 167, 205, 208, 235, 245, 247, 257–259

facilitators, 26, 30, 34, 105, 214–218, 221, 228, 230, 232, 233, 290, 292, 319, 321, 325, 329, 330

factors, 67, 68, 84–86, 94, 115, 155, 162, 163, 192, 206, 216, 253, 279, 280, 299, 317

fairness, 46, 82, 84, 96, 97, 283, 286

family, 16, 20, 36, 63, 136, 138, 148, 167, 172, 321

fears, 61, 64, 66, 67, 81–84, 86, 96, 108–110, 150, 157, 168, 170, 171, 261, 340

Features of Accelerated Learning programmes, 51

feedback, 32, 136–138, 147–149, 232–235, 244–246, 255, 258, 259, 277–279, 282, 284–285, 287–290, 293–296, 310–314, 316–319, 329, 330

  behavioural, 132

  candid, 167, 169

  leader, 277

  peer, 289, 290, 295

feedback activities, 75, 239

feedback methods, 233

feedback process, 278, 288, 330

feedback sessions, 84, 313, 317

feeling confident, 80, 81

feelings, 61, 62, 66, 68, 70, 71, 73, 75, 79–82, 97, 102, 111–113, 153, 162–163, 170, 171, 173–175, 254, 255

field, 5, 19, 31, 47, 60, 89, 90, 92, 97, 116, 136, 138, 169, 170, 185, 199

flow, 10, 62, 66, 87, 96, 244–249, 255, 258

flow states, 87, 245–246

food, 87, 97, 98, 104, 110, 120, 148

format, 29–31

forums, 31, 33, 169, 236–238, 240, 323, 326

framework, 10, 100, 123, 124, 158, 160, 177, 180–183, 227, 231, 338, 342

friends, 15–16, 20, 23, 33, 64, 83, 104, 112, 136, 137, 139, 148, 157, 167, 257–259, 263, 264

fun, 9, 18, 22, 26, 34, 35, 38, 73, 234, 243–244, 246, 254, 255, 257–260, 265, 266, 271, 278

functional learning paths, 197

functions, 45, 50, 54, 89, 90, 96, 126, 132, 182, 189–191, 200, 202, 205, 318, 319, 322, 324

G

games, 39, 47, 73, 76, 221, 228, 231, 234, 243–245, 254, 255, 263, 264, 271, 273, 278, 287

gamification, 14, 17, 38, 39, 46, 47, 177, 236, 237, 243–244, 249–251, 253, 255, 256, 259, 262, 263, 266, 268, 271–273

  maths teacher uses, 268, 269

gamification strategy, 39, 177, 247, 250, 252, 255–256, 258, 262–266, 268, 271–272

gaps, 52, 63, 109, 110, 156, 178, 180, 196, 198, 200, 205, 206, 337

gathering, 99, 100, 102, 144

generations, 9, 16, 18–24, 26, 27, 34, 47, 51, 66, 84, 216, 238

GIBS, 41, 42, 44, 46, 48, 52, 53, 57

Global leadership programme, 49, 52

goals, 110, 111, 125, 129, 143, 145, 147, 149, 152, 159, 160, 164, 245, 246, 255, 264, 265, 269, 298

  organisational, 7, 22, 169, 343

  strategic, 126, 183, 191

grade levels Programmes, 52

group members, 33

groups, 9, 10, 83–85, 212, 218, 219, 221, 230, 237, 241, 259, 260, 264, 289, 297, 321, 322, 324–326, 333, 334

group work, 33, 213, 228

guest speakers, 319, 325, 329, 330

guide, 14, 31, 68, 106, 107, 129, 161, 227, 288, 303–305, 308, 314, 343

guilds, 264, 266

H

habits, 27, 61, 62, 64, 99, 129, 156, 169, 337

higher level roles, 197

high-level design, 303, 321

high performer, new, 4, 338

holding authentic conversations, 119, 166, 168, 170–172, 175
HR Manager, 198, 200
HR manager's complaints, 179, 180
HR strategy, 124–126, 200

I

ICF. *See* International Coach Federation
ILP (Individual Learning Plan), 181, 183, 200
imagination, 38, 71, 72, 89, 137, 175, 254, 265
implementation, 6, 14, 73, 191, 262, 299, 304, 306, 307, 315, 319, 320, 331, 332, 334, 343, 345
important leadership skills, 54
improvement, team learning Business, 333
Individual Learning Plan (ILP), 181, 183, 200
Individual learning Team learning Project, 289
individuals, 9, 13, 29, 32, 33, 36, 45, 46, 132, 133, 188, 190, 207, 212, 238, 239, 245, 317, 323
  talented, 317, 318
individual values, 44
induction, 44, 46, 52, 134, 256
industries, 6, 30, 31, 34, 36, 41, 130, 244, 270, 317, 322, 330, 344
informal learning, 28, 57, 102, 221, 224, 235–238, 285
information, 17, 18, 21, 31, 71, 72, 99–101, 103–105, 129–131, 213–214, 223, 225–226, 230–232, 238, 288, 328, 329, 341–344
  new, 31, 76, 102, 105, 154, 207, 214, 231, 257
information technology, 21, 24, 41
informing learners, 228, 229
innovation, 6, 15, 51, 55, 56, 100, 121, 122, 130, 136, 142, 191, 193, 254, 264, 327, 333
input sessions, 322
Inspirational Leadership, 54, 327
instruments, 72, 77, 143
interact, 9, 16, 18, 21, 24, 26, 28, 33, 72, 92, 93, 257, 258, 261, 308, 313, 317
internal coaches, 48, 51, 149
International Coach Federation (ICF), 32, 143, 147
Internet, 21, 23, 24, 222
interventions, large-scale change, 3, 54
interviewees, 42, 44, 46, 53–55
Investec, 41, 42, 47–48, 50, 54

J

job, 19, 20, 23, 33, 36, 42, 43, 56, 57, 77, 216, 221, 278, 283, 284, 286, 288, 310, 312
job families, 194, 195
judgement, 4, 43, 55, 78, 150, 173, 211, 286, 338

K

key capabilities, 4
key customers, 122, 135, 136
key elements, 231, 316, 317, 340
key stakeholders, 183, 294, 313, 317, 320, 321, 326, 341
knowledge, 31, 32, 68–70, 101, 107, 140–141, 192, 193, 214–216, 226–227, 230–232, 283, 284, 286–289, 292–294, 310–312, 317–319, 330–332
  prior, 99, 100, 102, 229
  transfer of, 44, 277, 278, 283
knowledge assessment, 278, 287, 295, 312
knowledge level, 312
knowledge skills behaviours, 188
knowledge worker, 131, 190

L

leader boards, 39, 255, 260, 263, 266, 269
leaders, 4–6, 31, 32, 41–45, 48–53, 55–57, 82, 120–123, 127–128, 130, 143, 144, 212, 214–217, 283–284, 308–310, 313
  developing, 5, 53
  key, 122, 124
  mid-level, 6
  new, 5, 123, 124, 134
leadership, 5–7, 37, 38, 48, 49, 51, 53, 121, 122, 124, 128, 129, 181, 182, 184, 185, 189–192, 217, 307–309, 313, 314, 322
  coaching style of, 48, 128, 143, 149
  critical, 2, 316
  strategy sessions team development, 208
leadership behaviours, 128, 309
leadership brand, 128, 143, 204
leadership capability, 51, 219
leadership challenges, 5, 175
leadership commitment, 49, 140, 141

leadership competencies, 143, 185, 197, 204, 322

leadership development, 7, 126, 128, 140, 143, 145, 275, 299, 337

Leadership Development and Talent Management, 165

Leadership Development Programs, various, 47

leadership development session, 123, 141

Leadership Development Survey, 7, 32

leadership feedback multi-raters, 194

leadership learning, 307

leadership level, 182, 184, 190

leadership positions, 309, 315

leadership programmes, 5, 7, 48, 53, 117, 136, 168, 192

Leadership session, 128, 141
  facilitated, 290

leadership skills, 1, 44, 51, 54, 184, 322, 330
  good, 202

leadership stories, 239, 331

leadership style, 12, 124, 168, 170, 184

learner ability, 294

learner centric, 8, 27, 29

learners, 28–31, 33–35, 47–50, 98–102, 107–109, 213–222, 226–234, 236–238, 245–246, 268–270, 282–284, 286–289, 291–296, 310, 312–314
  at-risk, 268, 269
  coach, 314
  experiential, 26
  fast, 204, 317
  group of, 235, 237
  individual, 218, 307
  teach, 107, 284

learner self-assessment, 293

learners experience, 242

learners level, 269

learners teaching, 279, 287

learning, 7–10, 12–18, 25–30, 32–47, 53–57, 59–63, 81–87, 89–96, 123–130, 132–138, 143–148, 215–232, 275–283, 296–301, 307–318
  accelerating, 42, 54, 144
  blended, 33, 34
  brain processes, 99
  classroom, 38, 39
  coaching deepens, 143

community, 125, 135

continuous, 31, 37, 139

customise, 9, 12, 13, 87

end-user, 307

experiential, 22

formal, 224, 235, 236, 285

group, 10, 61, 208, 292

integration of, 49, 93

interval, 30, 227

ladder of, 227

levels of, 217, 227

link, 73, 313

mobile, 17, 34, 47, 236, 237

next-level, 322

organisational, 37, 129, 180, 239, 316

organisational capabilities, 184

organisation-led, 42

quantum, 213, 214

real, 237, 280

self-directed, 31, 38

spaced, 30, 227

sustainable, 13, 162, 223, 236, 285

sustained, 114, 314

team, 37, 46, 49, 125, 133

transformational, 305, 306, 309

value of, 42, 44, 276

virtual, 47, 332

learning academy, 321, 328

learning activities, 8, 40, 69, 93, 100, 116, 125, 132, 265, 282, 292

learning architecture, 12, 14, 140, 177–180, 219, 305

learning assessment, 12, 14, 177, 234, 275, 276, 286, 301, 313

learning audience, 217, 307, 308

learning buddy, 137

learning chain, 30, 223–225, 227, 230, 234, 287, 306, 310–311, 313, 314

learning champions, 1, 42, 53

learning climate, 214, 215

learning communities, 216

learning content, 17, 18, 50, 93, 126, 227

learning context, 61, 144, 220

learning contracts, 289, 295

learning criteria, 291, 333

learning culture, 8, 10, 12, 14, 36, 119–121, 125–128, 132, 139, 140, 142, 167, 178, 306 learning culture framework, 119, 124

learning cycle, 59, 63, 94, 98, 99, 104, 213, 313, 314

learning decisions, 7

learning department, 137

learning design, 14, 25, 35, 39, 89, 104, 107, 111, 125, 129, 211–213, 215, 303, 308, 309, 311

learning designers, 30, 95, 101, 212, 214–216
up-skill, 46

learning design for Accelerated Learning, 177, 212

learning design principles, 303, 312

learning environments, 8, 17, 38, 42, 44, 53, 55, 82, 213, 214, 216, 221, 228, 314, 318, 328

learning events, 100, 220, 232, 287, 297, 305, 307, 308
designing, 101
sequence of, 220, 227

learning experience, 28, 34, 35, 39, 44, 61, 93, 101, 102, 107–109, 135, 254, 255, 265, 266, 330, 339, 341, 342, 344, 345
accelerated, 61, 246
connected, 34
cross-functional, 206
current, 235
designing, 44, 212
dynamic, 175
implementing, 95
individualised, 311
mutual, 136

learning experiences change, 60

learning forums, 200, 209

learning framework, 13, 29, 37, 236, 311
accelerated, 10, 314

learning function, 7, 42, 54–56, 186, 211, 276, 280, 282, 305

learning influences, 59, 66, 67
various, 66, 84

learning interventions, 44, 57, 92, 115, 144, 178, 206
designing, 85, 127

learning involvement, 1, 54

learning journey, 10, 12, 14, 42, 67, 69, 123, 132, 136–138, 234, 313, 323, 330

learning landscape, 303, 306

learning management system (LMS), 32, 47, 126

learning methodologies, 46, 129, 318, 342

learning methods, 74, 208, 232, 239, 240, 306, 314

learning modules, 29, 222, 326

learning motivation, 21, 22

Learning nugget, 223, 310, 311

learning objectives, 115, 220, 236, 278

learning opportunities, 262, 317
informal, 216, 311, 314

learning organisation, 12, 29, 36–37, 40, 56, 120, 124, 125, 127, 134, 142, 179
systemic, 37

learning organisation mind-set, 36

learning outcomes, 219, 265, 284

learning partner, 64, 137, 139, 144, 168, 175

learning paths, 6, 181, 206

Learning Pathway, 9, 61, 197, 198

learning plans, 49, 184, 200, 207, 212, 328
strategic, 182, 300

learning platforms, social, 34, 45, 126

learning portal, 303, 332

learning practitioners, 57, 238, 242, 294

learning preferences, 70–71, 73, 75–76, 87, 207

Learning principles, 57, 98, 102, 106, 107, 111, 114, 116

learning professionals, 4, 19, 55, 180, 312

learning profile, 10, 12, 59, 66, 86, 217

learning programme design, 130, 252

learning programmes, 47, 85, 106, 115, 138, 177, 217, 251, 252, 255, 286, 309, 324, 325, 328
annual, 334
comprehensive Accelerated, 49
current, 317
current Accelerated, 41
designed intensive, 114
designing, 114
designing Accelerated, 10
intensive long-term, 318
week-long, 32

learning projects, 295, 325, 329, 331, 332

learning providers, 29, 206, 272, 277

learning relationship, 214

learning sessions, 85, 115, 135, 141, 144, 207, 221, 266, 316, 330

learning set, 217, 218, 230, 232, 237, 289, 290, 292, 293

learning space, 68, 138, 162, 218, 239

learning specialists, 31, 32, 56, 82, 127, 130, 183, 202, 212, 250

learning strategy, 125, 126, 183, 188, 305, 307, 312, 314

learning styles, 21, 30, 53, 61, 67, 73, 75–77, 86, 93, 152, 169, 215–217
  individual, 213, 215

learning teams, 315, 321, 332, 333

learning themes, 303, 340

learning theory, 35, 126

learning tools, 12, 31, 236, 272

learning transfer, 234

learnt, 4, 5, 7, 16, 18, 19, 21, 24, 25, 38, 184, 218, 220, 234, 242, 269, 270, 292, 293, 312

lessons, 5, 244, 268–270

lessons learnt, 31, 134, 315

level, 5, 127–130, 139–140, 187–192, 194–195, 199–202, 228–235, 265, 266, 268, 269, 276–280, 282–284, 287–288, 290–292, 294–296, 322, 323
  five, 266, 276
  higher, 84, 187, 197, 286
  lower, 195, 286, 339
  multiple, 202
  neural, 91
  right, 54, 121, 123, 181, 318
  skill, 87, 247
  strategic, 189
  team, 189

levelling, 39, 247

level of self-awareness, 219, 239, 296

levels of instruction, 228, 314

Liberty, 45–47, 54, 57

life, 18–21, 23, 41, 55, 56, 61–64, 68, 69, 79, 80, 106, 108, 111, 133, 136, 170, 239, 242

life coaching, 145, 239

lifelong learning, 56, 127

limbic system, 94, 96

line managers, 42, 48, 123, 127, 149, 150, 179, 183, 284, 289, 290, 295, 307, 308, 312, 313, 322, 325, 330

links, 86, 91, 92, 95, 98, 100, 108, 145, 148, 154, 223, 225, 227, 229, 230, 234, 240–242

LMS (learning management system), 32, 47, 126

loss, 83, 167, 170–171, 173, 226

M

making learning assessment decisions, 276

management, 23, 51, 185, 266, 331, 336

managers, 51, 52, 132, 133, 136, 137, 150, 188, 190–192, 198, 201–203, 278, 279, 287–291, 295, 296, 319, 328–329, 339–340, 344, 345

Manager's feedback, 141

Manages, 191, 196

Massive Open Online Courses. *See* MOOCs

Master Psychopharmacology Program (MPP), 30–31

mastery, 39, 132, 178, 249, 251, 254, 268, 271, 273
  personal, 37, 132, 169

mastery test, 268–269

MathLand, 268, 269

matrix, 187–189, 197

MCPs (mission-critical positions), 187–188, 219

Measuring ROI, 296, 299, 300

media, social, 15, 17, 24, 34

medium, 70, 72, 208

members, 19, 21, 24, 26, 33, 37, 237, 253, 326

memory, 38, 59, 61, 66, 72, 78, 89, 94, 96, 98, 102, 103, 106, 108–109, 225, 227
  working, 82, 94, 96, 100, 101, 104, 105, 107, 148

mentors, 32, 50, 136, 137, 150, 151, 199, 219, 246, 290, 317–320, 325, 327, 329, 332, 333, 345

Microsoft, 102, 255

millennials, 19, 21–23, 93, 245

mindfulness, 32, 105, 107, 344

mind tools, 217, 227, 228, 240

mirror neurons, 110, 111

mirror neuron system, 110

mission-critical positions. *See* MCPs

mobile devices, 16, 17, 24, 26, 34, 39, 85, 222, 231, 238

models, mental, 37, 128

modules, 46, 48, 49, 51, 275

MOOCs (Massive Open Online Courses), 28–29

motivation, 18, 25, 28, 35, 60, 61, 66, 67, 82, 86, 90, 94, 96, 146, 152, 243, 249–251

motivators, 81–84

motor cortices, 98, 99

movement, 39, 73, 115, 116, 221

MPP (Master Psychopharmacology Program), 30–31
multitasking, 104, 107

N

National Qualifications Framework. *See* NQF
natives, digital, 21, 23, 24
native speakers, 21, 23, 24
natural learning ability, 3
natural light, 114, 115, 221
nature, 49, 116, 147, 148, 151, 157, 194, 195, 237, 317, 320, 321, 323, 326, 330
NBI (Neethling Brain Instrument), 74
NEAs (Negative Emotional Attractors), 109, 110
Nedbank, 41, 43, 46–49, 55
Neethling Brain Instrument (NBI), 74
Negative Emotional Attractors. *See* NEAs
nervous system
  autonomic, 95
  somatic, 95
  sympathetic, 95, 96, 155
neural pathways, 101, 213, 214, 231
Neuro-Linguistic Programming, 74
Neurolinguistic Programming (NLP), 35, 74
neurons, 91, 95, 99, 103, 105, 110
neuroplasticity, 35, 103
neuroscience, 9, 30, 35, 48, 59, 66, 81, 89–94, 111, 138, 152, 231, 239
Neuroscience research, 114, 116, 117
new roles, 5, 126, 127, 170
next level leaders, 141
next level role, 181, 208, 290, 330
NLP (Neurolinguistic Programming), 35, 74
novices, 10, 101
NQF (National Qualifications Framework), 7, 180, 286
nuggets, learning chain links knowledge, 223, 311

O

objectives, 71, 220, 229, 329, 339, 340
objectivity, 201, 202, 295
office, 31, 33, 43, 221, 259, 261
on-boarding, 92, 95, 98, 247, 265
online learning, 8, 46, 52, 144, 265, 313

online learning experiences, 32
online learning programme, 31, 222
on-the-job learning, 231, 236, 313
operant conditioning, 251–253, 261
operations, 123, 186, 187, 189, 190, 196, 198, 315, 319
optimal experience, 62, 244, 245
optimise, 4, 9, 35, 77, 84, 87, 89, 138, 284, 314
option, 53, 67, 161, 166, 259, 261, 323, 324, 343–345
organisational, 32, 177, 206, 207, 239, 300, 320
organisational awareness, 4, 327
organisational capabilities, 181, 186
organisational change, 212
  frequent, 3
  strategic, 209
organisational competence audit, 182, 205
organisational competency audit, 205, 206
organisational culture, 44, 337
organisational learning operationalisation, 333
organisational level, 55, 206, 239
organisational structure, 189, 268
organisations, 4–8, 29–31, 40–42, 44–46, 48–49, 53, 54, 56–57, 120–130, 132–136, 142, 143, 178–190, 211, 239, 286, 287, 295–297
  high-performance, 9, 120, 166
organisation's ability, 36, 125
organizations, 60, 334
outcomes, 30, 31, 121, 122, 157–159, 161, 164, 174, 206, 209, 212, 265, 303, 304, 326, 328, 329, 338, 340
outputs, 188, 189, 192, 295, 299

P

paradigm shifts, 1, 13, 15, 27
parasympathetic nervous system (PNS), 95, 96, 152
participant reactions, 276, 277
participants, 24, 27, 31, 232, 233, 276, 278, 279, 290, 292, 293, 296, 297, 300, 315, 316, 318, 319, 321–326, 329–334, 344, 345
parties, 28, 164, 170, 171, 173–175, 319, 342
Passion4Development, 248, 266
PEAs (Positive Emotional Attractors), 109, 110
Peer review of behaviour change, 278

peers, 32, 201, 215, 216, 233, 278, 284, 288, 290, 300, 316, 330, 334
perceptions, 37, 66, 81, 95, 109, 113, 128, 166, 170, 171, 173, 277, 293
performance assessment, 287, 288, 311, 312
performance management, 15, 16
performance standards, 132, 166, 181, 182, 188, 191, 192
permission, 107, 138, 139
person, 87, 121, 122, 137, 139, 151–157, 163, 165, 170, 172, 173, 175, 181, 188, 189, 201, 202, 212, 213, 233, 234
personal influences, 336, 338, 342
personality preferences, 69, 86, 283
perspectives, 10, 12, 76, 146, 151, 153, 160, 169, 171, 212, 304, 305, 307, 308, 317, 342, 344
Perspective Taking Capacity (PTC), 147
phases, 53, 55, 156, 287, 293, 332
planning learning experiences, 212
plans, 43, 46, 70, 71, 123, 125, 135, 141, 156, 157, 174, 179, 191, 196, 200, 205, 207
  high-level programme, 326
platforms, 34, 38, 45–47, 56, 129, 238, 257, 264, 265, 270
  digital, 28, 29
players, 244, 249, 253, 255–258, 260–261, 263–266, 271
playfulness, 35, 38
PMO (project management officer), 321, 334
PNS (Parasympathetic nervous system), 95, 96, 152
podcasts, 18, 22, 24, 75, 222, 224, 236–238
PoE (Portfolio of Evidence), 203, 204, 278, 290
Portfolio of Evidence. See PoE
Positive Emotional Attractors. See PEAs
post-assessment, 278, 279
post-programme, learning priorities, 322
power, 2, 5, 37, 68, 83, 92, 97, 99, 143, 166, 216, 253, 260–262, 308, 311
preferences, 12, 23, 27, 60, 67, 69, 70, 73–76, 134, 155, 340
Prefers, 71, 76
pre-frontal cortex, 94–96, 98, 99, 340
presentations, 9, 31, 100, 123, 223, 226, 232, 242, 278, 288–290, 292–293, 298, 317, 327, 333

final, 303, 326, 333
pressure, 42, 71, 80–82, 168, 318, 323, 345
priorities
  strategic, 57, 177, 183, 343, 344
  strategic learning, 10, 12, 187, 198
prior learning, 228, 229
process skills, 306
productivity, 34, 187, 240, 248, 253, 254, 275, 279, 296, 319
products, 17, 31, 36, 43, 49, 122, 135, 136, 185, 186, 258, 259, 265
proficiency, 12, 84, 182, 200–201, 204
proficiency level, required, 200, 206
proficiency levels, 10, 14, 177, 181, 189, 198–200, 205
profile, 26, 67, 74, 268
programme, 7, 43, 45, 47–49, 51–53, 206, 208, 220–222, 232, 299–300, 317, 319–323, 325–326, 328–331, 333, 334
  accelerated learning XL, 49
  business school, 208, 321, 336
  culture change, 117
  eLearning, 271
  formal, 208
  leadership development, 194, 207
  part-time, 322, 323
programme participants, 303, 328, 331
progression, 249, 251, 268
project management, 43, 193, 206, 315, 321, 343
project management officer (PMO), 321, 334
project managers, 219, 313, 320, 321
project owner, 290, 318–320
project plans, 321
projects, 4, 6, 8, 51–53, 134, 135, 138, 232, 270–272, 290–293, 320–322, 324–329, 331–332, 334, 339, 342
  action-learning, 51
project teams, 54, 123, 134, 167, 169, 322, 323, 329, 341
  strategic, 121, 134
project work, 51, 207, 327, 332
providing learning guidance, 228, 231
psychometrics, 72, 201, 203, 278, 290, 322
PTC (Perspective Taking Capacity), 147
purpose, organisation's, 128, 181

Q

quadrant, 74, 256–257

qualifications, 7, 38, 45, 48, 192, 282, 284, 286

quality, 6, 7, 104, 114, 155, 186, 204, 207, 218, 279, 300, 337, 339, 340

quality of attention, 104

questions, critical, 282, 342, 344

R

recall, 4, 65, 66, 69, 104, 105, 132, 138, 144, 223, 225–227, 231, 235, 314, 345

recall of prior learning, 228, 229

refocus, 113, 114

regular feedback, 22, 53, 174, 201

reinforcement, 4, 69, 140, 141, 144, 169, 223, 225–228, 232, 234, 251, 313, 314

relatedness, 82, 83, 96, 97, 250

research, 3, 30, 33, 35, 38, 67, 69, 101, 104, 115, 116, 132, 133, 212, 213, 257–259, 336, 338

resources, 2, 7, 8, 83, 85, 137, 139, 156, 159, 161, 280, 283, 295–297, 319, 321, 324

additional, 13, 67, 75, 86, 92, 95, 98, 154, 162, 183, 282

respondents, 5, 7, 253, 275, 276

responses, 54, 61, 64, 65, 97, 109, 166, 175, 251–253, 255, 258

responsibility, 33, 56, 126, 134, 147–149, 155, 157, 158, 162, 195, 199, 295

result, 29, 31, 34, 35, 54, 56, 145–147, 163, 165, 168, 173, 249, 250, 277, 279, 280, 321, 323

retention, 30, 31, 38, 133, 150, 183, 189, 223, 227, 234, 235

retention of learning, 4, 107, 144, 177, 225, 227, 255

retrieval, 102, 228, 229, 234

revalue, 113, 114

review, 4, 30, 69, 157, 164, 167, 171, 174, 223, 225, 226, 230, 232, 233, 258, 259, 290, 292

rewards, 19, 83, 84, 97–98, 105, 244, 245, 252–253, 260–266, 270, 295

RMB, 41, 42, 44, 46–49, 51, 56

ROI, 7, 46, 53, 266, 276, 277, 280, 289, 298–300, 325

role profiles, 181, 189, 191, 194, 198, 322

roles, 12, 26, 55, 56, 146, 159, 181–183, 188–190, 194, 199, 200, 207, 218, 294, 295, 317, 318, 323–325, 343, 344

current, 43, 183, 200, 206, 207, 227, 297, 315, 318

key, 56, 124, 178, 320

organisation's, 69

S

sales e-learning programs, 47

SCARF, 81, 96, 109, 111, 338

SCM (Success Case Method), 297–298

scores, 260, 263, 271

Sector Education and Training Authority. *See* SETA

selection, 315, 323–324, 328, 331

selection process, 290, 318, 320, 325, 326, 328, 332

self-assessment, 75, 154, 169, 201, 278, 284, 287, 290

learning activity, 289

self-leadership, 44, 48, 53, 54, 141, 204

self-study, 22, 207, 208, 236, 237, 316

senior leaders, 5, 6, 48, 51–53, 125, 126, 128, 132, 135, 139, 300, 323, 332

senior levels, 43, 51, 187, 188, 323, 328

senior managers, 3, 32, 45, 51, 167, 294, 318, 331, 334, 336, 339, 345

sensations, emotional, 111, 112

sensory cortices, 98, 99

services, 17, 31, 36, 41, 43, 124, 135, 149, 167, 259, 261

sessions, 121, 134, 136, 137, 139, 147–149, 153, 157, 158, 164, 172, 174, 229, 322, 325–327, 330, 332

facilitated, 233, 290

set, 83, 84, 101, 103, 120, 121, 123, 133, 136–138, 172, 173, 219–221, 228, 236–238, 246, 289–290, 328, 329, 342, 343

SETA (Sector Education and Training Authority), 7, 50, 180, 183

shift, 1, 8, 9, 16, 27, 35, 36, 40, 42, 45, 46, 54, 103, 105, 124, 131, 300, 304

situations, 78, 83, 150, 155, 160–162, 165–167, 171, 173, 175, 219, 224, 233, 234, 236, 340, 342

skills, 6–7, 9, 10, 29–32, 43, 53, 54, 130–133, 137, 138, 178, 179, 183, 184, 189, 192, 194–195, 245–248, 283–287, 294
  current, 246, 247
  functional, 56, 193, 322
  important behavioural, 108
  key, 108, 130, 151, 152, 324
  new, 9, 64, 69, 83, 184, 207, 233, 234, 282, 287, 306
  scarce, 7, 30, 135, 178, 182, 205, 206
  technical, 47, 49, 52, 315, 316
skills factor, 247, 248
skills level, 199, 247
skills practice, 175
skills training, 107, 305
smartphones, 15, 17
SMEs (subject matter experts), 228, 231, 238, 272, 313, 324, 325
SNS (sympathetic nervous system), 95–97, 109, 152, 155
social engagement, level of, 237
social learning, 12, 27, 28, 32–34, 46, 129, 130, 235, 237
social networks, 17, 20, 23, 25, 89, 221, 238
solutions, 23, 31, 33, 71, 155, 160, 166, 244, 248, 260, 299, 317, 322, 323, 342
South African organisations, 1, 13, 41
space, 9, 38, 41, 83, 93, 100, 102, 107, 115, 146, 147, 152, 163, 173, 221, 228
specialists, 77, 95, 190, 202, 212, 318, 319, 326, 331
sponsors, 42, 51, 151, 317, 319, 321, 324, 327, 329, 332, 333
staff, 9, 47, 50, 55, 57, 121, 124, 126, 130, 132, 135, 136, 192, 197, 234, 239
stakeholders, 57, 123, 184, 256, 275, 295, 298, 299, 305, 323, 325, 331, 342–344
standards, 29, 83, 137, 189, 190, 198, 201
state, 95, 143, 217, 245–247, 250, 260
status, 66, 68, 82, 83, 96, 97, 260–263, 270
steps, 98–100, 112, 149, 153, 156, 172, 177, 217–218, 223, 227, 256, 265, 266, 298, 312, 341–343
  next, 161, 187, 330, 340
steps of programme planning, 235, 313
stimuli, 13, 64, 72, 94, 98, 228, 230
strategic challenges, 2, 317, 332

strategic change management, 168
strategic learning challenges, 55
strategic partners, 305
strategic projects, 49, 120–123, 136, 317, 318, 323–326, 334
strategic review sessions, 122, 123, 136
strategy, 6, 7, 17, 18, 45, 47, 105, 107, 122, 123, 125, 126, 181–183, 205, 206, 253, 254, 256, 258, 259, 270–272, 307
strengths, 48, 53, 61, 63, 77–81, 104, 110, 129, 134, 196, 200, 239, 240, 290, 330
stress, 66, 80, 81, 95–96, 108–109, 114, 158, 259, 318, 323
students, 17, 23, 26, 29, 39, 109
styles, 19, 67, 75, 76, 192, 218, 219, 330
subject matter experts. See SMEs
sub-projects, 123
Success Case Method. See SCM
suggestions, 125, 128, 130, 132–137, 161, 169, 290
suppliers, 130, 135, 136, 138, 166
support behaviour change, 313
support organisational change, 211
survey participants, 298
survival, 69, 94, 96, 97, 109, 110
sympathetic nervous system. See SNS
synthesise, 76, 288, 293, 341, 343, 344
systems, 18, 19, 27, 29, 36, 65, 66, 95, 125–127, 196, 198, 211–212, 264, 265, 270, 272, 304–308, 312–314
systems approach, 36, 37, 125, 132
systems thinking, 36–37, 43, 47, 340

T

Table, 24, 25, 68–71, 73–76, 83, 84, 96, 97, 99, 109, 110, 112–113, 191, 192, 208, 240, 251, 252, 257, 276, 277, 320, 321
tablet PCs, 17
tablets, 17, 21, 47
talent forums, 122, 123, 130, 141, 200, 203, 209, 275, 328
talent management, 49, 121, 122, 126, 151, 165, 275, 337
teachers, 19, 27, 31, 33, 34, 226
team-based strategic action learning projects, 51
team behaviours, 134, 306

team leader, 194, 308

team leadership, 190, 193

teams, 50, 51, 53, 54, 121–124, 129, 130, 133–134, 140, 141, 167–169, 190–191, 232, 239, 289–291, 317, 319, 324–326, 329–333
  core, 321, 331

team sessions, 134, 236, 237

team tools, 133, 134, 326

technical level, 190

technology, 21, 23–24, 43, 46, 91, 93, 126, 131, 136, 138, 191, 196, 237, 238, 315, 318, 319

technology support, 124, 138

technology user types, 18, 23, 24

temporal lobe, 98, 99

theory, self-determination, 250, 251

thinking, 8, 30, 36, 37, 60–62, 65, 66, 70–72, 74–77, 105, 106, 115, 146–148, 154–156, 168, 169, 173, 174, 338, 339, 344
  critical, 33, 55, 149, 215, 335, 337–339, 341, 344, 346
  systemic, 125

thinking brain, 94, 96

thinking questions, 156

thinking styles, 66, 73, 74, 162, 166

thought leaders, 57, 316, 317

threats, 94, 96–98, 109, 154, 201, 202

tips, 82–84, 138, 153, 162, 175, 201–203, 232, 238, 300, 326

tools, 13, 14, 23, 24, 26, 85, 125, 126, 130, 133, 134, 137, 138, 239, 240, 242, 288, 293, 337, 339–343, 345

topics, 29, 30, 45, 73, 100, 105, 106, 138, 161, 174, 229–231, 238, 241, 242, 268, 284, 325, 326, 345

training, 7, 22, 23, 101, 122, 123, 134, 136, 143, 145, 179, 180, 200–202, 248, 270, 276–280, 286, 287, 304, 305
  facilitator, 345
  soft skills behaviour, 314

training interventions, 179, 223

training programmes, 85, 90, 207, 236, 336, 337
  executive, 270

transfer, 7, 31, 34, 92, 122, 184, 228, 234, 235, 310, 312

transformation, 46, 78, 120, 123, 142, 211, 212, 218, 239, 304, 307–309, 313

transformation journey, 120, 122, 123

transition, 17, 25, 27, 53, 90, 145, 180, 305

traps, behavioural, 336, 337

trends, 8, 13, 33, 46, 49, 131, 222, 225, 239
  learning methodology, 1, 46
  new, 30, 47, 48, 53, 239, 240, 295

truth, 40, 112, 114, 163, 166, 170

tutorials, 226, 265

Twitter, 17, 34, 47, 258

types, 72, 74, 75, 98, 146, 147, 150, 155, 158, 192, 197, 203, 251–253, 256–258, 261, 262, 322, 324
  player, 256–257, 262, 265, 271

U

Unique learning profiles, 13, 59, 60, 67

Useful questions, 158, 161

users, 24, 25, 211, 217, 238, 252–253, 255, 261, 268, 270, 309, 313

V

value-added services (VAS), 17

value chain, 181, 182, 187, 211, 280, 287, 295

values, 21, 22, 56, 67–69, 113, 121, 134, 135, 141, 162, 163, 185, 186, 188, 189, 191, 192, 276, 280–283, 300, 301, 342–345
  monetary, 299
  organisational, 128, 170
  personal, 66, 68, 70

VAS (value-added services), 17

veteran, 19, 26, 27

video, 15, 18, 20, 23, 25, 26, 29, 46, 164, 214, 216, 217, 219–222, 236–238, 259, 285, 288

video games, 21, 23, 24, 247

vision, 7, 121, 123, 127, 140, 147, 181, 183, 189, 191, 193, 309

visual, 46, 60, 66, 73, 75, 230

W

well-thought-through change management strategies, 34

wikis, 24, 25, 126, 224, 236, 237

workers, 19, 23, 129–131

workforce, 19–21, 23, 52, 60, 186

workings, 59, 93, 94

workplace, 20, 39, 42, 44, 100, 144, 224, 234, 238, 260, 286, 287, 345
Workplace Skills Plan. *See* WSP
workshops, 22, 124, 134, 138, 139, 169, 226, 228, 251, 330, 342, 344, 345
world, 2, 5, 6, 9, 10, 16, 20, 21, 23, 60, 61, 90, 92, 93, 95, 101, 102, 165, 166, 169, 238, 242
  new, 305, 324
World Café, 48, 240, 241
WSP (Workplace Skills Plan), 181, 183, 209
www.youtube.com, 18, 23, 34, 93, 106, 121, 164, 214, 216, 217, 219–221, 237, 238, 285, 288, 296, 301

Y

YouTube, 18, 23, 34, 93, 164, 214, 216, 217, 219–221, 237, 238, 259, 261, 285, 288, 296, 301

ENDORSEMENTS FROM PEOPLE WHO HAVE READ THIS BOOK

"In this exceptionally readable book, Debbie Craig presents us with an appetising smorgasbord of important ideas. Visually engaging, accessible, and well-integrated, this is a thinker's goldmine. It's well worth reading – mindfully, thoughtfully, and attentively. Well done, Debbie!"

~ Dr Karl Albrecht, consultant, author, futurist, lecturer, and author of
Practical Intelligence: The Art and Science of Common Sense

"For me, this book bridges the gap between ideal theory and creating value through well-thought-through talent management principles. It is also practical and appealing, and should be read by all Human Resources practitioners. Brilliant work, Debbie!"

~ Gawie Herholdt, Group Effectiveness Manager: Harmony Gold, accountable for Talent
Management, Performance Management, and Organisational Effectiveness

"Both Debbie and Kerryn have again proved that they have thoroughly understood and grasped the ever-changing world of learning by presenting the reader with a fresh, well-balanced approach to learning development and growth, in their latest book.

"They present us, the reader, with a wealth of information, confronting us with the shift in learning and development to accelerated learning. The book illustrates in a well-integrated way the fact that real learning is a much more collaborative process than it used to be.

"The case studies are well interwoven with each other, taking the reader through the processes in a well synchronised way; and once through the initial stages, they can be implemented straight into the learning cycle.

"A book well worth reading and to have as a reference on your bookshelf.

"Well done, Debbie and Kerryn."

~ Prof. Sakkie van de Merwe, Managing Director of South African
Training Academy, an OD ETDP specialist training organisation.

"If human capability is the one strategic differentiator in the talent and knowledge century, our ability to constantly raise our workforces' strategic insights, level of commercial capability and abilities to lead and manage others, at a speed faster than our competitors, will be the enduring source of competitive advantage. Congratulations to Debbie Craig and Kerryn Kohl, who have captured the essence of accelerated learning, a process which, particularly in a dynamic markets context, is so important to change the status quo, where so many people have potential for greatness but have often lacked opportunities and mentorship."

~ Shaun Rozyn, Executive Director: Corporate Education,
Gordon Institute of Business Science

"This book brings a fresh approach to an old challenge of motivating fast learning and linking it to consistent results. With a stimulating and dynamic format – and great YouTube references! – Debbie and Kerryn bring valuable insights to anyone interested in making a difference by growing people to their potential."

~ Carmen Gomez Rodrigues, General Manager –
Southern Cone, Buckman Latin America

"Wow, what a wonderful approach to this new, modern world of learning! As organisations and individuals are on the cusp of change asking questions around Mastery, Autonomy, Purpose (by Dan Pink), this book will take you on a journey towards clarity and understanding that the world is changing and organisations need to become learning cultures to survive the ever present 'change' and subsequent integration. Kerryn, whom I have known and worked with since my arrival in South Africa, is passionate about the learning paradigms that face us in today's fast-paced world. Both Kerryn and Debbie have captured the key concepts in the fun-filled construct and learning playground this book inspires. Their passion is evident throughout, and I am privileged to be part of the story."

~ Karin Ovari, Regional Manager, Intertek Consulting & Training

"Talented and engaged employees are a key enabler in any organisation. Companies may have a great vision and a winning strategy, but people bring these to life. Debbie Craig has integrated the latest thinking on how we may develop and engage the talent in our organisations in order to ensure personal and organisational success. This book is a great contribution to the learning and development field."

~ Joan Peters, Leadership Academy Manager, Volkswagen Learning Academy

"In many ways this book reminded me of Peter Senge's The Fifth Discipline field book, which similarly inspired me a few years back. This book, however, is a very detailed , pragmatic and contemporary update integrating the realities of 21st century competitive learning landscape with exhilarating new approaches, techniques, tools, practices, qnd methods to achieve liberating yet learning-cenered breakthrough results at individual, team and organisational level.

"Chief Human Resource Officers as well as their peers, and Chief Learning Officers and their associated practitioners, will all benefit from not just reading this very compelling text but studying and applying all its valuable lessons in their quest both to accelerate learning and achieve tangible results."

"Wow! Sincerely, really, really enjoyed your book. So much useful specific contemporary detail and really consider the Blogs and many U Tube inserts and other web links to be both valuable, resourceful and provides this publication with distinctive nature.

~ Johan Ludike, Head of Talent Management, Yum University, Yum Brands Africa

"Why do we 'FACE' a global talent crisis? Why can't we match learning pathways to strategic challenges? Why can't we utilise people's natural learning ability? This book offers deep thoughts and practical approaches to accelerating learning in order to engage, develop and retain the talent we need. Numerous theories, tools, brain-break activities, programme examples and case studies are included. I am learning at the moment, and recommend this valuable publication as worth your time to read, think through, and practise. It will definitely contribute to your ambition of creating a learning organisation."

~ JianQin Yan, Human Resources and Administration
Director, Buckman Laboratories Chemicals Co., Ltd. Shanghai, China

"Accelerated Learning offers dynamic reading which jumps between traditional concepts, real life youth challenges and organisational culture and learning dilemmas regarding how to optimise potential resources and engage people in the long term. This book is a bridge between several generations, clarifying the way in which each can learn through different avenues and platforms. It offers a creative transformation process to accelerate learning and results. It offers a unique way of guiding the reader through sharing content, offering feedback opportunities, and providing several tools to explore topics further, such as decision making, collaboration, high performance, talent, coaching, conversations, culture, change, leadership, and innovation. It is full of surprises, rewards and interaction and fun!

"I have personally experienced the benefit of transformational leadership with Catalyst. This book continues their breakthrough thinking and can be a game changer for dealing with the next generation and creating a common language in order to increase the speed of learning and deliver results fast!"

~ Jorge Romero Alva, General Manager, Buckman Latin America, Mexico

"What an amazing read – it is truly a book that keeps on giving! It stimulates thinking about accelerated learning and is full of modern and practical content, presented in an easily accessible and understandable manner. And the gamification throughout the book places the reader in a milieu of an active learner through he experience of reading the book and accelerating one's own learning."

~ Liza Govender, Executive Manager: Talent, Transnet

"For organisations to become and to remain high performing in an ever-changing world demands a new approach to people development. There is an abundance of information available on tools, generational information, application of social media, and other topics.

This book pulls all this together and yet is based on sound pedagogical theory. It also adds valuable insights for South African leaders grappling with the double-edged sword of the dearth of talent and the need for accelerated learning. It is a mus- have on the bookshelf of talent managers and chief learning officers.

"Both Kerryn Kohl and Debbie Craig bring their valuable practical lessons learnt, their passion for this subject, and their deep expertise in this field to us in a practical and useful manner. I have had the fortune of working in organisations and in consulting for organisations in this field for over 20 years, and I wish I had had this book 20 years ago already!"

~ Lou-Anne Lubbe, previous MD, People & Organisation Talent, Accenture South Africa.

www.ingramcontent.com/pod-product-compliance
Lightning Source LLC
Chambersburg PA
CBHW082128210326
41599CB00031B/5906